THE FRANCIS TRILOGY
OF
THOMAS OF CELANO

The Life of Saint Francis
(1228–1229)

The Remembrance of the Desire of a Soul
(1245–1247)

The Treatise on the Miracles of Saint Francis
(1250–1252)

THE FRANCIS TRILOGY
OF
THOMAS OF CELANO

The Life of Saint Francis
The Remembrance of the Desire of a Soul
The Treatise on the Miracles of Saint Francis

Edited by
Regis J. Armstrong, O.F.M. Cap.
J. A. Wayne Hellmann, O.F.M. Conv.
William J. Short, O.F.M.

New City Press
Hyde Park, New York

Published in the United States by
New City Press, 202 Comforter Blvd., Hyde Park, New York 12538
©2004 Franciscan Institute of St. Bonaventure University, St. Bonaventure, NY

Cover design by Nick Cianfarani
Maps ©1998, Franciscan Friars of California

Library of Congress Cataloging-in-Publication Data:
  Thomas, of Celano, fl. 1257.
  [Selections. English. 2004]
  The Francis Trilogy : The life of Saint Francis, The rememberance of the desire of a
soul, The treatise on the miracles of Saint Francis / by Thomas of Celano ; edited by Regis
J. Armstrong, J. Wayne Hellmann, William J. Short.
        p.   cm.
  ISBN 1-56548-204-2
  1. Francis, of Assisi, Saint, 1182-1226.   2. Christian saints--Italy--Assisi--Biography.
  I. Armstrong, Regis J., II. Hellmann, J. Wayne.   III. Short, William J.   IV. Thomas, of
Celano, fl. 1257. Vita prima Sancti Francisci. English.   V. Thomas, of Celano, fl. 1257.
Vita secunda Sancti Francisci. English.   VI. Thomas, of Celano, fl. 1257. Tractatus de
Miraculis B. Francisci. English.   VII. Title.
  BX4700.F6F68E5   2004
  271'.302--dc22   2004049859

2d printing: July 2010

Contents

The Life of Saint Francis
(1228–1229)

The Remembrance of the Desire of a Soul
(1245–1247)

The Treatise on the Miracles of Saint Francis
(1250–1252)

Foreword

In the vast library of Christian spirituality, the literature surrounding Francis of Assisi is considerable. Curiously, much of that literature is biographical in nature. Even works dedicated to Franciscan spirituality rely more on his biographies than on his writings, and, of these, the three portraits of Thomas of Celano are foundational.

By the completion of *The Founder,* the second of the three volumes of *Francis of Assisi: Early Documents,* the possibility arose of placing the three major portraits of Thomas of Celano into one volume. After the completion of *The Prophet,* the third volume, that idea became imperative, as Thomas emerged as the most quoted writer of the developing Franciscan literary tradition of the first hundred and fifty years. To study Francis is, in a certain sense, to study Thomas. Bonaventure's compilations, the *Major* and *Minor Legenda* rely unabashedly on the writings of Thomas. Julian of Speyer, Henri d'Avranche, Ubertino da Casale, and Angelo Clareno incorporate incidents, vocabulary, and images of Francis into their works, while in his *The Kinship of Saint Francis,* Arnald of Sarrant boldly places Thomas as a Matthew figure among the four "Evangelists" of the Franciscan Gospels.

Placing these major texts of Thomas of Celano in one volume enables his genius to be appreciated and the contours of his interpretation of the spirit and personality of Francis to be clearly identified. Thomas emerges as a master of the ecclesial, historical and ascetical traditions as applied for an interpretation and understanding of Francis's life of holiness. All of the texts show Thomas to be a master of the popular memory of Francis's followers as he integrates their many memories into presentations aiding those followers in their own pursuit of virtue. All three works, however, also reveal Thomas to be a master of the folklore of the thirteenth century towns, villages, and countryside where the memory and popular cult of Francis flourished. All three portraits, then, bring the reader into three different arenas where the same memory of Francis touched lives of ecclesiastics, his male and female followers, and ordinary people.

Undoubtedly questions will arise in the minds of those who are captured by Thomas's literary genius, questions that will inevitably lead them to the larger three-volume set, *Francis of Assisi: Early Documents.* Why,

for example, did Francis's companions feel obliged to narrate other incidents in the saint's life or in their experience of him? Why did the brothers
mandate in 1260 the composition of a new, official biography? Why did
they put the "Thomas Trilogy" aside in 1266 in favor of Bonaventure's
portraits? Finally, why does that so-called "deleted" trilogy continue to
emerge throughout the next one hundred and twenty years or so? While
the answers to these questions remain as elusive as ever, hopefully the
presentation of *The Francis Trilogy* will enable readers to identify Thomas's
unique contributions to the rich inheritance of the Franciscan tradition.

The technical apparatus found in this compendium of Thomas's portraits of Francis is fundamentally the same as that found in *Francis of
Assisi: Early Documents.* The introductions and notes are basically the same,
although adjusted to the present text and excised of references to the
three volumes.

Regis J. Armstrong, O.F.M. Cap.

THE LIFE OF SAINT FRANCIS

(1228–1229)

Introduction

Brother Thomas of Celano (d. 1260) was the first to write a life of Saint Francis and the first to describe the earliest days of the life of his followers. With his masterful pen he laid the foundation for the rich Franciscan literary tradition of the 13th century by composing two major works: *The Life of Saint Francis,* commonly referred to as *The First Life* [*Vita Prima*], in 1229 and *The Remembrance of the Desire of a Soul,* commonly referred to as *The Second Life* [*Vita Secunda*] in 1247.[1] Thomas also wrote two other works on Saint Francis, *The Legend for Use in the Choir* [*Legenda ad Usum Chori*] in 1230 and *The Treatise on the Miracles* [*Tractatus de Miraculis B. Francisci*] in 1254. Except for his presence at the Pentecost Chapter at the Portiuncula in 1221 and for his part in the subsequent mission of the friars to Germany, there is little other known evidence about Thomas's life. No scholarly biography of his life has ever been written.[2]

Thomas's birth, into the noble family of the Conti dei Marsi, occurred sometime between 1185-1190. The city of his birth, Celano, is a small city in the Abruzzi, twenty miles southeast of Aquila in the mountains southeast of Rome.[3] His exceptional writing ability indicates Thomas received a solid liberal arts education in the basic curriculum of study in the Middle Ages, the *trivium* and *quadrivium,* possibly at the Benedictine monastery of Saint John the Baptist near Celano. His knowledge of the monastic literary tradition as well as his theological acumen supports the opinion that he studied theology, perhaps at Monte Cassino, Rome or Bologna.[4] Thomas probably includes himself in the remark he makes in *The Life of Saint Francis* that, at the Portiuncula, after Saint Francis returned from Spain in 1215 "some literate men and nobles gladly joined him."[5] Thomas prefaces this comment in a rare autobiographical reference by indicating that the God who brought Francis back from Spain to Italy "was pleased to be mindful of me and many others."[6]

During the Chapter of 1221 Thomas was among the brothers chosen for the mission to Germany.[7] After arrival in Germany, he was elected to the office of custodian to lead the friars of Worms, Speyer, and Cologne. Later, on the recommendation of Brother Caesar of Speyer, Thomas became the vicar of all the brothers of Germany. It is not known why he returned to Italy, but by July 16, 1228, he was most likely back in Assisi for the canonization of Saint Francis. His vivid and dramatic narration of the canonization event in Book Three of *The Life of Saint Francis* suggests an eyewitness account.[8]

Shortly before the July 1228 canonization and shortly after Pope Gregory IX's decree, *Recolentes qualiter,* of April 29, 1228, calling for a burial church to be built for Francis in Assisi, Gregory IX conferred upon Thomas the distinguished task of writing a life of the new saint.[9] Thomas, it would seem, was to complement the architectural celebration of Francis with the composition of a new literary monument. Both contributions, requested by Gregory IX within months of each other, were to help preserve the memory of the life and example of the Poverello.

Unlike the new burial church, *The Life of Saint Francis* was quickly completed, within six to eight months. On February 25, 1229, Gregory IX had already approved, confirmed and declared it official. By the next year, 1230, Thomas finished his second work on the life of Saint Francis, *The Legend for Use in the Choir.*[10] This second work was for use within the celebration of the Divine Office. It was written at the request of Brother Benedict of Arezzo, Minister of Romania and Greece.[11] In composing *The Legend for Use in the Choir* Thomas selected material from *The Life of Saint Francis* and divided it into nine lessons or selections so that it could be included among the readings of the breviary.[12] It is a shortened and concise version of *The Life of Saint Francis,* condensing certain sections for the readings on the feast of Saint Francis and during the octave, the eight days following the feast.

Fourteen years later, at the Chapter of Genoa in 1244, Thomas was again called. This time, it was not the pope but the brothers who sought his assistance. The General Minister, Crescentius of Jesi (1244-1247), acting on the direction of the General Chapter, called for a collection of the stories circulating about Francis and commissioned Thomas to capture those memories in his classical style of writing. Thomas dedicated his collection, *The Remembrance of the Desire of a Soul,* to Crescentius.[13]

Crescentius's successor, Brother John of Parma, further commissioned Thomas to write his fourth and final work on Francis, *The Treatise on the Miracles.* Although Thomas had reported on miracles in his earlier writings on Francis, he was asked to produce a systematic collection of all accounts of these extraordinary events during and after Francis's life that were circulating. Evidently, Thomas did not respond quickly to the request. According to the *Chronicle of the Twenty-Four Generals,* John had to make several requests.[14] The *Treatise on the Miracles* was finally confirmed by John of Parma at the General Chapter of Metz on May 31, 1254, twenty-five years after Gregory IX had confirmed and approved *The Life of Saint Francis.*[15]

It is not certain where Thomas was residing during these years. His literary activity provides clues. During the writing of *The Life of Saint Francis* and *The Legend for Use in the Choir,* Thomas probably lived in or near Assisi, where he could find the witnesses he needed. It is certain that he was living in Assisi in 1230 when Jordan of Giano visited there. Jordan reports that he "went to Brother Thomas of Celano, who gave him some relics of The Blessed Father Francis."[16] Fourteen years later, when commissioned by the Chapter of Genoa in 1244 the already famous writer would have returned to Assisi for the composition of *The Remembrance of the Desire of a Soul*. In the latter years of his life he would again have been in Assisi for the composition of *The Treatise on the Miracles*.[17] Some authors maintain that Thomas may be the author of *The Legend of Saint Clare*, who was canonized on August 15, 1255. Were this the case, he would again have found himself in Assisi where he could find the sources, witnesses and oral tradition he needed.[18]

Most likely Thomas lived his life between Assisi and Tagliacozzo, a town about fifteen miles west of his hometown of Celano. In Tagliacozzo, Thomas spent the last years prior to his death as chaplain to the Poor Ladies, the followers of Saint Clare, at the convent of San Giovanni di Val dei Varri.

Thomas died on October 4, 1260 in Tagliacozzo and was buried in the monastery of the Poor Ladies.[19] In 1516, long after the monastery was abandoned in 1476, the brothers transferred his bones to the church of Saint Francis in Tagliacozzo where his bones presently rest. Locally, Thomas continues to be honored as the saint who wrote about a saint.

The Life of Saint Francis (1229)

As the first written account of the life of Saint Francis, Thomas's work holds a place of honor. It holds a unique place in the historical sequence of the many other lives which would subsequently be written. This is not to argue that this text is more "historical" in the contemporary sense of that concept. More importantly, *The Life of Saint Francis* captures the first burst of enthusiasm in the new religious movement of the Lesser Brothers. It expresses the joy of the canonization and celebrates Saint Francis's memory. Its author is convinced that through Francis something new and refreshing entered into the spiritual communion of saints and into the visible life of the Church. In fact, Francis is the preeminent saint: "That is why every order, sex, and age finds in him a clear pattern of the teaching of salvation and an outstanding example of holy deeds."[20]

The Life of Saint Francis and the Early Development of the Order

Besides Francis, three other historical figures find an honored place within the pages of *The Life of Saint Francis*. They are: Clare of Assisi (1194-1253), Elias Buonbarone (1180-1253) and Hugolino dei Conti di Segni, who reigned as Pope Gregory IX from 1227-1241. At various points within the narrative Thomas accents their relationship to Francis and sings their praises.

Clare, still a relatively young woman while Thomas was writing in 1228, is praised as "bright in name, more brilliant in life, most brilliant in character." Numbers 18,19 and 20 in the First Book are dedicated to her and to her sisters at San Damiano. Again, after Francis's death near the end of Book Two, it is Clare and her sisters "who kissed his most splendid hands."[21] Clare and her sisters embody the grief of the whole church at the saint's death.

Thomas describes Brother Elias as "the one he chose for the role of mother to himself and had made a father of the other brothers."[22] Elias, appointed by Francis in 1217 as the first minister in the Holy Land, was already well known as a leader of the expansion of the Order. He led the Chapter of 1221 and organized the second and successful mission to Germany. Under his direction, the Order also spread to France, Spain, and in 1223 to England. Understandably, Thomas writes eloquently of the affectionate relationship between Elias and Francis. Elias hurries to Francis in his illness and receives an extraordinary blessing from his dying father: "I bless you, my son, in all and through all and just as the most High has increased my brothers in your hands, so too upon you and in you, I bless them all." Elias, like the biblical Jacob, becomes an instrument of Francis's blessing for all of the brothers.

Finally, Hugolino dei Conti di Segni is presented as the choice of Francis to be "father and lord over the whole religion and order of his brothers." Thomas writes that Hugolino "conformed himself to the ways of the brothers," was "humble with the humble and poor with the poor," and "a brother among brothers." This was the man, Thomas acknowledges, who "helped greatly to spread the Order."[23] Hugolino, born in 1155 at Anagni, son of the count of Segni and nephew of Pope Innocent III, had excelled in theology and canon law at Paris and Bologna. As cardinal bishop of Ostia, he gave proof of his great political skills as papal legate in southern Italy, Germany, Lombardy and Tuscany. He was also known to be intensely religious and in touch with contemporary spiritual movements. After he became cardinal protector of the Lesser Brothers in 1220, he threw his exceptional political weight behind the faltering fraternity. After Francis's first vicar, Peter di Catanio, died suddenly within a year of his appointment, it may have been Cardinal Hugolino who suggested that Elias become the new vicar.

The Life of Saint Francis in Service of the Church

The Life of Saint Francis, like the basilica raised in his honor, was a work intended by Pope Gregory for the whole Church. After Francis's canoniza-

tion on July 19,1228, Gregory exhorted the bishops of the world to promote the cult of the new saint in a letter dated February 21, 1229.[24] Only
four days later, on February 25, Gregory officially approved and promulgated *The Life of Saint Francis*. This context gives it an official ecclesial character.[25] Designed to appeal to the rich tradition of holiness manifested in
the lives of the saints, it reaches beyond the particular interests of Francis's followers to inspire men and women everywhere. Therefore, Thomas
situates the saint, Francis, within the ancient Christian tradition and
brings the freshness of his example into the life of the Church.

Unlike Thomas's later works on Francis, *The Life of Saint Francis* is not
written about Francis for the brothers at the request of the brothers. Only
about a fourth of the text treats Francis and his relationship with the
brothers. The rest is dedicated to conversion, promotion of the gospel, and
his example and teaching of Christian holiness.

In this context, the success of *The Life of Saint Francis* was important for
Gregory, not only for the promotion of the memory of Saint Francis and
the strengthening of the Franciscan Order in the Church, but also as a part
of his effort to promote spiritual renewal within the life of the Church. At
a time when heresies abounded, crusades failed and the struggle for
power between the Holy Roman Empire and the Papacy intensified, the
poor and humble follower of the gospel, Francis of Assisi, offered an alter-
native way of Christian living.

The Life of Saint Francis as Hagiography

To accomplish his purpose, Thomas draws from the memory of the
martyrs, the ascetics and the monks to illustrate that Francis is a saint
rooted in the tradition of the Church. Thomas explains that Francis's par-
ticipation in the same holiness as that of the great saints of memory is
based on a conversion that frees him from many burdensome cares and
leads him into the life of the Church where he hears the Word of God.

In his conversion Francis no longer lives as a "deaf hearer" of the gospel
but he becomes instead a bold proclaimer of the Word of God.[26] The gospel he
proclaims makes his hearers "children of peace."[27] Promoting the gospel
message of peace, Francis spends his life rebuilding the life of the Church
upon its solid and ancient foundation. His work of rebuilding three churches,
ones dedicated to the Virgin (Saint Mary of the Angels), to the apostles
(Saint Peter) and to a martyr (Saint Damian), renews the life of the Church
on its ancient foundations of the Virgin, the apostles and the martyrs.

Although there are canonical and hagiographical aspects to the text of
The Life of Saint Francis, these are not the only dimensions or perspectives
from which Thomas writes. He includes specific biographical and histori-

cal data. In these specifics about Francis and his early followers, Thomas
appeals to his own experience of Francis and, as he writes in the prologue,
to "trustworthy witnesses" who also would have themselves been readers
of his final text. Clearly, he had access to important textual sources within
the Order: the *Earlier Rule*, the *Later Rule*, the *Testament*, the *Admonitions*,
and *The Canticle of Creatures*.

The official canonical purposes and hagiographical elements Thomas
utilized to construct his text do not lessen the value of *The Life of Saint Francis* as a primary source for historical elements of Francis's life and of the
early life of the new fraternity. Thomas still presents a Francis situated in
real places and connected to his concrete historical contemporaries,
including early followers and many friends among ecclesiastical and lay
persons with authority and influence.

However, narrating historical events about Francis and the early brothers is not his primary purpose. The canonized Francis is no longer a simple
companion to his brothers. Now Francis is for the Church. For his sources,
therefore, Thomas went beyond the brothers to Pope Gregory IX, to
Bishop Guido II of Assisi, and certainly also to Clare. Although there is no
process of canonization extant, Thomas had access to the catalogue of
miracles which were read aloud at Francis's canonization, and these probably make up a good portion of Book Three.

The Life of Saint Francis is a grand tapestry of "trustworthy witnesses,"
varying literary and liturgical sources, multiple hagiographical traditions
and several ecclesial purposes. Although Thomas included historical data,
he intended primarily to announce Francis to the world. In the development of his text, he presents Francis as a model of conversion in order to
express the unique gospel message of Francis's life. Finally he captures
the moment of Francis's reception of the stigmata on La Verna. Thomas
wrote to increase the joy among the Christians of his day over Francis's
canonization. Likewise, it seems he hoped to solidify the spiritual identity
and mission of the Order in service of the life of the universal Church.

The Life of Saint Francis:
A Mirror of Incarnation, Passion and Resurrection

The Life of Saint Francis can be read from any of the perspectives mentioned above: historical, canonical or official, hagiographical, as well as
formational or pastoral. Structurally, it is divided into three books. Traditionally, this three-fold division is accented as chronological: 1) from his
youth to Christmas of 1223; 2) the last two years of his life from early 1224
to his death on October 4, 1226; 3) the canonization and the catalogue of
miracles read at the canonization on July 16, 1228.

The first two books differ in tone and purpose, but they are complementary treatises. Between the first two books there is a close thematic relationship. The third and last book, which narrates the celebration of Francis's 1228 canonization, appears to be an eyewitness account. This third book has a function different from that of the first two books. It is written in a different literary genre, that of miracle accounts, and differs in style from the other two. While the first and second books focus on Francis's life, the third recounts events in the Church after the death of Francis.

The theme of "the humility of the incarnation" uniquely identifies Book One, as Thomas summarizes the conversion, life, teaching and example of Francis. Humility enabled Francis to celebrate the birth of the Incarnate Word that he heard, preached, and lived throughout his life. Book One concludes with a vivid description of the great midnight Christmas liturgy of the cave at Greccio in which there is a wondrous vision: ". . . a little child lying lifeless in the manger . . . is awakened and impressed on their loving memory by His own grace through His holy servant Francis."[28] The gospel word heard and proclaimed through Francis's life of conversion brought about a marvelous vision of the Incarnation. Thomas explains through the life of Francis, how the Church, with all of creation, is renewed because the Word made flesh, long forgotten, comes to life again.

In Book Two the "charity of the Passion" predominates. The gospel word is no longer the commission to sell and give all goods to the poor. Rather, the Word is Christ on the Cross. This Word is experienced in a vision on La Verna. Francis sees what he hears. He comes to the mystical experience of both, the Word and the vision, in his own flesh, the stigmata. By the Word and the vision, Francis is transformed into the Incarnate and Crucified Christ. By employing the biblical image of the Seraph, an image rich in the contemplative tradition, Thomas identifies Francis's transformative experience as one of burning and intimate love.[29] The "charity of the Passion" is incarnated in Francis's own flesh, transporting him into the heavenly liturgy. In the prayer that concludes Book Two, Francis places his stigmata before Jesus Christ, Son of the most high Father. This is a form of intimate intercessory prayer that has salvific significance for all. In response, Christ Crucified is moved to "bear his own wounds to the Father, and because of this the Father will ever show us in our anguish His tenderness."[30]

Book Three, in the account of the canonization and the miracles, describes the liturgy of Francis that continues to be celebrated on earth. It captures that exuberance: "a new spirit was placed in the hearts of the elect and a holy anointing has been poured out in their midst."[31] There is new joy and power among those Francis left behind. As Francis is canonized, Christians of every vocation rejoice and the whole region is filled with new life and enthusiasm. At his tomb there is new life. Many people are healed and find consolation. The third book is a "Pentecost" experi-

ence. From this perspective, it flows from the first two books. After celebration of Francis's conversion leading to renewal of the Incarnation in
Greccio and after the celebration of new life in the transformation of
Francis in his stigmata and his *transitus* to the heavenly throne, there is
new faith, healing and life in the community left behind. In the third
book, the Church reaps the fruit of Francis's conversion and conformity to
Christ Crucified. Even in that time of crisis, a new grace of the Spirit is
alive in the Church.

Conclusion

Thomas of Celano's *The Life of Saint Francis* is a master's tapestry inter-
weaving multiple colored threads of hagiography, historical data, invitation toward gospel and ecclesial renewal, and identification of the mission
and formation of the brothers after Francis. The frame of this tapestry,
holding all together, is a profound theology of the Word and of the Cross,
fused into a Christology of Incarnation and Passion. Ultimately, the story of
Francis is an invitation to experience a love that radically transforms the
human person into the image of Christ Crucified, in intimate union with an
all-loving and merciful God. The differing threads within this tapestry provide multiple ways to understand, remember and celebrate Saint Francis.

There are many ways of approaching Thomas's portrait. While Augus-
tinian in nature, Thomas's anthropology draws the reader into a rich symbolic theology in which image, experience, and mysticism blend. His
theology of conversion and grace reveal themselves at every turn.[32]
Thomas describes Francis as God's instrument of ecclesial renewal and
reform and, in doing so, develops a strong theology of the Church upon
which later authors will build.[33] *The Life of Saint Francis* is a text that
demands the active cooperation of a reader. Not simply an encomium for
the newly proclaimed saint, Thomas's work is a stimulus for the
ever-struggling sinner—a testament of hope focused, as Francis would
have it, on the Christ he knew so intimately.

Notes

1. The editors have chosen to use the title used by Thomas in describing his major works. Since
there was no question of his writing a "second life" of Saint Francis at the time he wrote his "first
life," Thomas entitled his work, simply *The Life of Saint Francis*. When asked to supplement that
work with remembrances unknown or overlooked at the time, Thomas entitled his second work
The Remembrance of the Desire of a Soul. It is a title inspired by Isaiah 26: 8, "your name and your remembrance are the desire of my soul." Since the majority of this work is dedicated to Francis's pursuit of virtues—only the first twenty-five numbers of Thomas's work are "biographical" in
nature—Thomas's title expresses more fully its nature.
2. Studies on Thomas's life are few. The following are available: Sophronius Clasen, "Vom
Franziskus der Legende zum Franziskus der Geschicthe," *Wissenschaft und Weisheit*, 29

(1966):15-29; Engelbert Grau, "Thomas of Celano: Life and Work," trans. Xavier John Seubert, *Greyfriars Review* v.8, 2 (1994): 177-200; Giovanni Odoardi, "Tommaso da Celano e S. Francesco," in *Tommaso da Celano e la sua opera di biografo di S. Francesco.* Atti del Convegno di studio: Celano, Novembre 29-30,1982 (Celano,1985), 105-23; N. Petrone, "Note biografiche su fra Tommaso da Celano," in *Fra Tommaso da Celano storico-poeta e santo,* a cura di N. Petrone, Tagliacozzo 1992, 9-15.

    3. Cf. Odoardi, Giovanni, *Fra Tommaso da Celano, storico letterato poeta uomo di virtù* (Tagliacozzo: S. Francesco)1969.

    4. Cf. Odoardi, *Fra Tommaso,* 10.

    5. Thomas of Celano, *The Life of Saint Francis,* 57 (hereafter 1C).

    6. 1C 56.

    7. In naming those who were chosen to embark on a mission to Germany, Jordan lists in fourth place "Thomas of Celano, who later wrote both the first and the second legends of Saint Francis." Cf. Jordan of Giano, *Chronicle* 19 (hereafter ChrJG).

    8. 1C 124-126.

    9. It is interesting to note that Gregory's commission for the writing of a life of Francis followed the commission for the new basilica in Francis's honor. Both were commissioned shortly before Francis's canonization. Cf. W.R. Thomson, *Checklist of Papal Letters Relating to the Three Orders of Saint Francis: Innocent III-Alexander IV, AFH 64 (1971)* 367-580, specifically pages 383-384.

    10. Chiara Frugoni has suggested that *The Legend for Use in the Choir* (hereafter LCh) was written later, after the Treatise on the Miracles, that is, after 1253. She argues that the description of the stigmata indicates a later development. Cf. Chiara Frugoni, *Francesco e l'invenzione delle stimmate. Una storia per parole e immagini fino a Bonaventura e Giotto* (Torino 1993)171-173, 198-199.

    11. Cf. LCh 1 ; Michael Bihl, "De S. Francisci Legenda ad usum chori auctore Fr. Thoma celanensi, iuxta novum codicem senensem" in *Archivum Franciscanum Historicum* 26 (1933) 343-389.

    12. LCh has a few differences from 1C: in n. 11 the Seraph takes a more active role in the stigmata event, in n. 13 there is mention of placing Francis's body in the tomb; in nos. 14-16 new miracles are mentioned; in n. 17 there is allusion to Francis's death on a Sunday and there is allusion to the new church as Francis's burial place.

    13. Since Crescentius was replaced on July 13, 1247, the work was completed earlier in that year of 1247.

    14. Cf. *Chronica XXIV Generalium Ordinis Minorum, Analecta Francescana* III, 276.

    15. For the sake of completeness, it can here be mentioned that Thomas is also considered the poet of liturgical sequences, *Sanctitatis nova signa* and *Fregit victor.* Cf. *Analecta Francescana* X, 402-04 and pages 355-360 below. Also, since the 14th century, Thomas has been considered the poet of the sequence, *Dies Irae.* This, however, is doubtful. Cf. M. Inguanez and A. Amelli, "Il Dies irae in un codice del secolo XII," *Miscellanea Cassinese* 9 (1931) 5-11; K. Vellekoop, *Dies irae. Studien zur Frugeschichte einer Sequenz* (Bilthoven, 1978).

    16. Cf. ChrJG 59.

    17. Cf. *Preface* in *Analecta Franciscana* X, pp. v, xxiv-xxvi, xxxvi-xxxix.

    18. Cf. Francesco Pennacchi, *Legenda Sanctae Clare Virginis* (Assisi, 1910). Pennacchi, in the first publication of *The Legend of Saint Clare,* which was based upon the Assisi Codex 338, attributed the authorship to Thomas of Celano. Subsequent publications by other scholars have suggested other authors, both named and anonymous. A critical edition of the text is necessary before the question can be resolved. For a summary of the scholarship on *The Legend of Saint Clare* see Regis J. Armstrong, *Clare of Assisi: Early Documents* (St. Bonaventure, NY: Franciscan Institute Publications, 1993) 246-249.

    19. The tradition for the date of his death is October 4. In listings of the death dates of martyrs and saints used in the Franciscan Order, Thomas is listed under October 4. See *Martyrologium Franciscanum,* auctore Arturo a Monasterio, recognitum et auctum a Ignatio Beschin et Juliiene Palazzolo (Roma, Librariam Collegi S. Antonii, 1938) under October 4.

    20. Cf. 1C 90,119.

    21. Cf. 1C 117.

    22. Cf. 1C 98.

    23. Cf. 1C 99.

    24. Cf. *Sicut phialae aureae,* BF I 49.

    25. Because 1C was commissioned by a pope for purposes of church renewal, it is often called canonical. This does not mean the text is simply a tool for furthering church politics. It means the text emerges out of specific context for a specific purpose, in this case the promotion of a saint worthy of imitation by all people.

    26. Cf. 1C 22.

    27. Cf. 1C 23.

    28. Cf. 1C 86.

    29. Cf. J.A. Hellmann, "The Seraph in Thomas of Celano's *Vita Prima*" in *That Others May Know and Love: Essays in Honor of Zachary Hayes,* ed. Michael Cusato and F. Edward Coughlin (St. Bonaventure, NY: Franciscan Institute 1997) 23-41.

    30. Cf. 1C 118.

    31. Cf. 1C 89.

    32. Cf. François de Beer, *La Conversion de Saint François* (Paris: Editions Franciscaines, 1963).

    33. Cf. Regis J. Armstrong, "Clare of Assisi, the Poor Ladies, and Their Ecclesial Mission in the First Life of Thomas of Celano," *Greyfriars Review* 5:3 (1991) 389-424.

Prologue

[1] It is my desire to explain in orderly detail the acts and life of our most blessed father Francis: pious devotion and truth will always be my guide and instructor.[a] Since everything which *he did and taught* is retained fully in the memory of none, I have endeavored to set forth, insofar as I was able, though with unskilled words, at least those things which I heard from his own mouth or I learned from trustworthy and esteemed witnesses, just as the illustrious lord Pope Gregory has commanded.[b] But how I wish I were deserving to be a disciple of him who always avoided the obscurities of expression and the embellishments of language!

[2] I have divided everything that I was able to gather together about the blessed man into three books, and I have separated each book into individual chapters.[c] In this way the sequence of his various exploits will not be confused nor their truthfulness be brought into doubt. Accordingly, the first book follows an historical sequence and is devoted principally to the purity of his blessed way of life, to his virtuous conduct and his wholesome teaching. In this book I have also introduced a few of the many miracles which our Lord God deemed worthy to perform through him while he was *living in the flesh*. The second book, on the other hand, tells of his deeds from the next to last year of his life up to his happy death. The third book contains many miracles, while passing over in silence many others, which our most glorious Saint performed on earth while reigning *with Christ* in the heavens. Also recorded in this section are the veneration, honor, praise and glory paid to him by the blessed Pope Greg-

Acts 1:1

Phil 1:22

Rv 20:4

---

a. At the very outset, Thomas begins to follow the lines of traditional hagiography, in this instance, *The Life of Saint Martin of Tours* (+397) by Sulpicius Severus (+ c. 420).

b. The reference is to Pope Gregory IX, Hugolino dei Conti di Segni, whose papacy extended from March 19, 1227, until August 22, 1241. Born in 1170, he was a nephew of Pope Innocent III into whose service he entered after completion of his studies in Paris and Bologna. In 1217 Hugolino became the Papal Legate for Lombardy and Tuscany, and encountered Francis, Clare and their followers. Eventually he became their official protector.

c. The individual chapter is further divided into numbered subsections. All references to this text are to these numbered subsections.

ory, together with all the cardinals of the holy Roman Church, when they enrolled him in the catalogue of the saints. Thanks be to Almighty God, who always displays Himself *in His saints* as worthy of admiration and love.

Ps 68: 36

End of the Prologue.

The First Book

Chapter I
HOW HE LIVED IN THE CLOTHING AND SPIRIT OF THE WORLD

Jb 1:1

[1]In the city of Assisi, which is located in the confines of the Spoleto valley, *there was a man* named Francis. From the earliest years of his life his parents reared him to arrogance in accordance with the vanity of the age.[a] And by long imitating their worthless life and character he himself was made more vain and arrogant.[b]

A most wicked custom has been so thoroughly ingrained among those regarded as Christians, and this pernicious teaching has been so universally affirmed and prescribed, as though by public law, that, as a result, they are eager to bring up their children from the very cradle too indulgently and carelessly. For when they first begin to speak or babble, little children just born are taught shameful and detestable things by gestures and utterances. And when the time of weaning arrives, they are compelled not only to say but to devote themselves to things full of excess and lewdness. Compelled by the anxiety of youth, they are not bold enough to conduct themselves honorably, since in doing so they would be subject to harsh discipline. A secular poet puts it eloquently:

> Since we have grown up with the training of our parents,
> all sorts of evils pursue us from our childhood.[c]

---

a. Thomas does not give us a date for Francis's birth, but elsewhere he writes that Francis died in the twentieth year of his conversion (cf. n. 119), or twenty years after he had given himself perfectly to Christ (cf. n. 88). Since Francis's conversion took place when he was about 25 years old (cf. n. 2), and since he died on October 3, 1226, he must have been born in 1181 or 1182. Gregory the Great (+604), whose second book of his *Dialogues* is dedicated to a life of Benedict of Nursia (+546), treats the birth of Benedict in the same way, that is, without a date, cf. Gregory the Great, *Dialogue* II, Introduction.

b. The literary tradition of the Middle Ages and the strong influence of Saint Augustine of Hippo (+430) on medieval hagiography prompted Thomas to stress the power of evil operative upon the young Francis.

c. Seneca, *Ad Lucilium epistulae morales*, v 1, ep. 60, 1. The philosopher Seneca (+85 C.E.) enjoyed great popularity in the Middle Ages as a moralist and presumed correspondent of Saint Paul. Thomas calls him a poet because of several plays attributed to him. The quotation here is from his letters.

This is quite true, for the desires of parents are more injurious to their children, the more they yield gladly to lax discipline.

But even when the children advance a little more in age, they always fall into more ruinous actions by their own choice. For a flawed tree grows from a flawed root; and what was once badly corrupted can only with difficulty be brought back to the norm of justice.

But when they begin to enter the gates of adolescence, what sort of individuals do you imagine they become? Then, without question, flowing on the tide of every kind of debauchery, since they are permitted to fulfill everything they desire, they surrender themselves with all their energy to the service of outrageous conduct. For having become *slaves of sin* by a voluntary servitude, all the members of their body display the *weapons of iniquity,* and, displaying nothing of the Christian religion in their own lives and conduct, they content themselves with just the name of Christian. These wretched people generally pretend that they have done more wicked things than they actually have, so that they do not appear despicable by seeming innocent.[a]

Rom 6: 20

Rom 6: 13

[2]This is the wretched early training in which that man whom we today venerate as a saint—for he truly is a saint—passed his time from childhood and miserably wasted and squandered his time almost up to the twenty-fifth year of his life. Maliciously *advancing beyond* all of his *peers* in vanities, he proved himself a more excessive *inciter of evil* and *a zealous imitator* of foolishness. He was an object of admiration to all, and he endeavored to surpass others in his flamboyant display of vain accomplishments: wit, curiosity, practical jokes and foolish talk, songs, and soft and flowing garments. Since he was very rich, he was not greedy but extravagant, not a hoarder of money but a squanderer of his property, a prudent dealer but a most unreliable steward.[b] He was, nevertheless, a rather kindly person, adaptable and quite affable, even though it made him look foolish.[c] For this reason more than for anything else, many went over to him,

2 Mc 4:1, Gal 1: 14

Lk 19:20

---

a. Cf. Saint Augustine, *The Confessions:* "I pretended to obscenities I had not committed, lest I might be thought less courageous for being more innocent, and be accounted cheaper for being more chaste" (II, 3, 7). [This and all future quotations from *The Confessions* have been taken from: Augustine, *The Confessions,* translated with an introduction and notes by Maria Boulding, O.S.B. (Hyde Park, New York: New City Press,1997).]

b. Thomas returns to the examples of the earlier hagiographical tradition in which highlighting the goodness of a person before his conversion can be found. In this case there is a possible allusion to *The Life of Saint Anselm of Canterbury* (+1109) by Eadmer of Canterbury (+1124) in which he describes the saint as generous and reliable. Cf. Eadmer, *Life of Anselm* I, 1.

c. Sulpicius Severus described Martin as being "kept completely free from those vices in which that class of men [soldiers] become too frequently involved." *The Life of Martin* 2. [This and all future quotations from *The Life of Martin* have been taken from: "The Works of Sulpicius Severus," translated with Preface and Notes by Alexander Roberts, in *A Select Library of Nicene and Post-Nicene Fathers of the Christian Church,* Second Series, Volume XI, (New York: The Christian Literature Company, 1894).]

partisans of evil and inciters of crime. Thus with his crowded procession of misfits he used to strut about impressively and in high spirits, making his way through the streets of Babylon.[a]

Ps 33:13
$$\text{Then } \textit{the Lord looked down from the heavens}$$
and *for the sake* of His own *name*
He removed His own *anger far* from him,
and for His own *glory He bridled* Francis's mouth
so that he would *not perish* completely.
Is 48:9
The hand of the Lord was upon him,
Ez 1:3
a change of the right hand of the Most High,
Ps 77:11
that through him the Lord might give sinners confidence
in a new life of grace;
and that of conversion to God
he might be an example.[b]

Chapter II
HOW GOD VISITED HIS HEART THROUGH A BODILY ILLNESS
AND A VISION IN THE NIGHT

[3]That man was still boiling in the sins of youthful heat, and his unstable time of life was driving him without restraint to carry out the laws of youth. At the very time when he, not knowing how to be-
Rv 20:2
come tame, was aroused by the venom of the *ancient serpent,* the divine vengeance, or rather the divine anointing, came upon him.[c] This aimed, first of all, at recalling his erring judgment by bringing distress to his mind and affliction to his body, according to that proph-
Hos 2:6
ecy: *Behold I will hedge up your path with thorns, and I will stop it with a wall.*

Thus worn down by his long illness, as human obstinacy deserves since it is rarely remedied except through punishment, he began *to*

---

a. *The Confessions* (II, 3, 8): "With companions like these I roamed the streets of Babylon and wallowed in its filth as though basking amid cinnamon and precious ointments." See also *Lives of the Desert Fathers* VIII, 3, and Eadmer, *The Life of Anselm* II, 24 both of which refer to a pre-conversion state by the image of the "streets of Babylon."

b. In order to express the rhetorical and poetic quality of Thomas's work, the translators have broken the text into sense lines. By doing so they break with the customary way of presenting Thomas's work in order to express in a clearer way the beauty of the text. Cf. Introduction for explanation of sense lines.

c. Thomas uses the Latin word, *fervescere,* which literally means "to boil" to highlight the "boiling" passions of the adolescent Francis. In this sentence Thomas plays on two Latin words, *divina ultio* [divine vengeance] and *divina unctio* [divine anointing].

mull over within himself things that were not usual for him.[a] When he
had recovered a little and, with the support of a cane, had begun to
walk about here and there through the house in order to regain his
health, he went outside one day and began to gaze upon the surrounding countryside with greater interest. But the beauty of the
fields, the delight of the vineyards, and whatever else was beautiful
to see could offer him no delight at all.[b] He wondered at the sudden
change in himself, and considered those who loved these things
quite foolish.

    [4]From that day he began to regard himself as worthless and to
hold in some contempt what he had previously held as admirable
and lovable, though not completely or genuinely. For he had not yet
been freed from the *bonds of vanities* nor *had he thrown off from his neck
the yoke* of degrading servitude. It is difficult to leave familiar things
behind, and things once instilled in the spirit are not easily weakened. The spirit, even a long time after its early training, reverts to
them; and vice, with enough custom and practice, becomes second
nature.[c]

    Thus Francis still tried to avoid the divine grasp, and, for a brief
time losing sight of the Father's reproach while good fortune smiled
upon him, *reflected upon worldly matters.* Ignoring *God's plan,* he
vowed, out of vainglory and vanity, to do great deeds. A certain nobleman from the city of Assisi was furnishing himself on a large
scale with military weaponry and, swollen by the wind of *empty
glory,* he asserted solemnly that he was going to Apulia to enrich
himself in money or distinction.[d] When Francis heard of this, because he was whimsical and overly daring, he agreed to go with
him. Although Francis did not equal him in nobility of birth, he did
outrank him in graciousness; and though poorer in wealth, he was
richer in generosity.

Lk 12:17

Is 5:18; Gn 27:40

1 Cor 7:34; Wis 9:13

Gal 5:26

---

a. Medieval hagiography frequently describes illness as providing the occasion for conversion. In *The Life of Anselm* I,3, for example, Anselm actually prays for an illness in order to be received into the monastic way of life.

b. Gregory the Great writes of the early years of Benedict in a similar way: "While still living in the world, free to enjoys its earthly advantages, he saw how barren it was with its attractions and turned from it without regret." Cf. Gregory the Great, *Dialogue II*, Prologue. [This and all subsequent quotations will be taken from the following text: Gregory the Great, *Dialogues*, translated Odo John Zimmerman, O.S.B., *The Fathers of the Church*, vol. 39 (New York: Fathers of the Church, Inc., 1959).]

c. Cf. Cicero (+43 B.C.E.), *De finibus bonorum* V 25 74: "Even the votaries of pleasure take refuge in evasions: the name of virtue is on their lips all the time, and they declare that pleasure is only at first the object of desire, and that later habit produces a sort of second nature, which supplies a motive for many actions not aiming at pleasure at all." Cf. Macrobius, *Saturnalia* VII 9 7; Augustine, *Contra Julianum opus imperfectum* IV 103.

d. Apulia is located in the southeastern part of the peninsula. It is the place where Walter of Brienne, head of Innocent III's papal militia, was fighting against Markwald of Anweiler, seneschal of the German Empire. The latter claimed tutelage over the young Frederick II, who had been entrusted to the pope.

[5]One night, after Francis had devoted himself with all of his determination to accomplish these things and was eager, seething with desire, to make the journey, the One who had struck him with the *rod of justice* visited him in a *vision during the night* in the sweetness of grace.[a] Because he was eager for glory, the Lord exalted and enticed him to its pinnacle. For it seemed to him that his whole house was filled with soldiers' arms: saddles, shields, spears and other equipment. Though delighting for the most part, he silently wondered to himself about its meaning. For he was not accustomed to see such things in his house, but rather stacks of cloth to be sold. He was greatly bewildered at the sudden turn of events and the response that all these arms were to be for him and his soldiers. With a happy spirit he awoke the next morning. Considering his vision a prediction of great success, he felt sure that his upcoming journey to Apulia would be successful. *In fact he did not know what he was saying,* and as yet he did not at all understand the gift sent to him from heaven. He should have been able to see that his interpretation of it was mistaken. For, although the vision bore some semblance of great deeds, his spirit was not moved by these things in its usual way. In fact, he had to force himself to carry out his plans and undertake the journey he had desired.

Margin references: Is 10:24; Jb 4:13; 33:15; Mk 9:5

It is a fine thing
that at the outset mention be made of arms,
and very fitting
that arms be handed over
to a soldier about to do battle
with one strong and fully armed.
Thus,
like a second David
in the name of the Lord God of hosts
from the long-standing abuse of its enemies,
he might *liberate Israel.*

Margin references: Lk 11:21; 1 Sm 17:45; 1 Sm 17:26

---

a. The phenomenon of dreams, frequently found in medieval hagiography, is present throughout the Bible (e.g., Gn 28:12; 41:5; 47:7; 1 Kgs 3:15). Further information can be found in Martin Dulaey, "Sognes-Reves", in *Dictionnaire de Spiritualité Ascetique et Mystique XIV* (Beauchesne: Paris, 1990) 1054-1066. For other examples in medieval hagiography, cf. Eadmer, *The Life of Anselm* I,2; *Lives of the Desert Fathers* X:4.

Chapter III

HOW, CHANGED IN MIND BUT NOT IN BODY,
FRANCIS TALKED ALLEGORICALLY ABOUT THE TREASURE HE HAD FOUND
AND ABOUT HIS BRIDE

[6]Changed in mind but not in body, he now refused to go to Apulia and was anxious to direct his will to God's. Thus he retired for a short time from the tumult and business of the world and was anxious to keep Jesus Christ in his inmost self. Like an experienced merchant, he concealed *the pearl he had found* from the eyes of mockers and *selling all he had,* he tried to buy it secretly.   Mt 13:46

Now there was in the city of Assisi a man he loved more than all the rest. They were of the same age and the constant intimacy of their mutual love made him bold to share his secrets with him. He often brought him to remote places suitable for talking, asserting that he had found a great and valuable treasure. This man was overjoyed, and since he was so excited about what he heard, he gladly went with him whenever he was summoned. There was a cave near the city where they often went and talked together about the treasure.[a] The man of God, who was already holy because of his holy proposal, was accustomed to enter the cave, while his companion waited outside, and inspired by a new and extraordinary spirit he would pray to his *Father in secret.* He acted in such a way that no one   Mt 6:6
would know what was happening within. Wisely taking the occasion of the good to conceal the better, he consulted God alone about his holy proposal. He prayed with all his heart that the eternal and true God guide his way and *teach him to do His will.* He endured great   Ps 143: 10
suffering in his soul, and he was not able to rest until he accomplished in action what he had conceived in his heart. Different thoughts followed one after another, and their relentlessness severely disturbed him. He was burning inwardly with a divine fire, and he was unable to conceal outwardly the flame kindled in his soul. He repented that he had sinned so grievously and that he had offended *the eyes of majesty.* While his past and present transgressions   Is 3:8
no longer delighted him, he was not yet fully confident of refraining from future ones. Therefore, when he came back out to his companion, he was so exhausted from his struggle that one person seemed to have entered, and another to have come out.

---

a. Gregory the Great had described this period of Benedict's conversion in a similar way when writing of his flight to a "lonely wilderness" where he made his home in a "narrow cave." Cf. Gregory, *Dialogue* II 1. Thomas uses the word *crypta* to describe that place of solitude. It is translated in this instance as "cave." Its location and nature remain problematic.

[Ps 126:2]

[Mt 13:44]

[7]One day, when he had invoked the Lord's mercy with his whole heart, the Lord showed him what he must do. *He was filled with* such *great joy* that, failing to restrain himself in the face of his happiness, he carelessly mentioned something to others. Even though he could not remain silent because of the greatness of the love inspired in him, he nevertheless spoke cautiously and in riddles. Just as he spoke to his special friend about a *hidden treasure,* so he endeavored to talk to others in figures of speech. He said that he did not want to go to Apulia, but promised to do great and noble deeds at home. People thought he wanted to get married, and they would ask him: "Do you want to get married, Francis?" He replied: "I will take a bride more noble and more beautiful than you have ever seen, and she will surpass the rest in beauty and excel all others in wisdom."

[Jas 1:27]

[Mt 13:44]

[1 Tm 2:7]

[Eph 3:7]

Indeed
the *unstained bride* of God is
the true *religion* that he embraced,
and the hidden treasure *the kingdom of heaven,*
that he sought with great longing.
For it had to be that the gospel call be fulfilled
in the one who was to be
in faith and truth
a minister of the gospel.

Chapter IV
HOW AFTER HE SOLD ALL HIS BELONGINGS,
HE DESPISED THE MONEY HE RECEIVED

[Jb 12:5]

[8]Ah! Inclined and strengthened by the Holy Spirit the blessed servant of the Most High, seeing that the *appointed time* was at hand, followed that blessed impulse of his soul. Thus, as he trampled upon worldly things, he made his way to the greatest good. He could no longer delay, for by then a fatal disease had spread everywhere and infected the limbs of so many that, were the doctor to delay just a little, it would stifle breath and snatch life away.

After fortifying himself with the sign of the holy cross, he arose, and when his horse was made ready, he mounted it. Taking with him scarlet cloth to sell, he quickly came to a city called Foligno.[a] There after selling everything he brought in his usual way, this successful merchant even left behind the horse he was riding, when he had obtained his price. Starting back, he put down his bags and pondered conscientiously what to do about the money. In a wonderful way, in an instant, he turned completely to the work of God. Feeling the heavy weight of carrying that money even for an hour, and reckoning all its benefit to be like so much sand, he hurried to get rid of it. Returning toward the city of Assisi, he came across a church on the side of the road. It had been built in ancient times in honor of Saint Damian and was threatening to collapse because of age.[b]

[9] Arriving at this church, the new *knight of Christ,* aroused by piety at such a great need, entered it with awe and reverence.[c] He found a poor priest there, kissed his holy hands with great devotion, offered him the money he was carrying and explained his proposal in great detail.[d]

2 Tm 2:3

The priest was astounded and, surprised at this sudden conversion in incredible circumstances, he refused to believe what he was hearing. Because he thought he was being mocked, he refused to keep the money offered to him. It seemed to him that Francis, just the day before, was living outrageously *among his relatives and acquaintances* and *exalting his stupidity* above others. But Francis stubbornly persisted and endeavored to create confidence in his words. He pleaded, begging the priest with all his heart to allow him to stay

Lk 2:44

Prv 14:29

---

a. Foligno is located about 15 km or 9 miles east of Assisi. In modern use the term "scarlet" describes a vivid shade of red. Prior to the 16th century it referred to a bright dye, white, blue or green. The taste for the exotic that influenced Western fashion at the time of the Crusades brought from the East its first samples of damask, scarlet and crimson. All these rare fabrics were prized and very expensive.

b. The church of San Damiano was built in 1103 by a consortium of noble families that later entrusted it to the prior of San Rufino in Assisi and later to the city's bishop. It is difficult to know the condition of the church when Francis first entered it. For information concerning the origins and questions of the Church of San Damiano, see Marino Bigaroni, "San Damiano-Assisi: The First Church of Saint Francis," *Franciscan Studies* (1986) 45-97; Arnaldo Fortini, *Francis of Assisi,* translated by Helen Moak (New York: Crossroad, 1981), p. 215, j.

c. Thomas uses the word *pietas* here, a word he employs nineteen times in 1C. It is a difficult word to translate since our modern English word, piety, does not fully express the richness of a word that classical Roman writers associated with humility, religion and spirituality, and viewed as the bedrock of all social relationships. Cf. H. Hagenvoort, *Pietas: Selected Studies in Roman Religion,* (Leiden, E.J. Brill: 1980). For a thorough study of the word in the history of spirituality, see Irénée Noye, *"Piété," Dictionnaire de la Spiritualité Ascetique et Mystique.*

d. *Propositum,* a word Thomas uses twenty-two times in this work, does not always have the same meaning, cf. *Corpus des Sources Franciscaines I, Thesaurus Celanensis,* edited Georges Mailleux, (Louvain: Publications du CETEDOC, 1974). At times it refers to purpose, as in this instance, while at other times it suggests a plan or a proposal. The word takes on a technical sense when it refers to the *propositum vitae,* the primitive "rule," which Francis and his first brothers presented to Pope Innocent III. Cf. 1C 33.

with him for the sake of the Lord.[a] Finally the priest agreed to let him stay, but out of fear of Francis's parents did not accept the money. The true scorner of wealth threw it onto a window opening, since he cared for it as much as he cared for dust.[b]

For he desired
to possess wisdom, which *is better than gold,*
and *to acquire understanding,* which *is more precious than silver.*

Prv 16:16

Chapter V
HOW HIS FATHER PERSECUTED AND BOUND HIM

Acts 16:17; Mt 25:5

[10]While the *servant of the most high God was staying* there, his father went around everywhere like a diligent spy, wanting to know what had happened to his son. When he had learned that Francis was living in that place in such a way, he was *touched inwardly with sorrow of heart* and *deeply disturbed* by the sudden turn of events. *Calling together his friends* and *neighbors,* he raced to the place where the servant of God was staying.

Gn 6:6; Ps 6:4

Lk 15:6

The new athlete of Christ,[c] when he heard the threats of his pursuers and learned in advance of their coming, lowered himself into a hiding place, which he had prepared for himself for this very purpose, wanting *to leave room for their anger.* That pit was in the house and was known to only one person.[d] He hid in it for one month continually and scarcely dared to come out even for human needs. Whenever food was given he ate it in the secrecy of the pit, and every

Rom 12:19

---

a. Bernard of Clairvaux (+1153) writes of a similar desire expressed by Saint Malachy (+1148). Cf. Bernard, *The Life and Death of Saint Malachy the Irishman* 4. This text is important because it provides an example of the hagiographic style of Bernard of Clairvaux whose influence on the spiritual literature of the early thirteenth century—and hence on Thomas—was significant.

b. In the changing economy of the twelfth and thirteenth centuries, such an attitude toward money was common. Money was "portable" wealth and concern for it presented new temptations to greed and exploitation. Cf. Lester K. Little, *Religious Poverty and the Profit Economy in Medieval Europe* (Ithaca, NY: Cornell University Press, 1978), especially pp. 35-41; George Duby, *William Marshal: The Flower of Chivalry,* translated by Richard Howard (New York: Pantheon Books, 1985), pp. 87-90.

c. The image of a trained athlete appears in hagiography from the time of the martyrs to describe one involved in the struggle of the spiritual life. As one had to practice physical asceticism or self-discipline to be a strong athlete, so one had to do the same in the spiritual life. Bernard of Clairvaux portrays Malachy as an "athlete of the Lord," cf. Bernard of Clairvaux, *The Life and Death of Saint Malachy the Irishman* VIII, 16. [All passages from this text are taken from Bernard of Clairvaux, *The Life and Death of Saint Malachy the Irishman,* translated and annotated by Robert Meyer, (Kalamazoo: Cistercian Publications, 1978).] Felix, a monk of the eighth century, described the Anglo-Saxon saint, Guthlac (+714), as an "athlete of Christ," cf. Felix, *The Life of Saint Guthlac* 33. [All passages from this text are taken from: *Felix's The Life of Saint Guthlac,* text, translation and notes by Bertram Colgrave, (Cambridge: Cambridge University Press, 1985).]

d. This passage raises questions: the nature of the *fovea* [pit], its location, and the identity of the one person who knew of its existence. Subsequent writers attempt to bring clarity to these issues in their biographies of Francis.

service was provided to him in secret. He prayed with flowing tears[a] that *the Lord would free* him *from the hands of those persecuting* his *soul* and that he could favorably fulfill his fervent wishes. *Fasting and weeping,* he earnestly prayed for the Savior's mercy, and, lacking confidence in his own efforts, *he cast his care upon the Lord.* Though staying *in a pit and in darkness,* he was imbued with an indescribable happiness never before experienced. Then totally on fire, he abandoned the pit and openly exposed himself to the curses of his persecutors.

Ps 142:7

Jl 2:12

Ps 55: 23; Dn 2:22

[11]He rose, therefore, swift, energetic and eager, carrying *the shield of faith* for the Lord, and strengthened with the armor of great confidence, he set out for the city.[b] Burning with holy fervor, he began to accuse himself of idleness and sloth.

Eph 6:16

When all those who knew him saw him, they compared his latest circumstances with his former and they began to reproach him harshly.[c] Shouting that he was insane and out of his mind, *they threw mud from the streets and stones* at him. They saw him as changed from his earlier ways and weakened by starving his body. They blamed everything he did on starvation and madness.

Ps 18:43; Jn 8:59

But since *the patient person is better than the proud,* God's servant showed himself deaf to all of them, and neither broken nor changed by any wrong to himself he gave thanks to God for all of them.

Eccl 7:9

For in vain do the wicked persecute those striving for virtue,
for the more they are stricken, the more fully will they triumph.
As someone says, "Disgrace makes a noble mind stronger."[d]

[12]For some time rumor and gossip of this sort raced *through the streets* and *quarters of the city,* and the noise of that ridicule echoed here and there. The report of these things reached the ears of many, finally reaching his father. When he heard the name of his own son mentioned and that the commotion among the townspeople swirled around him, he immediately arose, not to free him, but rather to de-

Sg 3:2

---

a. For similar descriptions see Alan, Bishop of Auxerre, *Vita secunda s. Bernardi* 4; Eadmer, *The Life of Anselm* II,53; and Gregory the Great, *Dialogue II* 17.

b. Once again Thomas uses military images which were frequently used in medieval hagiography. Cf. Felix, *The Life of Saint Guthlac* 27: "Then girding himself with spiritual arms . . . he took the shield of faith." See also, Bernard of Clairvaux, *The Life and Death of Saint Malachy the Irishman* 26: "He puts on the weapons so mighty with God."

c. Geoffrey of Auxerre, author of Book Four of the *Vita prima s. Bernardi,* writes: "When his brothers and close relatives saw that [Bernard] was considering leaving the world and adopting this way of life, they began to use every means in their power to try and make Bernard change his mind."

d. Thomas seems to refer to Seneca's *Epistola Morales* 4, n.10:2: *Habet enim hoc optimum in se generosus animus, quod concitatur ad honestia* [For this is the best that the generous spirit has within itself, that it is urged toward honorable things].

stroy him. With no restraint, he pounced on Francis like a wolf on a lamb and, glaring at him fiercely and savagely, he grabbed him and shamelessly dragged him home. With no pity, he shut him up for several days in a dark place.[a] Striving to bend Francis's will to his own, he badgered him, beat him, and bound him.

As a result of this Francis became more fit and eager to carry out his holy plan. Neither the reproach of words nor the exhaustion of chains eroded his patience.

> Those taught to rejoice in suffering
> will not deviate from an upright intention and way of life
> nor be stolen from Christ's flock
> because of beatings and chains.

Ps 32:6
> Nor will they fear *in the flood of many waters*
> whose refuge from oppression is the Son of God,
> who always shows them his sufferings,
> greater than those they endure.

Chapter VI
HOW HIS MOTHER FREED HIM
AND HOW HE STRIPPED HIMSELF BEFORE THE BISHOP OF ASSISI

[13]When his father had left home for a little while on pressing family business, the man of God remained bound in the prison of his home.[b] His mother, who had remained at home alone with him, did not approve of her husband's action and spoke to her son in gentle words. After she saw that she could not dissuade her son from his

1 Kgs 3:26
proposal, *she was moved by* maternal *instinct*. She broke his chains and let him go free. Thanking Almighty God, he quickly returned to the place he had been before. Since he had passed the test of temptations, he now enjoyed greater freedom. Throughout these many struggles, he began to exhibit a more joyful appearance. From the in-

---

a. The same spirit of persecution by one's father appears elsewhere in hagiography. Cf. Eadmer, *The Life of Anselm* I,4: "That is to say, he stirred up in his father's mind so keen a hatred against him that he persecuted him as much, or even more, for the things he did well as for those which he did ill." [This and all future references are taken from: Eadmer of Canterbury, *The Life of Saint Anselm, Archbishop of Canterbury*, edited with introduction, notes by Richard Southern, (London, New York:Thomas Nelson and Sons Ltd, 1962).]

b. As a merchant in the cloth trade, Pietro di Bernardone may have traveled to cloth fairs in Champagne. He would have taken the usual trade route from the Mediterranean to the North Sea. Since the end of the 12th century Champagne had been the main center for trade between East and West. Trade fairs traveled from city to city: Troyes, Provins, Bar-sur-Aube and Lagny. Generally Italian businessmen were the driving force and the masters of trade traveling the passes of the Alps and Apennines, at times in harsh weather. They traveled alone or, because the road was dangerous, in caravans. Cf. Map B, p. 208.

juries inflicted he received a more confident spirit and, now free to go anywhere, he moved about with even greater heart.

Meanwhile, the father returned and, not finding him and heaping sin upon sin, he turned to reviling his wife. He raced to the place, shaking and screaming, so that if he could not call his son back, he might at least drive him from the area. But since *the fear of the Lord is* the assurance of fortitude, when the child of grace heard that his father in the flesh was coming to him, he went out on his own to meet his father crying out loudly that binding and beating lead to nothing. In addition, he declared he would gladly suffer anything for the name of Christ.

Prv 14:26

[14]When the father saw that he could not recall him from the journey he had begun, he became obsessed with recovering the money. The man of God had desired to spend it on feeding the poor and on the buildings of that place. But the one who did not love money could not be deceived even by this appearance of good, and the one who was not bound by any affection for it was not disturbed in any way by its loss. The greatest scorner of the things of earth and the outstanding seeker of heavenly riches had thrown it into the dust on the windowsill. When the money was found, the rage of his angry father was dampened a little and his thirsty greed was quenched a bit by its discovery. Then he led the son to the bishop of the city to make him renounce into the bishop's hands all rights of inheritance and return everything that he had.[a] Not only did he not refuse this, but he hastened joyfully and eagerly to do what was demanded.

[15]When he was in front of the bishop, he neither delayed nor hesitated, but immediately took off and threw down all his clothes and returned them to his father. He did not even keep his trousers on, and he was completely stripped bare before everyone. The bishop, observing his frame of mind and admiring his fervor and determination, got up and, gathering him in his own arms, covered him with the mantle he was wearing. He clearly understood that this was prompted by God and he knew that the action of the man of God, which he had personally observed, contained a mystery. After this *he*

---

a. This is a reference to Bishop Guido II, who was bishop of Assisi from 1204 until his death, July 30, 1228. A papal decree of May 12, 1198 addressed to his predecessor, Guido I, confirmed the many episcopal privileges by the bishop of Assisi. At the time of these events, Guido II possessed broad powers in both the ecclesiastical and civil worlds. Cf, *Regesta Honorii Papae III*, ii, P. Pressutti, Rome, 1895, n. 4958, p. 242 NV. I, p. 323. For information on the juridical procedures for bringing an accused person before the consuls or bishop, cf. Arnaldo Fortini, *Francis of Assisi*, translated by Helen Moak (New York: Crossroad, 1981), 222-230.

Ps 30:11   *became* his *helper.* Cherishing and comforting him, he embraced him
Col 3:12   in the depths of charity.

Look!
Now he wrestles naked with the naked.

1 Cor 7: 33

After putting aside all that is *of the world,*
he is mindful only of divine justice.[a]
Now he is eager to despise his own life,
by setting aside all concern for it.
Thus
there might be peace for him,
a poor man on a hemmed-in path,
and only the wall of the flesh would separate him
from the vision of God.

Chapter VII
HOW, WHEN CAPTURED BY BANDITS,
HE WAS THROWN INTO THE SNOW,
AND HOW HE SERVED LEPERS

[16]He who once enjoyed wearing scarlet robes now traveled about
half-clothed. Once while he was singing praises to the Lord in
French in a certain forest, thieves suddenly attacked him.[b] When
they savagely demanded who he was, the man of God answered con-
Ps 48:3; Mt 27:4   fidently and forcefully: "I am the herald *of the great King!* What is it to
you?" They beat him and threw him into a ditch filled with deep
snow, saying: "Lie there, you stupid herald of God!" After they left,
he rolled about to and fro, shook the snow off himself and jumped
out of the ditch. Exhilarated with great joy, he began in a loud voice
to make the woods resound with praises to the Creator of all.

---

a. The theme of nudity entered the language of spirituality through the literature of the early Christian
    martyrs, as can be seen in the *The Life of Polycarp* 13; *Acts of the Martyrdom of Perpetua and Felicitas* 10,
    20; *Martyrdom of SS. Carpus, Papylus, and Agathonice.* It entered into medieval literature through Saint
    Jerome, *The Life of Paula* and Saint Gregory the Great, *Homilia in Evangelium* 32 n. 2 (PL 76, 1233). Cf.
    Michel Mollat, *The Poor in the Middle Ages: An Essay in Social History,* translated by Arthur Goldhammer
    (New Haven and London: Yale University Press, 1986); Margaret Miles, *Carnal Knowing: Female
    Nakedness and Religious Meaning in the Christian West* (Boston, MA: Beacon Press, 1989).
b. The expression *lingua francigena,* translated in this text "French," refers to the language of Champagne.
    Francis may have learned French from his father or from accompanying him on his journeys to the trade
    fairs, cf. p. 192, b.

Eventually he arrived at a cloister of monks, where he spent several days covered with only a cheap shirt, serving as a scullery boy in the kitchen.[a] He wanted to be fed at least some soup. No mercy was shown him and he was not even able to get some old clothes. Not moved by anger but forced by necessity, he moved on to the city of Gubbio, where he obtained a cheap tunic from an old friend. Shortly afterward, when the fame of the man of God had grown far and wide and *his name was spread* among the people, the prior of that monastery, when he recalled the event and understood what had been done to the man of God, came to him and, out of reverence for the Savior, begged forgiveness for himself and his monks.

2 Chr 26:8; Lk 4:37

[17]Then the holy lover of profound humility moved to the lepers and stayed with them.[b] For God's sake he served all of them with great love. He washed all the filth from them, and even cleaned out the pus of their sores, just as he said in his *Testament*: "When I was in sin, it seemed too bitter for me to see lepers, and the Lord led me among them and I showed mercy to them." For he used to say that the sight of lepers was so bitter to him that in the days of his vanity when he saw their houses even two miles away, he would cover his nose with his hands.

Test 2

When he started thinking of holy and useful matters with the grace and *strength of the Most High*, while still in the clothes of the world, he met a leper one day. Made stronger than himself, he came up *and kissed him.*[c] He then began to consider himself less and less, until by the mercy of the Redeemer, he came to complete victory over himself.

Lk 1:35

Mk 14:45

While staying in the world and following its ways, he was also a helper of the poor. He extended a hand of mercy to those who had nothing and he poured out compassion for the afflicted. One day, contrary to his custom (since he was very polite), he rebuked a poor person seeking alms from him, and he was immediately *led to penance*. He began to say *to himself* that to refuse what was asked by

Mt 27:3

---

a. This may have been the monastery of *San Verecondo*, today *Vallingegno*, located just south of Gubbio. The Latin word, *garcio* [scullery boy], is a term of contempt for a certain class of workers regarded as unskilled and uncouth.

b. This may be the leper hospital of San Rufino dell'Arce near the Portiuncula or that of San Lazaro close to the Rivo Torto, or that of San Salvatore delle Mura, site of the present day Casa Gualdi which lies below Assisi and halfway to Saint Mary of the Angels. The precise location is still contested. In Assisi, as in other communes, harsh rules governed the whereabouts and movements of lepers. They were forbidden to enter the city.

c. Association with lepers and outcasts was seen as part of the life of Martin of Tours and, through him, entered into the pattern of medieval spirituality. Cf. Sulpicius Severus, *The Life of Martin* 18: "At Paris, again, when Martin was entering the gate of the city, with large crowds attending him, he gave a kiss to a leper, of miserable appearance, while all shuddered at seeing him do so."

Lk 7:49

Ps 14:1; Acts 5:4
someone begging in the name of such a great King would be both a
shame and a disgrace. And so he fixed this *in his heart:* to the best of
his ability, never to deny anything to anyone begging from him for
God's sake. This he did and with such care that he offered himself
completely, in every way, first practicing before teaching the gospel
counsel:[a] *"Give to the one who begs from you, and do not turn away from the*
Mt 5: 42 *one who wants to borrow from you."*

Chapter VIII
HOW HE BUILT THE CHURCH OF SAN DAMIANO,
AND OF THE WAY OF LIFE OF THE LADIES LIVING IN THAT PLACE[b]

[18]The first work that blessed Francis undertook,
after he had gained his freedom
from the hands of his carnally-minded father,
was to build a house of God.
He did not try to build a new one,
but he repaired an old one,
restored an ancient one.[c]
He did not tear out the foundation,
but he built upon it,
always reserving to Christ his prerogative,
although unaware of it,
for no one can lay another foundation,
but that which has been laid,
1 Cor 3:11 *which is Christ Jesus.*

When he had returned to the place mentioned where
the church of San Damiano had been built in ancient times,
he repaired it zealously within a short time,

---

a. The practice and the teaching of the gospel is a prominent theme of Christian hagiography. This can be seen in Gregory of Nyssa's (+394) *The Life of Moses*, II, 55: "The history all but cries out to you not to be presumptuous in giving advice to your hearers in your teaching unless the ability for this has been perfected in you by a long and exacting training such as Moses had." [This and all future passages from this text are taken from: Gregory of Nyssa, *The Life of Moses*, edited with translations, introductions, and notes by Abraham Malherbe and Everett Ferguson, (Paulist Press, NY, 1978).] Cf. Carolyn Walker Bynum, *Docere Verbo et Exemplo: An Aspect of Twelfth-Century Spirituality,* (Missoula, MT: Scholars Press, 1978).

b. Thomas uses the title, *Domina* [Lady] which traditionally referred either to princesses of blood or to nuns and canonesses. (See Du Cange, Glossarium mediae et infimae latinitatis, ed. L. Favre, (Graz,1883-1887). *Domina* 5, and *Domicellae* 2).

c. Thomas uses the adjective *novus* [new] thirty-nine times in this work emphasizing Francis as a "new knight of Christ" (n. 9), a "new athlete of Christ" (n. 10), and a "new evangelist" (n. 89). Integrally associated with him are a new: mystery (n. 85), song (n. 126), Bethlehem (n. 85), miracles (nn. 119, 121), vine (n. 74), light (nn. 119, 123), order (n. 74), joy (n. 119), waters (n. 151), teachings (n. 26), spirit (n. 6) and rite (n. 89).

aided by the grace of the Most High.[a]
This is the blessed and holy place where
the glorious religion and most excellent Order
of Poor Ladies and holy virgins
had its happy beginning,
about six years after the conversion of the blessed Francis
and through that same blessed man.

The Lady Clare,[b]
a native of the city of Assisi,
the most precious and strongest stone of the whole structure,
stands as the foundation for all the other stones.[c]
For
after the beginning of the Order of Brothers,
when this lady was converted to God
through the counsel of the holy man,
she lived for the good of many
and as an example to countless others.
Noble by lineage, but more noble by grace,[d]
chaste in body, most chaste in mind,
young in age, mature in spirit,
steadfast in proposal and most eager in her desire for divine love,
endowed with wisdom and excelling in humility,
bright in name, more brilliant in life, most brilliant in character.[e]
[19]A noble structure of precious pearls arose above this woman,
whose praise comes not from mortals but from God,   Rom 2:29
since our limited understanding is not sufficient to imagine it,
nor our scanty vocabulary to utter it.

---

a. Rebuilding churches was a medieval expression of piety. The eighth century author, Eddius Stephanus, for example, writes of the English saint Wilfrid (+710), that he first rebuilt a church at York and subsequently another in honor of Saint Peter and, finally, one in honor of Saint Mary. Cf. Eddius Stephanus, *The Life of Bishop Wilfrid*, text, translation and notes by Bertram Colgrave (Cambridge, New York: Cambridge University Press, 1985). Similar examples may be found in the following: Theodore of Cyrus, *A History of the Monks of Syria*, "Life of Julian," 13, translated by R.M. Price,(Kalamazoo: Cistercian Publications, 1985); Bernard of Clairvaux, *The Life of Saint Malachy the Irishman* VI, 12.

b. For further information on the life of Clare of Assisi, see *Clare of Assisi: Early Documents*, translated and edited by Regis J. Armstrong, (St. Bonaventure, NY: Franciscan Institute, 1993); Ingrid Peterson, *Clare of Assisi: A Biographical Study* (Quincy: Franciscan Press, 1993).

c. This may allude to 1 Kgs 7:9-10, a description of Solomon's temple, and Rv 21:19, a description of the city walls of the heavenly Jerusalem and thus would refer to the temples of the historical and the heavenly Jerusalem.

d. Cf. Jerome, *Paula* 1, "Noble in family, she was nobler still in holiness."

e. This is the earliest instance of the play on the name Clare or *Chiara* which is translated as "bright." Thus the Latin text: *Clara nomine, vita clarior, clarisima moribus.*

First of all,
the virtue of mutual and continual charity
that binds their wills together
flourishes among them.
Forty or fifty of them can dwell together in one place,
wanting and not wanting the same things
forming one spirit in them out of many.[a]
Second,
the gem of humility,
preserving the good things bestowed by heaven
so sparkles in each one
that they merit other virtues as well.[b]
Third,
the lily of virginity and chastity
diffuses such a wondrous fragrance among them
that they forget earthly thoughts
and desire to meditate only on heavenly things.
So great a love of their eternal Spouse arises in their hearts
that the integrity of their holy feelings keeps them
from every habit of their former life.
Fourth,
all of them have become so distinguished
by their title of highest poverty
that their food and clothing
rarely or never
manage to satisfy extreme necessity.[c]
[20]Fifth,
they have so attained the unique grace
of abstinence and silence
that they scarcely need to exert any effort
to check the prompting of the flesh

a. "*Idem velle atque idem nolle, ea demum firma amicitia est* [Wanting and not wanting the same thing—this is the foundation of a firm friendship]." This is a proverbial saying that Sallust places in the mouth of Cataline who urges his fellow conspirators in the name of friendship to join him in revolt, cf. Caius Crispus Sallust, *Bellum Catilinarium*, XX 4 (The Loab Classical Library) 33-34.

b. The monastic tradition presented humility as the foundation of all virtue, e.g. Bernard of Clairvaux, *Sermo I in Nativitate Domini* (PL 183:115): "Be eager to humble yourselves, for [humility] is the foundation and guardian of the virtues." "No gem," writes Bernard, "is more resplendent . . . than humility." Cf. Bernard, *De Consideratione ad Eugenium papam tertiam libri quinque* II 13. "What is as pure," he asks, "or as perfect as humility of heart?" Bernard, *In Annuntiatione, Sermo* III, 9. Thomas, however, places it in the second position in the life of the Poor Ladies even though he echoes the earlier approach in suggesting that humility "preserves the good things bestowed by heaven" and enables them to "merit other virtues as well."

c. In this instance the Latin *titulus* [title] is a canonical term signifying the source of one's adequate support. In the phrase *altissimae paupertatis titulo* [the title of the highest poverty] Thomas uses the term in a paradoxical way to indicate that the source of support of the Poor Ladies is poverty.

and to restrain their tongues.[a]
Sixth,
they are so adorned with the virtue of patience
in all these things,
that adversity of tribulation,
or injury of vexation
never breaks or changes their spirit.[b]
Seventh,
and finally,
they have so merited the height of contemplation
that they learn in it everything they should do or avoid,
and they know how to go beyond the *mind to God* with joy,   2 Cor 5:13
persevering night and day
in praising Him and praying to Him.

For the moment
let this suffice
concerning these virgins dedicated to God
and most devout servants of Christ.
Their wondrous life
and their renowned practices received from the Lord Pope Gregory,[c] at that time Bishop of Ostia,
would require another book
and the leisure in which to write it.

---

a. The vast amount of medieval literature on silence flows from the monastic tradition in which it was viewed as a form of abstinence. Cf. Carolyn Walker Bynum, *Holy Feast and Holy Fast: The Religious Significance of Food to Medieval Women* (Berkeley: University of California, 1987); Rudolph Bell, *Holy Anorexia* (Chicago: University of Chicago Press, 1985).

b. The cultivation of patience was seen as a primary means of identification with Christ. While strongly present in the literature of martyrdom, it entered into that of monasticism through the Desert tradition and became a prerequisite for the quiet of contemplation.

c. *Institutio* [practices] refers to the *Form of Life* given by Cardinal Hugolino to the Poor Ladies of San Damiano in 1219, cf. Hugolino "The Form and Manner of Life Given by Cardinal Hugolino (1219)" in *Clare of Assisi: Early Documents*, translated and edited by Regis J. Armstrong (St. Bonaventure: Franciscan Institute Publications, 1993) 89-100.

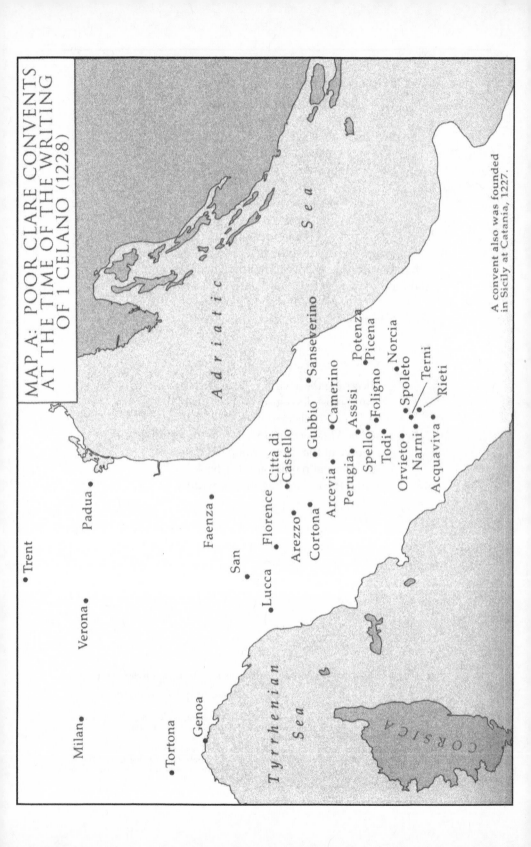

MAP A: POOR CLARE CONVENTS
AT THE TIME OF THE WRITING
OF 1 CELANO (1228)

A convent also was founded
in Sicily at Catania, 1227.

Adriatic Sea

Tyrrhenian Sea

CORSICA

Trent

Milan

Verona

Padua

Tortona

Genoa

Faenza

San

Lucca

Florence

Arezzo

Cortona

Città di Castello

Gubbio

Sanseverino

Arcevia

Camerino

Perugia

Assisi

Spello

Foligno

Potenza Picena

Todi

Norcia

Orvieto

Spoleto

Narni

Terni

Acquaviva

Rieti

Chapter IX

HOW, WHEN HE HAD CHANGED HIS HABIT,
HE REBUILT THE CHURCH OF SAINT MARY OF THE PORTIUNCULA,
AND HOW, WHEN HE HAD HEARD THE GOSPEL
AND LEFT BEHIND EVERYTHING,
HE DESIGNED AND MADE THE HABIT WORN BY THE BROTHERS

[21] Meanwhile, the holy man of God, having changed his habit and rebuilt that church, moved to another place near the city of Assisi, where he began to rebuild a certain church that had fallen into ruin and was almost destroyed. After a good beginning he did not stop until he had brought all to completion.[a]

From there he moved to another place, which is called the "Portiuncula," where there stood a church of the Blessed Virgin Mother of God built in ancient times. At that time it was deserted and no one was taking care of it.[b] When the holy man of God saw it so ruined, he was moved by piety because he had a warm devotion to the Mother of all good and he began to stay there continually.[c] The restoration of that church took place in the third year of his conversion. At this time he wore a sort of hermit's habit with a leather belt. He carried a staff in his hand and wore shoes.

[22] One day the gospel was being read in that church about how the Lord sent out his disciples to preach. The holy man of God, who was attending there, in order to understand better the words of the gospel, humbly begged the priest after celebrating the solemnities of the Mass to explain the gospel to him. The priest explained it all to him thoroughly line by line. When he heard that Christ's disciples should not *possess gold* or *silver* or *money, or carry on their journey a wallet or a sack, nor bread nor a staff,* nor *to have shoes* nor *two tunics,* but that they should preach *the kingdom of God* and *penance,* the holy man, Francis, immediately *exulted* in the *spirit of God.*[d] "This is what I want," he said, "this is what I seek, this is what I desire with all my heart." The holy fa-

Mt 10:9-10

Lk 9:2; Mk 6:12

Lk 1:47

---

a. While Thomas uses the Latin word, *habitus,* taken here in the material sense of habit as clothing, it implies also a juridical change: Francis is now under Church protection. The church is probably the church of Saint Pietro della Spina, in the fields beyond Assisi not far from the Rivo Torto. It was cared for by the Benedictines.

b. The first mention of this church in the archives of Assisi occurs in 1045, although it is not listed until 1150 as among the churches of the area. There is a legend that it was built at the direction of Pope Liberius (352-366) by some hermits who upon their arrival from the Holy Land placed a "little piece [*portiuncula*]" of stone there from the place of the Dormition of the Blessed Virgin. Another legend maintains that Saint Benedict enlarged it in 516. The present building, however, dates from the 10th century. At the time of Francis, this church was also dependent on the Benedictine abbey of Mt. Subasio.

c. For Thomas's use of *pietas* [piety] cf. p. 189, c.

d. Rather than a single gospel text, this is a collection of phrases borrowed from the three Synoptics. Traditionally it is held that this event took place on the feast of the apostle, Saint Matthias, February 24.

2 Cor 7:4

Ex 3:5

Gal 5:24

ther, *overflowing with joy,* hastened to implement the words of salvation, and did not delay before he devoutly began to put into effect
what he heard.[a] Immediately, *he took off the shoes from his feet,* put
down the staff from his hands, and, satisfied with one tunic, exchanged his leather belt for a cord. After this, he made for himself a
tunic showing the image of the cross, so that in it he would drive off
every fantasy of the demons.[b] He made it very rough, so that in it he
might *crucify the flesh with its vices* and sins. He made it very poor and
plain, a thing that the world would never covet. As for the other
things he heard, he set about doing them with great care and reverence. For he was no deaf hearer of the gospel; rather he committed
everything he heard to his excellent memory and was careful to carry
it out to the letter.[c]

Chapter X
HIS PREACHING THE GOSPEL AND ANNOUNCING PEACE
AND THE CONVERSION OF THE FIRST SIX BROTHERS

Sir 23:22

Mk 6:41

Mt 4:17

[23]He then began to preach penance to all with a fervent spirit and
joyful attitude. He inspired his listeners with words that were simple
and a heart that was heroic. His word was like *a blazing fire,* reaching
the deepest parts of the heart, and filling the souls of all with wonder. He seemed entirely different from what he had been, and *looking
up to heaven* he refused to look down upon earth. It is truly amazing
that he first *began to preach* where he had learned to read as a little
boy, and where at first he was reverently buried.

---

a. Thomas now relies upon Athanasius's (+373) *The Life of Antony* (+356), a text which not only established
   the framework of Christian hagiography but also had an enormous influence on the development of
   religious life. "[Antony] went into the church pondering these things, and just then it happened that the
   gospel was being read, and he heard the Lord saying to the rich man, 'If you would be perfect, go, sell what
   you possess and give to the poor, and you will have treasure in heaven.' It was as if by God's design he held
   the saints in his recollection and as if the passage were read on his account. Immediately Antony went out
   from the Lord's house and gave to the townspeople the possessions he had from his forebears." Athanasius,
   The Life of Antony 2. [This and all further quotations are taken from *Athanasius: The Life of Antony and the
   Letter to Marcellinus,* translation and introduction by Robert C. Gregg, preface by William A. Clebsch (New
   York, Ramsey, Toronto: Paulist Press, 1980).]
b. Throughout his writings Thomas frequently refers to struggles with demons, a theme that was expressed
   throughout medieval hagiography because of the influence of Athanasius's *The Life of Antony* in which
   demons occupy an important place.
c. Cf. Sulpicius Severus, *The Life of Martin,* 2: ". . . iam tum Evangelii non surdus auditor [He was no deaf
   hearer of the gospel]." For the important role of memory in ancient and medieval learning, see Mary
   Carruthers, *The Book of Memory: A Study of Memory in Medieval Culture* (Cambridge: Cambridge
   University Press, 1990).

Thus;
a blessed beginning was confirmed
by a more blessed end.[a]
Where he learned, there he also taught;
and where he began, there he blessedly ended.

In all of his preaching, before he presented the word of God to the assembly, he prayed for peace saying, *"May the Lord give you peace."* He always proclaimed this to men and women, to those he met and to those who met him. Accordingly, many *who hated peace* along with salvation, *with the Lord's help* wholeheartedly embraced peace. They became themselves *children of peace,* now rivals for eternal salvation.[b]

2 Thes 3:16

Ps 120:7

Mk 16:20, Lk 10:6

[24]Among these there was a man from Assisi with a holy and simple character, who was the first to follow devoutly the man of God.[c]

After him, brother Bernard, embracing *the delegation of peace,* eagerly ran after *the holy man of God* to gain *the kingdom of heaven.*[d] He had often received the blessed father as a guest, had observed and tested his life and conduct. Refreshed by the fragrance of his holiness, he conceived fear and gave birth to the spirit of salvation. He used to see him praying all night long, sleeping rarely, praising God and the glorious Virgin, His mother. He was amazed and said, *"This man truly is from God."* So he hurried *to sell all* he had and distributed it to the poor, not to his relatives. Grasping the title of a more perfect way, he fulfilled the counsel of the holy gospel: *"If you wish to be perfect, go and sell* all *you own, and give to the poor, and you will have treasure in heaven; then come, follow me."* When he had done this, he joined the holy man, Francis, in the same life and habit, and was always with him, until the brothers increased in number and he, with the obedience of his devoted father, was sent to other regions.[e]

Lk 14:32

Lk 4:34;
Mt 13:44-46

Lk 23:47

Mt 13:46

Mt 19:21

---

a. The church of Saint George, which stood on the site of the present Blessed Sacrament Chapel in the basilica of Saint Clare, was near the house of Pietro Bernardone and included a school which Francis attended. Clare went to the church to hear him preach and it was there that he was first buried in 1226 and there that his canonization took place in 1228.

b. The proclamation or greeting of peace is a theme frequently present in medieval hagiography. Cf. William of Saint Thierry, Arnold of Bonval, Geoffrey of Auxerre, *Vita prima s. Bernardi* XXIII; Cf. Bernard, *The Life of Malachy* VIII.17

c. The identity of this first companion remains unknown. He is never mentioned again in any writing, not even by Thomas himself. It has been suggested that after his initial enthusiasm he left Francis's company.

d. This is a reference to Bernard, son of Quintavalle di Berardello, a wealthy, educated noble and a member of a family that was prominent in Assisi.

e. *Sanctus* can mean "saint" and, as such, refer to the title conferred by canonization. It may also simply mean "holy" and, thus, refer more generally to a holy person.

His conversion to God stood out as a model
for those being converted
in the way he sold his possessions
and distributed them to the poor.

Mt 2:10

The holy man Francis *rejoiced with very great joy*
over the arrival and conversion of such a man,
because the Lord seemed to be caring for him,
giving him a needed companion

Sir 6:14

and a *faithful friend.*

²⁵Immediately another man from the city of Assisi followed him. This man was highly respected in his way of life, and what he began in a holy fashion he completed within a short time in an even holier

Mt 25:19

way.[a] Not *much later,* brother Giles followed, *a simple and upright man*

Jb 2:3

who feared God.

[He lived for a long time:

Ti 2:12

he was holy, living *justly* and *piously.*
He left us examples of perfect obedience,
work, including work with his hands,
solitary life, and holy contemplation.][b]

When one other, brother Philip, joined them, he brought their

Is 6:6-7

number to seven.[c] The Lord touched his *lips with the coal* that cleanses, so that he might speak of Him in words that were sweet and flowing with honey.[d] Understanding and interpreting the holy Scriptures, *al-*

Jn 7:15

though he had not studied, he became an imitator of those whom the

Acts 4:13

Jewish leaders considered *ignorant* and *without learning.*

---

a. This may be Peter di Catanio di Guiduccio, who joined Francis with Bernard on April 16, 1208. He served as vicar during Francis's early absences and later accompanied him to Egypt and Syria in 1219. When Francis resigned his office in 1220, Peter was named his vicar. He died on March 10, 1221, at the Portiuncula where he is buried.

b. Giles was received into the Order on April 23,1208, and died on April 27, 1262. This sentence, then, is an interpolation. Thomas could not have written in 1229 about Brother Giles's long life at this early date.

c. Philip the Tall, *Filippo Longo,* accompanied Francis to the Rieti Valley and, in 1209, to Rome. He served as Visitator of the Poor Ladies of Saint Damian in 1219 and again from 1228 to 1246. He died in 1259.

d. The Latin word *mellifluous,* flowing with honey, appears three times in the 1C: in this paragraph, in referring to Francis's words at Greccio (n. 86) and in those of Pope Gregory IX at Francis's canonization (n. 125). It is used frequently in Cistercian literature, especially by Bernard of Clairvaux, the "Mellifluous" Doctor.

Chapter XI
THE SPIRIT OF PROPHECY AND THE ADMONITIONS OF SAINT FRANCIS

[26]Day by day the blessed father Francis was being *filled* with the *consolation* and the grace of the *Holy Spirit*, and, with all vigilance and concern, he was forming his new sons with new instruction, teaching them to walk with steady steps the way of holy poverty and blessed simplicity.[a]

One day he was marveling at the Lord's mercy in the kindness shown to him. He wished that the Lord would show him the course of life for him and his brothers, and he went to a place of prayer, as he so often did.[b] He remained there a long time *with fear and trembling* before *the Ruler of the whole earth*. He recalled *in the bitterness of* his *soul the years* he spent badly, frequently repeating this phrase: *"Lord, be merciful to me, a sinner."* Gradually, an indescribable joy and tremendous sweetness began to well up deep in his heart.

> He began to lose himself;
> his feelings were pressed together;
> and that darkness disappeared
> which fear of sin had gathered in his heart.
> Certainty of the forgiveness of all his sins poured in,
> and the assurance of being revived in grace was given to him.
> Then he was caught up above himself and totally engulfed in
> light,
> and, with his inmost soul opened wide,
> he clearly saw the future.
> As that sweetness and light withdrew,
> *renewed in spirit,*
> he now seemed to be *changed into another man.*[c]

[27]He returned and said to the brothers with joy: *"Be strong,* dear brothers, and *rejoice in the Lord.* Do not be sad, because you seem so few, and do not let my simplicity or yours discourage you. The Lord has shown me that God will make us grow into a great multitude, and will spread us to the ends of the earth. I must also tell you what I

Margin references:
Acts 9:31
Tb 13:6
Zec 4:14
Is 38:15
Lk 18:13
1 Sm 10:6; Ps 51:12
Eph 6:10
Phil 3:1

---

a. Cf. p.196, c.

b. This place of prayer was probably Poggio Bustone in the Rieti Valley. Francis passed this area on his way to or from Rome.

c. The language here is reminiscent of Gregory the Great whose theology of compunction and contemplation influenced much of the later tradition. Cf. Gregory, *Dialogue* II 35: ". . . the light of holy contemplation enlarges and expands the mind in God until it stands above the world."

Rv 7:9

saw about your future, though it would please me more to remain silent, if charity did not compel me to tell you. *I saw a great multitude* of people coming to us, wishing to live with us in the habit of a holy way of life and in the rule of blessed religion. Listen! The sound of them is

Sg 2:14; Gn 8:3

still *in my ears*, their *coming and going* according to the command of holy obedience. I seemed to see highways filled with this multitude

Acts 2:5

gathering in this region *from* nearly *every nation*. Frenchmen are coming, Spaniards are hurrying, Germans and Englishmen are running, and a huge crowd speaking other languages is rapidly approaching."[a]

When the brothers heard this, they were filled with wholesome joy, either because of the grace which the Lord God had conferred on His holy one, or because they eagerly thirsted for the profit of their neighbors, whom they wanted to increase in number daily in order

Acts 2:47

to *be saved.*

[28]And the holy man said to them: "So that we may give thanks   LR VI
faithfully and devotedly[b] to the Lord our God for all His gifts and that you may know how our present and future brothers should live, understand this truth about the course of things to come. In the beginning of our way of life together we will find fruit that is very sweet and pleasant. A little later fruit that is less pleasant and sweet will be

Lam 1:20

offered. Finally, fruit *full of bitterness* will be served, which we will not be able to eat. Although displaying some outward beauty and fragrance, it will be too sour for anyone to eat. As I told you, the Lord

Gn 12:2

certainly will make us grow into *a great nation*. But in the end it will turn out as follows: it is like a man who tosses his nets into the sea or

Lk 5:6

a lake and catches *a great number of fish*. When he has loaded them all into his boat, he is reluctant to carry them all because of their great number. So *he would pick out* for his *baskets* the larger ones and those

Mt 13:47-48

he likes, but the others he would *throw out.*"

All these things the holy man of God predicted.
How brightly their truth shines!
How they came true in events is clear

---

a. A similar vision can be found in the *Vita prima s. Bernardi* IX in which the universal appeal to and attraction of many followers demonstrate the fruits of holiness and confirm credibility. The author writes of Bernard: "Longing for his work to bear rich fruit filled his heart and, as he stood still and closed his eyes in prayer, he saw coming down the mountains round about and down into the valley below such a great company of men of every type and standing that the valley could not hold them all."

b. References on the inside margin point out passages found in other writings that influenced Thomas in the composition of this work. Direct references are indicated in the text with an open bullet.

to those who reflect in the spirit of truth.
See how *the spirit of prophecy rested* on Saint Francis!   Is 11:2

Chapter XII
HOW HE SENT THEM IN PAIRS THROUGH THE WORLD,
AND HOW THEY CAME TOGETHER AGAIN IN A SHORT TIME

[29] At that same time, another good man entered their religion, and they increased their number to eight.[a] Then the blessed Francis called them all to himself and told them many things about *the kingdom of God,* contempt of the world, denial of their own will, and subjection of the body. He separated them into four groups of two each.   Acts 1:3

"Go, my dear brothers," he said to them, *"two by two* through different parts of the world, *announcing peace* to the people and *penance for the remission of sins.* Be *patient in trials,* confident that the Lord will fulfill His plan and promise. Respond humbly to those who question you. *Bless those who persecute you.* Give thanks to those who harm you and bring false charges against you, for because of these things an *eternal kingdom is prepared* for us."   Lk 10:1 / Acts 10:36 / Mk 1:4; Rom 12:12 / Rom 12:14 / Mt 25:34

LR III 10-14

Accepting the command of holy obedience *with* much *joy and gladness,* they humbly prostrated themselves on the ground before Saint Francis. Embracing them, he spoke sweetly and devotedly to each one: *"Cast your care upon the Lord, and he will sustain you."* He used to say this phrase whenever he transferred brothers by obedience.   1 Mc 5:54 / Ps 55:23

[30] Then brother Bernard with brother Giles hastened on the way to Santiago;[b] Saint Francis with one companion chose another part of the world.[c] The other four, two by two, went to other regions.

Only a short time had passed when Saint Francis began desiring to see them all. *He prayed to the Lord,* who *gathers the dispersed of Israel,* mercifully to bring them together soon. So it happened in a short time: they came together at the same time according to his desire, without any human summons, *giving thanks to God.*   Ex 8:30 / Ps 147:2 / Col 3:17

---

a. It is difficult to establish the identity of the individual brothers as they appear in Thomas's account. Leaving aside the anonymous man (cf. n. 24), there are now seven companions—Bernard, Giles and Philip, whom Thomas identifies, and four unidentified brothers who, together with Francis, make eight.

b. This is Santiago de Compostela, the shrine to Saint James the Apostle, in northwestern Spain. After Jerusalem it was the most popular place of pilgrimage in the Middle Ages.

c. Francis may have gone to the Rieti Valley. His companion seems to have been Philip the Tall.

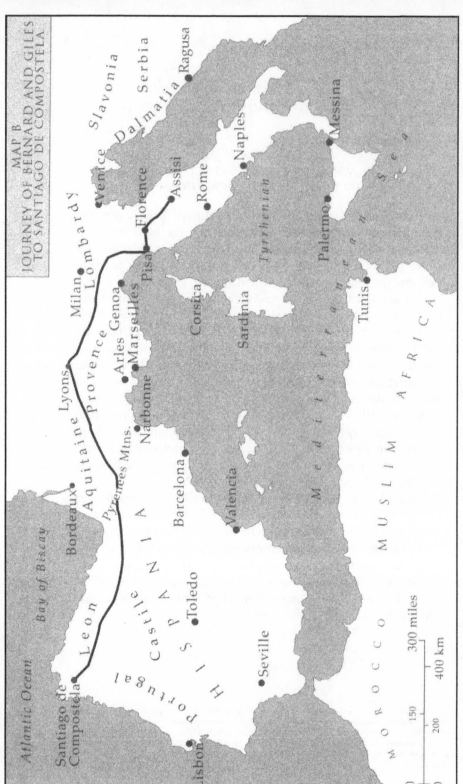

The route shown on this map is that followed by the majority of pilgrims from Italy over the Alps and through Provence to Hispania (Spain), and it is most likely that Bernard and Giles would have travelled this route (1Cel 30). It is also likely that Francis would have travelled part of this route when he tried to reach Morocco and the Miramamolin in 1213 or 1214 (1Cel 56).

ER XVIII

                            Coming together in one place,   1 Cor 11:20
they celebrate with great joy on seeing their devoted shepherd,
and they are amazed that
the same desire to come together moved all of them in this way.
They report the good things
which *the merciful Lord* was doing for them,   Ps 115:5
and if they had been somewhat negligent and ungrateful,
they humbly ask and carefully accept
correction and punishment from the holy father.[a]

They always acted in this way when they came to him, and they did not hide from him the least of their thoughts or even immediate impulses of their souls. When they had fulfilled *everything which* had been *commanded,* they regarded themselves as *useless servants.* For a   Lk 17:10 pure spirit so possessed that whole first school of blessed Francis that, though they knew how to carry out things that were useful, *holy* and *just,* they were completely ignorant of how to rejoice over them   Phil 4:8-9 with vanity. The blessed father, embracing his sons with unbounded love, began to open up to them his proposal and to show them what the Lord had revealed to him.

[31]Immediately four other good and sound men *were added* to them   Acts 2:41 as followers of the holy man of God. On that account, a loud cry began among the people and the fame of the man of God began to spread far and wide. At that time Saint Francis and his brothers felt great *gladness and* unique *joy* whenever one of the faithful, *led by the*   Lk 1:14; Mt 4:1 *Spirit* of God, came and accepted the habit of holy religion, whoever the person might be: rich or poor, noble or insignificant, wise or simple, cleric or illiterate, a layman of the Christian people. This was a great wonder to those of the world and an example of humility, challenging them to the way of a more reformed life and to penance for sins.

                            No lowliness of birth,
no weakness of poverty
stood in the way of building up in God's work
the ones *God* wanted *to build up,*   Acts 20:32

---

a. Through a curious shift into the present tense, Thomas seems to suggest that what he describes in this passage became the "ritual" of the chapters celebrated by the early fraternity. The "chapter" comes out of the earlier monastic tradition in which monks gathered together to hear a reading of a "chapter" of the monastic rule, confessed their faults and received correction.

a God who delights to be

with *the simple* and those rejected by the world.

Prv 3:32

Chapter XIII

HOW HE FIRST WROTE A RULE WHEN HE HAD ELEVEN BROTHERS,
AND HOW THE LORD POPE INNOCENT CONFIRMED IT,
AND ABOUT THE VISION OF A TREE

Acts 2:47

[32]When blessed Francis saw that the Lord God was *daily increasing* their numbers, he wrote for himself and his brothers present and future, simply and in few words, a form of life and a rule.[a] He used primarily words of the holy gospel, longing only for its perfection. He inserted a few other things necessary for the practice of a holy way of life. Then he went to Rome with all his brothers, since he greatly desired that the Lord Pope Innocent the Third confirm for him what he had written. There was in Rome at this time the venerable bishop of Assisi, Guido by name, who honored Saint Francis and all the brothers in everything and revered them with special love. When he saw Saint Francis and his brothers, he reacted strongly at their arrival, as he did not know the reason for it. He feared they wanted to leave their homeland, where the Lord had begun to perform great things through his servants. He greatly rejoiced to have such men in his diocese, for he relied most of all on their life and character. But when he heard the cause and understood their proposal, *he rejoiced greatly in the Lord* and promised to give them advice and to offer his support. Saint Francis also approached the reverend lord bishop of Sabina, named John of Saint Paul, who, among the other princes and great men at the Roman Curia, seemed to look down on the things of earth and love the things of heaven.[b] The bishop received him kindly and charitably[c] and praised highly his wish and proposal.

Phil 4:10

LR X 5

---

a. These are the very terms used by Francis in The *Testament* to describe the document, the *propositum vitae*, presented by the first brothers to Pope Innocent III.

b. Giovanni de Colonna was known as John of Saint Paul since he was a Benedictine monk of the Monastery of Saint Paul Outside the Walls. A personal friend of Bishop Guido and a confidant of Pope Innocent III and knowledgeable and active in the apostolic movements of the period, he became Cardinal Bishop of Sabina in 1204. He died in 1215. The quotation is taken from the medieval Postcommunion Prayer for the Second Sunday of Advent.

c. Thomas describes John of Saint Paul receiving Francis *benigne et caritative* [kindly and charitably], in other words, with the same dispositions Francis demands of a minister responding to a brother who is experiencing difficulties, cf. LR X 5.

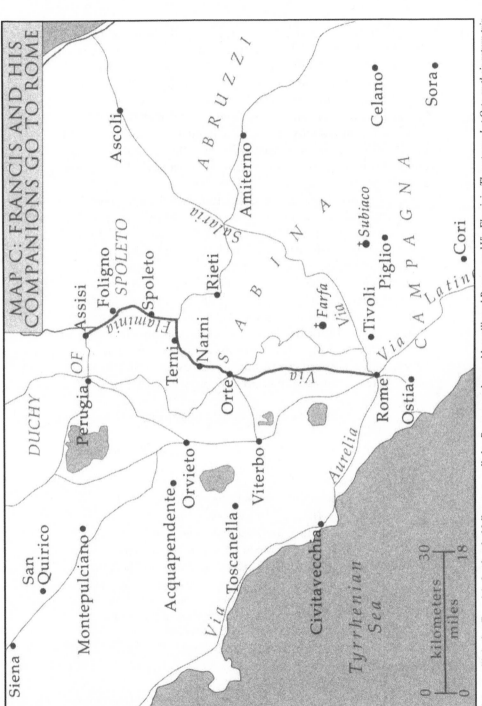

MAP C: FRANCIS AND HIS COMPANIONS GO TO ROME

It is most likely that Francis's first band of followers travelled to Rome over the aged but still used Roman road Via Flaminia. They stopped at Orte on their return trip (1 Cel 34).

1 Cor 1:2

Dt 7:12,13; Lk 10:17

1 Sm 3:19

Gn 20:16

Dn 4:7-8

Lk 7:11-12

Jdt 10:14

[33]The bishop of Sabina, a far-sighted and discerning man, questioned him about many things, urging him to turn to the monastic or eremitical life. But Saint Francis, as much as he could, humbly refused his urging. He did not despise what was urged on him, but he was intently seeking other things, moved by a loftier desire. That lord marveled at his enthusiasm and, fearful that the holy man might fail in such a lofty proposal, he pointed out smoother paths. Finally, won over by his perseverance, the bishop agreed to his pleas and from then on strove to promote his interests before the lord pope.

Presiding over *God's Church* at that time was the lord Pope Innocent the Third, a glorious man, prolific in learning, brilliant in speech, burning with zeal for justice in matters which the cause of the Christian faith demanded. When he recognized the wish of the men of God, he first considered the matter and then gave his assent to their request, something he completed by a subsequent action. Exhorting and then warning them about many things, he blessed Saint Francis and his brothers and said to them: "Go with the Lord, brothers, and as the Lord will see fit to inspire you, preach penance to all. When the almighty *Lord increases* you in numbers and grace, come back to me *with joy,* and I will grant you more things than these and, with greater confidence, I will entrust you with greater things."[a]

The Lord was truly *with* Saint Francis
wherever he went,
gladdening him with revelations and encouraging him with gifts.
For when he had gone to sleep one night,
he seemed to be walking down a road,
and alongside it stood *a tree of great height.*
That *tree was lovely and strong,*
thick and *exceedingly high.*
It came about that when he *approached* the tree
and stood under it and *marveled at its beauty* and height,
the holy man himself rose to so great a height
that he touched the top of the tree.
Taking it into his hand, he easily bent it to the ground.
It really happened this way,
when the lord Innocent,

---

a. Thus Pope Innocent III gave oral approval to the document or *propositum vitae* that Francis and his brothers brought him. This event took place in either 1209 or 1210.

a very high and lofty tree in the world,
bent himself so kindly to his wish and request.

Chapter XIV
HIS RETURN FROM THE CITY OF ROME TO THE SPOLETO VALLEY
AND OF A STOP ALONG THE WAY

[34] Saint Francis with his brothers
rejoiced greatly at the task and the favor
given by so great a father and lord.
They *gave thanks* to Almighty *God,*							Acts 27:35
who places the lowly on high
and raises up mourners to health.							Jb 5:11

He immediately went to visit the tomb of Saint Peter, and after
praying there he left the city. Setting out with his companions, he
took the road to the Spoleto Valley. As they were going, *they discussed*
among themselves the many gifts of different kinds the merciful God			Lk 24:17
granted them. They had been graciously received by Christ's vicar,
the lord and father of the whole Christian nation. How could they
carry out his advice and commands? How could they sincerely keep
the rule they had accepted and steadfastly safeguard it? How could
they walk before the Most High in all holiness and religion? Finally,
how could their life and conduct, by growth in the holy virtues, be an
example to their neighbors?

By the time Christ's new students in the school of humility had
finished their disputation, the day was far spent *and the hour was late.*
They arrived at *a deserted place.* They were hungry and exhausted from		Mt 14:15
the weariness of their journey and could not find any food, as that
place was far removed from people's homes. But God's grace was
looking after them, for suddenly they met a *man* carrying *bread in his*
hand, and *he gave it* to them and left.[a] They honestly did not recognize		1 Kgs 10:3, 4;
him and, marveling in *their hearts,* they all eagerly encouraged each		Mk 14:13
other to a greater trust in divine mercy.							Ps 35:25

After eating the food and being much strengthened by it, they
went on to a place near the city of Orte, where they stayed for about
fifteen days. Some of them went into the city to acquire the neces-

---

a. The conviction that God provides for the journey of those dedicated to him is another frequent theme in
   hagiography. Cf. *Desert Fathers* I 47; II 9; VIII 5, 6, 38-41, 44-47; X 8; XII 4, 14-15.

sary food. They brought back to the other brothers the small amount
they managed to obtain by going door-to-door and they ate together

Acts 24:3; Is 30:29 *with gratitude* and *joyful hearts.* If anything remained, since they could
not give it to anyone, they stored it in a tomb, which had once held
the bodies of the dead, so they could eat it at another time. The place
was deserted and abandoned, and hardly anyone ever visited it.

35They had great joy, because they saw nothing and had nothing
that could give them empty or carnal delight.[a] There, they began to
have commerce with holy poverty.[b] Greatly consoled in their lack of

1 Cor 7:33 all *things of the world,* they resolved to adhere to the way they were in
that place always and everywhere. Only divine consolation delighted

1 Pt 5:7 them, having put aside all *their cares* about earthly things. They decided and resolved that even if buffeted by tribulations and driven by

Eccl 3:5 temptations they would not withdraw *from* its *embrace.*

Even though the delight of that place could have greatly spoiled
true spiritual vigor, it did not capture their affection. They left the
place, so the continuity of a longer stay would not tie them even by
appearance to some kind of ownership. Then following their blessed
father, they entered the Spoleto Valley. These true proponents of justice conferred together about whether they should live among people or go off to solitary places. Saint Francis did not put his trust in

Ps 88:14 his own efforts, but with holy *prayer coming before* any decision, he

2 Cor 5:15 chose not *to live for himself* alone, but for the one *who died for all.* For he
knew that he was sent for this: to win for God souls which the devil
was trying to snatch away.

Chapter XV
ON THE FAME OF BLESSED FRANCIS
AND OF THE CONVERSION OF MANY TO GOD,
AND HOW THE ORDER WAS NAMED THE LESSER BROTHERS
AND HOW BLESSED FRANCIS FORMED THOSE ENTERING RELIGION

36Francis, Christ's bravest knight,
went around the cities and villages,
proclaiming the kingdom of God

Mt 9:35

---

a. A possible allusion to Seneca, *Epistolae morales,* Liber 1, epistola 2,6: *Honesta res laeta paupertas* [An upright thing is joyful poverty]. As frequently in the writings of Francis, poverty is here linked with joy. Cf. Adm XXVII.

b. The Latin text reads: *Coeperunt propterea cum sancta paupertate ibidem habere commercium.* Thomas uses the word *commercium* to evoke the ideas of contract and covenant.

and *preaching peace*   Mt 9:35; Acts 10:36
and penance *for the remission of sins,*   Mk 1:4
not in the persuasive words of human wisdom
but in the learning and *power of the Spirit.*   1 Cor 2:4

He *acted confidently* in all matters because of the apostolic authority   Acts 9:28 granted him. He did not use fawning or seductive flattery. He did not smooth over but cut out the faults of others. He did not encourage but struck at the life of sin with a sharp blow, because he first convinced himself by action and then convinced others by words. Not fearing anyone's rebuke, he spoke the truth boldly, so that even well-educated men, distinguished by fame and dignity, were amazed at his words and were shaken by a healthy fear in his presence.

Men ran, women also ran,
clerics hurried,
and religious rushed to see and hear the holy one of God,
who seemed to everyone a person of another age.[a]
People of all ages and both sexes hurried to behold the wonders
which the Lord worked anew in the world through his servant.

At that time,
through the presence of Saint Francis and through his reputation,
it surely seemed a new light had been sent from heaven to earth,
driving away all the darkness
that had so nearly covered that whole region
that hardly anyone knew where to turn.
Deep forgetfulness of God
and lazy neglect of his commandments
overwhelmed almost everyone,
so that they could barely be roused from old, deep-seated evils.
[37]He gleamed   Sir 50:6; Prv 7:9
like a shining *star in the darkness of night*   Jl 2:2
and *like the morning spread over* the darkness.[b]

---

a. Eadmer of Canterbury offers a similar picture of people of all ways of life coming to Anselm. Cf. Eadmer, *The Life of Anselm*, I, 22.

b. These images, inspired by Gregory IX's proclamation, *Mira circa nos*, issued at Francis's canonization, reflect Thomas's theology of reform in which images of light-darkness, fertility-aridity, death-life were so prominent. Thomas raises Francis to the level of a theological-historical exemplar who begins a reform of the Church during his earthly life and who leaves behind a *forma* or model by which this reform is to be continued.

Thus, in a short time,
the appearance of the entire region was changed
and, once rid of its earlier ugliness,
it revealed a happier expression everywhere.
The former dryness was put to rout
and a crop sprang up quickly in the untilled field.

Zec 8:12 Even the uncultivated *vine* began
Lv 1:9 to produce buds with a *sweet-smell* for the Lord,
and when it had produced *flowers of sweetness,*
Sir 24:23 it brought forth equally *the fruit of honor and respectability.*
Is 51:3 *Thanks and the voice of praise* resounded everywhere,
as many,
casting aside earthly concerns,
gained knowledge of themselves
in the life and teaching of the most blessed father Francis
and aspired to love and reverence for their Creator.

Many people,
well-born and lowly, cleric and lay,
driven by divine inspiration,
began to come to Saint Francis,
for they desired to serve
under his constant training and leadership.[a]
All of these
the holy one of God,
like a fertile stream of heavenly grace,
watered with showers of gifts
and he adorned the field of their hearts
with the flowers of perfection.

Ex 38:23 He is without question an *outstanding craftsman,*
for through his spreading message,
the Church of Christ is being renewed in both sexes
according to his form, rule and teaching,
and there is victory for the triple army of those being saved.[b]
Furthermore,

---

a. Cf. Eadmer of Canterbury, *The Life of Anselm* 1, 22, 31.

b. This may be an allusion either to the three ranks in the church (clergy, religious, laity) or to the three Franciscan Orders (Lesser Brothers, Poor Ladies, and Lay Penitents).

to all he gave a norm of life
and to those of every rank
he sincerely pointed out the way of salvation.

[38]But the subject at hand is primarily the Order that he accepted and retained as much out of love as out of profession. What was that Order? He himself originally planted the Order of Lesser Brothers and on the occasion of its founding gave it this name.[a] For when it was written in the Rule, "Let them be lesser . . . ," at the uttering of this statement, at that same moment he said, "I want this fraternity to be called the Order of Lesser Brothers."

Test 19

They were truly lesser who, by being subject to all, always sought the position of contempt, performing duties which they foresaw would be the occasion of some affront. In this way they might merit to be grounded on the solid rock of true humility and to have the well-designed spiritual structure of all the virtues arise in them.

Yes, the noble building of charity rises
upon the foundation of perseverance;   Eph 2:20
and in it *living stones,*   1 Pt 2:5
gathered from every part of the world,
have been built into a dwelling place of the Holy *Spirit.*   Eph 2:22
What a great flame of charity burned in the new disciples of
Christ!
What great love of devout company flourished in them![b]
When they all gathered somewhere
or met each other on the road (which frequently happened),
in that place a shoot of spiritual love sprang up,
scattering over all love the seeds of real delight.

What more can I say?
There were
chaste embraces, delightful affection, a holy kiss,
sweet conversation,
modest laughter, joyful looks, *a clear eye,*   Mt 6:22

---

a. *Ordo Fratrum Minorum* is translated as Order of Lesser Brothers. "Friars Minor," the commonly accepted title of the First Order of Saint Francis, reflects the early English translations of *frater* as "friar" and the diminutive *minor* as "minor."

b. A spirituality of mutual love and affection characterizes the monastic tradition especially in the literature of the twelfth century Cistercian reform. Cf. *Lives of the Desert Fathers,* XX, 8 and *The Life of Bernard,* 14.

Prv 15:4-1   a supple spirit, *a peaceable tongue, a mild answer,*
                a single purpose, prompt obedience, and untiring hands.

[39] Since they looked down on all earthly things and never loved themselves selfishly, they poured out all their loving affection in common, hiring themselves out for wages to provide for their brothers' needs. They gathered together out of desire and were delighted to stay together; but they found being apart a burden, parting bitter, and separation hard.

But these obedient knights never dared to put anything before the orders of obedience: before the word of obedience was uttered, they prepared themselves to carry out the order. They almost ran headlong to carry out what they were asked with no thought of contradicting it, knowing nothing about distinguishing precepts.[a]

As followers of most holy poverty, since they had nothing, they loved nothing; so they feared losing nothing. They were satisfied with a single tunic, often patched both inside and out. Nothing about it was refined, rather it appeared lowly and rough so that in it they seemed completely *crucified to the world.* They wore crude trousers with a cord for a belt. They held firmly to the pious proposal of remaining this way and having nothing more. So they were safe wherever they went. Disturbed by no fears, distracted by no cares, they awaited the next day without any worry.[b] Though frequently on hazardous journeys, they were not anxious about where they might stay the next day. Often they needed a place to stay in extreme cold, and a baker's oven would receive them; or they would hide for the night humbly in caves or crypts.

During the day those who knew how worked with their own hands, staying in the houses of lepers or in other suitable places, serving everyone humbly and devoutly. They did not want to take any job that might give rise to scandal;[c] but rather always doing what was holy and just, honest and useful, they inspired all they dealt with to follow their example of humility and patience.

LR V 4
Test 16
Gal 6:14
ER VII

---

a. This comment suggests that, already at the time of Thomas's writing, the Order had a number of brothers who argued about the prescriptions of LR and Test. The lack of legal precision in the document approved by Pope Innocent III and the ambiguous nature of Test confirm that, as many maintain, the Founder saw commitment to the gospel life as a work of the Holy Spirit. Cf. LR X 8.

b. Cf. Seneca, *Epistulae morales* I ep. 12 n. 9: *Ille beatissimus est et securus sui possessor, qui crastinum sine sollicitudine expectat* [That person is most happy and in secure possession of his self who awaits the next day without great concern].

c. ER VII prohibits them from being treasurers, overseers, or having any kind of supervisory position in a house. It adds: "Let them be subject to all in the same house."

[40]The virtue of patience so enveloped them that they sought to be where they would suffer persecution of their bodies rather than where their holiness would be known and praised, lifting them up with worldly favor. Often mocked, objects of insult, stripped naked, beaten, bound, jailed,[a] and not defending themselves with anyone's protection, they endured all of these abuses so bravely that from their mouths came only the *sound of praise and thanksgiving.*

They never or hardly ever stopped praying and praising God. Instead, in ongoing discussion, they recalled what they had done. They gave thanks to God for the good done and, with groans and tears, paid for what they neglected or did carelessly. They would have thought themselves abandoned by God if they did not experience in their ordinary piety that they were constantly visited by the spirit of devotion. For when they felt like dozing during prayer, they would prop themselves up with a stick, so that sleep would not overtake them. Some anchored themselves with cords, so furtive sleep would not disturb prayer. Some bound themselves with irons; and others shut themselves in wooden cells.

Whenever their moderation was upset, as normally happens, by too much food or drink, or if they went over the line of necessity because of weariness from travel, they punished themselves severely with many days of fasting. They strove to restrain the burning of the flesh by such harsh treatment that they did not hesitate to strip themselves on freezing ice, and to cover themselves in blood from gashing their bodies with sharp thorns.[b]

[41]They so spurned earthly things that they barely accepted the most basic necessities of life; and, as they were usually far from bodily comfort, they did not fear hardship. In all these things, they sought *peace* and meekness *with all.* Always doing what was *modest and peaceful,* they scrupulously avoided all scandal. For they hardly spoke even when necessary; nor did anything harmful or useless *come out of their mouth,* so that in all their life and action nothing immodest or unbecoming could be found. Their every act was disciplined, their bearing modest. With eyes fixed on the ground and their minds set on heaven, all their senses were so subdued that they scarcely allowed themselves to hear or see anything except what their holy purpose demanded.

Is 51:3

Heb 12:14; Jas 3:17

Mt 4:4

---

a. This passage is reminiscent of Paul's Second Letter to the Corinthians 11:23-27 in which he reflects on his sufferings for the gospel.
b. In his description of the brothers throwing themselves into freezing water or into thorn bushes, Thomas combines accounts of the actions of Benedict and of Bernard. Cf. Gregory the Great, *Dialogue* II 2; Alan, Bishop of Auxerre, *Vita secunda s. Bernardi* III.

Among them there was
no envy, no malice, no rancor,
no mocking, no suspicion, no bitterness.
Instead, there was
great harmony, constant calm,
Is 51:3
thanksgiving, and songs of praise.
These are the lessons by which the devoted father
instructed his new sons
not so much *in words* and *speech*
1 Jn 3:18
but in deed and truth.

Chapter XVI
CONCERNING THEIR STAY IN RIVO TORTO
AND ABOUT SAFEGUARDING POVERTY

[42]Blessed Francis gathered with the others in a place called Rivo
Torto near the city of Assisi.[a] In this place there was an abandoned
hut. Under its cover lived these despisers of great and beautiful
houses, protecting themselves from the torrents of rain. As the saint
said, "It is easier to get to heaven from a hut than from a palace."[b] All
his sons and brothers were living in that same place with the blessed
2 Cor 11:27
Father, *with great labor*, and lacking everything. Often they were deprived of the comfort of bread, content with turnips they begged in
their need here and there on the plain of Assisi. The place in which
they were staying was so narrow that they could barely sit or sleep in
it.

Yet there was no complaining about this,
no grumbling;
but with peaceful heart,
the soul filled with joy
preserved the virtue of patience.[c]

---

a. Rivo Torto, a crooked, snake-like stream below the road from Assisi to Panzo, flows down into the Umbrian
Valley not far from San Damiano.

b. A similar saying is attributed to "a certain hermit" by Peter Cantor (+1197): *"Melius et tutius prosilitur in
caelum de turgurio quam de palatio* [It is better and safer to proceed into heaven from a simple hut than from
a palace]" Cf. Peter Cantor, *Verbum abbreviatum* 86.

c. These words are taken from the hymn from the Common of Several Martyrs, *Sanctorum Meritis: Non
murmur resonat, non querimonia/Sed corde tacito, mens bene conscia/Conservat patientiam* [No grumbling
resounds, no complaint/But with silent heart, the mind well attuned/Preserves patience].

Saint Francis used to engage carefully in a daily, or rather, constant examination of himself and his followers. Allowing nothing dangerous to remain in them, he drove from their hearts any negligence. Unbending in his discipline, he *was* watchful *of his guard* at every hour. For if, as happens, any temptation of the flesh struck him, he would immerse himself in a ditch filled in winter with ice, remaining in it until every seduction of the flesh went away. The others avidly followed his example of mortifying the flesh.[a]

Is 21:8

[43]He taught them to mortify not only vices and to check the promptings of the flesh, but also to check the external senses, through which death enters the soul. At that time the emperor Otto passed through that area, traveling in great pomp and circumstance to receive the crown of an earthly empire. The most holy father and his followers were staying in that small hut next to the very parade route. He did not go outside to look and did not allow the others to do so, except for one who, without wavering, proclaimed to the emperor that his glory would be short-lived.[b] The glorious holy one, living within himself and walking in *the breadth of his heart,* prepared in himself a worthy *dwelling place of God.*[c] That is why the uproar outside did not seize his ears, nor could any cry intrude, interrupting the great enterprise he had in hand. Apostolic authority resided in him; so he altogether refused to flatter kings and princes.

Ps 119:45
Eph 2:22

[44]He always strove for holy simplicity, refusing to allow the narrow place to restrict *the breadth of his heart.* For this reason, he would write the names of the brothers on the beams of that little house so that each would know his place when he wished to pray or rest, and the confines of the place would not disturb the silence of the spirit.

Ps 119:45

One day while they were staying there, a man came leading an ass to the little shelter where the man of God and his companions were staying. To avoid being sent away, the man urged the ass to enter by saying, "Get inside, for we shall do well for this place!" When the

---

a. The mortification of the flesh is a prominent theme throughout medieval hagiography and Thomas's descriptions of these practices of Francis are not unlike those described by *Vita prima s. Bernardi* III or recommended by Bernard himself, *On Consideration* IV 6, 21.

b. The emperor Otto IV (1198-1218) passed through the duchy of Spoleto at the end of September 1209, but the event related here probably took place in 1210 during another of Otto's passages. In Roman triumphal processions, a slave would whisper into a general's ear admonishing him that the glory of his triumph would be brief. Francis's refusal to flatter the emperor is reminiscent of Saint Martin of Tours: "It is almost a miracle that a bishop should not have succumbed to the temptation of flattering an emperor." Cf. Sulpicius Severus, *The Life of Martin* 20.

c. Gregory writes of Benedict in similar terms: *solus habitavit secum* [alone he lived with himself], thus accentuating the strong place of solitude in the monastic tradition. Cf. Gregory, *Dialogue* II 3. The same is written of Bernard: *libere secum habitans et deambulans in latitudine cordis sui* [living freely with himself and walking in the broad expanse of his heart] Cf. *Vita prima s. Bernardi* III 1, 2.

holy Francis heard this statement, he took it seriously, since he knew the man's intention: the man thought that the brothers wanted to

Is 5:8

stay there to expand the place by *joining house to house*. Immediately

1C 21

Saint Francis left the place, abandoning it because of what the peasant had said. He moved to another place, not far away, which was called "Portiuncula," where, as told above, he had repaired the church of Saint Mary a long time before. He wanted *to own nothing* so

2 Cor 6:10

that he could *possess everything* more fully in the Lord.

Chapter XVII

HOW BLESSED FRANCIS TAUGHT THE BROTHERS TO PRAY
AND ABOUT THE OBEDIENCE AND PURITY OF THE BROTHERS

Lk 11:1

[45]The brothers at that time begged him *to teach* them *how to pray,*

Prv 20:7

because, *walking in simplicity* of spirit, up to that time they did not know the Church's office. Francis told them: *"When you pray, say 'Our*

Test 5

Mt 6:9

Father' and 'We adore you, O Christ, in all your churches throughout the whole world, and we bless you, for by your holy cross you have redeemed the world.' " The brothers, devout disciples of their master, strove diligently to observe this. For they attempted to fulfill completely not only the things he told them as brotherly advice or fatherly commands, but even those things he thought or meditated upon, if they could know them by some indication. The blessed father told them that true obedience is not about just what is spoken but also about what is thought, not just what is commanded but what is desired, that is: "If a brother subject to a prelate not only

Adm III

hears his words but understands his will, he should immediately ready himself fully for obedience, and do whatever by some sign he knows the other wants."

For this reason, in whatever place a church had been built, even when they were not near it, but could glimpse it from a distance, they would turn toward it. Prostrate on the ground, bowing inwardly and outwardly, they would adore the Almighty saying, "We adore you, O Christ, in all your churches . . ." just as their holy father taught them. What is just as striking is that wherever they saw a cross or the sign of a cross, whether on the ground, on a wall, in the trees or roadside hedges they did the same thing.

[46]In this way holy simplicity filled them,
innocence of life taught them,

and purity of heart so possessed them
that they were completely ignorant of duplicity of heart.
For just as there was in them *one faith,*
so there was *one spirit,*   Eph 4:3-5
one will, one charity, continual unity of spirit,
harmony in living, cultivation of virtues,
agreement of minds, and piety in actions.

For example, they often used to confess their sins to a certain secular priest, even when his wickedness had been reported to them by many people. He had a very bad reputation and was despised by everyone else because of the enormity of his misdeeds. But they did not wish to believe it; so they did not stop confessing their sins to him as usual, nor stop showing him proper reverence.

One day he, or another priest, said to one of the brothers, "Watch out, brother, don't be a hypocrite!" The brother immediately believed that he was a hypocrite because of the priest's statement. For this reason, he was crying and weeping day and night, moved by deep sorrow. When the brothers asked him what caused such grief and unusual gloom, he answered, "A priest told me something that has upset me so much that I can hardly think about anything else." The brothers kept trying to console him and urged him not to believe it. But he said, "How can you say that, brothers? A priest told me this. Could a priest lie? Since a priest does not lie, we must believe what he said." Remaining for a long time in this simplicity, he finally gave in to the words of the blessed father who explained to him the priest's statement and wisely excused his intention. For in almost any case of disturbance of mind in one of the brothers, at his *burning words* the   Ps 119: 140
clouds would break up and clear weather would return.

Chapter XVIII
ABOUT THE FIERY CHARIOT
AND THE KNOWLEDGE
THAT BLESSED FRANCIS HAD
OF THOSE ABSENT

Gn 17:1

Prv 10:9

Mt 6:9

[47]*Walking before God with simplicity*
and among people with confidence,
the brothers merited at that time to rejoice in a divine revelation.
They were on fire with the Holy Spirit
and with prayerful voices sang the *"Our Father"*
in the melody of the Spirit.
They did this at all hours and not simply those assigned,
since earthly concerns and the nagging anxiety of cares
troubled them little.

2 Kgs 2:11-14

Lk 2:8; Mt 24:4

1 Cor 11:20;
Lk 22:23

One night the blessed father Francis was away from them in body. About midnight, some of the brothers were sleeping and others were praying in silence with deep feeling, when a brilliant *fiery chariot* entered through the little door of the house, and moved *here and there* through the little house two or three times. On top of it sat a large ball that looked like the sun, and it made the night bright as day.[a] *Those who were awake* were dumbfounded, while those sleeping woke up *in a fright*, for they sensed the brightness with their hearts as much as with their bodies. *They gathered together* and *began to ask each other* what all this *meant*. From the strength and grace of such great light, the conscience of each was revealed to the others.

At last they understood, realizing that the soul of the holy father radiated with great brilliance. Thus, thanks to the gift of his outstanding purity and his deep piety for his sons, he merited the blessing of such a gift from the Lord.

1 Cor 14:25

[48]They learned time and again by clear signs and their own experience that the hidden *recesses of their hearts* were not hidden from their most holy father.

1 Cor 14:25

How often he knew the deeds of absent brothers,
not by human teaching but the revelation of the Holy Spirit!
He opened up the hidden *recesses of their hearts,*

---

a. Light expresses the splendor and glory of God in which saints, after the example of Elijah, are frequently bathed after long periods of prayer. Cf. *Lives of the Desert Fathers,* II, 9; *Guthlac* 50; *The Life of Anselm,* I, 16; *The Life of Malachy the Irishman* XXIX 65.

and examined their consciences![a]
How many he warned in their dreams,
both ordering what they should do
and forbidding what they should not!
How many future evil deeds he foretold
of those whose present deeds seemed so good in appearance!
So too did he announce
the future grace of salvation to many,
since he foresaw the ending of their misdeeds.
In fact, if someone in a spirit of purity and simplicity
merited enlightenment,
he would gain a singular consolation from a vision of him,
something not experienced by others.

I shall report just one of the many stories that I have learned from the reports of reliable witnesses. At one time, brother John of Florence was appointed by Saint Francis as minister of the brothers in Provence. He celebrated a chapter of the brothers in that province, and the Lord God with his usual favor opened the *door of eloquence* for him and made all the brothers willing and attentive listeners. Among them was a certain brother priest named Monaldo, distinguished by a brilliant reputation and by an even more brilliant life. His virtue was grounded in humility, aided by frequent prayer, and preserved by the shield of patience.

Col 4:3

Also at that chapter was brother Anthony whose *mind* the Lord *had opened to understand the Scriptures* and *who poured forth* among all the people *sweet words* about Jesus, *sweeter than milk and honey.*[b] He was preaching to the brothers fervently and devoutly on the verse, *"Jesus of Nazareth, king of the Jews."* Brother Monaldo glanced at the door of the house in which the brothers *were all gathered.* He saw there with his bodily eyes blessed Francis lifted up in the air with his hands extended as if on a cross, blessing the brothers. *All of them* seemed *filled with the consolation of the Holy Spirit* and were so taken with the joy of salvation that they believed readily what they heard regarding the vision and the presence of the glorious father.

Lk 24:45
Ps 45:2; Ps 19:11

Jn 19:19
Jos 9:2

Acts 9:31

---

a. Throughout the hagiographic tradition the texts frequently speak of the saint's ability to read hearts. Cf. *Lives of the Desert Fathers*, XII, 10; Gregory, *Dialogue* II 20; Eadmer of Canterbury, *The Life of Anselm* I,8; Alan, Bishop of Auxerre, *Vita secunda s. Bernardi* XII; and Bernard, *The Life of Saint Malachy*, XV, 35.

b. A reference to Brother Anthony of Lisbon or Padua. He was born in Lisbon, Portugal, in 1195. Inspired by the news of the first Franciscan martyrs in Morocco, Anthony left the Canons Regular and joined the Order in 1220. He died in 1231 and was canonized in the following year.

[49]I shall relate only one account, undoubtedly true, about how he knew the hidden recesses of troubled hearts, something that many often experienced.

There was a certain brother named Riccerio, noble by birth but more noble in character, a lover of God and despiser of himself. With a devout spirit he was led wholeheartedly to attain and possess the favor of the blessed father Francis. He *was quite fearful* that the holy man Francis would detest him for some secret reason and thus he would become a stranger to the gift of his love. That brother, since *he was fearful,* thought that any person the holy man Francis loved intimately was also worthy to merit divine favor. On the other hand, he judged that someone to whom he did not show himself kindly and pleasant would incur the wrath of the supreme Judge. This brother turned these matters over in his heart; he *silently* spoke *of these matters* to himself, but revealed to no one else his secret thoughts.

[50]One day the blessed father was praying in his cell and that brother came to the place disturbed by his usual thoughts. *The holy one of God* knew both that the brother had come and understood what was twisting in his heart. So the blessed father immediately called him to himself. "Let no temptation disturb you, son," he said to him, "and do not be troubled by any thought. You are very dear to me and you should know that, among those dearest to me, you are worthy of my love and intimacy. Come to me confidently whenever you want, knowing you are welcome, and, in this intimacy, speak freely." That brother was amazed and from then on became even more reverent. The more that he grew in the holy father's grace, the more he began to enjoy God's mercy with confidence.

> How bitterly they feel your absence, holy father,
> who completely despair
> of ever finding anyone like you on earth!
> We ask you, through your intercession,
> help those covered by the harmful stain of sin.
> Though you were already filled
> with the spirit of all the just,[a]
> foreseeing the future
> and knowing the present,

Jdt 8:8

Lk 2:25

Gn 24:45

Lk 4:34

---

a. Cf. Gregory the Great, "Dialogue" II 8: "*Vir iste spiritu iustorum omnium plenus fuit* [that man was filled with the spirit of all the just]." Also, *The Life* of William the Great (+1157), *Acta Santorum*, 3rd Edition (Paris, Rome: 1863-1870), February 10 II, p. 464: "*omnium iustorum spiritu plenus fuit* [he was filled with the spirit of all the just]."

to avoid all boasting
you always displayed the image of holy simplicity.
But let us return now to the matters mentioned above,
following again the order of our story.

Chapter XIX
HIS WATCHFULNESS OVER THE BROTHERS,
SCORN FOR HIMSELF, AND TRUE HUMILITY

[51]Blessed Francis returned in body to his brothers, whom, as was said above, he never left in spirit. Asking carefully and in detail about all their doings, he was always moved by a wholesome curiosity about those in his charge. If he found something inappropriate was done, he did not leave it unpunished. He first discerned any spiritual vices. Then he judged those of the body, and finally uprooted any occasions that might open the way to sin.

He zealously and carefully safeguarded Lady Holy Poverty. In order to avoid the superfluous, he would not even permit a small plate to remain in the house if, without it, he could avoid dire need. He said it was impossible to satisfy necessity without bowing to pleasure. He rarely or hardly ever ate cooked foods, but if he did, he would sprinkle them with ashes or dampen the flavor of spices with cold water.[a] Often, when he was wandering through the world to preach *the gospel of God,* he was called to a dinner given by great princes who venerated him with much fondness. He would taste some meat in order to observe the holy gospel.[b] The rest, which he appeared to eat, he put in his lap, raising his hand to his mouth so that no one could know what he was doing. What shall I say about drinking wine, when he would not allow himself to drink even enough water when he was burning with thirst?

[52]Now as to *his bed:* wherever he received hospitality, he refused to use a straw mattress or blankets. The naked ground received his naked body, with only a thin tunic between them. Sometimes when he would refresh his small body with sleep, he would often sleep sitting up, not lying down, using a stone or a piece of wood as a pillow.

Rom 1:1

R XIV,3; LR III,14

Lk 10:7-8

Sg 1:11

---

a. This approach to food reflects the early Christian ascetical tradition. Cf. Marcianus, 21 in *History of the Monks of Syria.*

b. Francis placed this teaching in both rules. This distinguishes Francis from the Cathars who refused to touch meat.

As normally happens, sometimes the craving to eat something came upon him, but afterwards he would barely allow himself to eat it. Once, because he was ill, he ate a little bit of chicken. When his physical strength returned, he entered the city of Assisi. When he reached *the city gate,* he commanded the brother who was with him to tie a cord around his neck and drag him through the whole city as if he were a thief, loudly crying out: "Look! See this glutton who grew fat on the flesh of chickens that he ate without your knowledge." Many people ran to see this grand spectacle and, groaning and weeping, they said: "Woe to us! We are wretches and our whole life is steeped in blood! With excess and drunkenness we feed our hearts and bodies to overflowing!" *They were touched in their hearts* and were moved to a better way of life by such an example.

⁵³He often did things in this way both to despise himself fully and to invite others to everlasting honors. Toward himself *he had become like a broken vessel,* burdened by no fear or concern for his body. He would zealously expose himself to insults so that he would not be forced by self-love to lust for anything temporal. A true scorner of himself, he taught others to despise themselves by word and example. To what end? He was *honored by all* and merited high marks from everyone. He alone considered himself vile and was the only one to despise himself fervently. Often honored by others, he suffered great sorrow. Shunning human praise, he had someone, as an antidote, revile him. He would call one of the brothers to him, saying, "I command you under obedience to insult me harshly and speak the truth against their lies." When the brother, though unwilling, called him a boor and a useless hired-hand, he would smile and clap loudly, saying: *"May the Lord bless you,* for you are really telling the truth; that is what the son of Pietro Bernardone needs to hear." Speaking in this fashion, he called to mind the humble origins of his birth.

⁵⁴In order to show himself contemptible and to give others an example of true confession, when he did something wrong he was not ashamed to confess it in his preaching before all the people. In fact, if he had perhaps thought ill of someone or for some reason let slip a harsh word, he would go with all humility to the person of whom he had said or thought something wrong and, confessing his sin, would ask forgiveness. His conscience, a witness of total innocence, guarding itself with *all care,* would not let him rest until it gently healed the wound of his heart. In every type of praiseworthy deed he wished to

Lk 7:12

Acts 2:37

Ps 31:13

Lk 4:15

Adm V, XIII, XV
XX, XXIII, XXIV

Adm XII, XIX

Nm 6:24; Ps 128:5

2 Cor 8:7

be outstanding, but to go unnoticed. In every way he fled praise to avoid all vanity.

> Woe to us who have now lost you,
> O worthy father,
> model of all kindness and humility!
> Since we did not strive to know you when we had you,
> we have lost you by *a just judgment!*

Dt 16:18

Chapter XX
THE DESIRE TO UNDERGO MARTYRDOM
WHICH TOOK HIM FIRST TO SPAIN AND THEN JOURNEYING TO SYRIA;
AND HOW GOD SAVED SAILORS FROM DANGER,
MULTIPLYING THEIR SUPPLY OF FOOD

> [55] Burning with divine love,
> the blessed father Francis was always eager
> to *try his hand at brave deeds*,
> and walking *in the way of* God's *commands*
> with heart wide-open,
> he longed to reach the summit of perfection.

Prv 31:19

Ps 115:32

In the sixth year of his conversion, burning with the desire for holy martyrdom, he wished to take a ship to the region of Syria to preach the Christian faith and repentance to the Saracens and other unbelievers.[a] But after he had boarded a ship to go there, contrary winds started blowing, and he found himself with his fellow travelers on the shores of Slavonia.[b]

When he realized that he had been cheated of what he desired, after a little while he begged some sailors going to Ancona to take him with them, since there were hardly any ships that could sail that year to Syria. But the sailors stubbornly refused to do so since he could not pay them. The holy one of God, trusting God's goodness, secretly boarded the ship with his companion. By divine providence, a man arrived unknown to anyone, who brought the food needed. He called over a person from the ship, *a God-fearing man. "Take with you* all these

---

a. Probably in 1212. The desire for martyrdom is a theme at the very heart of the pursuit of religious life. Thus hagiography is filled with examples of men and women who desired to give their lives for Christ. Cf. Athanasius, *The Life of Antony*, 46; *Vita prima s. Bernardi* X.

b. Present day Dalmatia, it was called Slavonia at the time. It is east of Italy, across the Adriatic Sea. Since he left from Ancona, Francis would not have covered more than 150 km/95 mi.

Tb 1:1; Tb 11:4

things," he said, "and in their *time of need* faithfully give them to those poor men hiding on your ship."

Sir 8:12

A great storm arose and they had to spend many days *laboring at the oars.* They had used up all their food. Only the food of the poor Francis remained. Owing to divine grace and power, his food multiplied so much that, although there were still many days of sailing remaining, it fully supplied the needs of them all until they reached the port of Ancona. When the sailors realized that they had escaped the dangers of the sea through God's servant Francis, they gave thanks *to almighty God,* who is always revealed through his servants as awesome and loving.

Mk 6:48

Sir 50:19

[56]Francis, *the servant of the most high,* left the sea and began to walk *the earth. Furrowing with the plough* of the word, *he sowed the seed* of life, bearing blessed *fruit.* Soon many good and suitable men, cleric and lay, *fleeing the world* and courageously escaping the devil, by the grace and will of the Most High, followed him devoutly in his life and proposal.

Dn 3:93

Dt 21:3

Mt 13:3

2 Pt 1:4

Though the shoot of the gospel was producing choice fruit in abundance, it did not stifle his highest purpose, the burning desire for martyrdom. Not *too long after* this, he began to travel towards Morocco[a] to preach the gospel of Christ to the Miramamolin and his retinue.[b] He was so carried away with desire that he would sometimes leave behind *his companion on the journey* and hurry ahead, intoxicated in spirit, in order to carry out his purpose. But the good God, out of pure kindness, was pleased to be mindful of me and many others.[c] After he reached Spain God *withstood him to his face,* striking him with illness, and called him back from the journey he had begun.[d]

Mt 25:19

2 Cor 8:19

Gal 2:11

[57]Shortly afterwards when Francis returned to the Church of Saint Mary of the Portiuncula, some literate men and nobles gladly

---

a. To go to Morocco, Francis most likely followed the route to Santiago de Compostella. See Map B, p. 208. Morocco, during Francis's time, was ruled by the reformist movement of the al-Muwahhidun. From this Arabic term is derived the name "Almohads" by which they are designated in western literature. Their military occupation of North Africa was begun in 1129. They seized Tunis and Tripoli in 1159 and created for the first time in North Africa a single state. During these years of Francis's life, under the reign of Muhammad al Nasir (1199-1213), the Almohad army was invincible and the empire at its zenith of material and cultural success.

b. "Miramamolin" refers to "Amir al-Mu'minin," which translates as "Commander of the Believers." It is a religious title somewhat parallel to "sultan," which is a title for one who holds political power. "Miramamolin" can serve as a protocol title for a caliph.

c. In this passage Thomas makes a rare, personal reference to himself and to his own relationship to Francis.

d. Thomas does not provide information about the nature of this illness. Later, in *The Treatise on the Miracles* 34 (hereafter 3C), he says that it was "a very grave illness." "For after suffering privation and weakness," he writes, "and having been driven from a lodging place by the incivility of the host, he lost his speech for three days." But Thomas says little else.

joined him.[a] He received such men with honor and dignity, since he himself was very noble and distinguished in spirit, and respectfully gave to each his due. In fact, since he was endowed with outstanding discernment, he wisely considered in all matters the dignity of rank of each one.

But still he would not rest from carrying out fervently the holy impulse of his spirit. Now in the thirteenth year of his conversion, he journeyed to the region of Syria, while bitter and long battles were being waged daily between Christians and pagans.[b] Taking a companion with him, he was not afraid to present himself to the sight of the Sultan of the Saracens.[c]

> Who is equal to the task of telling this story?
> What great firmness he showed standing in front of him!
> With great strength of soul he spoke to him,
> with eloquence and confidence
> he answered those who insulted the Christian law.

Before he reached the Sultan, he was captured by soldiers, insulted and beaten, but was not afraid. He did not flinch at threats of torture nor was he shaken by death threats. Although he was ill-treated by many with a hostile spirit and a harsh attitude, he was received very graciously by the Sultan. The Sultan honored him as much as he could, offering him many gifts, trying to turn his mind to worldly riches. But when he saw that he resolutely scorned all these things like dung, the Sultan was overflowing with admiration and recognized him as a man unlike any other. He was moved by his words *and listened to him very willingly.*   Mk 6:20

> In all this, however,
> the Lord did not *fulfill* his *desire,*   Ps 127:5
> reserving for him the prerogative of a unique grace.[d]

---

a. Thomas may have been among some of the educated noblemen to receive the habit from Francis himself.

b. The journey to Syria took Francis to Damietta (Dimyat), a town in Lower Egypt situated on the eastern arm of the Nile near its mouth. This was an important town even before the Muslim conquest. As key to Egypt, it was the object of frequent naval raids, at first from the Byzantines and subsequently from Crusaders. Curiously, Thomas uses the word *paganos* [pagans], while Francis uses *infideles* [non-believers].

c. The Sultan whom Francis met was Malik al-Kamil (1180-1238). In 1218, upon the death of his father al-Adil, al-Kamil became Sultan of Egypt and supreme head of the Ayubid realm. In 1219 the Fifth Crusade succeeded in capturing the town of Damietta. For two years, al-Kamil was able to hold them at bay from his new camp, al-Marssura, south of Damietta, until the combined forces of other Ayubid princes reached Egypt in August 1221. They completely circled the crusaders and after heavy fighting the crusaders were forced to surrender on August 27, 1221. This brought the Fifth Crusade to an inglorious end. Francis visited al-Kamil at his camp Al-Marssura before the arrival of the other Ayubid forces. Cf. H. L. Gottschalk, *Al-Malik al Kamil von Egypten und seine Zeit*, Wiesbaden, 1958. Cf. Historia Occidentalis, 593ff.; 617ff.

d. An allusion to the reception of the stigmata as a different martyrdom.

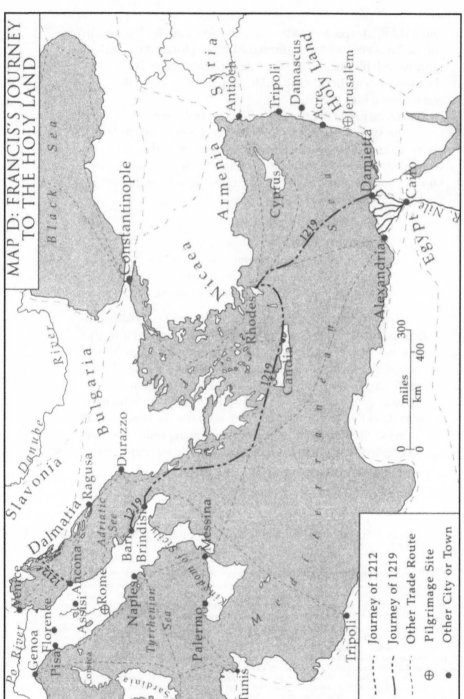

MAP D: FRANCIS'S JOURNEY TO THE HOLY LAND

Francis's first efforts to travel to the Holy Land failed when his ship was blown ashore at Dalmatia and the winds for continuing were not favorable (probably in late 1212). He was finally successful in joining the Fifth Crusade at Damietta in the summer of 1219. He probably left from Bari or Brindisi in a ship which hugged the shoreline as far as Rhodes and then crossed the Eastern Mediterranean.

Journey of 1212
Journey of 1219
Other Trade Route
⊕ Pilgrimage Site
• Other City or Town

MAP E: FRANCIS & THE FIFTH CRUSADE AT DAMIETTA

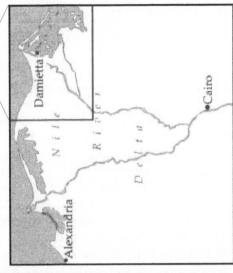

Area of Detail
Shown at Right

Alexandria

Damietta

Nile River Delta

Cairo

1 Celano 57 narrates Francis's journey to the Fifth Crusade and his dramatic crossing of the battle lines in order to visit the Sultan.

Mediterranean Sea

Contemporary Shoreline

Shoreline ca 1200

Shoreline ca 1200

Christian Camp

Damietta

Muslim Camp

Burah

Fāriskūr

Nile River

Delta

Nile River

Sharamsāh

Baramūn

Mansūrah

Nile

Chapter XXI
PREACHING TO THE BIRDS AND THE OBEDIENCE OF CREATURES

Acts 2:41

[58]While many *were joining* the brothers, as already related, the blessed father Francis was travelling through the Spoleto valley. He reached a place near Bevagna, in which a great multitude of birds of different types gathered, including doves, crows, and others commonly called *monaclae.*[a] When Francis, the most blessed servant of God, saw them, he ran swiftly toward them, leaving his companions on the road. He was a man of great fervor, feeling much sweetness and piety even toward lesser, irrational creatures. When he was already very close, seeing that they awaited him, he greeted them in his usual way.[b] He was quite surprised, however, because the birds did not take flight, as they usually do. Filled with great joy, he humbly requested that they listen to the word of God.

1C 23

Among many other things, he said to them: "My brother birds, you should greatly praise your Creator, and love Him always. He gave you feathers to wear, wings to fly, and whatever you need. God made you noble among His creatures and gave you a home in the purity of the air, so that, though you neither *sow nor reap,* He nevertheless protects and governs you without your least care." He himself, and those brothers who were with him, used to say that, at these words, the birds rejoiced in a wonderful way according to their nature. They stretched their necks, spread their wings, opened their beaks and looked at him. He *passed through their midst,* coming and going, touching their heads and bodies with his tunic. Then he blessed them, and having made the sign of the cross, gave them permission to fly off to another place. The blessed father, *however, went* with his companions along their way *rejoicing* and *giving thanks to God,* Whom all creatures revere by their devout confession.

Lk 12:24

Lk 4:30

Acts 8:39; 27:35

He was already simple by grace, not by nature. After the birds had listened so reverently to the word of God, he began to accuse himself of negligence because he had not preached to them before. From that day on, he carefully exhorted all birds, all animals, all reptiles, and also insensible creatures, to praise and love the Creator, because daily, *invoking the name* of the Savior, he observed their obedience in his own experience.

Acts 22:16

---

a. These are shiny black crows tinged with purple. The various manuscript readings for the name of this bird leave us only three choices: the jackdaw, the "grolle" or the magpie.

b. That is, with the greeting: "The Lord give you peace," cf. 1C 23, p. 203

⁵⁹One day he came to a village called Alviano to preach the word of God. *Going up to a higher place* where all could see him, he called for silence. All remained silent and stood reverently. But a large number of swallows nesting there were shrieking and chirping. Since blessed Francis could not be heard by the people, he said to the noisy birds: "My sister swallows, now *it is time* for me also to speak, since you have already said enough. *Listen to the word of the Lord* and stay quiet and calm until *the word of the Lord is completed.*" Immediately those little birds fell silent — to the amazement and surprise of all present — and did not move from that place until the sermon was over. Those men who *saw* this *sign* were filled with great wonder, saying: *"Truly, this man is* holy, and a friend of the Most High."[a]

With great devotion they hurried to touch at least his clothes, while *praising and blessing God*. It was certainly a marvel that even irrational creatures recognized his feeling of piety toward them, and sensed the sweetness of his love.

⁶⁰Once while he was staying near the town of Greccio, a certain brother brought him a live rabbit caught in a trap. Seeing it, the most blessed man was moved with tenderness. "Brother rabbit," he said, "come to me. Why did you let yourself get caught?" As soon as the brother holding it let go, the rabbit, without any prompting, took shelter with the holy man, as in a most secure place, resting *in his bosom.* After it had rested there for a little while, the holy father, caressing it with motherly affection, let it go, so that now free it would return to the woods. As often as it was put on the ground, it rushed back to the holy man's lap, so he told the brothers to carry it away to the nearby forest. Something similar happened with another little rabbit, a wild one, when he was on the island in the Lake of Perugia.[b]

⁶¹He had the same tender feeling toward fish. When he had the chance he would throw back into the water live fish that had been caught, and he warned them to be careful not to be caught again. One time while he was sitting in a little boat at the port on the Lake of Rieti, a fisherman caught a large fish, commonly called a *tinca,* and reverently offered it to him.[c] He accepted it gladly and gratefully, calling it "brother." He put it back in the water next to the little boat,

Jgs. 13:16

Tb 12:20

Is 1:10

2 Chr 36:21

Mt 12:38

Lk 23:47

Lk 24:53

2 Sm 12:3; Lk 16:23

---

a. Suetonius, "Life of Julius Caesar," Book 2, 94:10 in *The Lives of the Caesars* in which Caesar silences noisy frogs so that he can speak. Cf. *Suetonius*, Vol. I, The Loeb Classical Library translated by J.C. Rolfe, (Cambridge: Harvard University Press, 1950).

b. This lake is also known as Lake Trasimene, cf. Map D, p. 232. Not far from Cortona, it is the largest lake found in the peninsula of Italy. On its largest island, Isola Maggiore, Francis spent the Lent of 1211 or 1213.

c. A *tinca* or "tench" is a common European freshwater fish of the carp family.

Ps 113:2   and with devotion blessed *the name of the Lord.* For some time that
fish did not leave the spot but stayed next to the boat, playing in the
water where he put it until, at the end of his prayer, the holy man of
God gave it permission to leave.

> Thus the glorious father Francis,
> walking in the way of obedience,
> and embracing the yoke of complete submission to God,
> was worthy of the great honor before God
> of having the obedience of creatures.[a]

Water was changed into wine for him once at the hermitage of
Sant'Urbano when he was suffering from a severe illness. Once he
tasted it, he recovered so easily that everyone believed it was a divine
miracle, as it indeed was.

> He is truly a saint,
> whom creatures obey in this way:
> at his wish
> the very elements convert themselves
> to other uses.[b]

Chapter XXII

HIS PREACHING AT ASCOLI AND HOW THE SICK WERE HEALED,
EVEN WHEN HE WAS AWAY, BY ITEMS HE HAD TOUCHED WITH HIS HAND

[62]At the time the venerable father Francis preached to the birds,
Mt 9:35   as reported above, he went around *the towns and villages,* sowing the
seed of divine blessings everywhere, until he reached the city of
Ascoli. There he spoke the word of God with his usual fervor. By a
Ps 77:11   change *of the right hand of the Most High,* nearly all the people were
filled with such grace and devotion that they were *trampling each*
Lk 12:1   *other* in their eagerness to hear and see him. Thirty men, cleric and
lay, at that time received the habit of holy religion from him.

---

a. The obedience of animals is considered a sign of holiness in the *Dialogues* of Sulpicius Severus, PL 20:193.

b. Bede, *The Life of Cuthbert:* "If someone serves the Creator of all creatures, faithfully and wholeheartedly, it
is no wonder that every creature should serve his commands and desires." Cf. B. Colgrave, *Two Lives of
Saint Cuthbert* (Cambridge Harvard University Press, 1940), 224.

MAP F
WHERE FRANCIS PREACHED
ACCORDING TO 1 CELANO

To Bologna

Ancona

Gubbio

Lago di Trasimeno

Perugia

Assisi

Bevagna

Ascoli

Alviano

Rieti

L. di Vico

To Rome

To Rome

1 Celano speaks specifically of Francis preaching in only five places: Bevagna (1Cel 58), Alviano (1Cel 59), Ascoli (1Cel 62), Ancona (1 Cel 77), and Gubbio (1 Cel 86).

So great was the faith of men and women
and so great the devotion of their hearts
towards the holy one of God,
that a person was considered fortunate
Mt 9:21   who was able to touch *at least his clothing.*
When he entered a city,
clergy rejoiced, bells rang,
men exulted, women rejoiced, and children clapped.
Often taking branches from trees and singing psalms,
they went out to meet him.

The perversity of heretics was shamed,
the faith of the Church was extolled
and, as believers rejoiced, heretics hid.[a]

The marks of his holiness were so clear in him that no one dared
Nm 27:22   to speak against him, as *the assembly of the people* paid attention to him
alone. He put the faith of the Holy Roman Church above and beyond
all things, preserving, honoring and following it, since the salvation
of all who would be saved was found in it alone. He honored priests
and affectionately embraced every ecclesiastical order.

[63]The people used to bring him loaves of bread to bless, which
they kept for a long time, and, on tasting them, they were cured of
various diseases.

Driven by great faith, people often tore his habit until sometimes
he was left almost naked. Even more remarkable is that health was
restored to some people through some thing that the holy father had
touched with his hands.

There was a pregnant woman living on a small farm in the Arezzo
area. At the time of childbirth she was in labor with such excruciat-
ing pain that she hovered between life and death. *Her neighbors and*
Lk 1:58   *relatives heard* that the blessed Francis was going to pass by there on
Acts 28:6   his way to a hermitage.[b] *While they were waiting* the blessed Francis
Mt 2:12   went to that place *by another route.* He had gone on horseback because
he was weak and sick. When he reached that place, he sent one of

---

a. This paragraph interrupts the narrative sequence or "historical order" of Thomas's portrait in order to extol
the magnificence of Francis's moral virtues. In doing so Thomas goes beyond the first of two requirements
for canonization established by Pope Innocent III: "virtue of behavior and the virtue of signs, that is, works
of mercy during life and miraculous signs after death". Cf. Innocent III, Letter of Canonization, January 12,
1199, in *Regesta Pontificium Romanorum*, vol. I (Berlin, 1874), p. 55, no. 573. The narration of these
miracles performed by Francis during life will continue until paragraph 71.

b. The city of Arezzo is on the way to the hermitage at La Verna. Cf. Map F. p. 237.

the brothers, named Peter, to return the horse to the man who had lent it to him out of sincere charity.

When returning the horse brother Peter went down the road near the house where the woman was suffering. The men of that area saw him and raced to meet him, thinking that he was blessed Francis. When they realized that he was not, *they were sorely disappointed. They* Mt 18:31 *began to inquire among themselves* if they could find some item that Lk 22:23 blessed Francis's hand had touched. *They had spent* quite a bit of time Mt 24:45 in this search, when they finally discovered the bridle reins which he had held in his hand while riding. Pulling the bridle from the horse's mouth, they placed on the woman the reins which he had held in his very hands. At this, the danger passed, and the woman gave birth in great joy and good health.

[64]Gualfreduccio was an inhabitant of Città della Pieve, a man who was *religious, worshiping and fearing God with all his household.* He had a Acts 10:2 cord at his home that blessed Francis once used as a belt. Many men and not a few women in that area suffered from various diseases and fevers. That man went to the houses of the sick and gave the sufferers water to drink which had been touched by the cord or mixed with its threads. And in this way all of them *in the name of Christ* regained 1 Pt 4:14 their health.

These things happened, moreover, in the absence of blessed Francis. There are so many others that they could not all be mentioned even briefly in a very long story. But we shall now include in this book a brief mention of those things that *the Lord our God* worked Ps 99:9 through his presence.

Chapter XXIII
HOW HE HEALED A LAME MAN AT TOSCANELLA AND A PARALYZED MAN AT NARNI

[65]Once when the holy man of God, Francis, was travelling far and wide through the land, proclaiming *the good news of the kingdom of God,* Lk 4:43 he came to a city called Toscanella. As he was sowing the seed of life as usual, a knight of that same city took him in as his guest. The man Lk 7:12 *had only one son,* who was lame and had no bodily strength. Although the young boy was no longer being breast-fed, he was still sleeping in a cradle. The father of the boy, seeing the man of God was endowed with such holiness, humbly *fell down at his feet,* begging him for his Ru 3: 7-8

son's health. For a long time the holy man Francis refused to comply, considering himself useless and unworthy of such power and grace. But at last, overcome by the persistence of the father's entreaties, Saint Francis prayed, laid hands on the boy and, blessing him, *lifted him up*. Immediately the boy, *in the name of our Lord Jesus Christ* stood up healed and, with the onlookers rejoicing, began to walk all around the house.

Acts 3:7

Acts 4:19

66Once the *man of God* Francis came to Narni and remained there for several days. A man of that city named Pietro was *bedridden as a paralytic*. Over a five-month period this man had been so deprived of the use of all his members that he could not get up at all or even move. He had completely lost the use of his feet, hands, and head. He could only move his tongue and blink his eyes. Hearing that Saint Francis had come to Narni, he sent a message to the bishop of the city requesting him, for the sake of divine piety, to send the servant of *the most High God* to him. He believed that seeing him and being in his presence would free him from the bonds of that paralysis. And so it did! The blessed Francis came to him, made the sign of the cross over him from head to toe, and, as the affliction vanished, immediately *restored* him to *his earlier health*.

1 Kgs 9:6

Mt 9:2

Lk 8:28

Mt 12:13

Chapter XXIV
HOW HE GAVE SIGHT TO A BLIND WOMAN AT NARNI
AND HEALED A CRIPPLED WOMAN AT GUBBIO

67A woman of that same city, afflicted with blindness, received the sign of the cross made by the blessed Francis over her eyes. She merited to receive immediately the sight for which she longed.

At Gubbio, there was a woman with both hands so crippled that she was unable to handle anything with them. When she heard that Saint Francis had entered the city, she immediately ran to him. With a sad and mournful face she showed him her crippled hands and begged him to touch them. He was moved with great piety. He touched her hands and healed them. The woman immediately returned home full of joy, made a cheesecake with her own hands, and offered it to the holy man.[a] He kindly took a little of that cake and told her to eat the rest of it with her family.

---

a. The scene recalls the cure of Peter's mother-in-law. Cf. Mk 1:31.

Chapter XXV

HOW HE FREED A BROTHER FROM A FALLING SICKNESS OR A DEMON
AND HOW HE FREED A POSSESSED WOMAN AT SAN GEMINI

[68]One of the brothers often suffered from a terrible affliction,
dreadful to see. I do not know quite what I should call it, since there
are some who believe it was an evil demon. He would often fall, look-
ing around with a pitiful expression, and *roll around foaming at the*   Mk 9:19
mouth. Sometimes his limbs would contract and then stretch out;
sometimes they would be bent and twisted and, at other times, rigid
and hard. Sometimes, when he was completely stretched out and
rigid with his feet level with his head, he would be lifted into the air
as high as a man stands and then suddenly bounce back to the
ground. The holy father Francis took pity upon his serious condition,
went to see him and, after praying, signed him and blessed him. The
man was suddenly healed. Afterwards he never had any trouble
from that illness.

[69]One day the most blessed father Francis was passing through
the diocese of Narni. He came to a village called San Gemini. While
he was proclaiming there the *good news of the kingdom of God,* he, along   Lk 4:43
with three of the brothers, received hospitality from a man *fearing*
and serving God. This man enjoyed a very good reputation in the area.   Acts 10:2
His wife, however, was *troubled by a demon,* as all the people living in   Mt 15:22
the area were aware. Her husband pleaded with blessed Francis for
her, trusting that through his merits she would be set free. But since
the blessed Francis preferred in his simplicity to be held in contempt
rather than to be lifted up by worldly honor for some display of holiness, he refused to do it. Yet God was involved in the case! Since so
many people kept asking, he gave in to their pleas. He called over the
three brothers who were with him. He set one in each corner of that
house. "Brothers," he said to them, "let us pray to the Lord for this
woman, that God may *shake off* the devil's *yoke* from her 'to His praise   Gn 27:40
and glory.' "[a] He added: "Let us stand apart in the corners of the
house to prevent the evil spirit from fleeing or deceiving us by trying
to hide in the corners."

When *the prayer was finished,* blessed Francis, *in the power of the*   Jdt 6:16
Spirit, approached the woman, who was twisting miserably and   Rom 15:13, 19
screaming horribly. *"In the name of our Lord Jesus Christ,"* he said, *"I*   Acts 16:18
command you, demon, under obedience, *to come out from her* and not

---

a. A reference to the *Suscipiat* response of the Liturgy of the Eucharist.

Gn 39:12 trouble her any more." He had scarcely uttered the words when the demon *went out*. It did so with such swiftness and with such a furious roar, that on account of the sudden cure of the woman and the immediate obedience of the demon, the holy father thought he was deceived. So he left that place right away, ashamed. Divine Providence arranged it that way so he could not boast vainly.

That is why when blessed Francis passed through that same place on another occasion and brother Elias was with him, that woman, hearing of his arrival, *got up immediately,* ran down the street, and *cried out after him,* asking him to speak to her. But he refused to do so, knowing that she was the woman from whom he had once, by divine power, driven out a demon. She *kissed his very footprints, giving thanks to God* and his holy servant Francis, who had *freed her from the hand of death.* At last, brother Elias forced him by his pleas; and blessed Francis spoke to her after being reassured by many about the affliction that was mentioned and her deliverance.

Acts 9:34
Mt 15:23
Est 13:13
Acts 28:15
Hos 13:14

Chapter XXVI
HOW HE ALSO DROVE OUT A DEMON AT CITTÀ DI CASTELLO

[70] At Città di Castello also there was a woman who was possessed by a demon.[a] When the most blessed father Francis was in that city, the woman was led to the house where he was staying. But the woman *stood outside* and began to gnash her teeth and howl in a horrible voice with a twisted face, which is *usual with unclean spirits.* Many people from the city, both women and men, came to plead with Saint Francis on the woman's behalf. That evil spirit had troubled her for a long time by twisting her body and disturbed the people themselves with its howling. The holy father sent out to her the brother who was with him, since he wished to check whether it was a demon or the woman's deception. When that woman saw the brother, she began to mock him, since she knew that he was hardly the holy man, Francis. Meanwhile, Francis had been praying and once his prayer was finished he came outside. The woman started to shake and roll on the ground, since she could not bear his power. Saint Francis called her to himself, saying: "In virtue of obedience, I command you, *evil spirit:*

Jn 20:11
Mt 10:1; Jn 19:40
Mk 5:8

a. Città di Castello was an important center of the Tiber Valley. It is situated on the most convenient and direct route from Saint Mary of the Angels to La Verna. Francis must have passed this way frequently. Cf. Map F, p. 237.

come out of her." The evil spirit released her immediately without harm, and departed, furious.

Thanks be *to almighty God* who *works all things* in everyone. But we have not chosen to describe miracles — they do not make holiness but show it—but rather to describe the excellence of his life and the honest form of his manner of living. Passing over the miracles, because they are so numerous, let us return to narrating the works *of eternal salvation.*[a]

Sir 50:19; 1 Cor 12:11

Heb 5: 9

Chapter XXVII
THE PURITY AND STEADFASTNESS OF HIS MIND,
HIS PREACHING IN FRONT OF THE LORD POPE HONORIUS;
AND HOW HE COMMITTED BOTH HIS BROTHERS AND HIMSELF
TO THE PROTECTION OF THE LORD HUGO, BISHOP OF OSTIA

[71]*The man of God,* the blessed Francis,
had been taught not to seek his own salvation,
but what he discerned would help the salvation of others.

1 Sm 9:6, 10

More than anything else he desired
to be set free and to be with Christ.
Thus his chief object of concern was

Phil 1:23

to live free from all things *that are in the world,*
so that his inner serenity would not be disturbed

1 Jn 2:15

even for a moment
by contact with any of its dust.[b]
He made himself insensible to all outside noise,
gathering his external senses into his inner being
and checking the impetus of his spirit,
he emptied himself for God alone.

In the clefts of the rock he would build his nest
and *in the hollow of the wall* his dwelling.
With blessed devotion he visited the heavenly mansions;

Sg 2:14

and, totally *emptied* of *himself,*

Phil 2:7

he rested for a long time in the wounds of the Savior.
That is why he often chose solitary places
to focus his heart entirely on God.

---

a. At this point Thomas leaves his narration of Francis's miracles and virtues.

b. Thomas uses the image of dust to describe money (n. 9) and, in this instance, worldly distractions. Cultivation of a serene interior peace is the reason for seeking solitary places. Cf. Gregory the Great, *Dialogue* II 3.

But he was not reluctant,
when he discerned the time was right,
to involve himself in the affairs of his neighbors,
and attend to their salvation.
For his safest haven was prayer;
not prayer of a fleeting moment, empty and proud,
but prayer that was prolonged,
full of devotion, peaceful in humility.
If he began at night,
he was barely finished at morning.
Walking, sitting, eating, drinking,
he was focused on prayer.
He would spend the night alone praying
in abandoned churches and in deserted places
where,
with the protection of divine grace,
he overcame his soul's many fears and anxieties.[a]

Ez 21:24

[72]He used to struggle *hand to hand* with the devil who, in those places, would not only assault him internally with temptations but also frighten him externally with ruin and undermining.[b] The brave knight of God knew that his Lord could do all things in all places; thus he did not give in to the fears but said in his heart: "You, evil one! You cannot strike me with your evil weapons here any more than if we were in front of a crowd in a public place."

1 Cor 7:32; Acts 13:5

He was extremely determined and paid no attention to anything beyond *what was of the Lord.* Though he often preached *the word of God* among thousands of people, he was as confident as if he were speaking with a close friend. He used to view the largest crowd of people as if it were a single person, and he would preach fervently to a single person as if to a large crowd. Out of the purity of his mind he drew his confidence in preaching and, even without preparation, he used to say the most amazing things to everyone. Sometimes he prepared for his talk with some meditation, but once the people gathered he could not remember what he had meditated about and had nothing

---

a. Unceasing prayer and all night vigils characterize the prayer of the saints in the hagiographic tradition. For example, Sulpicius Severus describes the prayer of Martin of Tours: "In fact he did not indulge either in food or sleep, except insofar as the necessities of nature required. . . . Never did a single hour or moment pass in which he was not either actually engaged in prayer; or, if it happened that he was occupied with something else, still he never let his mind loose from prayer." Cf. Sulpicius Severus *The Life of Martin* 26.

b. This experience of temptation is also common among the saints and is described as direct and immediate. Once again the examples of Antony, Martin, and Benedict are paramount. Cf. *The Life of Antony,* 9; *The Life of Martin* 22; and *Dialogue* II 8.

to say. Without any embarrassment he would confess to the people that he had thought of many things before, but now he could not remember a thing. Sometimes he would be filled with such great eloquence that he moved the hearts of his hearers to astonishment. When he could not think of anything, he would give a blessing and send the people away with this act alone as a very good sermon.

[73]Once he came to the city of Rome on a matter concerning the Order, and he greatly yearned to speak before the Lord Pope Honorius and the venerable cardinals.[a] Lord Hugo, the renowned bishop of Ostia, venerated the holy man of God with special affection. When he learned of his arrival, Lord Hugo was filled with fear and joy, admiring the holy man's fervor yet aware of his simple purity. *Trusting* to the mercy *of the Almighty* that never fails the faithful *in time of need,* he led the holy man before the Lord Pope and the venerable cardinals.

2 Mc 8:18; Sir 8:12

Lk 7:15

As he stood in the presence of so many princes of the Church, blessed Francis, after receiving permission and a blessing, fearlessly *began to speak.*

> He was speaking with such fire of spirit
> that he could not contain himself for joy.
> As he brought forth the word from his mouth,
> he moved his feet as if dancing,
> not playfully but burning with the fire of divine love,
> not provoking laughter but moving them to tears of sorrow.
> For many of them *were touched in their hearts,*
> *amazed* at the grace of God
> and the great *determination* of the man.

Acts 2: 37

Acts 4:13

The venerable lord bishop of Ostia was waiting fearfully, praying to God that they would not despise the blessed man's simplicity; for both the glory and the disgrace of the holy man would reflect on himself, since he was the father set *over the* saint's *household.*

Lk 12: 42

> [74]For Saint Francis clung to the bishop
> as *a son* does to his father
> and *an only child to its mother,*
> safely resting and *sleeping in the lap* of his kindness.
> The bishop filled the role and did the work of a shepherd,

Lk 7:12

2 Sm 12:3

a. A reference to Honorius III, immediate successor to Innocent III, and pope from July 18, 1216, to March 8, 1227.

but left the name of shepherd to the holy man.
Blessed Francis would foresee needs,
but that blessed lord would deliver
what was foreseen.
There were many who plotted to destroy

Ps 144:12   *the new planting* of the Order at its beginning.

Jer 2:21   There were many trying to suffocate the *chosen vineyard*
which the Lord's hand had so kindly planted anew in the world.
There were many trying to steal and eat its first fresh fruit.
But all of these opponents were *slain with the sword*
of the venerable father and lord

Acts 5:36   *and their efforts came to naught.*
For he was a river of eloquence,
a wall of the Church,
a spokesman for truth,
and a lover of the humble.

That was a memorable and blessed day when the holy man of God committed himself to such a venerable lord. Once this lord was acting in Tuscany as legate of the Apostolic See, as he frequently did. Blessed Francis, not yet having many brothers and intending to go to France,[a] reached Florence where the bishop was then staying. At that time the two of them were not yet joined by close friendship, but their shared reputation for holy living joined them in mutual and affectionate charity.

[75]Upon entering a city or area, it was blessed Francis's custom to visit the priests or bishops. Upon hearing there was such a great pontiff in Florence, he presented himself to the bishop's kindness with great reverence. When the lord bishop saw him, he received him humbly and devoutly, just as he always did for those professing holy religion, especially those carrying the noble banner of blessed poverty and holy simplicity. Now the bishop was concerned *to provide for*

2 Cor 8:14   *the needs* of the poor and to handle their affairs in a special way. So he carefully inquired the reason for the blessed man's arrival there and

Lk 12: 49   graciously understood his proposal. He perceived in the holy man

1 Sm 18:1   someone who, more than others, spurned all earthly things, one who was burning with the fire which Jesus *sent down to the earth.*

---

a. Here *France* refers to the property of the kings of France, which after the 15th century came to be called Ile-de-France: Paris and a broad area around it.

From that moment, his soul *was joined to the soul* of the holy man.[a] Sincerely asking for his prayers, the bishop freely offered the holy man his protection in all things. Then, the lord bishop advised him not to complete the journey he had begun, but rather to be vigilant, to care for and protect those whom the Lord God had entrusted to him.

When the holy man Francis saw that this revered lord had such a devout attitude, sweet affection, and powerful words, he *rejoiced*   Mt 2:11 *greatly. Falling at his feet,* he handed over and entrusted himself and   Acts 10:25 his brothers wholeheartedly to the bishop.

Chapter XXVIII
THE SPIRIT OF CHARITY
AND THE FEELING OF COMPASSION FOR THE POOR
THAT GLOWED IN HIM
AND WHAT HE DID WITH THE SHEEP AND THE LAMBS

[76]*The father of the poor,*   Jb 29:16
the poor Francis,
conforming himself to the poor in all things,
was distressed to see anyone poorer than himself,
not out of any desire *for empty glory,*   Gal 5:26
but from a feeling of simple compassion.
Though he was content with a ragged and rough tunic,
he often wished to divide it with some poor person.

This richest poor man, moved by a great feeling of pity, in order to help the poor in some way, used to approach the rich people of this world during the coldest times of the year, asking them to loan him their cloaks or furs. As they responded even more gladly than the blessed father asked, he used to say to them, "I shall accept this from you only on the condition that you never expect to have it returned." The first poor man who happened to meet him, he would then clothe with whatever he had received, exulting and rejoicing.

---

a. As the Scriptural allusion suggests, Thomas likens the friendship between Francis and Hugolino to that of David and Jonathan. "When David had finished speaking, the soul of Jonathan was bound to the soul of David, and Jonathan loved him as his own soul," (1 Sm 18:1).

He was deeply troubled whenever he saw one of the poor insulted or heard *a curse* hurled at any creature. It happened that a certain brother insulted a poor man begging alms, saying: "Are you sure that you are not really rich and just pretending to be poor?" When Saint Francis, *the father of the poor,* heard this, he was deeply hurt and he severely rebuked the brother who had said these things. Then he ordered the brother to strip naked in front of the poor man and to kiss his feet, to beg his forgiveness. He used to say: "Anyone who curses the poor insults Christ whose noble banner the poor carry, since Christ *made himself poor for us in this world."* That is also why, when he met poor people burdened with wood or other heavy loads, he would offer his own weak shoulders to help them.

[77] The holy man overflowed with the spirit of charity, bearing within himself a deep sense of piety not only toward other humans in need but also toward mute, brute animals: reptiles, birds, and all other creatures whether sensate or not. But among all the different kinds of creatures, he loved lambs with a special fondness and spontaneous affection, since in Sacred Scripture the humility of our Lord Jesus Christ is frequently and rightly compared to the lamb. He used to embrace more warmly and to observe more gladly anything in which he found an allegorical likeness to the Son of God.

Once he was making a journey through the Marches of Ancona and *preached the word of the Lord* in the city. Then he took the road toward Osimo, with lord Paul, the one whom he had *appointed minister* of all the brethren in that province. He came upon a shepherd in the fields pasturing a flock of goats. There was one little sheep walking humbly and grazing calmly among these many goats. When blessed Francis saw it, he stopped in his tracks, *and touched with sorrow in his heart,* he groaned loudly, and said to the brother accompanying him: "Do you see that sheep walking so meekly among those goats? I tell you, in the same way our Lord Jesus Christ, *meek and humble,* walked among the Pharisees and chief priests. So I ask you, my son, in your love for Him to share my compassion for this little sheep. After we have paid for it, let us *lead* this little one *from the midst* of these goats."

[78] Brother Paul was struck by his sorrow and also began to feel that sorrow himself. They had nothing except the cheap tunics they wore and they were concerned about how to pay for the sheep, when suddenly a traveling merchant arrived and offered to pay for what they wanted. Taking up the sheep, they *gave thanks to God* and after reaching Osimo made their way to the bishop of the city, who re-

ceived them with great reverence. Now the lord bishop was surprised both at the sheep *the man of God* was leading and at the affection for it that was leading him to do this. But when the servant of Christ recounted the long parable of the sheep, the bishop *was touched in his heart* by the purity of the man of God, and *gave thanks to God.* 2 Kgs 24:9 Acts 2:37 Acts 27:35

The next day, on leaving the city, the man of God began to wonder what to do with the sheep. On the advice of his companion and brother, he entrusted it to the care of the maidservants of Christ in the cloister of San Severino. The venerable servants of Christ gladly received the little sheep as a great *gift from God.* They devotedly cared 2 Mc 15:16 for the sheep for a long time and made a tunic from its wool, a tunic they sent to the blessed father Francis at the church of Saint Mary of the Portiuncula at the time of a chapter meeting. The holy man of God received the tunic with great reverence and high spirits, hugging and kissing it, and invited all those around him to share this great joy.

⁷⁹On another occasion he was traveling through the Marches and the same brother was gladly accompanying him when he came across a man on his way to market. The man was carrying over his shoulder two little lambs bound and ready for sale. When blessed Francis heard the bleating lambs, *his innermost heart was touched* and, 1 Kgs 3:26 drawing near, he touched them as a mother does with a crying child, showing his compassion. "Why are you torturing my brother lambs," he said to the man, "binding and hanging them this way?" "I am carrying them to market to sell them, since I need the money," he replied. The holy man asked: "What will happen to them?" "Those who buy them will kill them and eat them," he responded. At that, the holy man said: "No, this must not happen! Here, take my cloak as payment and give me the lambs." The man readily gave him the little lambs and took the cloak since it was much more valuable. The cloak was one the holy man had borrowed from a friend on the same day to keep out the cold. The holy man of God, having taken the lambs, now was wondering what he should do with them. Asking for advice from the brother who was with him, he gave them back to that man, ordering him never to sell them or allow any harm to come to them, but instead to preserve, nourish, and guide them carefully.

Chapter XXIX
THE LOVE THAT HE HAD TOWARD ALL CREATURES
FOR THE SAKE OF THE CREATOR
AND A DESCRIPTION OF BOTH ASPECTS OF HIS PERSON

⁸⁰To enumerate and recount all the things
our glorious father Francis did
and taught while *living in the flesh*
would be a lengthy or an even impossible task.
Who could ever express the deep affection he bore
for all things *that belong to God?*
Or who would be able to tell
of the sweet tenderness he enjoyed
while contemplating in creatures
the wisdom, power, and goodness of the Creator?
From this reflection
he often overflowed
with amazing, unspeakable joy
as he looked at the sun,
gazed at the moon, or observed the stars in the sky.
What simple piety!
What pious simplicity!

Even for worms he had a warm love, since he had read this text
about the Savior: *I am a worm and not a man.* That is why he used to
pick them up from the road and put them in a safe place so that they
would not be crushed by the footsteps of passersby.

What shall I say about the other lesser creatures? In the winter he
had honey or the best wine put out for the bees so that they would
not perish from the cold. He used to extol the artistry of their work
and their remarkable ingenuity, giving glory to the Lord. With such
an outpouring, he often used up an entire day or more in praise of
them and other creatures. Once the three young men *in the furnace of
burning fire* invited all the elements *to praise and glorify* the Creator of
all things, so this *man, full of the spirit of God* never stopped *glorifying,
praising, and blessing* the Creator and Ruler of all things in all the elements and creatures.

⁸¹How great do you think was the delight the beauty of flowers
brought to his soul whenever he saw their lovely form and noticed
their sweet fragrance? He would immediately turn his gaze to the
beauty of that flower, brilliant in springtime, sprouting *from the root of*

Phil 1:22

Mt 22:21

Sir 18:2

Ps 22:7

CtC

Dn 3:17;3:51

Jesse. By its *fragrance* it raised up countless thousands of the dead. Whenever he found an abundance of flowers, he used to preach to them and invite them to praise the Lord, just as if they were endowed with reason.

Fields and vineyards,
rocks and woods,
and all *the beauties of the field*,
flowing springs and blooming gardens,
earth and fire, air and wind:
all these he urged to love of God and to willing service.
Finally, he used to call all creatures
by the name of "brother" and "sister"
and in a wonderful way, unknown to others,
he could discern the *secrets of the heart* of creatures
like someone who has already passed
into the freedom of the glory of the children of God.

O good Jesus,
with the angels in heaven
he now praises you as wonderful,
who, when *placed on earth,*
preached you as lovable to all creatures.

[82] Whenever he used to say *your name, O holy Lord,* he was moved in a way beyond human understanding. He was so wholly taken up in joy, filled with pure delight, that he truly seemed a new person of another age.[a]

For this reason he used to gather up any piece of writing, whether divine or human, wherever he found it: on the road, in the house, on the floor. He would reverently pick it up and put it in a sacred or decent place because the name of the Lord, or something pertaining to it, might be written there.

Once a brother asked why he so carefully gathered bits of writing, even writings of pagans where the name of the Lord does not appear. He replied: "Son, I do this because they have the letters which make the glorious *name of the Lord God.* And the good that is found there

Margin references:
Is 11:1
2 Cor 2:14
Sir 24:19
1 Cor 14:25
Rom 8:21
Jb 20:4
Ps 8:2; Is 6:3
est 12; 1LtCl 12; rd 35; 1LtCus 5
Dt 5:11

---

a. In this paragraph, Thomas underscores Francis's reverence not only for the written word of Scripture, a theme frequently offered in his writings, cf. 1LtCl 6; 2LtCl 6; 1LtCus 5; LtOrd 35-37, but for any written articulation of God's name. At the same time, he draws attention to the medieval custom of preserving Sacred Scripture in a special place of honor in each church, i.e., the aumbry.

does not belong to the pagans nor to any human being, but to God alone 'to whom belongs every good thing.' "[a]

What is even more amazing is this: when he had letters written as greetings or admonitions he would not allow a single letter or syllable to be erased from them even when they included a repetition or mistake.

[83]How handsome,
how splendid!

2 Sm 6:22
How *gloriously he appeared*
in innocence of life,
in simplicity of words,
in purity of heart,
in love of God,
in fraternal charity,
in enthusiastic obedience,
in agreeable compliance,
Jgs 13:6
in angelic appearance.

Friendly in behavior,
serene in nature,
affable in speech,
generous in encouragement,
Prv 11:13
faithful in commitment,
prudent in advice,
efficient in endeavor,[b]
Est 2:15
he was *gracious in everything!*

Tranquil in mind,
pleasant in disposition,
sober in spirit,
2 Tm 1:7
lifted in contemplation,
tireless in prayer,
he was fervent in everything!

a. Although the statement is an echo of ER XVII 18, it also resonates with the long-standing tradition of Christian education and the appropriation of pagan language and learning found in the practices of the Middle Ages. This is expressed in Saint Augustine's *On Christian Doctrine* and Hugh of Saint Victor's *Didiscalion.*

b. These two attributes, *"in consiliis providus, in negotiis efficax* [prudent in advice, efficient in endeavor]" are taken from William of Saint Thierry, Arnold of Bonval, Geoffrey of Auxerre, *Vita prima s. Bernardi* III 1,1. In this same passage, William, author of the First Book, also describes, as does Thomas, Bernard's physical appearance and inner strengths. Cf. PL 185: 303.

Firm in purpose,
consistent in virtue,
persevering in grace,
he was the same in everything!

Swift to forgive,   Jas 1:19
slow to grow angry,
free in nature,
remarkable in memory,
subtle in discussing,   Wis 7:22; 7:23
careful in choices,
he was simple in everything!

Strict with himself,
kind with others,
he was discerning in everything!

He was very eloquent, with a cheerful appearance and a kind face; free of laziness and arrogance. He was of medium height, closer to short,[a] his head was of medium size and round. His face was somewhat long and drawn, his forehead small and smooth, with medium *eyes* black and *clear.* His hair was dark; his eyebrows were straight, and his nose even and thin; his ears small and upright, and his temples smooth. *His tongue was peaceable,* fiery and sharp; *his voice* was powerful, but *pleasing,* clear, and musical.[b] His teeth were white, well set and even; his lips were small and thin; his beard was black and sparse;[c] his neck was slender, his shoulders straight; his arms were short, his hands slight, his fingers long and his nails tapered. He had thin legs, small feet, fine skin and little flesh.[d] His clothing was rough, his sleep was short, his hand was generous.

Mt 6:22

Prv 15:4

Sg 2:14

Because he was very humble, he showed *meekness to all people,* and duly adapted himself to the behavior of all. Holy among the holy, *among sinners he was like one of them.*

Ti 3:2

Wis 4:10; Gn 3:22

---

a. A similar description can be found of Bernard of Clairvaux, cf. *Vita prima s. Bernardi* III 1,1.

b. The same adjectives are used again in Thomas's description of Francis proclaiming the gospel of the Nativity at Greccio. Cf. n. 86 below.

c. For a similar passage see *Vita prima s. Bernardi* III 1,1.

d. Another passage similar to the *Vita prima s. Bernardi* III 1,1. Although Thomas knew this work, as is obvious from the similar pattern Thomas provides in describing Francis's appearance and inner strengths, a comparison of both texts shows that Thomas portrays Francis differently.

Help sinners,
O lover of sinners,
most holy father.
We beg you,
by your glorious prayers,
raise up mercifully
those you see miserable in the filth of misdeeds!

Chapter XXX
THE MANGER HE MADE IN CELEBRATION OF THE LORD'S BIRTHDAY

[84] His highest aim, foremost desire, and greatest proposal was
to pay heed to the holy gospel in all things and through all things,
to follow the teaching of our Lord Jesus Christ
and to retrace His footsteps completely
with all vigilance and all zeal,
all the desire of his soul
and all the fervor of his heart.

Francis used to recall with regular meditation the words of Christ
and recollect His deeds with most attentive perception.
Indeed, so thoroughly did the humility of the Incarnation
and the charity of the Passion
occupy his memory
that he scarcely wanted to think of anything else.

We should note then, as matter worthy of memory and something to be recalled with reverence, what he did, three years prior to
his death, at the town of Greccio, on the birthday of our Lord Jesus
Christ. *There was a certain man in that area* named John who *had a good
reputation* but an even better manner of life. Blessed Francis loved
him with special affection, since, despite being a noble in the land
and very honored in human society, he had trampled the nobility of
the flesh under his feet and pursued instead the nobility of the spirit.
As usual, blessed Francis had John summoned to him some fifteen
days prior to the birthday of the Lord. "If you desire to celebrate the
coming feast of the Lord together at Greccio," he said to him, "hurry
before me and *carefully make ready* the things I tell you. For I wish to
enact the memory of that babe *who was born in Bethlehem*: to see as
much as is possible with my own bodily eyes the discomfort of his

Jb 1:1; Phil 4:8

Prv 24:27

Mt 2: 1,2

infant needs, how he *lay in a manger,* and how, with an ox and an ass standing by, he rested on hay." Once the good and faithful man had heard Francis's words, *he ran quickly* and prepared in that place all the things that the holy man had requested.[a]

Lk 2:7
Jn 20:4

⁸⁵ Finally, *the day of joy* has drawn near,
the time of exultation *has come.*
From many different places the brethren have been called.
As they could,
the men and women of that land with exultant hearts
prepare candles and torches to light up that night
whose shining star has enlightened every day and year.
Finally, the holy man of God comes
and, finding all things prepared,
he saw them and was glad.
Indeed, the manger is prepared,
the hay is carried in,
and the ox and the ass are led to the spot.
There simplicity is given a place of honor,
poverty is exalted,
humility is commended,
and out of Greccio is made a new Bethlehem.

Tb 13:10; Sg 2:12
Jn 8:56

The night is lit up like day,
delighting both man and beast.
The people arrive, ecstatic at this new mystery of new joy.
The forest amplifies the cries
and the boulders echo back the joyful crowd.
The brothers sing, giving God due praise,
and the whole night abounds with jubilation.
The holy man of God stands before the manger,
filled with heartfelt sighs,
contrite in his piety,
and overcome with wondrous joy.[b]
Over the manger the solemnities of the Mass are celebrated
and the priest enjoys a new consolation.

Ps 139:12
Mk 1:24

---

a. At this point Thomas once again makes an unexpected shift into the present tense, suggesting that what had happened at Greccio had become an annual event. This text could be a description of the ceremony repeated each Christmas at Greccio in memory of Francis's action.

b. This description of Francis's experience at Greccio is reminiscent of one of Bernard of Clairvaux on Christmas eve. Cf. *Vita secunda s. Bernardi* 2.

[86]The holy man of God is dressed in the vestments of the Levites, since he was a Levite, and with full voice sings the holy gospel.[a] Here is his voice: a powerful voice, *a pleasant voice,* a clear voice, a musical voice, inviting all to the highest of gifts. Then he preaches to the people standing around him and pours forth sweet honey about the birth of the poor King and the poor city of Bethlehem. Moreover, burning with excessive love, he often calls Christ the "babe from Bethlehem" whenever he means to call Him Jesus. Saying the word "Bethlehem" in the manner of a bleating sheep, he fills his whole mouth with sound but even more with sweet affection. He seems to lick his lips whenever he uses the expressions "Jesus" or "babe from Bethlehem," tasting the word on his happy palate and savoring the sweetness of the word. The gifts of the Almighty are multiplied there and a virtuous man sees a wondrous vision.[b] For the man saw a little child lying lifeless in the manger and he saw the holy man of God approach the child and waken him from a deep sleep. Nor is this vision unfitting, since in the hearts of many the child Jesus has been *given over to oblivion.* Now he is awakened and impressed on their loving memory by His own grace through His holy servant Francis. At length, the night's solemnities draw to a close and everyone went home with joy.

[87]The hay placed in the manger there was preserved afterwards so that, through it, the Lord might restore to health the pack animals and the other *animals* there, as He *multiplied his* holy *mercy.* It came to pass in the surrounding area that many of the animals, suffering from various diseases, were freed from their illnesses when they ate some of this hay. What is more, women who had been suffering with long and hard labor had an easy delivery after they placed some of this hay upon themselves. Finally, an entire group of people of both sexes obtained much-desired relief from an assortment of afflictions.

At last, the site of the manger was consecrated as a temple to the Lord. In honor of the most blessed father Francis, an altar was constructed over the manger, and a church was dedicated.

Sg 2:14

Ps 31:13

Ps 36:7-8

---

a. With this description of Francis in the vestments of a Levite, Thomas is the first to suggest that Francis was a deacon. *Levita* [Levite or deacon] refers to the Old Testament Levite, one set aside for service within the Temple. Thus the text is ambiguous in nature. Later texts, e.g. Julian of Speyer's *The Life of Saint Francis* 55 (hereafter LJS), and Bonaventure's *Major Legend* X, 7 (hereafter LMj) are more precise in identifying Francis as a deacon. How and when he was ordained is not known.

b. This may possibly be John of Greccio himself about whose background nothing is known.

This was done
so that where animals *once ate the fodder of the hay,*   Dn 5:21
there humans henceforth
for healing of body and soul
would eat the flesh
of the immaculate and spotless lamb,
our Lord Jesus Christ,
who *gave Himself for us*   Ti 2:14
with supreme and indescribable love,
who lives and rules with the Father and the Holy Spirit as God,
eternally glorious forever and ever.
Amen.
Alleluia, Alleluia.

Here ends the first book of the life and deeds of blessed Francis.

The Second Book

Chapter I
[THE CHARACTER OF THIS BOOK,
THE TIME WHEN SAINT FRANCIS BLESSEDLY DIED,
AND HIS ACHIEVEMENTS][a]

[88]In the previous book, which by the Savior's grace we have brought to a fitting conclusion, we have written down the story of the life and deeds of our blessed father Francis up to the eighteenth year of his conversion. In this book, we shall add a brief account of his remaining deeds, beginning with the next to last year of his life, as we have been able to determine them. For now we intend to note only those things that seem more important so that those who wish to say more about them may always find something to add.

For in the one thousandth, two hundredth, and twenty-sixth year
of the Incarnation of the Lord,
in the fourteenth year of the indiction,[b]
on the fourth day before the Nones of October,[c]
a Sunday,
our most blessed father Francis
departed from the prison of the flesh
and soared to the dwellings of the heavenly spirits.
This happened in the city of Assisi where he was born
at Saint Mary of the Portiuncula
where he first planted the Order of Lesser Brothers,

---

a. In a number of manuscripts this explanatory heading is missing.

b. An indiction was a recurring cycle of fifteen years and was spoken of as "a cycle of indiction." The number attached to it indicated the specific year within the cycle, as in this instance, the 14th year within the indiction. Thomas follows the Roman or Papal indiction according to which an indiction is determined by adding 3 to the year in question, that is, 1226 plus 3. The sum is then divided by 15. The number of the indiction, then, was 82 and within that 82nd cycle, it was the 14th year.

c. Nones was the ninth day before the Ides, hence the fifth day of every month except for March, May, July and October, when it was the seventh; in this case, then, the fourth day before the Nones would be October 4. Since each day began at sunset, our modern calendar would consider it October 3.

twenty years after he embraced Christ completely
following the life and *footsteps* of the Apostles,   1 Pt 2:21
bringing to perfect completion what he had begun.
In that city,
with hymns and praises,
his holy and sacred body was laid to rest
and honorably enclosed.
There it glitters
with many miracles
to the glory of the Almighty.
Amen.

[89]From the first flower of his youth, he was given little or no instruction *in the way of God* or knowledge of Him. He remained for quite some time in natural simplicity and the heat of vices. By the *change* brought about in him by the power of *the right hand of the Most High he was justified from sin.* And by the grace and *power of the Most High* he was filled with divine *wisdom* beyond all others of his time. As the teachings of the gospel had declined seriously in practice—not just in some cases but in general everywhere—*this man was sent* from God so that everywhere, throughout the whole world, after the example of the Apostles, *he might bear witness to the truth.* And so it was, *with the Christ leading,* that his teaching showed clearly that all *the wisdom of the world* was *foolish,* and quickly, he turned all toward the true *wisdom of God through the foolishness of his preaching.*

Bar 3:13

Rom 6:7; Lk 1:35
Dt 34: 9

Jn 1:6:7
Dn 9:25

1 Cor 1: 21

In these last times,   1 Pt 1:5
a new Evangelist,
like one of the rivers of Paradise,
has poured out   Gn 2:10
the streams of the gospel   Is 44:3
in a holy flood over the whole world.[a]
He preached the way of the Son of God   Est 13:4
and the teaching of truth in his deeds.
In him and through him

---

a. These passages are indicative of the renewal theme in Thomas's portrait. In addition to repeating the theme of newness (cf. 196, c), Thomas now introduces an apocalyptic tone by referring to "these last times" and to many prophetic themes. The inspiration for these passages may come from Pope Gregory IX's *Mira circa nos,* the papal decree of canonization, in which Francis is portrayed as God's instrument "at the eleventh hour." Cf. infra pp. 565 -569.

an unexpected joy and a holy newness
came into the world.
A shoot of the ancient religion
suddenly renewed the old and decrepit.
A new spirit was placed in the hearts of the elect
Ez 11:19; 36:26   and a holy anointing *has been poured out in* their *midst.*
Gal 1:1:0   This holy *servant of Christ,*
Gn 1:14   like one of the *lights of heaven,*
shone from above with a new rite and new signs.
The ancient miracles have been renewed through him.
In the desert of this world
a fruitful vine has been planted
in a new Order but in an ancient way,
bearing *flowers, sweet*
Sir 24:23; Ps 52:10   with the *fragrance* of holy virtues
Ez 17:6,7   and *stretching out* everywhere *branches* of holy religion.

Jas 5:17   [90] Although *like us, subject to suffering,* he was not satisfied with observing the ordinary precepts. Rather, overflowing with burning charity, he set out on the way of full perfection, reached out for the
Ps 119:96   peak of perfect holiness, and *saw the goal of all perfection.* That is why every order, sex, and age finds in him a clear pattern of the teaching of salvation and an outstanding example of holy deeds. If people in-
Prv 31:19; 1 Cor   tend to put *their hand to difficult things,* and strive *to seek the higher gifts*
12:31   of a more excellent way, let them look into the mirror of his life, and learn all perfection.[a] There are some who tend to lower, more level paths, fearing to walk the steep route and climb to the summit of the mountain: they too shall find in him suitable reminders. Finally, those who *seek signs* and miracles, let them ask his holiness, and they
1 Cor 1:22   will receive what they request.

Yes, his glorious life reveals in even brighter light
the perfection of earlier saints;
the passion of Jesus Christ proves this,
and His cross shows it clearly.
For the venerable father was in fact marked in five parts of his body
with the marks of the passion and the cross,
as if he had hung on the cross with the Son of God.

---

a. In this passage Francis is proposed for the first time as a mirror for those seeking perfection, an image that develops in importance in subsequent Franciscan literature.

This is a great sacrament, Eph 5:32
and evidence of the grandeur of a special love.
But there is hidden here some secret;
here is concealed some awesome mystery,
one we believe is known to God alone,
though it was partly revealed by the Saint to one person.
For this reason it is useless to try to praise him,
whose praise is from the One Who is
the praise of all, their origin and greatest honor,
the giver of the gifts of light.
Now *blessing God, holy, glorious,* and true, Lk 24:53; Is 58:13
let us return to our story.

Chapter II
THE HIGHEST DESIRE OF BLESSED FRANCIS
AND HOW IN OPENING THE BOOK
HE UNDERSTOOD THE LORD'S WILL FOR HIM

[91]At one time the blessed and venerable father Francis, with worldly crowds gathering eagerly every day to hear and see him, sought out a place of rest and secret solitude. He desired to free himself for God and *shake off any dust that clung to him* from the time spent Lk 10:11 with the crowds.[a] It was his custom to divide the time given him to merit grace and, as seemed best, to spend some of it to benefit his neighbors and use the rest in the blessed solitude of contemplation. *He took with him* only a few companions—who knew his holy way of Lk 9:28; Mk 14:33 living better than others—so that they could shield him *from the interruption and disturbance of people,* respecting and protecting his si- Ps 91:6; 30:21 lence in every way.

After he had been there for some time, through unceasing prayer and frequent contemplation, he reached intimacy with God in an indescribable way. He longed to know what in him and about him was or could be most acceptable to the *Eternal King.* He sought this dili- Ps 29:10 gently and devoutly longed to know in what manner, in what way, and with what desire he would be able to cling more perfectly to the Ps 73:28 *Lord God,* according to His *counsel* and the *good pleasure* of His will. This Sir 40:25 was always his highest philosophy; this was the highest *desire* that always *burned* in him as long as he lived. He asked the simple and the Nm 11:4

---

a. Cf. Gregory the Great, *Diaolgues*, Prologue (PL 77:152A).

wise, the perfect and the imperfect, how he could reach the *way of truth* and arrive at his greater proposal.

Ps 119:30

⁹²Since he was the most perfect among the perfect, he refused to think he was perfect and thought himself wholly imperfect. He could *taste and see* how pleasing, *sweet and good* the God of Israel is to those who are of sincere heart and who *seek Him* in true purity and *in pure simplicity*.

Ps 34:9

Ps 73:1

Wis 1:1

He felt pouring down on him from above a sweetness and delight rarely given to even a few, and it made him lose himself completely. He was filled with such joy that he wished by any means to pass over entirely to that place where, in passing out of himself, he had already partially gone. This man, having *the spirit of God,* was ready to endure any suffering of mind and bear any affliction of the body, if at last he *would be given the choice* that the *will of the heavenly Father* might be *fulfilled* mercifully in him. So one day he approached the sacred altar which had been built in the hermitage where he was staying and, taking up the volume where the holy Gospels were written, he placed it reverently upon the altar.

1C 26

1 Cor 7:40

Jos 24:15

Mt 6:14

Then he prostrated himself with his heart as much as his body *in prayer to God,* asking in humble prayer that *God in His kindness—the Father of mercies and the God of all consolation*—be pleased to show him His will. He prayed earnestly that at the first opening of the book he would be shown what was best for him to do, so that he could bring to complete fulfillment what he had earlier simply and devotedly begun. In this he was led by the spirit of the saints and holy ones, as we read they did something similar with sincere devotion in their desire for holiness.[a]

Lk 6:12; Jl 2:13

2 Cor 1:3

⁹³*Rising from prayer in a spirit of humility and with a contrite heart,* he prepared himself with the sign of the holy cross. He took the book from the altar, and *opened it with reverence* and fear. *When he opened the book,* the first passage that met his eye was the passion of our Lord Jesus Christ that tells of the suffering he was to endure. To avoid any suspicion that this was just a coincidence, he opened the book a second and a third time. Every time he found either the same text or one that was similar. This *man filled with the spirit of God* then understood that he would *have to enter into the kingdom of God through many trials,* difficulties and struggles.

Lk 22:45; Dn 3:39

Rv 5:7; 5:8

Gn 41:38

Acts 14:21

---

a. This approach to the Scriptural text has its roots in Saint Augustine. Cf. *The Confessions* VIII, 12, 29: "For on leaving it I had put down there the book of the apostle's letters, I snatched it up, opened it and read in silence the passage on which my eyes first lighted."

The brave knight *was not disturbed by oncoming battles,* nor was he downcast in his spirit as he was about to *fight the wars of the Lord* in the camps of this world.

Eccl 8:8

1 Sm 25:28

> He was not afraid that he would yield to the enemy
> since he had long struggled beyond human strength
> not even to give in to himself.
> He was so filled with fire that,
> even if in preceding ages
> there had been a companion with a proposal equal to his,
> no one has been found whose desire was greater than his.
> He found it easier to do what is perfect
> than to talk about it;
> so he was constantly active
> in showing his zeal and dedication in deeds, not in words,
> because words do not do what is good,
> they only point to it.
> Thus he remained undisturbed and happy,
> singing *songs of joy in his heart* to himself and to God.
> For this reason he was found worthy of a greater revelation,
> since he rejoiced over a small one;
> *faithful in a small thing,*
> *he was placed over greater ones.*

Eph 5:19

Lk 19:17

Mt 25:21

Chapter III
THE VISION OF A MAN HAVING THE IMAGE OF A CRUCIFIED SERAPH

[94]While he was staying in that hermitage called La Verna, after the place where it is located, two years prior to the time that he returned his soul to heaven, he saw *in the vision of God* a man, *having six wings like a Seraph, standing over* him, *arms extended and feet joined,* affixed to a cross. *Two of his wings* were raised up, *two were stretched out over his head as if for flight,* and *two covered his* whole *body.* When the blessed servant of the most High saw these things, he was filled with the greatest awe, but could not decide what this vision meant for him. Moreover, he greatly rejoiced and was much delighted by the kind and gracious look that he saw the Seraph gave him.[a] The Ser-

Ez 1:1; 8:1

Is 6:2

---

a. The "seraph" or "seraphim" belong to the highest choir of angels. These angels, most intimately present to God, are found in the biblical tradition, especially in visions of God. Cf. Is 6:1-13; Ez 1:5-14, 1:22-25; and Rv 4:6-9.

aph's beauty was beyond comprehension, but the fact that the Seraph was fixed to the cross and the bitter suffering of that passion thoroughly frightened him. Consequently, he got up both sad and happy as joy and sorrow took their turns in his heart. Concerned over the matter, he kept thinking about what this vision could mean and
Ps 143:4   his *spirit was anxious* to discern a sensible meaning from the vision.

While he was unable to perceive anything clearly understandable from the vision, its newness very much pressed upon his heart. Signs of the nails began to appear on his hands and feet, just as he had seen them a little while earlier on the crucified man hovering over him.

[95] His hands and feet seemed to be pierced through the middle by nails, with the heads of the nails appearing on the inner part of his hands and on the upper part of his feet, and their points protruding on opposite sides. Those marks on the inside of his hands were round, but rather oblong on the outside; and small pieces of flesh were visible like the points of nails, bent over and flattened, extending beyond the flesh around them. On his feet, the marks of nails were stamped in the same way and raised above the surrounding flesh. His right side was marked with an oblong scar, as if pierced with a lance, and this often dripped blood, so that his tunic and undergarments were frequently stained with his holy blood.[a]

Sadly, only a few merited seeing the sacred wound in his side during the life of the crucified servant of the crucified Lord. Elias was fortunate and did merit somehow to see the wound in his side.[b]
1 Jn 1:1   Rufino was just as lucky: he *touched it with his own hands.* For one time, when the same brother Rufino put his hand onto the holy man's chest to rub him, his hand slipped, as often happens, and it chanced that he touched the precious scar in his right side. As soon as he had touched it, the holy one of God felt great pain and pushed
Gn 19:16   Rufino's hand away, crying out *for the Lord to spare him.*

---

a. For extensive study on the stigmata see Octavian Schmucki, *The Stigmata of Saint Francis of Assisi: A Critical Investigation in the Light of Thirteenth-Century Sources.* Translated by Canisius Connors. (St. Bonaventure, NY: The Franciscan Institute, 1991).

b. In Book Two, Thomas gives importance to Elias Buonbarone (+1253), who was born in either Assisi or in Cortona. Shortly after the first missionary Chapter in 1217, Elias departed for the Holy Land to serve as Minister for the new venture. Later, during his own 1219-1220 visit in the East, Francis met Elias and brought him back to Italy. In 1221, after the death of his first vicar, Francis appointed Elias. Elias presided at the Chapter of Mats in 1221, which furthered the missionary activity of the Order into Germany. After Francis's death, the Pentecost Chapter of 1227 elected John Parenti, Minister from Spain, to be the Minister General. Elias was engaged by Gregory IX to oversee the building of a new basilica in honor of the new saint. In 1232, Elias was elected to succeed John Parenti. During his tenure as Minister General, Elias promoted theological studies and missionary expansion into Asia and Africa. In 1239, the brothers, distressed by his abuse of authority and his autocratic use of visitators, requested Pope Gregory IX to depose Elias from his office. After he was removed, Elias sided with the Emperor Frederick II in his political dispute with Gregory IX. Gregory IX excommunicated him. Elias died reconciled and absolved in Cortona on April 22, 1253.

He hid those marks carefully from strangers, and concealed them cautiously from people close to him, so that even the brothers at his side and his most devoted followers for a long time did not know about them.

Although the servant and friend of the Most High saw himself adorned with such magnificent pearls, like *precious stones,* and marvelously decorated *beyond the glory and honor of all others,* still his heart did not grow vain. *He did* not *seek* to use this to *make himself appealing* to anyone in a desire for vainglory. Rather in every way possible he tried to hide these marks, so that human favor would not *rob him* of the grace *given* him.

^(96)He would never or rarely reveal his great secret to anyone. He feared that his special friends would reveal it to show their intimacy with him, as friends often do, and he would then lose some of *the grace given to him.* He always carried in his heart and often had on his lips the saying of the prophet: *"I have hidden your words in my heart to avoid any sin against You."*

Whenever some people of the world approached him and he did not wish to speak with them, he would give this sign to the brothers and sons staying with him: if he recited the verse mentioned above, immediately they would dismiss politely those who had gathered to see him. He had learned through experience that one cannot be a spiritual person unless one's secrets are deeper and more numerous than *what can be seen on the face* and by their appearance can be judged in different ways by different people. For he had met some people who agreed with him outwardly but inwardly disagreed, applauding him to his face but laughing behind his back. These brought *judgment upon themselves* and made honest people seem somewhat suspect to him.

So it is that malice often attempts to smear sincerity
and because of the lies of many,
the truth of the few *is not believed.*

2 Chr 9:9

Sir 3:19; Ps 8:6

Gal 1:10

Mt 6:18; 6:19

Rom 12:3; 2 Cor 7:9

Ps 119:11

2 Cor 10:7

1 Cor 11:29

2 Thes 2:11

Chapter IV
THE FERVOR OF BLESSED FRANCIS AND THE DISEASE OF HIS EYES

[97]During this same period his body began to be afflicted with different kinds of illness, and more severe than usual. Since he had *over many years chastised his body and brought it into subjection,* he suffered infirmities often. During the course of the eighteen years which by then had passed, his *flesh* rarely or never *had any rest,* as he traveled through many *distant regions,* so that the *willing spirit,* the devout spirit, and the *fervent spirit which dwelt within him* might scatter everywhere the *seed of the word of God. He filled the* whole *world* with the gospel of Christ, in the course of one day often *visiting* four or five *towns and villages,* proclaiming to every one the *good news of the kingdom of God,* edifying his listeners by his example as much as by his words, as he made of his whole body a tongue.

There was in him such harmony of flesh with spirit
and such obedience that,
as the spirit strove to reach all holiness,
the flesh did not resist
but even tried to run on ahead,
according to the saying:
For you my soul has thirsted;
and my flesh in so many ways!
Repeated submission became spontaneous,
as the flesh, yielding each day,
reached a place of great virtue,
for habit often becomes nature.[a]

[98]According to the laws of nature and the human condition *day by day* the body must *decay* though *the inner being is renewed.* So the precious *vessel* in which the heavenly *treasure was hidden* began to shatter all over and lose all its strength. Yet *when a man has finished, then he will begin* and when he has finished, then he will start to work. And so the *spirit* became *willing* in the *flesh that was weak.* He so desired the salvation of souls and longed to benefit his neighbors that, even though he could no longer walk on his own, *he went through the towns* riding on a little donkey.

Marginal references:
Rom 15:23; 1 Cor 9:27
2 Cor 7:5
Gn 41:46
Acts 18:25; Rom 8:11
Lk 8:11 Mt 26:41; Wis 1:7
Mk 6:6
Lk 8:1
Ps 63:2
2 Cor 4:16
Mt 13:44
Sir 18:6
Mt 26:41
Lk 9:6

---

a. Cf. n. 4 above; Augustine, *Treatise on John's gospel,* Tract 44 n. 1 (PL 35, 1744); Cicero, *De Finibus bonorum* V 25 74; Macrobius, *Saturnalia* VII 9 7. The passage also appears in *Vita prima s. Bernardi* IV 20 and Alan, Bishop of Auxerre, *Vita secunda s. Bernardi* IV 16 [PL 185, 238, 479].

The brothers often advised him, urging him to give some relief to his frail and weakened body through the help of doctors. But he absolutely refused to do this. His noble spirit was aimed at heaven and he only *desired* to be set free and *to be with Christ.* But he had not yet **Phil 1:23** *filled up in his flesh what is lacking in the sufferings of Christ,* even though **Col 1:24** *he bore the marks on his body.* So *God multiplied* his *mercy* on him, and he **Gal 6:17; Ps 36:8** contracted a serious disease of the eyes.[a] Day after day the disease grew worse and seemed to be aggravated daily from lack of treatment. Brother Elias, the one he chose for the role of mother to himself and had made a father of the other brothers,[b] finally forced him not to refuse medicine but to accept it *in the name of the Son of God.* **1 Jn 5:13** Through Him it was created, as it is written: *The Most High created* medicine *from the earth and the wise will not refuse it.* The holy father **Sir 38:4** then gladly agreed with him and humbly accepted his direction.

Chapter V
HOW HE WAS RECEIVED AT THE CITY OF RIETI
BY THE LORD HUGOLINO, BISHOP OF OSTIA,
AND HOW THE HOLY MAN DECLARED
THAT HE WOULD BE BISHOP OF THE WHOLE WORLD

[99]Many came with their medicines to help him but no remedy could be found. So he went to the city of Rieti where a man was staying who was said to be the greatest expert in curing that disease. When he arrived there he was received kindly and respectfully by the whole Roman Curia, which was then staying in that city. He was especially well received by Lord Hugolino, the bishop of Ostia, who was renowned for his upright conduct and holy life.

Blessed Francis, with the consent and approval of the Lord Pope Honorius, chose this man as father and lord over the whole religion and order of his brothers because blessed poverty greatly pleased him and holy simplicity received his greatest reverence.

---

a. The disease has been diagnosed as ophthalmia, a severe inflammation of the eyeball or the mucous membrane lining the inner surface of the eyelids and covering the front part of the eyeball.

b. Placing Elias in the role of "mother" is consistent with Francis's understanding of the way in which each of the brothers should "love and care" for one another, cf. ER IX 11; LR VI 8; RH 1, 2, 10.

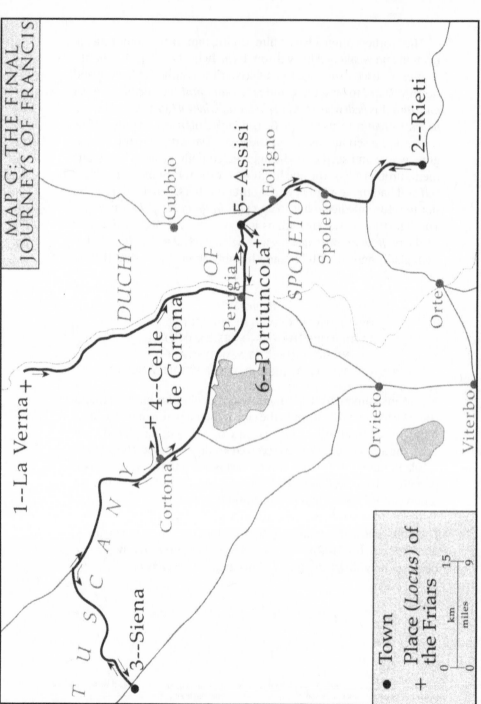

MAP G: THE FINAL JOURNEYS OF FRANCIS

1--La Verna +

4--Celle de Cortona +

Cortona

3--Siena

T U S C A N Y

D U C H Y

Gubbio

Perugia

6--Portiuncola +

O F

5--Assisi

Foligno

S P O L E T O

Spoleto

2--Rieti

Orte

Orvieto

Viterbo

• Town

+ Place (*Locus*) of the Friars

0   km   15
0   miles   9

1 Celano 99-108 relates that at the end of his life Francis travelled through Tuscany and the Duchy of Spoleto. After receiving the stigmata on Mt. LaVerna (1), Francis travelled to several places in the region: to Rieti (2), then north and west to Siena (3), then back to Celle de Cortona (4), on to Assisi (5), and finally to the Portiuncula (6).

That lord conformed himself to the ways of the brothers.
In his desire for holiness
he was simple with the simple,
humble with the humble,
and poor with the poor.
He was a brother among brothers,
the least among the lesser,[a]
and in his life and habits strove to behave
as one of them
as much as was possible.

He took care to plant this holy religion everywhere
and in faraway places his glowing reputation,
from an even more glowing life,
helped greatly to spread the Order.
The Lord *gave* him *a learned tongue.*   Is 50:4
With it he confounded the opponents of truth,
refuted *the enemies of the cross of Christ,*   Phil 3:18
led the strangers back to the way,   Dt 22:1
made peace between those in conflict,
and bound together those in peace
in a stronger *bond of love.*   Hos 11:4
In the Church of God
he *was a lamp burning and shining,*   Jn 5:35
a *chosen arrow*   Is 49:2
ready *at the right time.*   Ps 32:6
Many times he took off his fine clothes
and, dressed in rough garments
and with bare feet,
like one of the brothers,
he went *asking for terms of peace.*   Lk 14:32
He used to do this with great care whenever necessary
between neighbor and neighbor,   Jer 7:5
and always between God and the people.
For this reason
God *chose him*   Sir 45:4

---

a. The phrase "the least among the lesser" is a play on words since the comparative form of the adjective "*minores*" is also used as a noun to designate the followers of Francis. The idea here is that the bishop was more a lesser brother than the other brothers.

Acts 5:11

Ps 110:7; Rv 13:7

2 Tm 3:16

Ez 31:8; Ps 110:3

Jer 2:21

Ps 80:12; 18:20

Mt 24:45; Ps 145:15

Mt 4:1

Acts 13:9

Is 52:10

2 Cor 5:14

Gn 49:26

> to be the pastor *of all His* holy *church*
> and *lifted up his head among the tribes of the people.*

[100]The blessed father Francis foretold this in words and foreshadowed it in action so that it would be recognized as *inspired by God* and done by the will of Christ Jesus. It happened in this way. The Order and religion of the brothers had begun to spread by the grace of God. Like a *cedar in the garden of God* it lifted its crown of merit *into the heavens,* and like *a chosen vineyard* it stretched out its holy *branches to the ends of the earth.*[a]

At that time Saint Francis approached the lord Pope Honorius, who was then at the head of the Roman Church, humbly asking him to appoint the lord Hugolino, bishop of Ostia, as father and lord for him and his brothers. The lord Pope bowed to the holy man's request, and kindly agreeing, entrusted to the bishop his authority over the Order of the brothers. Like *a prudent and faithful servant set over the family* of the Lord, the bishop accepted it reverently and devoutly. He strove in every way to administer the *food* of eternal life *in due season* to those entrusted to him. The holy father for this reason subjected himself to him in every way and venerated him with wonderful and reverent affection.

Blessed Francis was *led by the Spirit* of God with which *he was filled.* Therefore he saw long before what was later to appear *in the sight of all.* For whenever he wanted to write to him, impelled by the needs of the Order they both served, or, more often, moved *by the love of Christ* which he felt so strongly toward him, he would never allow him to be called in his letters "Bishop of Ostia and Velletri" as others did in customary greetings. Instead, taking up the topic, he used to say; "To the Most Reverend Father, Lord Hugolino, Bishop of the Whole World."

Often he would greet him with unheard-of blessings, and although he was a son in his loyal submission, he would sometimes console him with a fatherly word at the prompting of the Spirit so that he could *strengthen* him *with the blessings of the fathers until the desire of the everlasting hills should come.*

[101]That same lord also felt great love for the holy man and therefore was pleased with whatever the blessed man did or said, and was deeply moved at the mere sight of him. He swears that no matter

---

a. In order to experience the fullness of affective, poetic and religious power conveyed by a simple biblical allusion, see the beautiful allegory of the cedar, (Ez 31:9) to which Thomas alludes here.

how disturbed or troubled he became, when he saw or talked to Saint Francis the clouds inside him would break up and clear weather would return; his depression would vanish and joy would pour down over him.

This man *ministered* to blessed Francis, *as a servant to his lord,* and, whenever he saw him, he offered the reverence due to *an apostle of Christ.* Bowing before him both outwardly and inwardly, he would often kiss his hand with his consecrated lips.

With devotion and care, he tried to find a way for the blessed father to regain the earlier health of his eyes, knowing he was *a holy and just* man, *very much* needed and useful to the Church of God. He shared in worrying about him with the whole assembly of the brothers, *pitying the sons* because *of their father.* Then he advised the holy father to take care of himself and not to refuse the things needed to treat his illness, because neglecting them would not be considered praiseworthy but sinful. Saint Francis humbly observed what such a revered lord and a beloved father told him. From then on he more carefully and freely did what was needed for his treatment. But now the illness had grown so bad that any relief at all required the greatest expertise and demanded the most bitter medicine. This is what was done: his head was cauterized in several places, his veins opened, poultices applied, and drops poured into his eyes. Yet *he had no improvement but kept getting steadily worse.*

Lk 12:37

1 Cor 1:1

Acts 3:14

Neh 2:2

Ps 103:13

Ps 89:23

Mk 5:26

Chapter VI
THE CONDUCT OF THE BROTHERS ATTENDING SAINT FRANCIS
AND THE WAY HE DECIDED TO LIVE

¹⁰²For nearly two years he endured these things
with complete patience and humility,
in all things giving thanks to God.
But in order to be able
to devote his attention to God more freely,
he entrusted his own care to certain brothers,
who with good reason were very dear to him.
Thus he could more freely explore in frequent *ecstasy of Spirit*
the blessed dwelling places of heaven,
and, in the abundance of grace,
stand *in heavenly places*
before the gentle and serene *Lord of all things.*

Tb 2:14; 1 Thes 5:18

2 Cor 5:13

Eph 1:3

2 Mc 14:35

1 Mc 5:50

These brothers were *men of virtue,* devoted to God,
pleasing to the saints, and well-liked by people.
The blessed Father Francis *rested* upon them

Jgs 16:29

as a *house* upon four *pillars.*[a]
I omit their names for the present, out of regard for
modesty,
which is a close friend of these spiritual men.
Modesty is the beauty of all ages,
a witness of innocence,
the sign of a pure mind,

Prv 22:15

the rod of correction,
the special glory of conscience,
the protector of reputation,
and the mark of thorough integrity.

Acts 2:44

This virtue graced those men and made them loveable and kind to people. This grace *they all held in common,* but a particular virtue also adorned each one. One had outstanding discernment, another had extraordinary patience, one was famous for his simplicity, and the last had great physical strength along with gentleness of spirit. These men vigilantly, zealously, and eagerly protected the peace of mind of the blessed father, cared for him in his illness, and spared no pain or labor in offering themselves completely to the saint's service.

Jn 11:9

[103] In the sight of God and the people *of this world*
the glorious father had been made perfect in grace.
In all that he did he glowed brilliantly,
yet he always kept thinking
about how to undertake even more perfect deeds.

Gn 32:2

Like a soldier, well-trained in *the battle camps of God,*
challenging the enemy,
he wanted to stir up fresh battles.

Dn 9:25

With *the Christ as leader,*
he resolved "to do great deeds,"
and with weakening limbs and dying body,
he hoped for victory over the enemy in a new struggle.
True bravery knows no real limits of time,
for its hope of reward is eternal.

1C 7

---

a. The four pillars refer to the four brothers who nursed Francis. Traditionally, these brothers are identified as Angelo Tancredi, Rufino, Leo, and either Bernard or John.

He burned with a great desire to return to his earliest steps toward humility; *rejoicing in hope* because of his boundless love, he planned to call his body back to its original servitude, although it had now reached its limit. He cut away completely the obstacle of all cares and silenced the noise of all concerns. When he had to relax this rigor because of illness, he used to say: "Let us begin, brothers, to serve the Lord God, for up until now we have done little or nothing." *He did not consider that he had already attained* his goal, but tireless in a proposal of holy newness, he constantly hoped to begin again.

Nm 11:4; Mt 2:10

Rom 12:12

Phil 3:13

> He wanted to return to serving lepers
> and to be held in contempt, just as he used to be.
> He intended to flee human company
> and go off to the most remote places,
> so that,
> letting go of every care
> and putting aside anxiety about others,
> for the time being
> only the wall of the flesh would stand between him and God.[a]

[104]He saw many rushing for positions of authority. Despising their arrogance, he strove by his own example to call them back from such sickness. Indeed, he used to say that it was a good and acceptable thing in God's sight to take care of others. He held it was appropriate for some to take on the care of souls as long as in this *they sought* nothing *of their own will,* but in all things constantly obeyed God's will. Such people should consider in the first place their own salvation and aim for the growth of their subjects, not their applause. They should seek *glory* before *God,* not honor from people, never desiring but fearing the office of prelate. If given to them it would humble them, not exalt them; were it taken away, it would not leave them dejected, but uplifted.

Phil 2:21

Rom 4:2

Adm IV; ER XVII

He maintained it was dangerous to direct others and better to be directed, especially in these times when malice is *growing so much* and wickedness *is increasing.* It hurt him that some had abandoned their *early deeds* and, in the midst of new discoveries, had forgotten their original simplicity. That is why he grieved over those who now sank to the level of what was low and cheap, although they once had

2 Thes 1:3

Rv 2:5

---

a. This passage is reminiscent of the vocabulary of monasticism which viewed the practice of prayer and asceticism in terms of the angelic life, that is, in terms of sharing in the angelic ministry of adoration and of serving those in need of God's mercy. Cf. 1C 15.

striven for higher things with all their desire. They had abandoned true joy and were running here and there, wandering through the fields of an empty freedom. So he prayed for God's mercy to set his sons free and fervently begged that they be preserved in the *grace* Rom 12:3 *given to them.*

Chapter VII
HOW HE CAME TO ASSISI FROM SIENA
AND CONCERNING THE CHURCH OF SAINT MARY OF THE PORTIUNCULA
AND THE BLESSING OF THE BROTHERS

[105] Six months before the day of his death, he was staying in Siena for treatment of his eye disease. But then all the rest of his body started to show signs of serious illness. His stomach had been destroyed, and his liver was failing. He was vomiting a lot of blood, so much that he seemed close to death. On hearing of this in a place far away, brother Elias rushed to his side. At his arrival the holy father had recovered so much that they left that area and went together to Mt 25:5 Le Celle near Cortona.[a] After reaching the place he *stayed for a while,* but then the swelling began in his abdomen, his legs, and his feet. His stomach became so weak that he could hardly eat any food at all. At that point, he asked brother Elias to have him carried to Assisi. The good son did what the kind father commanded and, when ev-
Est 8:15; 2 Cor 7:6 erything was ready, led him to the place he longed for. *The city rejoiced*
Dn 3:51 *at the arrival* of the blessed father and all the people with one voice
Lk 1:10; Mk 1:24 *praised God,* since *the whole multitude of the people* hoped that *the holy one of God* would die close to them, and this was the reason for such great rejoicing.

Jb 26:11 [106] And so it was also the *will of God*
that his holy soul, freed from the flesh,
Mt 3:2 would pass over to *the kingdom of heaven*
from that place
Phil 1:24 where, while *still living in the flesh,*
he had first been given the knowledge of higher things
and had the oil of salvation poured out upon him.
Mt 5:3 He knew that the *kingdom of heaven*
Ez. 34:13 was established in every *corner of the earth*

---

a. Francis first came to "Le Celle" of Cortona in 1211. At that time it was probably the site of some small buildings [*celle*], most likely mills harnessing the stream of water that flows beside them.

and he believed that divine grace was given
to God's chosen ones in every place.   Rom 8:33
Yet he knew from his own experience
that the place of the church of Saint Mary of the
Portiuncula
was especially full of grace
and filled with visits of heavenly spirits.
So he often told the brothers:
"See to it, my sons, that you never abandon this place.
If you are driven out from one side,
go back in from the other,
for this *is truly a holy place*   Ez 42:13
and *the dwelling place of God.*   1 Chr 29:1
Here the Most High increased our numbers
when we were only a few;   1 Chr 16:19
here He *enlightened the hearts* of his poor ones   Eph 1:18
with the light of His wisdom;
here He kindled our wills with the fire of His love;
here all who pray wholeheartedly will receive what they ask,
while offenders will be severely punished.
Therefore, my sons, hold this place, *God's dwelling,*   1 Kgs 8:30; 8:33
as worthy of all honor
and *here praise God*   Jer 29:13
in cries of joy and praise   Ps 42:5
with your whole heart."   Jer 29:13

[107] As his illness grew worse, he lost all bodily strength, and deprived of all his powers, he could not even move. One of the brothers asked him what he would prefer to endure: this long-lasting illness or suffering a martyr's cruel death at the hands of an executioner. "My son," he replied, "whatever is *more pleasing to the Lord my God* to   Dt 13:18; Rom 12:1
do with me and in me has always been and still is dearer, sweeter, and more agreeable to me. I desire to be found always and completely in harmony with and obedient to God's will alone in everything. But to suffer this illness, even for three days, would be harder for me than any martyrdom. I am not speaking about its reward but only of the *pain* and suffering *it causes."*   Dn 3:50

O martyr,
martyr laughing and rejoicing,
who endured so gladly
what was bitter and painful
for others to see!

Not one of his members remained without great pain and suffering; his bodily warmth gradually diminished, and each day he drew closer to his end. The doctors were amazed and the brothers were astonished that the spirit could live in flesh so dead, since with *his flesh*
Jb 19:20   *all consumed* only skin *clung to his bones.*

[108]When he saw his final day drawing near,
as shown to him two years earlier by divine revelation,
Mk 3:13   he *called to him* the brothers he *chose.*
Jn 19:11   He blessed each one as it was *given* to him *from above,*
just as Jacob of old, the patriarch, blessed his sons.
He was like another Moses
about *to ascend the mountain*
Dt 32:49   *that the Lord had shown* him,
when imparting blessings on the children of Israel.

When brother Elias sat down on his left side with the other brothers around him, the blessed father crossed his arms and *placed his*
Gn 48:14   *right hand on* Elias' *head.* He had lost the sight and use of his bodily eyes, so he asked: "Over whom am I holding my right hand?" "Over brother Elias," they replied. "And this is what I wish to do," he said,
Eph 4:6   "I bless you, my son, *in all and through all,* and just as the most High has increased my brothers and sons in your hands, so too, upon you and in you, I bless them all. May the king of all *bless you in heaven and*
Ps 113:6; Tb 9:9   *on earth.* I bless you as I can, and more than I can, and what I cannot
Dn 14:37   do may the One who can do all things do in you. *May God remember* your work and labors, and may a place be reserved for you among *the*
Heb 2:2   *rewards of the just.* May you receive every blessing you desire and may your every worthy request be fulfilled."
Eccl 9:22   "Good-bye, all my sons. Live *in the fear of God* and remain in Him
Sir 27:6; Ps 22:12   always, for a great *test* will come upon you and tribulation is drawing
Mt 10:22   near! Happy are those *who will persevere* in what they have begun: many will be separated from them by the scandals that are to come. But now I am hurrying to the Lord *and I am confident that I am going to*
Ps 30:9; Rom 1:19   *my God whom I have served in my spirit."*

He was staying then in the palace of the bishop of Assisi, and he asked the brothers to carry him quickly to the place of Saint Mary of the Portiuncula. For he wanted to give back his soul to God in that place where, as noted above, he first came to know perfectly *the way of truth.*

1C 88,106

Ps 19:30

Chapter VIII
WHAT HE DID AND SAID AT HIS BLESSED DEATH

[109]Twenty years had now passed since his conversion, and his time was ending just as it had been shown to him by God's will. For, once the blessed father and brother Elias were staying at Foligno, and one night while they were sleeping, a priest of venerable appearance and great age dressed in white clothing appeared to brother Elias. "Get up, brother," he said, "and tell brother Francis that eighteen years have passed since he renounced the world and clung to Christ. He will remain in this life only two more years; then he will go *the way of all flesh when the Lord calls* him to Himself." So it came to pass that, at the established time, the *word of the Lord* spoken long before now *was fulfilled.*

Jos 23:14; Gn 3:9

2 Chr 36:21

After he had rested a few days in that place he so longed for, knowing *the time* of his death *was close at hand,* he called to him two brothers, his special sons, and told them to sing *The Praises of the Lord* with a loud voice and joyful spirit, rejoicing at his approaching death, or rather at the life that was so near.[a] He himself, as best he could, broke into that psalm of David: *"With a loud voice I cried to the Lord; with a loud voice I beseeched the Lord."*

Heb 9:9

Ps 142:2-8

There was a brother there whom the holy man loved with great affection. Seeing what was happening and realizing the saint was nearing the end, he grew very concerned about all the brothers and said: "Oh, kind father, your sons will now be *without a father,* and will be deprived *of the true light* of their eyes! Remember the orphans you are leaving behind;[b] forgive all their faults, and gladden them all, whether present or absent, with your holy blessing." The holy man answered: "See, my son, I am being called by God. I forgive all my brothers, present and absent, all their faults and offenses, and I ab-

Lam 5:3

1 Jn 2:8

---

a. This refers to the CtC to which Francis added, on his deathbed, the verse: "Praised be You, my Lord, through our sister Bodily Death . . ."

b. Cf. Sulpicius Severus, *Letter* II, *To the Deacon Aurelius,* 10. This is in reference to the death of Saint Martin of Tours.

solve them insofar as I am able. When you give them this message, bless them all for me."

¹¹⁰Then he ordered the book of the Gospels to be brought in. He asked that the Gospel according to John be read to him, starting with the passage that begins: *Six days before the Passover,* Jesus, knowing that the hour had come for him to pass from this world to the Father.^a This was the very gospel his minister had planned to read, even before he was told to do so; that was the passage that met his eye as he first opened the book, although he had the complete Bible from which to read the gospel. Then he told them to cover him with sackcloth and to sprinkle him with ashes, as he was soon to become *dust and ashes.*

Many brothers *gathered* there, for whom *he was* both father and *leader.* They stood there reverently, all awaiting his blessed *departure* and happy *end.* And then that most holy soul was released from the flesh, and as it was absorbed into the abyss of light, his body *fell asleep in the Lord.*

One of his brothers and followers, a man of some fame, whose name I will conceal for now since he does not wish to glory in such fame while still *living in the flesh,* saw the soul of the most holy father *rise straight to heaven over many waters.* It was *like a star* but as big as the moon, with *the brilliance of the sun,* and *carried up* upon *a small white cloud.* ^b

¹¹¹Let me cry out therefore:
"O what a glorious saint he is!
His disciple saw his soul *ascending into heaven:*
beautiful as the moon,
bright as the sun,
glowing brilliantly as *it ascended* upon *a white cloud!*
O true *lamp* of the world,
shining more brilliantly than the sun in the *Church of Christ!*
Now, you have withdrawn the rays of your light,
as you withdraw into that luminous homeland.

Margin references: Jn 12:1; Jn 13:1; Sir 10:9; 17:27; Dt 31:11; Acts 14:11; Sir 33:24; Acts 7:60; Gal 2:20; Jos 8:20; Ps 29:3; Sir 50:6; 1 Cor 15:41; Rv 14:14; Acts 2:34; Sg 6:9; Rv 14:14; Sg 3:6; Mt 5:15; Rom 16:16

a. Thomas creates some confusion here. The first words of the quotation are from Jn 12:1, whereas what follows is from Jn 13:1ff. It is difficult to know if Francis wanted his brothers to read only the pericope of Jesus washing the feet of the Apostles or that which follows. Since Francis quotes John's Last Supper discourse so frequently in his writings, it seems plausible that he wanted to hear it during his last moments.

b. The soul of a saint in death moves to heaven in light. Cf. Gregory the Great, *Dialogue* II, 35: "In the dead of night he suddenly beheld a flood of light shining down from above more brilliant than the sun, and with it every trace of darkness cleared away. As he gazed at all this dazzling display, he saw the soul of Germanus, the Bishop of Capua, being carried by angels up to heaven in a ball of fire."

You have exchanged our poor *company*
for that *of the angels* and saints!
In your glorious goodness and great renown,
do not put aside care for your sons,
though you have put aside flesh like theirs.
You know, you truly know,
the danger in which you have left them;
for it was your blessed presence alone
that always mercifully relieved
their countless labors and frequent troubles!
O truly merciful and most holy father,
you were always kind and ready
to show mercy and forgive your sinful sons!
We bless you therefore, worthy father,
as you *have been blessed* by the Most High,
Who *is God over all things blessed forever. Amen."*

Heb 12:22

Tb 8:17; Gn 27:27

Rom 9:5

Chapter IX
THE LAMENT OF THE BROTHERS AND THEIR JOY
WHEN THEY PERCEIVED THAT FRANCIS BORE
THE SIGNS OF THE CROSS IN HIS BODY
AND ABOUT THE WINGS OF THE SERAPH

[112]At Francis's death,
*a whole crowd of people praising God
came together and said:*
"You, *our Lord and God, be praised and blessed,*
for you have given us unworthy ones so precious a remnant!
Praise and glory to you, O ineffable Trinity!"

Acts 21:30; Mi 5:7;
Lk 2:13

Dn 3:57; Ps 41:14

The whole city of Assisi rushed down *as a group* and *the entire region* hurried to see *the wonderful works of God* which *the Lord of majesty* gloriously displayed in his holy servant. Each person burst into a song of joy at the urging of a *joyful heart,* and all of them had their *desire fulfilled* and blessed the almighty Savior. Still his sons were mourning, bereft of so great a father, and showed the deep feeling of their hearts in groaning and tears.

Mt 8:34

Mt 3:5; Acts 2:11

Is 2:10

Lam 5:15

Phil 4:19

Then incredible joy lightened their grief!
A new miracle
turned their minds to amazement.
Their mourning turned into song,
their weeping to jubilation.
For they had never heard or read in Scripture
about what their eyes could see:
they could not have been persuaded to believe it
if it were not demonstrated by such clear evidence.
In fact,
there appeared in him
the form of the cross and passion
of the spotless lamb
who washed away the sins *of the world.*
It seemed
he had just been taken down from the cross,
his hands and feet pierced by nails
and his right *side*
wounded *by a lance.*

Est 13:17

1 Pt 1:19

Rv 1:5

Jn 19:34

They looked at his skin which was black before but now shining white in its beauty, promising the rewards of the blessed resurrection. They saw *his face* like *the face of an angel,* as if he were not dead, but alive. All his limbs had become as soft and moveable as in childhood innocence. His muscles were not taut, as they usually are in the dead, his skin was not hard, his limbs were not rigid but could be easily moved back and forth.

Acts 6:15

[113] *All the people saw* him glowing with remarkable beauty and his flesh became even whiter than before. It was even more wonderful for them to see in the middle of his hands and feet not just the holes of the nails, but the nails themselves formed by his own flesh, retaining the dark color of iron, and his right side red with blood. These signs of martyrdom did not provoke horror, but added great beauty and grace, like little black stones in a white pavement.

Ex 33:10

His brothers and sons hurried to him and, weeping together, kissed the hands, the feet, and the right side of their dear father who had left them. The wound in his side made them remember the One who poured out *blood and water* from His own side and *reconciled the world* to the Father.

Jn 19:34; 2 Cor 5:19

People considered it a great gift to be allowed to kiss or even to see the sacred *marks of Jesus* Christ which Saint Francis *bore in* his own *body.*

Gal 6:17

And seeing them,
who would not be moved to joy rather than tears?
And if moved to tears,
would that not be more
from gladness than sadness?
Whose heart would be so iron-hard
that it would not be moved to groan?
Whose *heart* would be so much *like stone*
that it would not break with sorrow,
that it would not burn with divine love
or would not be strengthened with good will?
Who would be so dull-witted and senseless
as not to realize the obvious truth?
He is a saint!
If he was so honored with a unique gift on earth,
he must *be exalted* with unspeakable glory *in heaven.*
[114]This is a unique gift,
a sign of special love:
to decorate the knight with the same arms of glory
that in their great dignity belong to the King alone![a]
This is a miracle worthy of *everlasting remembrance*
and a sacrament to be remembered
with unceasing and wondering reverence.
It presents to the eyes of faith
that mystery in which *the blood of the spotless lamb,*
flowing abundantly through the five wounds,
washed away the sins *of the world.*
O sublime splendor of the living cross,
giving life to the dead!
Its burden presses so lightly and hurts so sweetly
that through it dead flesh lives
and the weak spirit grows strong.

Ez 11:19

Is 33:5

1C 5

Ps 112:7

1 Pt 1:19

Rv 1:5

---

a. These "arms of glory," now identified with the stigmata, were foreseen in Francis's dream at the outset of his journey to Apulia.

You have made radiantly beautiful
Lk 7:47 this man who *loved* You *so much!*
Glory and blessing to God,
Rv 5:13; Rom 16:27 *who alone is wise,*
Sir 36:6 and *gives new signs and works new wonders*
to console the weak with revelations
and to raise their hearts to the love of things unseen
Ps 139:14 through *wonderful works* that are seen.[a]
O wonderful and loving plan of God!
To allay suspicion about the newness of this miracle,
Jn 3:13; 3:31 there first appeared mercifully in the One *from heaven*
what later appeared wondrously in the one who lived on earth.
2 Cor 1:3 The true *Father of mercies*
wanted to show how worthy of reward is the one
Mt 22:37 who strives *to love* Him *with his whole heart;*
worthy to be placed closer to Himself
in the highest order of supercelestial spirits.[b]

We too will certainly be able to reach these heights if, like the Ser-
Ez 1:22; 1:23 aphim, we *spread two wings over our heads:* that is, following blessed
Francis's example, in every good work we have a pure intention and
upright conduct, and, directing these to God, we strive untiringly to
please God alone in all things.[c] These two wings must be joined for us
Jas, 1:17 to cover our heads because *the Father of lights* will not accept our activity as upright without a pure intention nor vice versa, since He says:
If your eye is sound, your whole body will be full of light; but if your eye is evil,
Mt 6:22-23 *your whole body will be full of darkness.* That *eye* is *not sound* if it does not
see what should be seen, because it does not know the truth, or if it
looks at what should not be seen, because it does not have a pure in-

a. This echoes the Preface for Christmas: *Per hunc in invisibilium amorem rapiamur* [Through this we are lifted up into an invisible love].

b. The seraphim are found in the highest choir of angels, the choir closest to the divine majesty of God. Here Thomas places the life of Francis and especially the manifestation of the stigmata into the broader context of salvation history by showing how his life and its events participate in the mystery of divine love.

c. Thomas follows an allegorical and pedagogical explanation of the visions in Is. 6:1-13; Ez 1:5-14; 1:22-25; and Rv 4:6-9. Here at the end of Book Two, Thomas returns to comment on the significance of the seraph which, within the description of Francis's reception of the stigmata, he had introduced in n. 94 above. With the words, "We too will certainly be able to reach these heights . . ." Thomas proceeds to apply an allegorical interpretation of the seraph's six wings which invites the reader to follow Francis and to participate in the mystery of communion with Christ's passion and Cross. The allegorical interpretation of the seraph's wings originated with Pseudo-Dionysius, *Celestial Hierarchy* 7.1; 13.1; 15.2; in *Pseudo-Dionysius: The Complete Works*, translated by Colm Luibheid (New York: Paulist Press, 1987). It was continued in the West by Gregory the Great, *Homilia 34 in Evangelia, PL* 76:1246-49, 1252-53; Alan of Lille, *De Sex Alis Cherubim PL* 210:266-80, esp. 267-268; and Richard of Saint Victor, *The Mystical Ark* 1. 10, in *Richard of Saint Victor: The Twelve Patriarchs, The Mystical Ark, Book Three of the Trinity*, translated by Grover Zinn, (New York: Paulist Press, 1979).

tention. An open mind will judge neither as sound; the first is blind and the second evil. *The feathers* of *the wings* are the love of the saving and merciful Father and the *fear of the Lord*, the terrible judge. These lift the souls of the chosen above things of earth while restraining evil thoughts and ordering chaste affections.

Ez 1:23-24

Sir 1:11

The *other two wings* are for flying: showing a double charity to our neighbor, refreshing the soul with the *word of God* and nourishing the body with material aid. These *wings* are rarely *joined together,* since one person could hardly do both. The *feathers* of these wings are varied works of counsel and help offered to our neighbor.

Is 6:2

Lk 4:4

Ez 1:11

The last *two wings* are *to cover the body* that is bare of merits. This happens regularly as it is stripped naked whenever sin breaks in, but is then clothed again in innocence through contrition and confession. The feathers of these wings are the wide range of affections arising from hatred of sin and developing a longing for justice.

Ez 1:11

[115] Our blessed father Francis fulfilled all these things completely: he had both the image and the form of the Seraph and, remaining on the cross, he merited to fly away to the highest order of spirits. He was always upon his cross, never shirking labor or pain, fulfilling to the utmost the Lord's will in and about himself.

The brothers who lived with him know
that daily, constantly, talk of Jesus was always on his lips,
sweet and pleasant conversations about Him,
kind words full of love.
Out of the fullness of the heart his mouth spoke.
So the spring of radiant love
that filled his heart within
gushed forth.
He was always with Jesus:
Jesus in his heart,
Jesus in his mouth,
Jesus in his ears,
Jesus in his eyes,
Jesus in his hands,
he bore Jesus always in his whole body.
Often he sat down to dinner
but on hearing or saying or even thinking "Jesus"
he forgot bodily food,

Ez 33:32

Mt 12:34

as we read about another saint:
"Seeing, he did not see; hearing, he did not hear."[a]
Often as he walked along a road,
thinking and singing of Jesus,
he would forget his destination
and start inviting all the elements
to praise Jesus.
With amazing love he bore

Lk 2:19
1 Cor 2:2

in his heart and always held onto
Christ Jesus and Him crucified.
For this reason,
he, above others, was stamped with Christ's brilliant seal

2 Cor 5:13

as, in *rapture of spirit,*
he contemplated in unspeakable and incomprehensible glory
the One sitting "at the right hand of the Father,"

Lk 1:32

the Most High *Son of the Most High,*
Who, with the Father, "in the unity of the Holy Spirit,
lives and reigns," conquers and commands,
God eternally glorified *throughout all the ages.*

Dn 3:52; 3:90

Amen.

Chapter X

THE MOURNING OF THE LADIES AT SAN DAMIANO
AND HOW HE WAS BURIED WITH PRAISE AND GLORY

[116]His brothers and sons had assembled with *the whole multitude of*

Ez 27:33

people from the neighboring cities, rejoicing to take part in such solemn rites. They spent that entire night of the holy father's death in the praises of God. The sweet sound of jubilation and the brightness of the lights made it seem that angels were keeping vigil.

Jn 21:4; Acts 2:6

When day was breaking, the multitude of the city of Assisi *gathered* with all the clergy. They lifted his sacred body from the place where he had died and carried it with great honor to the city, singing hymns

Jos 6:20

and praises *with trumpets blaring. They all took branches* of olive and

Jn 12:13; Mt 21:8

other trees and solemnly followed the funeral procession, bringing even more candles as they sang songs of praise in loud voices.

---

a. Similar descriptions can be found describing Bernard of Clairvaux, cf. *Vita prima s. Bernardi* IV, *Vita secunda s. Bernardi* IV.

With the sons carrying their father and the flock following the shepherd who was hastening to *the Shepherd of them all,* he arrived at the place where he first planted the religion and the Order of the consecrated virgins and Poor Ladies. They laid him out in the church of San Damiano, home to those daughters he gained for the Lord. The small window was opened, the one used by these servants of Christ *at the appointed time* to receive the sacrament of the Lord's body. The coffin was also opened: in it lay hidden the treasure of supercelestial powers; in it he who had carried many was now carried by a few.

Ez 37:24

2 Sm 24:15

The Lady Clare!
Clearly a woman of true brilliance and holiness,
the first mother of all the others,
the first plant of that holy Order:
she comes with her daughters
to see the father
who would never again
speak to them or return to them,
as he was quickly going away.
[117]They looked upon him,
groaning and weeping with great *anguish of heart.*

Ps 38:9

"Father, O father, what shall we do?" they *began to cry out.* "Why are you abandoning us poor women? We are forsaken! To whom are you entrusting us?[a] Why didn't you send us ahead of you in joy to the place you are going, instead of leaving us behind in sorrow? What would you have us do, enclosed in this cell, without your usual visits? *All consolation* ebbs away along with you, just as no solace remains for us who are buried to the world! Who will comfort us in so great a poverty, poverty of merit as much as of goods?

Jos 3:3

2 Cor 1:5

"O father of the poor! O lover of poverty! Who will help us in temptation? You, who experienced so many temptations! You, who were such a careful judge of temptations! Who will comfort us in the midst of distress? *You, who were so often our help in times of distress!* What bitter separation, what painful absence!

Jb 29:16

Ps 46:2

"O death, dreadful death! You are killing thousands of his sons and daughters by taking away their father! *Our* poor *efforts* bore fruit through him, and you rush to tear him far from us, beyond recall!"

Jer 7:3,5

---

a. Cf. Sulpicius Severus, *Letter* III 10. "Before the death of Saint Martin, the monks cry out: 'Why are you abandoning us, father? To whom have you left your forsaken?' "

The virgins' modesty overcame their tears.

Zec 12:10

To grieve too much *over him* was unbecoming,
for at his passing
a host of angels rushed to greet him,
and *the citizens of heaven*

Eph 2:19

and members of God's household rejoiced.[a]
Thus,
torn between sorrow and joy,
they kissed his most splendid hands
that glittered with rare jewels and shining pearls.[b]
Once he was taken away,
the door
that never again will suffer such pain,

Mt 25:10

was closed on them.

O how great was the grief of all at the misery of these women!
How full was their mourning and the piety of their outcry!
Above all how great was the wailing of his grieving sons![c]
The sadness of each was shared by all,
since no one could keep from crying

Is 33:7

when even *the angels of peace wept bitterly.*

Bar 3:35; Ps 45:16

[118]Finally all reached the city
and *with* great *joy and gladness*

Mt 27:59

laid the most holy *body* in a sacred place
about to become even more sacred.[d]
In the past he had brightened that place wonderfully
with instruction by his holy preaching.

Jn 1:9

There he now *enlightens the world*
with a multitude of new miracles

Rv 16:14

glorifying the Most High *God Almighty.*
Thanks be to God.
Amen.

---

a. A phrase borrowed from the seventh responsory for Matins of the Feast of Saint Martin of Tours, November 11, "at whose passing the corps of saints sings, the choir of angels rejoices, the host of all the heavenly virtues and worshippers gather to meet him."

b. This is a passage taken from the second responsory and the second antiphon of the third nocturn for the feast of Saint Agnes, Virgin and Martyr: "rare jewels . . . glittering and shining, precious pearls."

c. Sulpicius Severus, *Letter* III 18: "How great was the grief of all, above all how great was the wailing of the grieving monks."

d. The holy place where he was buried was the church of Saint George.

Now look at what I have done, most holy and blessed father,
I have seen you through to the end with fitting and worthy
praises,
inadequate though they be,
and I have written down your deeds
telling the story as well as I could.
Please allow me,
pitiful as I am,
to follow you worthily in the present,
that I may mercifully merit joining you in the future.

O loving one,
bear in mind your poor sons
for whom, without you,
their one and only consolation,
there is little comfort.
Even though you,
their primary and prized portion,
have joined the choirs of angels,
and are seated with the apostles on a *throne of glory,*   Dn 3:53,54
they still lie *in a muddy swamp,*   Ps 40:3
enclosed in a dark cell,
tearfully crying out to you:
"O father,
place before Jesus Christ, son of the Most High Father,
His sacred stigmata;
and show Him the signs of the cross on your hands, feet, and side,
that He may mercifully bare His own wounds to the Father,
and because of this
the Father *will ever show us* in our anguish
His tenderness.   Jb 33:26
Amen.
So be it, so be it."[a]   Ps 72:19

Here Ends the Second Book.

---

a. Except for the last words—"the Father will ever show us in our anguish His tenderness," which replaces "He will give us one who is able to take the place of such a father," this prayer of Francis's orphaned followers is copied from an antiphon, *Plange turba paupercula,* composed by Gregory IX immediately after the saint's death. Luke Wadding, following Salimbene, thought the antiphon was written in 1239 for the chapter that was convened to choose a successor to Brother Elias. It dates from 1227 and preceded the election of John Parenti, the first successor of Francis.

The Third Book

[119]Francis, the most glorious father,
in the twentieth year of his conversion,

Lk 23:45

as he most blessedly *commended his spirit* to heaven,
brought a blessed beginning to an even more blessed end.

Ps 8:6

There, *crowned with honor and glory*

Ez 28:14

and granted a place *among the stones of fire,*
he stands by the throne of God,
devoted to dealing effectively with the concerns
of those he left on earth.
What could be denied him?
Stamped with the holy stigmata,
he reflects the image of the One,
co-equal with the Father,
Who *is seated at the right hand of the majesty on high,*
the brightness of his glory and the image of the divine *substance,*

Heb 1:3

Who *cleanses us from all sin.*
Why would he not be heard?
Conformed to the death of Christ Jesus

Phil 3:10

by sharing in His sufferings,
he displays His sacred wounds in his hands, feet, and side.
He gladdens the whole world
with the gift of new joy,
and offers to all the benefits of true salvation.
He floods the world with the brilliant light of miracles,
a true star glowing brightly over the whole earth.
The world once mourned when robbed of his presence

Ps 50:1

and saw itself overwhelmed by the dark abyss *at his setting,*

Is 16:3

but now it seems like the *light of midday.*

With new light rising,
the world is growing bright in these shining rays[a]
and feels all the darkness leave.
Now, all its complaints have stopped;
Blessed be God!   Ps 66:20

Every day, everywhere people rejoice anew
as the world is filled to overflowing with holy gifts from him.
From East and West they come,   Mt 8:11
from North and South: Gn 13:3; Ez 48:31
those helped by his patronage come
to attest to these things in *witness to the truth.*   Jn 5:33
While he *lived in the flesh,*   Phil 1:22; 1 Pt 4:2
this great lover of the things of heaven
held nothing of the world as his own,
so that he could possess the greatest good of all
more fully and more joyfully.
For this reason he has become in all things
what he did not want to be in few things,
and has exchanged time for eternity.
He helps everyone, everywhere.
He is near to everyone, everywhere.
Yet this lover of true unity
is not divided by being shared.[b]
[120]*While he still lived among sinners,*   Wis 4:10
he traveled the whole world preaching;
but now reigning with the angels on high,   Ps 149:1
he flies quicker than a thought as the herald of the Great King,
bringing wonderful gifts to all peoples.
For this reason,
all peoples honor, venerate, glorify and praise him.
They all share now a common good.
Who can estimate the quantity

---

a. This is a clear reference to the hymn of praise of the Easter Mystery at the paschal candle, the *Exultet.*

b. This is reference to the medieval liturgy of Holy Saturday in which a rod with three tapers was carried in procession into the church. During the procession, the Deacon would chant *Lumen Christi* three times and each time would light one of the tapers. At a certain point in chanting the *Exsultet,* the Deacon lit the paschal candle with one of these candles and chanted: "*Qui licet sit divisus in partes, mutuati tamen luminis detrimenta non novit* [This (triple candle) although it might be divided in parts, does not suffer loss through sharing its light].

or tell the quality of the miracles
the Lord has chosen to work everywhere through him?

Just in France, Francis has worked so many miracles that the
Frankish king and queen and all the nobility hasten to kiss and venerate the pillow that Saint Francis used during his illness.[a] There also
the world's wise and literate, whom Paris usually produces more
abundantly than the whole world, humbly and devotedly venerate,
admire, and revere Francis, an uneducated man, a friend of true simplicity and whole-hearted sincerity.

He is truly "France-ish" whose heart was so frank and free.[b]
Those who experienced the greatness of his soul know well how free
and freeing he was in everything, how intrepid and fearless in all
circumstances.[c] With great strength and bravery he trampled upon
every worldly thing.

And what can I say of other parts of the world? Disease disappears
and illness flees simply by means of his cord, and both men and
women are freed from distress merely by invoking his name.

¹²¹ At his tomb new miracles occur constantly
and, as the prayers increase,
remarkable aid is given to body and soul.
The blind recover sight,
the deaf regain hearing,
the lame walk again,
the mute speak,
those with gout jump,
lepers are cleansed,
those with swelling see it reduced,
and those suffering the burden of many different diseases

(Jer 1:18) (Mt 11:5)

a. The king of France here is probably Saint Louis IX (+1270) and the "queen" Blanche of Castille, his mother (+1252). At the time Thomas was writing in 1228, the king was no more than fourteen years old. The text seems to say that the relic was kept in France and exposed for the veneration of the faithful. According to 3C 37-39, Lady (Brother) Jacopa dei Settesoli came to see Francis as he lay dying. Among the things she brought him was a pillow for his head.
b. Thomas engages in a wordplay here that is nearly impossible to translate. The word for Francis in Latin, *Franciscus,* is closely related to the word for a Frenchman in medieval Latin, *Francus,* as in the phrase *rex Francorum,* and literally translates as the diminutive "little Frenchman." But the adjectival form *francus* means "noble" and "free." Hence there are four meanings being put into play here: French, noble, free, and Francis. One could translate this opening line as "Truly was he French," "Truly was he free," and "Truly was he noble." The meaning of a name was extremely important in the Middle Ages. Here, as earlier in the case of Clare, Thomas surely sees more than a fanciful etymology.
c. In Francis's name, Thomas sees two qualities, namely independence with regard to himself and discernment with regard to the initiatives of his neighbor. In the Latin text these two qualities are *liber* [free] and *liberalis* [freeing].

obtain the relief for which they have longed.
His dead body heals living bodies,
just as when living it raised dead souls.

The Roman Pontiff heard of these things and understood:
he, chief pontiff of all,
leader of Christians,
lord of the world,
shepherd of the Church,
the anointed of the Lord,   1 Sm 24:11
and the Vicar of Christ.
He rejoiced and exulted, dancing with joy,
for in his own day he was seeing
1C 18   the Church of God being renewed
with new mysteries that were ancient wonders.
This was happening because of his own son,
the one he had
carried in his sacred womb,
held in his lap,
nursed with the word,
nurtured on the food of salvation.
The other keepers of the Church also heard this,
those who are
the shepherds of the flock,
defenders of the faith,
friends of the bridegroom,   Jn 3:29
his supporters,
the poles of the earth,
the venerable Cardinals.
They rejoiced with the Church and shared the Pope's delight,
giving glory to the Savior who chose
with supreme, unfathomable wisdom,
supreme, incomprehensible grace,
and supreme, boundless goodness,
the foolish and lowly of the world   1 Cor 1:27; 1:28
in order *to draw* the strong *to Himself.*   Jn 12:32
The entire world heard of this and applauded,
and every realm subject to the Catholic faith,
overflowed *with joy,*
flooded with holy *comfort.*   2 Cor 7:4

[122]But then there came a rapid change in events, as a new problem rose up in the world.[a] The joyful peace was quickly shaken as the
torch of envy was lit and the Church was torn apart by internal warfare among its members. The Romans, that fierce and rebellious people, struck with their usual savagery against their neighbors and

1 Mc 14:31

boldly *stretched forth their hands against the holy places.*[b] The great Pope
Gregory tried to restrain this rising evil, to control the savagery, and
to stop the attacks, to safeguard the Church of Christ like a fortified
tower. Danger multiplied, destruction increased, and in the rest of

Ps 129:4

the world sinners *lifted up their necks* in rebellion against God. What
could he do? With great experience, he gauged the future and as-
sessed the present, deciding to abandon the City to the rebels so as to
free the world and defend it from more rebellion. He went to the city
of Rieti, where he was received with fitting honor. From there he
continued on to Spoleto, where everyone honored him with great
reverence. He stayed there for several days to organize the Church's
cause. Then, accompanied by the venerable cardinals, he kindly paid
a visit to the handmaids of Christ, dead and buried to the world.[c]

2 Cor 8:2

Their holy way of life, their *highest poverty,* and their renowned way of
living moved him to tears along with his companions, encouraging
them to despise worldly things and enkindling in them love for the
life of chastity.

O lovable humility, nurse of all graces!
The prince of the whole world,
successor of the prince of the Apostles,
visits the poor women,
going to the lowly, humble and enclosed!

---

a. The German emperor Frederick II controlled northern Italy and, through his mother, the Kingdom of the
Two Sicilies; he exercised a vise-like grip on the Papal States. He invaded the Papal States and from a
distance exercised his influence on the people of Rome, who revolted on Easter Monday 1228 during the
papal Mass in Saint Peter's Basilica. Gregory IX did not return to Rome until 1230. Thus, Thomas refers to
the people stretching "forth their hands against the holy places."

b. This passage is reminiscent of Bernard of Clairvaux's comments to Pope Eugene III about the Romans in
his work *De consideratione ad Eugenium III,* IV c. 2, n.2. "What shall I say of the people? They are Romans.
I could say nothing more concise or express anything more openly than what I feel about your parishioners.
What is better known to the world than the impudence and arrogance of the Romans! They are a nation
hostile to peace, one that is merciless and unmanageable, completely ignorant of what it means to be
subject unless they are incapable of resisting." Elsewhere he writes: "These people are hateful of heaven
and earth, for they raise their hands against both: disrespectful toward God, irreverent toward the sacred,
rebellious toward one another, envious toward their neighbors, inhumane toward foreigners."

c. A reference to the Poor Ladies of the monastery of Saint Paul, near Spoleto.

Worthy of *a good judgment,*   Dt 16:18

an example of this humility is rare,

not seen for many ages.

[123] After that he hurried on, he hurried to Assisi, where a glorious treasure was being kept for him, to make all his suffering and pressing trials disappear. On his arrival, the whole region rejoiced, the city *was*   Ps 126:2
filled with gladness, a great crowd of people joined the joyful celebration, and the bright day grew brighter with new lights. Everyone went forth *to meet him* and joined in solemn vigil. The devoted group of poor   2 Kgs 4:26
brothers went out to meet him, each one singing sweet songs to *the Lord's anointed.* The Vicar of Christ reached the place and first going   1 Sm 24:11
down to the tomb of Saint Francis, he eagerly paid his respects with great reverence. Groaning deeply, he struck his breast, and breaking into tears, he bowed his venerable head in an outpouring of devotion.

Meanwhile, a solemn assembly was called for the canonization of the saint and the eminent body of cardinals met frequently to consider the matter.[a] Many who had been freed from their illnesses through the holy man of God came from far and wide, and from here and there countless miracles gleamed: these miracles were heard, verified, accepted, and approved.

But then a new problem arose and, obliged by the duties of office, the blessed Pope had to go to Perugia, only in order to be able to return once again to Assisi with *more abundant* and special *grace* for the   Rom 5:20
most important task.[b] Another meeting was called in Perugia. The sacred consistory of cardinals met in the chambers of the Lord Pope to consider the cause. All were in agreement. They read the miracles with great reverence; they extolled the life and conduct of the holy man with the highest praise.

[124] "The holy life of this holy man," they said, "does not require the evidence of miracles *for we have seen it with our eyes and touched it with our hands* and tested it with truth as our guide." They all leapt to   1 Jn 1:1
their feet with tears of joy; and in their *tears* there was a great *blessing.*   Heb 12:17
They immediately fixed the blessed date when they would fill the whole world with blessed joy.[c]

---

a. Gregory continued the work of his predecessors, Innocent III and Honorius III by further revising the canonization process. All three insisted on two things: virtue of behavior and the virtue of signs, that is, works of mercy during life and miraculous signs after death. Undoubtedly Gregory gathered the cardinals to consider these two requirements.

b. From June 13 to July 13, 1228, Gregory continued to be involved in matters of state.

c. The day of the canonization was set for July 16, 1228.

The solemn day arrives, "A day held in reverence by every age,"[a] showering the earth and even the heavenly mansions with ecstatic rejoicing. Bishops gather, abbots arrive, prelates from the most remote areas appear; a king's presence is noticed, with a noble crowd of counts and dukes.[b] All accompany the lord of the whole earth, and with him enter the city of Assisi in a happy procession. They come to the place prepared for this solemn meeting and the glorious crowd of cardinals, bishops, and abbots gathers around the blessed pope.[c] A distinguished assembly of priests and clerics is there, a happy and sacred gathering of religious men, and the modest presence of veiled consecrated women, a great crowd from every people:

2 Chr 4:18   an almost *numberless multitude of both sexes.* They are running from all
Jgs 16:27   over, and in this crowd every age is represented enthusiastically. *The*
Jb 3:19   *small and the great are there; the servants and those freed from their masters.*

[125]The supreme pontiff,
bridegroom of the Church of Christ *is standing,*
Ps 45:10   surrounded *with* such *variety* of children,
Is 62:3; Rv 14:14   *a crown of glory* on his head
Sir 45:14   *marked with the sign of holiness.*
He stands adorned with the pontifical regalia
Ex 40:13   and clothed in *holy vestments*
Sir 45:13   with *settings of gold, the work of a jeweler.*
1 Sm 24:11   He stands there, *the Lord's anointed,*
Ps 45:10; Is 4:2   *gilded in magnificence and glory*
Sir 45:13   and covered *with precious stones* cut and sparkling,
catching the eyes of all.
Cardinals and bishops surround him,
Is 61:10   *clothed* with *jewels* glittering
on garments gleaming white as snow,
offering an image of the beauty of heaven,
displaying the joy of the glorified.
1 Sm 12:19   *All the people* are waiting for *the cry of joy,*
Jer 25:10   *the song of gladness,*

---

a. This phrase, *Toto venerabilis aevo,* is another echo of the Easter liturgy, which is taken from the hymn *Salve festa dies* by Venantius Fortunatus, bishop of Poitiers in 599. In this passage Thomas shifts again to the present tense for dramatic narrative.

b. John of Brienne was crowned king of Jerusalem on October 3, 1210. Toward the end of his life, he became a disciple of Francis and was buried in the basilica dedicated to the saint.

c. The canonization took place near the church of Saint George.

a new song,
a song full of sweetness,
a song of praise,   Ps 26:7
a song of everlasting blessing.

Pope Gregory first preaches *to all the people* with deeply felt words   Heb 9:19
sweeter than honey, proclaiming the praises of God in a resonant
voice. He praises the holy father Francis in noble words. Recalling his
way of life and speaking of his purity, he is drenched in tears. His sermon begins with the text: *"Like the morning star in the midst of clouds,*
like the full moon, like the shining sun, so in his days did he shine in the tem-
ple of God."[a]   Sir 50:6-7

At the end of this *speech, so true and worthy of complete acceptance,* one
of the subdeacons of the lord Pope, Ottaviano by name, reads in a   1 Tm 1:15
loud voice the miracles of the Saint to the whole assembly.[b] Lord
Ranieri, a Cardinal-deacon, a man of keen intelligence, of outstanding piety and conduct, speaks about them with sacred eloquence, his
eyes welling with tears.[c] The shepherd of the Church is overcome
with joy, with deep sighs rising from the bottom of his heart and, often sobbing, breaks out in tears. The other prelates of the Church
were also pouring out a flood of tears that dripped onto their sacred
vestments. Then all *the people are weeping,* tired out with eager expec-   1 Sm 11:5
tation.

[126]At that moment the blessed Pope cries out in a ringing voice,
and *raising* his hands *to heaven* proclaims: "To the praise and glory of   2 Mc 3:20
God almighty, Father, Son, and Holy Spirit, the glorious Virgin
Mary, the blessed Apostles Peter and Paul, to the honor of the glorious Roman Church! On the advice of our brothers and other prelates,
we decree that the most blessed father Francis, whom the Lord has
glorified in heaven and we venerate on earth, shall be enrolled in the
catalogue of saints, and his feast is to be celebrated on the day of his

---

a. Anonymous, *The Life of Gregory IX* which provides a further description of the pope's role in the
   canonization of Francis, cf. Infra, pp. 603-604. The biblical reference is to Simon the High Priest in whose
   days the temple was renewed, cf. Sir 50:1-23. It is used in the papal declaration of Francis's canonization,
   Mira circa nos, cf.
b. Ottaviano degli Ubaldini di Mugello was a cousin of Innocent III, and was later made cardinal by Innocent
   IV. Salimbene writes that Gregory IX held him in high regard. Cf. *Chronicle of Salimbene of Adam*
   translated by Joseph L. Baird, Giuseppe Baglivi, and John Robert Kane (Binghamton, NY: Center for
   Medieval and Renaissance Studies, 1986), 386.
c. The Cistercian Ranieri Capocci of Viterbo, made cardinal in 1216, was a good friend of the Order. He is the
   author of the hymn *Plaude turba paupercula* and the antiphon *Caelorum candor splenduit* in honor of
   Francis.

death." At this announcement, the reverend cardinals join the pope in singing the *Te Deum laudamus* in a loud voice.

Is 17:12; Lk 2:13

And there rises the cry of *many peoples* praising God;
the earth echoes the booming sound,
the air is filled with jubilation,
and the ground is soaked with tears.

Ps 33:3

Jb 38:7

They sing new songs
and the servants *of God rejoice*
in the melody of the Spirit.[a]
Sweet sounding instruments are playing
as hymns are sung with musical voices.

Ex 29:18

A *very sweet fragrance is flowing there*
and an even more pleasant melody is echoing there,
moving everyone deeply.
The day is breaking, colored with radiant sunbeams.
There are green *branches* of olive

Mt 21:8

and fresh boughs *of other trees.*
There all are dressed in festive clothing, shining brightly,
while the blessing of peace gladdens the spirits of all.

Is 6:1

Ps 73:17

Nm 29:39

Jb 40:22; Is 1:15

Sir 50:13

Lk 24:52,53; 2 Mc 3:22

Sir 50:22

The blessed Pope Gregory then comes down from the *high throne,* and by the lower steps *enters the sanctuary to offer prayers and sacrifices,* and with his blessed lips kisses the tomb holding the sacred body dedicated to God.[b] *He offers many prayers* and celebrates the sacred mysteries. Around him stands *a ring of brothers, praising, adoring and blessing almighty God, who has done wondrous things through all the earth.*

Mt 27:25; Lk 18:43

*All the people
echoed the praise of God,*
offering gifts of thanks to Francis
in honor of the Most High Trinity.
Amen.

---

a. The use of a biblical expression (Ps 33:3; 96:1; 98:1) may be no more than a rhetorical device here. This does not necessarily exclude the hypothesis that we have an allusion to the pieces composed by Gregory IX himself for the canonization. These were later incorporated into the Office for the Feast of Saint Francis: the hymn *Proles de caelo*, the responsory *De paupertatis horreo*, and the prose composition *Caput draconis*.

b. This sanctuary is the church of Saint George. Thomas states that the pope entered *per inferiores gradus* (by the lower steps). The author's care for detail and his keen interest in each scrap of information suggest his presence at the ceremonies he describes.

These things happened in the city of Assisi, in the second year of the pontificate of the Lord Pope Gregory the Ninth, on the seventeenth day of the calends of the month of August.[a]

---

a. That is, July 16, 1228.

The Miracles of Saint Francis

2 Cor 8:9; 13:13

Dn 9:25

[127]Humbly calling upon *the grace of Jesus Christ our Lord,* we shall briefly but accurately describe the miracles that were read in the presence of the Lord Pope and announced to the people, both in order to arouse *fitting devotion* among those living and to strengthen the faith of those to come.

Chapter I
THE CRIPPLED WHO WERE HEALED

The very same day on which the sacred and holy body of the blessed father was laid away as a most precious treasure, anointed with heavenly ointments rather than with those found on earth, a young girl was brought there who, for over a year, had suffered a deformity in her neck so hideous that her head rested on her shoulder and she could only look up sideways. She put her head for a little while beneath the coffin in which the precious body of the saint rested, and through the merits of that most holy man she was immediately able to straighten her neck, and her head was restored to its proper position. At this the girl was so overwhelmed at the sudden change in herself that she started to run away and to cry. There was a depression in her shoulder where her head had been when it was twisted out of position by her prolonged affliction.

[128]In the district of Narni there was a boy whose leg was bent back so severely that he could not walk at all without the aid of two canes. He made his living by begging; he had been burdened with that affliction for many years, and he had no idea who his father and mother were. This boy was completely freed from his affliction by the merits of our blessed father Francis so that he could walk about freely without any support from the canes and did so praising and blessing God and His saint.

[129] A certain Nicolò, a citizen of Foligno, was so crippled in his left leg that it caused him extreme pain; as a result he spent so much on doctors in his endeavor to restore his health that he went more deeply into debt than he could ever hope to pay. Finally, when the help of physicians had proven worthless, he was suffering such extreme pain that his neighbors could not sleep at night because of his moaning cries. Then dedicating himself to God and to Saint Francis, he had himself carried to the tomb of the saint. After spending a night in prayer at the saint's tomb, his crippled leg was cured and, overflowing with joy, he returned home without a cane.

[130] A boy had one leg so deformed that his knee was pressed against his chest and his heel against his buttocks. He came to the tomb of the blessed Francis, while his father was mortifying his own flesh with a hair shirt and his mother was performing severe penance for him. Suddenly the boy had his health so fully restored that he could run through the streets, healthy and happy, *giving thanks to* God and Saint Francis.

Acts 28:15

[131] In the city of Fano there was a man who was crippled with his legs doubled-up under him. They were covered with sores that gave off such a foul odor that the hospice staff refused to take him in or keep him. But then he asked the blessed father Francis for mercy and, through his merits, in a short time he rejoiced in being cured.

[132] There was also a little girl in Gubbio; her hands and all her limbs were so crippled that for over a year she was totally unable to use them. Carrying a wax image, her nurse brought her to the tomb of the blessed father Francis to seek the favor of a cure.[a] After she had been there for eight days, on the last day all her limbs were restored to their proper functions so that she was considered well enough to return to her activities.

[133] There was a boy from Montenero lying for several days in front of the doors of the church where the body of Saint Francis rested. He could not walk or sit up, since he was completely paralyzed from the waist down. One day he got into the church and touched the tomb of the blessed father Francis. When he came back outside, he was completely cured. Moreover, the young boy himself reported that while he was lying in front of the tomb of the glorious Saint, a young man was there with him clothed in the habit of the friars, on top of the tomb. The young man was carrying some pears in his hands, and he

---

a. In the Middle Ages there was a widespread custom that people who visited a shrine would offer an amount of wax, metal, bread or oil equal to the weight of the sick person for whom they were praying. The weighing was even accompanied by a special ritual. The same custom is mentioned in 1C 140, 146, 149.

called the boy. Offering him a pear, he encouraged him to get up. The boy took the pear from the young man's hand, and answered: "See, I am crippled and cannot get up at all!" He ate the pear given to him, and then started to put out his hand for another pear that the young man offered him. The young man again encouraged him to stand up, but the boy, feeling weighed down with his illness, did not get up. But while the boy reached out his hand, the young man holding out the pear took hold of his hand and led him outside. Then he vanished from sight. When the boy saw that he was cured, he began to cry out at the top of his voice, telling everyone what had happened to him.

[134]There was a woman from the village of Coccorano who was brought to the tomb of the glorious father on a stretcher; for, except for her tongue, all her limbs were totally paralyzed. After *she stayed a while* before the tomb of the most holy man, she stood up, entirely cured.

Mt 25:5

After another citizen from Gubbio brought his crippled son on a stretcher to the tomb of the holy father; he received him back whole and sound, though before he had been so crippled and deformed that his legs were completely withered and drawn up under him.

[135]Bartolomeo from the city of Narni was poverty-stricken and indigent. One day after he had been sleeping in the shade of a nut-tree he awoke to find himself so crippled he could not walk at all. As the disease spread, his leg and foot wasted away; they grew crooked and withered and he could not feel the cutting of a knife, nor was he afraid of burns from a fire. One night the saintly Francis, the true lover of the poor and the father of all the needy, appeared to him *in a dream.* He ordered him to go to a certain bathing pool, because, moved by piety at the man's misery, he wanted to free him there from his illness. When he awoke, *he did not know what to do,* so he told the whole story of the vision to the bishop of the city. The bishop urged him to hurry to the pool as he was ordered and, making the sign of the cross, blessed him. Leaning on a stick, he set out to drag himself to the place as best he could. As he moved along sadly, worn out by great effort, *he heard a voice saying to him:* "Go on in the peace of the Lord. I am the one to whom you vowed yourself." When the man drew near to the pool, it was night and he took the wrong road. *He heard a voice again telling him* that he was not on the right road, and it directed him to the pool. When he reached the place and entered the pool, he felt a hand placed upon his foot and another that gently pulled his leg. He was immediately freed, and he jumped out of the pool, praising and blessing the all-powerful Creator and His servant,

Dn 2:19

Lk 9:33; Acts 5:7

Acts 9:4

Acts 9:4

blessed Francis, who had received such grace and power from Him. That man, who was already mature, had been crippled and begging for six years.

Chapter II
THE BLIND WHO RECEIVED THEIR SIGHT

[136] A woman named Sibilla suffered from blindness in her eyes for many years. She was led to the tomb of the man of God, blind and dejected. She recovered her sight and, rejoicing and exulting, returned home.

At the tomb of the holy body, a blind man from Spello recovered his sight, which he had lost long before.

Another woman, from Camerino, was totally blind in her right eye. Her parents covered the damaged eye with a cloth that the blessed Francis had touched. After making a vow, they gave thanks to the Lord God and Saint Francis for restoring her sight.

A similar thing happened to a woman from Gubbio who, after making a vow, rejoiced on recovering her vision.

A citizen of Assisi was blind for five years. While the blessed Francis was still living, he was friendly to him, so whenever he prayed to the blessed man, he would recall their former friendship. He was cured as soon as he touched his tomb.

Albertino from Narni was totally blind for about a year, for his eyelids hung down over his eyes. Vowing himself to the blessed Francis, his sight was immediately restored; then he prepared himself and went to his glorious tomb.

Chapter III
THOSE POSSESSED BY DEMONS

[137] *There was a man* in the city of Foligno named Pietro, who, either to fulfill a vow or as a penance imposed on him for his sins, went one time on a pilgrimage to the shrine of Blessed Michael the Archangel.[a] He stopped at a fountain, and since he was thirsty and weary from his journey, he had started to drink the water of that fountain when he saw himself drinking up demons. He was possessed by them for three years, and he used to do things dreadful to see and worse to

Jb 1:1

---

a. At Monte Gargano in the province of Foggia, Apulia.

tell. When he came to the sepulcher of the most holy Father, the demons were furious and mauled him savagely. By an outstanding
miracle, he was marvelously delivered from them when he touched
the tomb.

[138]A woman in the city of Narni was driven by a most violent
madness, and since she was out of her mind, would do dreadful
things and say very inappropriate things. Blessed Francis appeared
to her in a vision and said: "Make the sign of the cross!" "I can't," she
replied. The Saint himself made the sign of the cross on her and
drove out all trace of her insanity and the phantoms of the demons.

Many other men and women who were harassed by torments of
evil spirits and led astray by their tricks were rescued from their
power through the outstanding merits of the holy and glorious father.

However, since deception frequently comes into question with
people of this kind, we shall pass them by with this brief account,
and go on to the most impressive cases.

Chapter IV
THOSE SICK UNTO DEATH WHO RECOVERED,
A MAN WITH SWELLING,
ONE MAN WITH DROPSY, AN ARTHRITIC, THE PARALYZED,
AND THOSE AFFLICTED WITH VARIOUS OTHER ILLNESSES

[139]A little boy named Matteo, from the city of Todi, *lay on his bed*
for eight days as if dead. His mouth was tightly closed; he could see
nothing, the skin on his face and hands and feet became as black as a
kettle, and everyone despaired of his life. But when his mother made
a vow, he recovered with amazing speed. He had been throwing up
putrid blood from his mouth so that it seemed as if he were losing his
intestines. His mother immediately knelt down and humbly called
on Saint Francis. As soon as she arose from prayer, the little boy
opened his eyes, looked around, and took his mother's breast. In a
little while the black skin peeled off, his flesh returned to the way it
was, and he was once again strong and healthy. As soon as he started
to improve, his mother asked him: "Who cured you, my son?" In answer he lisped: "Cecco, Cecco." Again she asked him: "Whose servant are you?" Again he answered: "Cecco, Cecco." Since he was just
a baby, he could not speak distinctly, and so in trying to pronounce
the name of "Francesco," he left out half of it.

Nm 12:6

Mt 9:2

[140]There was a young man who had been up on a very high place and fell from there and lost the use of all his limbs as well as his ability to speak. For *three days he neither ate nor drank* nor felt anything, so that they thought he was dead. His mother, without even seeking the aid of a doctor, asked blessed Francis to cure him. After she had made a vow the young man was restored to her, alive and sound, and she began to praise the all-powerful Savior.

Acts 9:9; Mt 11:18

Another man by the name of Mancino was so sick and so near death that everyone gave up all hope for him. But he invoked as well as he could the name of the blessed Francis and he was immediately restored to health.

A boy from Arezzo by the name of Gualtiero was suffering from prolonged fever and so tormented by a multiple abscess that all the doctors gave up hope for him. But his parents made a vow to blessed Francis, and he recovered the health they so longed for.

Another man, who was near death, made a wax image, and before it was even finished, he was entirely relieved of his unbearable pain.[a]

[141]A woman was confined to bed for many years by illness, unable to turn or move at all. She vowed herself to God and the blessed Francis. She was freed from her illness and resumed her usual activities. In the city of Narni, there was a woman who for eight years had a hand so withered that she could not use it at all. The blessed Francis appeared to her *in a vision,* stretching out his hand to her, and thereby made her withered hand able to work as well as her other one.

Acts 18:9

A young man in the same city was in the grip of a very serious illness for ten years; his whole body was so swollen that no medicine brought him any relief. After his mother made a vow, he received the relief of health through the merits of blessed Francis.

There was a man in the city of Fano suffering from dropsy, whose limbs were horribly swollen. Through blessed Francis he obtained a complete cure of his illness.

A citizen of Todi suffered from such an acute arthritic condition that he could neither sit nor lie down at all. The severity of the affliction grew so serious as to cause ever-increasing stiffness and it seemed he would become entirely helpless. He called doctors and took baths. He tried all kinds of medicines, but none of these brought

---

a. A person unable to visit a shrine would have a wax image made as a substitute to stand near the saint's tomb, a practice reflected in the "vigil light" candles in churches.

him any relief. One day while the priest was visiting, he made a vow to Saint Francis, asking to be restored to health. Soon after finishing his prayers to the Saint, he realized that he had been restored to health.

[142]There was a woman in the city of Gubbio who lay paralyzed. After she invoked the name of blessed Francis three times, she was freed from her infirmity and cured.

A man by the name of Bontadoso suffered such agonizing pains in his feet and toes that he could not walk or bend over and could neither eat nor sleep. A woman visited him one day and suggested that he vow himself to the blessed Francis with all his heart, if he wished to find quick relief from his sufferings. But that man, beside himself with pain, cried: "I do not believe that he is a saint!" But the woman stubbornly insisted that he make the vow. He finally vowed himself in this way: "I vow myself to Saint Francis and I believe he is a saint, if he frees me from this illness in three days." Through the merits of the Saint of God, he was soon cured, and was able to eat and sleep, *giving glory to almighty God.*

Jn 9:24; Rom 4:20

[143]A man was seriously wounded in the head by a metal arrow that had gone through his eye socket and lodged in his head. He could get no relief from the doctors. So with humble devotion he vowed himself to the Saint of God, Francis, hoping to be helped by the Saint's intercession. He then lay down to rest a little, and *while he was sleeping,* he *was told* by Saint Francis to have the arrow pulled out through the back of his head. The next day he did *as he was told in the dream,* and without great difficulty he obtained relief.

Gn 31:24

Gn 31:10

[144]A man from the village of Spello, named Imperatore, suffered for two years with such a severe rupture that all his intestines protruded through the side of his body. He could not keep them in place for any length of time so he had to wear a truss to hold them in. He went to doctors to seek relief, but they kept asking for more than he could afford to pay; in fact, he did not have enough left to live on or to eat for more than a day, so he gave up all hope of getting any help from them. Then he turned to seek divine help, and while on the road or at home or wherever he was, he humbly called upon blessed Francis. After a short time, it turned out that through the grace of God and the merits of blessed Francis he was restored to full health.

[145]A brother in the March of Ancona, who had vowed obedience in the ranks of our Order, suffered so greatly from a painful ulcer in his side that all hope of a cure had been given up by his physicians

because the infection had spread so far.[a] So he asked his minister, under whose obedience he lived, for permission to visit the place where the body of the most blessed Father rested, for he was confident that he would obtain the favor of a cure through the merits of the Saint. But his minister forbade him to go for fear his condition would grow worse from the hardships of the journey, for it was the season of rain and snow. Since the brother felt badly about not receiving permission to go, the holy Father Francis one night stood by him. "My son," he said, "do not worry about such things any more. Take off that fur you are wearing, remove that dressing and the bandages holding it, and keep your Rule; then you will be cured."[b] When he arose in the morning he did just as he was told, and *gave thanks to God* for his immediate cure.

Acts 27:35

Chapter V
THE LEPERS WHO WERE CLEANSED

[146] At San Severino in the March of Ancona there was a young man named Atto who was covered with leprosy; everyone was convinced he was a leper, for such was the opinion of the doctors. All his limbs were swollen and distended, and, since his blood vessels were protruding, he looked at everything with an unpleasant expression. He could not walk, but spent all his time in misery upon his sickbed, a cause of great sorrow and pain to his parents. His father, torn with unremitting grief, did not know what to do for him. Finally he felt in his heart that he should dedicate him completely to the blessed Francis. So he said to his son: "My son, do you want to vow yourself to Saint Francis, who is famous everywhere for his many miracles, that he may be pleased to deliver you from this suffering?" He answered: "Yes, I want to, father." Immediately the father had them fetch a piece of paper and he took measurements of his son's height and width. He then said: "Sit up, my son, and vow yourself to blessed Francis. When you are cured, you will take him a candle as large as you are every year as long as you live." At his father's bidding he sat up as best he could and, folding his hands, he humbly begged blessed Francis for mercy. After the measurements had been taken

---

a. He is the only brother who appears in this series of miracles. Another was the object of a miracle in those occurring during Francis's life, cf. 1C 68.

b. This admonition to keep the Rule is probably based on the fact that the brother was wearing a fur which would be considered a *vestis mollis* [soft garment] rather than a *vestis vilis* [coarse garment] contrary to LR II 13-15.

and he had finished his prayers, he was cured of his leprosy on the spot. He got up, *giving glory to God* and to blessed Francis, and *joyfully* started *to walk about.*

In the city of Fano there was a young man named Buonuomo whom all the doctors claimed was a paralytic and a leper. He was devoutly offered to blessed Francis by his parents, and he was cured of his leprosy and the paralysis vanished; he recovered his health completely.

Chapter VI
THE MUTE WHO BEGAN TO SPEAK
AND THE DEAF WHO BEGAN TO HEAR

Jn 9:1

[147]At Città della Pieve there was a boy who was very poor and a beggar. *From birth* he had been completely mute and deaf. His tongue was so short and stubby that, to those who many times examined it, the tongue seemed to be completely cut out. Late one evening the boy went to the house of a man named Marco, who lived in the same village. Using the signs the mute ordinarily use, the boy begged Marco to take him in; he inclined his head to one side, and put his hands under his cheek to indicate that he wanted to sleep there that night. That man gladly *received him into his house,* and was happy to keep him, for he found the young man to be a great help around the house. The boy had a *good disposition,* and although he was deaf and mute from infancy, he understood orders by means of signs. One evening that man was dining with his wife, while the boy stood by. The man said to his wife: "I would consider it the greatest miracle if blessed Francis were to give back to this boy his speech and hearing."

Jude 6:19

1 Kgs 11:28

2 Sm 15:7

Gn 8:15

Ps 69:31

Ps 36:7; Is 14:7

Acts 3:10

[148]He added: "*I vow to the Lord* God that if blessed Francis in his goodness will do this, for the love of him I will always hold this boy dear and support him all the days of his life." A marvelous promise indeed! When he had finished, the boy immediately *spoke up:* "Long live Saint Francis!" Then, looking up, he said: "I see Saint Francis standing above me here; he came to give me speech." Then the boy added: "What will I tell the people?" The man answered: "*You shall praise God* and *you shall save* many *people."* The man, *happy and joyful,* got up and told everyone what had happened. All the people came running, for they had seen the boy many times before when he was unable to speak. *Filled with wonder* and amazement, they humbly

sang praise to God and to blessed Francis. The boy's tongue had grown so that he could use it to speak; and he began to form words as if he had been talking all his life.

[149]There was another boy, named Villa, who could neither speak nor walk. His mother made a wax image for him and carried it with great reverence to the resting place of the blessed father Francis. When she returned home, she found her son walking and talking.

There was a man in the diocese of Perugia who was unable to utter a word. His mouth was always open, and he gaped and gasped horribly, for his throat was swollen and inflamed. When he came to the place where the most holy body rested and started going down the steps to the tomb, he vomited much blood. And he was entirely cured and began to speak, opening and closing his mouth in a normal way.

[150]A woman suffered great pains in her throat. Due to a violently feverish condition, her tongue stuck to her palate and withered. She could neither talk, nor eat, nor drink. Although poultices were applied and various medicines were tried, they gave her no relief from her illness. Finally she vowed herself to Saint Francis in her heart, since she could not speak. Suddenly there was a rattling noise and a small round stone came out of her throat; this she took in her hand and showed to everyone and soon she was entirely well.

In the town of Greccio there was a young man who had lost his speech and hearing and even his memory, so that he neither understood nor grasped anything. His parents had great faith in Saint Francis, and they vowed the boy to him with humble devotion. After they made this vow, through the favor of the most holy and glorious Father Francis, he was richly blessed with the use of all the faculties of which he had been deprived.

To the praise, glory and honor of Our Lord Jesus Christ, whose kingdom and empire remains firm and immovable forever and ever. Amen.

End.

[EPILOGUE]

[151]We have said a little about the miracles of our blessed father Francis, and have left out much, to inspire in those who wish *to follow his footsteps* an eagerness to seek the grace of new blessings. Thus he,

1 Pt 2:21

who so magnificently renewed the whole world by word and example, life and teaching, might always graciously water the souls of

Ps 119:132 those *who love the name of the Lord* with new showers of heavenly gifts.

For the love of the Poor Crucified, and by His sacred *stigmata*

Gal 6:17 which the blessed Father Francis *bore in* his *body*, I ask all those who

Gal 1:20; Lk 18:13 read, see or hear these words, to remember *me, a sinner, before God.*
Amen.

Rv 5:13   *Blessing and honor* and all praise

Rom 16:27   *to the only wise God,*
                                    Who always with great wisdom

1 Cor 12:6   *works all things in all* to His glory.
                                         Amen. Amen. Amen.

THE REMEMBRANCE

OF THE DESIRE OF A SOUL

(The Second Life of Saint Francis)

(1245–1247)

Introduction

The Chronicles of Salimbene degli Adami, written between 1283 and 1288, notes that Crescentius ordered Thomas of Celano to undertake the task of re-presenting the remembrances sent to him.[1] Thomas himself indicates that the choice of his role was that of the chapter itself: "The holy gathering of the last general chapter and you, most reverend father, chose to charge us, insignificant as we are, to write down the deeds as well as the words of our glorious father Francis, for the consolation of our contemporaries and the remembrance of future generations."[2] The result of Thomas's endeavor was a new, long and complicated text, completed shortly before the General Chapter of Lyons in July of 1247. Thomas entitled his third composition, *The Remembrance of the Desire of a Soul.*

The task, then, given to Thomas was formidable. In addition to receiving this commission from the General Minister, not the Pope, Thomas was now fifteen years older and had seen the fraternity change. The tumultuous years of Elias's term as General Minister (1232-1239), the sudden death of his successor, Albert of Pisa (1239), the sweeping changes of Haymo of Faversham (1239-1244), and his sudden death all had left their impressions. The interventions of Pope Gregory, moreover, especially that of *Quo elongati*,[3] had debilitating effects. Thomas's purposes, therefore, were quite different. *The Remembrance of the Desire of a Soul* is neither a continuation nor a complement to his earlier work, *The Life of Saint Francis.* The questions underlying the composition of *The Remembrance of the Desire of a Soul* were not so much about the life of Francis but about the way of life he founded.

Sources

"This work," Thomas states, "contains some marvelous details about the conversion of Saint Francis not included in earlier legends written about him because they were never brought to the author's attention." Besides traces from *The Life of Saint Francis,* in Book One Thomas takes advantage of material from *The Anonymous of Perugia* and *The Legend of the Three Companions.*[4] In these he was confronted with new information not only about Francis's youth and conversion, but also the beginnings of the primitive fraternity. This can be seen, for example, in the accentuation of Francis's baptismal name, John, in the experience of the Crucified in San Damiano, and in his dealings with both Popes Innocent III and Honorius III. He incorporates the information offered in *The Anonymous of Perugia* and *The Legend of the Three Companions,* as well as presenting a new chronological order.

In Book Two Thomas shifts his attention from specifically biographical information to a more thematic presentation of ideals. "We will attempt," he proposes in his Prologue, "to express and carefully state the good, pleasing, and perfect will of our most holy father. This concerns both himself and his followers, the exercise of heavenly discipline and that striving for highest perfection which he always expressed in love for God and in living example for others." To accomplish this, Thomas relies heavily on *The Assisi Compilation*. Even a cursory examination of incidents found in both *The Assisi Compilation* and *The Remembrance of the Desire of a Soul* reveals subtle differences but general dependency. *The Assisi Compilation* offers simple, colloquial, and immediate presentations of these incidents. To these Thomas brings his eloquent and literary style as well as his facility with Scripture to re-present the same stories within the framework of his specific purposes.[5] Many times, he omits the details of *The Assisi Compilation*, especially geographical ones that are not pertinent.[6] Sometimes he changes certain details in order to accentuate his themes;[7] at others, he shortens descriptions to develop more clearly their theological significance.[8]

While a more precise, in-depth comparison of *The Anonymous of Perugia*, *The Legend of the Three Companions*, *The Assisi Compilation*, and *The Remembrance of the Desire of a Soul* needs to be done, the inter-dependence of these texts is evident. The letter at the beginning of *The Legend of the Three Companions* attests to a block of information sent in response to Crescentius's request. That could easily have been the data of *The Legend of the Three Companions* edited to include much of the *The Anonymous of Perugia*, as well as that of *The Assisi Compilation*. In the final analysis, Thomas's work reflects the input of Francis's companions, crafted, however, according to Thomas's own design. Little wonder, then, that Thomas concludes his work with a prayer of the saint's companions. It adroitly omits any mention of "we who were with him," and so it may be seen as a prayer of Thomas himself as well as of any of Francis's companions.

Vision

Aside from the Prologue (2C 1-2) and the lengthy concluding prayer (2C 221-224), Thomas divides this work into two disproportionate sections. Book One is made up of only twenty-three paragraphs (2C 3-25) that, as noted, are biographical in nature. Book Two, on the other hand, contains one hundred and ninety-nine paragraphs (2C 26-220) presented in a thematic vein. Of these, six numbers (2C 114-220) describe Francis's death and, in two manuscripts, his canonization.

Two contemporary interpretations of *The Remembrance of the Desire of A Soul* exist. In that of François DeBeer, Thomas centered his material around the theme of conversion and, from that starting-point organized into two books to address two themes: initial conversion and the lifetime embrace of conversion.[9] The other is of Engelbert Grau who cites a passage in Thomas's introduction to Book Two for his interpretation: "I consider blessed Francis the holiest *mirror* of the holiness of the Lord, the *image of his* perfection."[10] "It is the intention of the author," Grau maintains, "to hold up a 'mirror of perfection' of Francis's exemplary life to the friars of the second generation who had not personally experienced or known him in his lifetime."[11] Both perspectives offer an understanding of the biographical material in Book One portending the thematic material of Book Two. In other words, the first provides insights into the nature and the foundation of Gospel life, while the second addresses practical attitudes and behaviors that can assist or impede the living out of the Gospel.

Thomas adjusts and nuances the information of the Companions to present a new perspective on Francis's vocation, its prophetic dimension. His baptism is a call to a prophetic generosity that embraces fellow prisoners, a poor knight, the beggars before Saint Peter's, and, most challenging of all, lepers. It is a call to overcome temptations, to reject the worldly career of knighthood, and to see beyond his carousing friends to Christ. Only then is Francis led by the Spirit to enter the church of San Damiano where "with the lips of the painting, the image of Christ crucified spoke to him . . . calling him by name"[12] From Christ, he receives a command that will direct him the rest of his life.[13] It takes him before the bishop where he proclaims God as his Father, pledges to go to the Lord naked· and begins serving the common Lord of all and begging leftovers from door to door. Thus Thomas interprets these events teaching the nature of Francis's prophetic vocation as rooted in baptism. As he opens himself in generosity to others, his vocation is to allow himself to be moved by the Spirit in Christ to the Father.

Thomas moves quickly in narrating Francis's prophecy concerning the virgins who would live in San Damiano, his example in attracting Bernard of Quintavalle and others, and his discourse before the pope. Curiously, Thomas devotes significant time to describing the role of the Portiuncula (2C 18-20) and the vision of the small black hen and her unruly chicks. In doing so, he provides two symbols that guide his thought in Book Two: the Portiuncula that represents the Church in which the Gospel life is discovered and lived, and the small black hen referring to Francis himself unable to defend with his wings.

Book Two moves to many particulars and examples of what this vocation in prophetic baptismal grace can mean for the brothers in the course of everyday life. The material from which Thomas drew offered him memories of everyday events in Francis life, experienced for the most part in intimate and private settings known particularly to "we who were with him." This second book has its own introduction, but almost every delineated thematic section also has its own introduction.[14] These are key to understanding Thomas's theological perception of events remembered about Francis. In *The Remembrance of the Desire of a Soul,* unlike in his *Life of Saint Francis,* Thomas seems more interested in showing the power of God's intervening and prophetic grace that begins in baptism and progressively develops through life. This grace of conversion is not a private matter, but is shared grace to be further developed among brothers who in dialogue mutually listen to the Gospel and entrust themselves to the Church. This is the foundation for the life of the Lesser Brothers, and in Francis's vocation the brothers can find their own call.

Thus a dynamic exchange takes place between the two books in which a theme developed in the second book can be found in seminal form in the first. Book One begins with Francis in comparison to John the Baptist (2C 3-4), while Chapter I of Book Two begins describing Francis's spirit of prophecy (2C 27-54). The correspondence continues as Thomas highlights the image of Martin of Tours (2C 5-6) and develops the theme of poverty (2C 55-93). His new spiritual energy (2C 7) finds inspiration in prayer (2C 94-101), his Catholic faith (2C 8) in Sacred Scriptures (2C 102-111); his religious spirit overcoming both temptation and himself (2C 9) in varied temptations (2C 112-124); and his service of lepers (2 C 9) in his true spiritual joy (2C 125-134). Finally, there is his response to Christ's command and his new family of brothers (2 C 7-17) which prompts a consideration of the virtues of the new fraternity: humility (2C 139-150), obedience (2C 151-154), simplicity (2C 189-203), special devotions (2C 196-203) and care for the Poor Ladies (2C 204-207).

Although Thomas constructed Book Two according to a thematic, not without relationship to Book One, he never had far from his mind the central concern of the brothers of his day, the problem of interpreting provisions of the *Rule*.[15] There is no rupture with the past, but rather in the past the future is already gestating. The foundation, however, is Christ in the grace of baptism, becoming ever more present and finally giving to each person his or her own *mandatum* within the deepest recesses of the soul. This is the lesson he wishes to communicate to his brothers who struggle with the identity of their vocation in the tumultuous period of the 1240's.

Thomas concludes Book Two with a description of Francis's death. It is the one place in *The Remembrance of the Desire of a Soul* that Thomas extensively uses what he had earlier written in *The Life of Saint Francis*. This indicates that Thomas took his new task seriously, to write about Francis from the memories of others and to present them in a new way for a new time. In Book One, even in our day, he reveals the ever-increasing gift of grace deep in the heart of the baptized, and in Book Two he motivates the grace-filled believer into action. In both books, however, remembrance of Saint Francis stirs the desire of every soul, eternal life.

Conclusion

The Remembrance of The Desire of a Soul: the title is provocative. Thomas's work is undoubtedly one of remembrance, a collage of the memories of Francis's companions stitched together in Thomas's unique style. Nonetheless, is it not difficult and, at the same time, intriguing to determine the soul possessing such desire? Is the desire of the companions? Of Thomas? Of Francis himself? Or did Thomas see his work as a means of stirring the memories of those who would read his work and, in so doing, re-enkindling the desire deep in their own souls?

In the final analysis, *The Remembrance of the Desire of a Soul* is a piece of spiritual literature that resonates deeply with those attempting to define the spirituality of Francis of Assisi. As it embraces a profoundly theological approach by seeing baptismal grace as the lynchpin of Francis's life, it also provides an anthropological dimension that provides insight into the saint's human nature and experience, or, as Ewert Cousins expresses it, "the inner dimension of the person . . . [where] ultimate reality is experienced."[16] While it must be read in the context of the historical milieu of the middle of the thirteenth century, Thomas's accentuation of the rich symbols that fill its history make it a text of contemporary relevance.

Notes

1. Salimbene degli Adami, *Chronicle,* 166: "In the year of the Lord 1244, Brother Haymo of England, general minister of the Order of Lesser Brothers, died, and elected in his place was Brother Crescentius of the March of Ancona, who was an old man. Crescentius then commanded Brother Thomas of Celano, who had written the first Legend of Saint Francis, to write another book, because many things about Saint Francis had been discovered which had never been written. And so Thomas of Celano wrote a very beautiful book about the miracles, as well as the life of Saint Francis, which he entitled the 'Remembrance of the Blessed Francis in the Desire of the Soul.' "

2. 2C 1.

3. Cf. FA:ED I 570-575. cf. supra, 15-18.

4. Jacques Dalarun notes that in 2C there are three episodes taken from 1C, five from AP, thirty-four from L3C, and eighty-seven from AC. One hundred one are without earlier recognizable sources, thus giving the text a total of 230 narrative episodes. Cf. Jacques Dalarun, *La Malavventura di Francesco d'Assisi: Per Un Uso Storico delle Leggende Francescane* (Milano: Edizioni Biblioteca Francescana, 1996), 92. The editors of this volume have assiduously studied the Latin texts of these works and attempted to bring the translations of each into uniformity so that their interdependence is obvious.

5. The simple statement found in AC 68 *Nolite facere amplius dicere* [Don't make me tell you again] is changed in 2C 44 to *Quid vultis ut iterum dicam?* (Mt 20:32; Jn 9:27) [Do you want me to say it again?]

6. E.g. 2C 31, 37, 40, 44, 75, 91, 122, 126, 181.

7. For example, in 2C 45 Thomas changes "a certain brother" (AC 73) to "two brothers" travelling to Greccio to catch a glimpse of Francis. "Two brothers" travelling together is more in accord with the Gospel injunction (Lk 10:1) and Thomas's earlier reiteration of it in 1C 29. In another instance, Thomas changes the occasion of Francis's appearing as a poor, humble pilgrim before the brothers at Greccio from Christmas (AC 74) to Easter (2C 61). This allows him to place greater emphasis on the example of Francis as a pilgrim, an important point in LR VI 2.

8. E.g. 2C 21-22, 59, 64, 73, 100, 151, 165. In 2C 21-22, the story of the brother dying of hunger, Thomas recasts AC 50 in order to accentuate Francis's image as a shepherd in caring for his sheep. In 2C 38, the story of the young woman coming to Francis with a complaint about her cruel husband, Thomas re-orders AC 69. In Thomas's rendering, Francis is sensitive to the "delicate and tender" woman who dies on the same day as her husband. In this way, Thomas emphasizes their celibate lives as a sacrificial offering, the "one as a morning holocaust, and the other as an evening sacrifice."

9. François De Beer, *La Conversion de Saint François selon Thomas de Celano* (Paris: Éditions Franciscaines, 1963).

10. 2C 26.

11. Engelbert Grau, "Thomas of Celano: Life and Work," GR 8:2 (1994): 190.

12. Cf 2C 10.

13. The Latin word *mandatum* [command] is significant in 2C where it is used far more than in 1C. See infra 2C 5, 163 a.

14. Cf. 2C 27 For specific introductions to the various individual narratives in which Thomas theologically contextualizes the various memories of Saint Francis, see the following: 2C 27 (prophecy), 55 (poverty), 94 (prayer), 102 (Scripture), 115 (temptation), 125 (spiritual joy),135 (hiding the stigmata), 140 (humility), 151 (obedience), 159 (idleness), 165 (love for creatures),

172 (charity), 189 (simplicity), 201 (devotion to Eucharist), 202 (devotion to relics), 203, (devotion to the cross), and 204 (the Poor Ladies).

15. Throughout Book Two, Thomas makes many allusions or direct references to LR, the Rule confirmed by Pope Honorius III with the papal decree, *Solet annuere,* cf. FA:ED I, 99-106. Cf. 2C 58, 66, 69, 72, 80, 81, 91, 131, 152, 175.

16. Ewert Cousins, "Preface to the Series." *Christian Spirituality.* Vol I. Origins to the Twelfth Century. Ed. Bernard McGinn, et al., (New York: Crossroad, 1985), xiii.

The Remembrance of the Desire of a Soul

Prologue

IN THE NAME OF OUR LORD JESUS CHRIST. AMEN.

TO THE GENERAL MINISTER OF THE ORDER OF THE LESSER BROTHERS
HERE BEGINS THE PROLOGUE

[1]The holy gathering of the last general chapter and you, most reverend father,[a] chose to charge us, insignificant as we are, to write down the deeds as well as the words of our glorious father Francis, for the consolation of our contemporaries and the remembrance of future generations.

We, more than others, learned these things through constant living together and mutual intimacy with him over a long time.[b] We hastened with humble devotion to obey this sacred command: it would be wrong to neglect it in any way. But on further considering the weakness of our capacities we are struck with a justified fear that such a worthy topic, handled in an unworthy manner, should be tainted by our efforts and become distasteful to others. We fear that, like food full of *delicious flavors,* it may be rendered tasteless by incompetent servants, and that our efforts will be criticized as presumption, rather than obedience.

Wis 16:20

---

a. For information on the request for information on Francis of the previous General Chapter of Genoa and the General Minister, Crescentius of Iesi, in 1244. This text of *The Remembrance of the Desire of a Soul* was presented to Crescentius of Iesi before the General Chapter of 1247, when John of Parma was elected in his place. The translation is based on the critical text of the AF X, 129-268.

b. This first number echoes the letter dated August 11, 1246, from Greccio attached to L3C, cf. L3C 1. See conclusion of the whole work, 2C 221-224, infra, 310-11. The *Prayer of the Companions.*

Blessed father, if the results of so much labor were to be examined only by your kind self, and did not have to be presented to a public audience, we would gladly be instructed by your correction and rejoice in your approval. Who can examine closely and balance carefully such diverse words and deeds, so that *all* listeners would *be of one mind?* We simply want to benefit each and everyone. So we beg those who read this to interpret it kindly and to bear with or correct the simplicity of the narrator so that reverence for the person who is our subject may remain intact. Our memory, like that of ignorant people, is blunted by the passage of time and cannot attain the heights of his profound words or due praise for his marvelous deeds. Even a quick and well-trained mind could hardly grasp these things, even if directly confronted with them. By your authority, you repeatedly ordered us to write. Now, pardon us publicly for our clumsy mistakes.

2 Mc 14:20

²In the first place, this work contains some marvelous details about the conversion of Saint Francis not included in earlier legends written about him because they were never brought to the author's attention. Then we will attempt to express and carefully state the *good, pleasing and perfect will* of our most holy father. This concerns both himself and his followers, the exercise of heavenly discipline, and that striving for highest perfection which he always expressed in love for God and in living example for others. Here and there, according to the opportunity, we have included a number of his miracles. We describe in a plain and simple way things that occur to us, wishing to accommodate those who are slower and, if possible, also to please the learned.

Rom 12:2

We beg you, therefore, kind father, consecrate with your blessing this small gift of our work—small, but not to be despised—which we gathered with no small labor. Correct its errors. Trim away the superfluous.

Thus things well said will be approved
by your learned opinion, and
like your name,
Crescentius,
they will build to a crescendo
and everywhere *increase and multiply in Christ.*

Gn 1:22,28; Acts 12:24;
Eph 2:20-21

Amen.

Here ends the Prologue

The First Book

THE REMEMBRANCE OF THE DESIRE OF A SOUL[a]
THE DEEDS AND WORDS
OF OUR MOST HOLY FATHER

His Conversion

Chapter I
HOW HE WAS AT FIRST CALLED JOHN,
AND LATER FRANCIS;
WHAT HIS MOTHER PROPHESIED ABOUT HIM,
WHAT HE HIMSELF PREDICTED WOULD HAPPEN TO HIM,
AND HIS PATIENCE WHILE IN CHAINS.

[3]"Francis"
was the name of this servant and friend of the Most High.
Divine Providence gave him this name,
unique and unusual,

1C 120   that the fame of his ministry should spread even more rapidly
throughout the whole world.
He was named *John* by his own mother
when, being *born again through water and the Holy Spirit*[b]   Jn 3:5
he was changed from a *child of wrath*   Eph 2:3
into a child of grace.[c]

---

a. This title, *Memoriale in Desiderio Animae* [The Remembrance of The Desire of a Soul], is inspired by the Vulgate version of Is 26:8: *nomen tuum et memoriale tuum in desiderio animae* [your name and your memory are the desire of the soul]. This is how the editors have chosen to entitle this whole work in order to capture its nature as a work of remembrance of Francis rather than as a life of Francis. This passage serves as a means of approaching the text since Book One (2C 1-25) begins by concentrating on the name, Francis, as a means of indicating the saint's vocation; while Book Two (2C 26-224) does so by reflecting on the importance of remembrance as a tool of honor and of love (2C 26).

b. This is the first reference to Francis's baptism. Since there is no record of it, scholars conjecture that it took place in the church of Santa Maria del Vescovado. Since the Duomo of San Rufino was being repaired, Santa Maria del Vescovado became the pro-cathedral. The baptismal font was later transferred back to San Rufino where it remains to this day. Cf. Omer Englebert, *Saint Francis of Assisi: A Biography*, trans. Eve Marie Cooper, 2nd Edition revised and augmented by Ignatius Brady and Raphael Brown (Chicago: Franciscan Herald Press, 1965), 405-406.

c. In contrast with 1C, Thomas now accents baptismal grace as operating within Francis from the very beginning. His baptismal name of *John* is actually more significant because it identifies this grace as prophetic.

This woman was
a friend of all complete integrity,
with some of the virtue of Saint *Elizabeth*,
of whom we read in Scripture,
she was privileged to resemble and act,
both in the *name* she gave her *son*
and in her prophetic spirit.[a]
For when her neighbors were admiring
Francis's greatness of spirit and integrity of conduct
she asked them,
as if prompted by divine premonition,
"What do you think this son of mine *will become?*[b]
You will see
that he shall merit to become a *son of God!"*
In fact this was the opinion of many,
whom Francis pleased, by his very fine efforts, as he grew older.
He completely rejected
anything that could sound insulting to anyone.
No one felt a young man of such noble manners
could be born of the stock
of those who were called his parents.

The name *John,*
refers to the mission which he received;[c]
the name *Francis*
to the spread of his fame which quickly reached everywhere,
once his turning to God was complete.[d]
Thus,
he used to keep the feast of John the Baptist
more solemnly than the feasts of all other saints,
because the dignity of this name

Lk 1:57-63

1C 2; L3C 2

Lk 1:66

L3C 2

Mt 5:9, Lk 20:36

---

a. In 1C 13, Francis's mother tried by "gentle words" to dissuade "her son from his intention," and, although unsuccessful, she "broke his chains and let him go free." In this text, Francis's mother is much more positive about his call. She is thus presented in the classical role of a saint's mother, e.g. the mothers of Saints Bernard and Dominic.

b. In this text, as in AP, L3C, AC, paragraphs paralleling earlier texts are indicated in the margins by a reference to the text. Where a verbal dependence on an earlier text is present, the text is emboldened and the reference is found in the margin.

c. The Hebrew name *John* was translated by Saint Jerome as *"the grace of the Lord,"* or *"grace is his."* In this context, Thomas sees his baptismal name as referring to Francis's prophetic mission. Cf. Jerome, *Liber de Interpretatione de Nominibus Hebraicis* 8,7; 9:25; *Corpus Christianorum Latinum* 3, 1972, 20.

d. For an understanding of the name *Francis*, see 1C 120, as well as FA:ED I 290 b.

marked him with a trace of mystical power.[a]
This observation is worthy of note:
among all those born of women   Mt 11:11
there has never been one greater than John
and among all the founders of religious communities
there has never been one more perfect than Francis.

[4]John
prophesied enclosed within the hidden confines
of his mother's womb.   Lk 1:41
Francis,
still unaware of God's guidance
foretold things to come
while held in an earthly prison.

L3C 4   Once there was a great massacre in a war between the citizens of
Perugia and Assisi.[b] Francis was captured along with many others,
and, chained with the rest of them, endured the squalor of prison.
His fellow captives were overcome with sadness, weeping bitterly
over the fact of their imprisonment, but Francis *rejoiced in the Lord,*   Ps 35:9
laughing and making fun of his chains. His unhappy companions re-
buked him as he reveled in his chains, and thought he was out of his
mind. Francis answered them prophetically: "What do you think
makes me so happy? I'm thinking about something else: some day
the whole world will worship me as a saint!" And now that is true;
everything he said has been fulfilled.

L3C 4   Among the others who were then imprisoned with him there was
an arrogant and utterly unbearable knight. Everyone else decided to
avoid him but he could not wear down Francis's patience; he toler-
ated the intolerable man and restored the others to peace with him.

What a *chosen vessel of all virtues;*   Sir 24:25; Acts 9:15
able to contain *every grace!*
Already he pours out charisms in all directions!

---

a. The frequent use of the adverb *iam* [already] and expressions such as *ab initio* [from the beginning]
indicate important differences between Thomas's portrayals of Francis's conversion. In 1C, the
conversion moves gradually with numerous new beginnings, but in 2C his conversion moves
decisively from one beginning. Thomas not only highlights the prophetic dimension of Francis's
baptismal name, but also the "mystical power" associated with it.
b. For background information on the war between Assisi and Perugia see L3C 4.

Chapter II
HOW HE CLOTHED A POOR KNIGHT
AND HOW HE SAW A VISION OF HIS CALLING WHILE STILL IN THE WORLD

⁵After a short time
freed from his chains,
he became more generous to the needy.
Already he resolved   1C 17; L3C 3
never to *turn his face away from any poor person*
who asked anything "for the love of God."

Tb 4:7; Sir 4:5

One day he met a poor, half-naked knight, and moved by piety,
for love of Christ, he generously gave him the finely tailored clothes
he was wearing. Did he do any less than the great Saint Martin?^a
They did the same thing, with the same purpose, though in different
ways.

Francis first gave away his clothes,
then everything else;
Martin gave away everything else^b
and then gave away his clothes.
Both lived *poor and humble* in this world
and both *entered heaven rich.*^c
Martin was poor, but a knight,
and clothed a poor man with part of his clothes.
Francis was rich, but not a knight,   L3C 6
and he clothed a poor knight with all of his clothes.
Both of them,

Is 16:14

---

a. Cf. Sulpicius Severus describes the generosity of Saint Martin of Tours (+397) in the following manner: "Accordingly, at a certain period, when he had nothing except his arms and his simple military dress, in the middle of winter, . . . he happened to meet at the gate of Amiens a poor man destitute of clothing. . . . He had nothing except the cloak in which he was clad, for he had already parted with the rest of his garments for similar purposes. Taking, his sword therefore he cut his cloak into two equal parts, and gave one part to the poor man, while he again clothed himself with the remainder." *The Life of Martin* 3. [This and other quotations from *The Life of Martin* and from the *Letters* have been taken from: "The Works of Sulpicius Severus," translated with Preface and Notes by Alexander Roberts, in *A Select Library of Nicene and Post-Nicene Fathers of the Christian Church,* Second Series, Volume XI, (New York: The Christian Literature Company, 1894).]

b. Sulpicius Severus, *Life of Martin* 3: "He had nothing except the cloak in which he was clad, for he had already parted with the rest of his garments for similar purposes."

c. Sulpicius Severus, *Letter III:* "Martin, poor and insignificant on earth, has a rich entrance granted him into heaven." This famous phrase, *pauper et humilis caelum dives ingreditur* [poor and humble he entered heaven rich] appears twice in the Office of Saint Martin. See Responsory VIII at Matins and Antiphon V at Lauds. With a change of name, it is also used for the Alleluia verse in a Mass of Saint Francis. See *Second Mass,* Gradual versicle as found in the Liturgical Texts, cf. FA:ED I 349.

1C 5

having carried out Christ's command[a]
deserved to be visited by Christ in a vision.[b]
Martin was praised for his perfection
and Francis was graciously invited to what was still missing.

[1C 5, 7; LJS 3; AP 5; L3C 5]

[6] A little later, he saw in a vision a beautiful palace, and there he saw various suits of armor and a lovely bride.[c] In that same dream Francis was *called by name* and was attracted by the promise of all these things. He therefore tried to go to Apulia[d] in order to gain knighthood, and richly outfitted, he hastened to achieve the honors of knightly rank. The spirit of the flesh prompted him to give an interpretation of the flesh to the vision. In fact, in the *treasury of God's wisdom* something even more magnificent was hidden there.

Gn 4:17

Col 2:2-3

[AP 6; //L3C 6]

As he slept one night, someone spoke to him a second time in a vision and asked him with concern where he was going. He explained his plan and said he was going to Apulia to become a knight. The other *questioned him anxiously* **"Who can do more for you, the servant or the lord?" "The lord!"** said Francis. **"Then why do you seek the servant** instead of the lord?" Francis then asked: **"Lord, what do you want me to do?"** And the Lord said to him: **"Go back to the land** *of your birth* because I will fulfill your dream in a spiritual way."

Lk 7:4

Acts 9:6

Gn 32:9

He turned back without delay
becoming even now *a model* of obedience.
Giving up his own will
he changed from Saul to Paul.
Paul was thrown to the ground
and his stinging lashes bore fruit in soothing words;[e]

1 Pt 5:3

---

a. This text emphasizes Christ's *mandatum* [command], a word used thirteen times in 2C, while it is used only four times in 1C. Moreover, Francis is "called by name" in this text. Thus Francis's conversion is connected to his encounter with Christ. This differs from 1C in which more emphasis is placed on the initiative of Francis's *propositum* [proposal], a word that appears twenty-two times in that earlier text and only eight times in 2C. On *propositum*, see FA:ED I 189 d.

b. Sulpicius Severus, *The Life of Martin* 3: "In the following night, when Martin had resigned himself to sleep, he had a vision of Christ arrayed in that part of his cloak with which he had clothed the poor man. . . . After this vision the sainted man was not puffed up with human glory, but, acknowledging the goodness of God in what had been done, and being now of the age of twenty years, he hastened to receive baptism." In this text Thomas puts more emphasis on knighthood, a theme also found in AP 6 and L3C 5.

c. Thomas builds on information supplied by the Three Companions (cf. L3C 5) which introduces the presence of a bride into the dream. In doing so, he introduces the theme of an espousal that he accentuates in describing Francis's commitment to Lady Poverty. This theme was quite prominent in the spiritual literature of the time, cf. Jean Leclercq, *Monks and Love in Twelfth-Century France: Psycho-Historical Essays* (Oxford: Oxford at The Clarendon Press, 1979); and Ann W. Astell, *The Song of Songs in the Middle Ages* (Ithaca and London: Cornell University Press, 1990), 73-104.

d. For information on Apulia, see FA:ED I 185 d.

e. A word play: *verbera dura verba dulcia* [stinging lashes . . . soothing words].

while Francis turned his fleshly weapons into spiritual ones,
and, instead of knightly glory,
received a divine rank.[a]
To the many who marveled at his unusual joy,   L3C 5
he said that he was going to become a great prince.

Chapter III
HOW A CROWD OF YOUNG PEOPLE
CHOSE HIM AS THEIR LORD SO THAT HE WOULD FEED THEM,
AND HOW HE CHANGED.

Eph 4:13   [7]He started to change into the *perfect man,*
and became a different person.[b]
When he returned home,
Ez 23:17   the *sons of Babylon* followed him,
and dragged him, though unwilling, in one direction
while he was heading in another.

Earlier he had been the ringleader of Assisi's frivolous young   1C 2; L3C 7
crowd. They still invited him to their dinner parties, in which the
suggestive and vulgar were always served. They chose him as their
leader, since they had often experienced his generosity, and knew for
sure he would pay all their expenses. They made themselves obedi-
Lk 15:16   ent so they could *fill* their *bellies,* and made themselves subject so they
could gorge themselves. Not wanting to seem stingy, Francis did not
reject the honor. Even while meditating on sacred things, he maintained his courtly manners. He set out a sumptuous dinner, with
Is 28:8; Prv 26:11   double portions of the most elegant food, and *stuffed to the point of*
Gn 10:11   *vomiting,* they dirtied *the streets of the town* with their drunken songs.
Gn 38:18; Ex 12:11   As their lord, *bearing a staff in his hands,* Francis followed them. But
gradually he withdrew bodily as he had already mentally turned deaf
1 Chr 23:30   to those things, while he *sang to the Lord* in his heart.
So much divine sweetness poured over him—as he later re-   L3C 7
counted—that he was struck dumb and could not move. A burst of
spiritual energy rushed through him, snatching him into the un-

---

a. The Latin reads: *divinum praesidatum* [a divine rank], the only time the word *praesidatum* appears
   in the works of Thomas of Celano. It may be interpreted as Francis's becoming a feudal lord over a
   conquered territory, that is, over himself.
b. In 2C 6 Francis is "changed from Saul to Paul." In this passage, another change is highlighted, i.e.
   into "the perfect man." All of these transformations led to the "mysterious change" that occurs in
   Francis in 2C 10.

seen.[a] It was so powerful it made him consider earthly things unimportant and utterly worthless.

What amazing generosity of Christ!
To those who do small things
He *gives the greatest gifts.*
In the flood of many waters
He *saves* and lifts up *His own.*
Christ *feeds the crowds with loaves and fishes*
and does not drive away sinners from his table.
When they *seek to make him king,*
He flees and *goes up the mountain to pray.*
These are *mysteries of God* toward which Francis reaches,
and he is led to unknowingly *perfect knowledge.*

2 Pt 1:4

Ps 32:6

Jn 17:10-12

Mt 14:15-21;
Mk 6:33-44;
Lk 9:12-17; Jn 6:5-13

Mt 9:10-13;
Lk 5:29-32, 15:2

Mt 14:23; Jn 6:15

Col 2:2

Jb 22:2

Chapter IV
HOW HE DRESSED IN POOR GARMENTS AND ATE WITH THE POOR
IN FRONT OF THE CHURCH OF SAINT PETER,
AND THE GIFT HE OFFERED THERE

[8]Already he was an outstanding lover of the poor
and his sacred beginning gave a glimpse
of what would be fulfilled in the future.
He often stripped himself to clothe the poor.
Although he had not yet made himself one of them
he strove to be like them with his *whole heart.*

Mt 22:37; Lk 10:27

L3C 10

Once on pilgrimage to Rome, out of love for poverty he took off his fine clothing and dressed himself in a poor man's clothes. He happily settled among the poor in the square in front of the church of Saint Peter, a place where the poor are abundant. Considering himself one of them, he eagerly ate with them. If his embarrassed friends had not restrained him, he would have done this many times.

L3C 10

When he approached the altar of the Prince of the Apostles, he was surprised that people gave such small gifts. He threw in a whole handful of money, showing that the one God honored above others should be honored by all in a special way.

st 6-10; L3C 8, 57

Showing *due honor*, he often gave liturgical vestments to poor priests, even to those of the lowest rank.

Rom 13:7

---

a. The Latin text *sed ipsum ad invisibilia raptans* is an allusion to the Preface of Christmas: "In him we see our God made visible and so are caught up in the love of the God we cannot see."

As he was to be entrusted
with the mission of an apostle,
he was completely Catholic in faith.
From the very beginning
he was full of reverence
for God's ministers and ministries.

1C 33, 36, 43;
LJS 28, 46
Off Vesp 1 1

Chapter V
HOW THE DEVIL SHOWED HIM A WOMAN WHILE HE WAS PRAYING
AND THE ANSWER WHICH GOD GAVE HIM,
AND WHAT HE DID FOR LEPERS

[9]Under his worldly clothing
he wore a religious spirit;
leaving public places
he sought places of solitude,
where he was often instructed by visits of the Holy Spirit.
He was drawn away,
lured by that remarkable delight
that from the very beginning flowed over him abundantly
and never left him as long as he lived.

As he began to visit hidden places conducive to prayer, the devil struggled to drive him away with an evil trick. He made Francis think of a horribly hunchbacked woman who lived in town and whose looks scared everyone. The devil threatened that he would become like her if he did not turn back sensibly from what he had begun. But, *strengthened by the Lord,* he rejoiced at a response of healing and grace. "Francis," God said to him *in spirit* "you have traded what you loved in a fleshly, empty way for things of the spirit, *taking the bitter for the sweet.* If you want to come to know Me, despise yourself. For when the order is reversed, the things I say will taste sweet to you even though they seem the opposite." He was moved to obey immediately the divine command, and was led through experience to the truth of these things.

Among all the awful miseries of this world Francis had a natural horror of lepers, and one day as he was riding his horse near Assisi he met a leper on the road. He felt terrified and revolted, but not wanting to transgress God's command and break the sacrament[a] of His word, he dismounted from his horse and ran to kiss him. As the leper *stretched out his hand, expecting something,* he *received* both *money* and a

Eph 6:10

Mt 22:43

Prv 27:7

Est 8:4; Acts 3:5;
Gn 43:21

1C 6; LJS 4

L3C 12

1C 17; LJS12; L3C

---

a. The Latin text reads *sacramentum* [sacrament], a word that appears fourteen times in Thomas's portraits of Francis and with a variety of meanings. At times it refers to the stigmata (1C 90, 114; 2C 203), to the Eucharist (2C 185, 201; 3C 28, 40), and, at other times, to actions or deeds containing a deeper symbolic meaning as in this instance (2C 9, 68, 126).

kiss. Francis immediately *mounted his horse* and although the field was wide open, without any obstructions, when he looked around he could not see the leper anywhere.[a]

> *Filled with joy* and wonder at this event,
> within a few days he deliberately tried to do something similar.
> He made his way to the houses of the lepers[b]
> and, giving money to each,
> he also *gave a kiss on the hand* and mouth.
> Thus he *took the bitter for the sweet*
> and courageously prepared to carry out the rest.

(margins) 1C 17 — Test 3; L3C 11 — 2 Cor 7:4 — Sir 29:5 — Prv 27:7

Chapter VI
THE IMAGE OF THE CRUCIFIED WHICH SPOKE TO HIM, AND THE HONOR THAT HE GAVE TO IT.

[10]With his heart already completely changed—soon his body was also to be changed—**he was walking** one day by **the church of San Damiano**,[c] which was abandoned by everyone and almost in ruins. *Led by the Spirit* he went in to pray and knelt down devoutly before the crucifix. He was shaken by unusual experiences and discovered that he was different from when he had entered. As soon as he had this feeling, there occurred *something unheard of in previous ages*: with the lips of the painting, **the image** of Christ **crucified spoke to him**. "**Francis**," it said, *calling him by name*, "**go rebuild My house;** as you see, **it is all being destroyed**." Francis was more than a little stunned, trembling, and stuttering like a man out of his senses. He prepared himself to obey and pulled himself together to carry out the command. He felt this mysterious change in himself, but he could not describe it. So it is better for us to remain silent about it too. From that time on, compassion for the Crucified was impressed into his holy soul. And we honestly believe the wounds of the sacred Passion were impressed deep in his heart, though not yet on his flesh.

(margins) 1C 6 — 9; LJS 6; L3C 13 — Mt 4:1 — Jn 9:32 — Is 40:26 — L3C 14

> [11]What an admirable thing,
> *unheard of in earlier ages!*
> Who would not be amazed at this?
> Who ever heard of anything like it?

(margin) Jn 9:32

---

a. Gregory the Great relates the story of the monk Martirio (or Martino) who carried Christ, disguised as a leper, on his shoulders. When the monk tries to detain him, he disappears. Cf. Gregory the Great, *Homilia in Evangelium* II, 39: 10 (PL 76: 1300).
b. See FA:ED I 195 b for information on the leper colonies of Assisi during Francis's time.
c. For background on the church of San Damiano, see FA:ED I 189 b.

Who could ever doubt that Francis,
as he returned to his homeland,
already appeared crucified?
Christ spoke to him from the wood of the cross
in a new and unheard of miracle,[a]
even when to all appearances,
he had not yet completely forsaken the world.
From that very hour
Sg 5:6 his *soul melted*
as the Beloved spoke to him.
A little while afterward   1C 94, 95
his heart's love
showed in the wounds of his body.

From then on, he could not hold back his tears, even weeping   LCh 10; L3C 14; A
loudly over the Passion of Christ, as if it were constantly before his
eyes. He filled the roads with his sobbing, and, as he remembered the
wounds of Christ, he would take no comfort. Once, upon meeting a
close friend, he explained the reason for this sorrow, moving him
also to bitter tears.

He does not forget to care for that holy image
nor hesitate to carry out the command.   L3C 13
Lk 19:15 He *gives* the priest *money* to buy a lamp and some oil,
lest the sacred image lack, even for a moment, the honor of light.
He then runs quickly to fulfill the rest,   1C 18; LJS 13; L3
working tirelessly to rebuild that church.
Gn 15:1 Although *the divine word spoken* to him
was really about that Church
Acts 20:28 *which* Christ *acquired with* His own *blood,*[b]
he did not immediately reach that level,
Rom 8:9 but moved gradually *from flesh to spirit.*

---

a. In 2C 11 Christ's speaking to Francis from the cross is described as an "unheard-of miracle." In 1C 112 Thomas writes of the stigmata as "a new miracle." This is an example of how references in 1C to later events in Francis's life are linked to earlier events in 2C.

b. Another example of Thomas's developing ecclesiology and theology of renewal that permeate his writings. Cf. Regis J. Armstrong, "Clare of Assisi, The Poor Ladies, and Their Ecclesial Mission in the *First Life* of Thomas of Celano," GR 5:3 (1991): 389-424.

Chapter VII
HOW HIS FATHER AND HIS BROTHER IN THE FLESH PERSECUTED HIM.

[10, 12; LJS 7, 8]

[AP 9; L3C 23]

[1C 14-15; LJS 9; AP 8; L3C 19]

[L3C 20]

[L3C 21]

[L3C 20]

[L3C 23]

[1 Tm 2:10]

[Wis 5:4]

[Ps 109:28]

[1 Kgs 3:1]

[Acts 10:27]

[Jn 13:19; Mt 6:9]

[Phil 3:8; 1:21]

[1 Sm 2:27]

[1 Sm 2:27]

[12]But, now that he was set upon *works of piety,* his father in the flesh began to persecute him. *Judging it madness* to be a servant of Christ, he would lash out at him with curses wherever he went. The servant of God then called a lowly, rather simple man to help him. Substituting him for his father, he asked him for a blessing whenever his father cursed him. He turned into deeds the words of the prophet, revealing the meaning of that verse: *Let them curse; you give your blessing.*

The *man of God* gave back to his father the money he wanted to spend for work on the church. He did this on the advice of the bishop of the town,[a] a very devout man, because it was wrong to spend ill-gotten gain for sacred purposes.[b] Within earshot of *many who had gathered about,* he declared: *"From now on I will say* freely:[c] '*Our Father who art in heaven',* and not 'My father, Pietro di Bernardone.'* Look, not only do I return his money; I give him back all my clothes. I will go to the Lord naked."

Oh how free is the heart of a man for whom Christ is already enough!

The *man of God* was found to be wearing a hair shirt under his clothes, rejoicing in the reality of virtue rather than in its appearance.

His brother in the flesh, just like his father, hounded him with poisoned words.[d] One winter's morning, when he saw Francis praying, covered with pitiful rags and shivering with cold, that wicked man said to a neighbor: "Tell Francis that now he should be able to sell you a penny's worth of sweat!" When the *man of God* heard this, he was very happy, and answered with a smile: "Actually, I'll sell it at a higher price to my Lord!"

Nothing could have been closer to the truth!
He not only *received*
a hundredfold in this life,
but even a thousand times more,

---

a. For information concerning the bishop of Assisi, Bishop Guido II, see AP 17, *supra,* 41 d.

b. Cf. Gratian, *Decretum, C.* 14, q. 5, c. 1-5. Thomas's statement can be taken in two ways. (a) Francis should not use for sacred purposes what he has taken from his father without his consent; or, (b) Francis should not dedicate to a sacred purpose money that his father had acquired by cheating customers and sharp business practice. In either case, it is tainted money.

c. Thomas adds *libere* [freely] to this phrase, which he omits in 1C 15, prompting some to speculate that he echoes his description of Francis as *liber et liberalis* [free and freeing] found in 1C 120.

d. Cf. L3C 23.

Mt 19:29

and in the world to come *eternal life*
not only for himself,
but also for many others.

Chapter VIII
HOW HE OVERCAME FEELINGS OF SHAME,
AND HIS PROPHECY ABOUT THE POOR VIRGINS

1 Sm 2:27

Jas 3:1

Jer 23:9; Acts 2:13, 15

Gn 23:10

¹³ He struggled to turn his earlier, luxurious way of life in a differ-
ent direction, and to lead his unruly body back to its natural goodness.^a One day the *man of God* was going through Assisi begging oil to
fill the lamps in the church of San Damiano, which he was then rebuilding. He saw a crowd carousing by the house he intended to enter. Turning bright red, he backed away. But then, turning his noble
spirit toward heaven, he rebuked his cowardice and *called himself to
account.* He went back immediately to the house, and frankly explained to all of them what had made him ashamed. Then, *as if drunk
in the Spirit,*^b he spoke in French, and asked for oil, and he got it.^c He
fervently encouraged everyone to help repair that church, and *in front
of everyone* he cried out in French that some day that place would be a
monastery of Christ's holy virgins.^d

L3C 24

1C 18; LJS 13

L3C 24

Is 4:4

Ps 45:1

Whenever he was
filled with *the fire of the* Holy *Spirit*
he would speak in French,
bursting out in fiery *words,*
for he could foresee
that he would be honored
with special reverence by that people.

---

a. In this passage Thomas accents a theme found in Athanasius's *Life of Anthony* 20, that the return to natural goodness highlighted that the Lord "may recognize his work as being just the same as he made it." Athanasius, *Life of Anthony and The Letter to Marcellinus,* translation and introduction by Robert C. Gregg, preface by William A. Clebsch (New York, Ramsey, Toronto: Paulist Press, 1980), 47.
b. See the Ambrosian hymn *Splendor Paternae Gloriae,* for Monday Lauds in the Roman Office: *laeti bibamus sobriam ebrietatem Spiritus* [as joyful people, let us drink the sober drunkenness of the Spirit].
c. For the use of French see FA:ED I 194 b. Although this incident is found in L3C 24, Thomas emphasizes the role of the Holy Spirit in prompting Francis to burst into French.
d. Curiously, Clare's *Testament* refers to this same prophecy of Francis, but suggests that it was already a monastery. Cf. Clare, *Testament* 13 in *Clare of Assisi: Early Documents.*

Chapter IX
HOW HE BEGGED FOOD FROM DOOR TO DOOR.

[14]Once he began serving
the common Lord of all,
he loved doing what was common,
and avoided singularity in everything,
which reeks of every vice.[a]

L3C 22

He continued the sweaty work of repairing that church as Christ had commanded him, and from being over-delicate he changed into a rough and work-worn man. The priest who had that church saw him worn out with constant labor and, moved to piety, began to serve him each day some of his own food, although nothing very tasty, since he was poor. Francis appreciated the priest's concern and welcomed his kindness, but said to himself: "**You won't find a priest like this everywhere, always bringing you food! This is not the life for someone** professing **poverty;**[b] you'd better not get used to this, or you'll slowly return to what you've rejected, and you'll drift back to your easy ways! Get up, stop being lazy, and beg scraps from door to door!"

L3C 22

He went through Assisi **begging** leftovers **from door to door.** When he saw his bowl filled with all kinds of scraps, he was at first *struck with revulsion;* but he *remembered God* and, overcoming himself, ate it with spiritual relish.

Jb 7:4; Ps 77:4

Love softens all,[c]
and changes the bitter to sweet.

t 3; L3C 11; 2C 9

Chapter X
HOW BROTHER BERNARD GAVE AWAY HIS PROPERTY

1C 24; L3C 27

[15]Bernard from the town of Assisi, who later became a son of perfection, planned to reject the world perfectly, thanks to the example

---

a. *Singularitas* [singularity] is difficult to translate. In Thomas's use, it means being eccentric or odd, behaving in a way that draws attention to one's self. It does not speak against being an individual, as much as addressing individualism. It appears again in this text as a vice to be avoided, cf. 2C 14, 28, 29, 144, 162. It is a word that frequently appears in monastic writings in both positive and negative senses, cf. Jean Leclercq, *Études sur Le Vocabulaire Monastique du Moyen Âge* (Rome: Herder, 1961).

b. This is the first time that this specific, more canonical phrase, *paupertatem profitens* [professing poverty], is applied to Francis in the literature, and suggests a shift in emphasis from the practice of a virtue to a more canonical or juridical sense.

c. This echoes, by way of antithesis, the saying of Vergil: *Omnia vincit amor.* [Love conquers all], cf. Vergil, *Ecologues* X: 69.

of the *man of God*.[a] He humbly sought advice: "Father, **if someone** L3C 28
had held a certain lord's possessions for a long time, and **no longer**
wishes to keep them, what would be the best thing to do?" The *man*
of God replied that all those things should be returned to the lord who
gave them. Bernard said to him: "I know that everything I have was
given to me by God and on your advice I am now ready to return all to
Him." The saint replied: "If you want to prove your words with
deeds, let us go into the church tomorrow at dawn, take up the Gospel Book, and seek the counsel of Christ." *When morning had broken* AP 10; AP 11; L3
they went into the church and, after preparing with a devout prayer,
they opened the book of the Gospel, ready to act on **whatever coun-**
sel should first come to them. When they opened the book, **Christ** 1C 24,92,93
openly gave them His counsel: *If you wish to be perfect, go and sell* all
you own, and give to the poor.[b]

They repeated this a second time, and found: *Take nothing for your*
journey. They tried a third time, and found: *If anyone would follow me,*
let him deny himself. Bernard immediately carried out all these things,
without neglecting a single iota of this counsel. In a short time, many Off Vesp 1 IV
turned away from the weary cares of the world toward an infinite
Good, *returning to their homeland* with Francis as their guide. It would
take too long to describe how each of them attained *the prize of their*
heavenly calling.

1 Sm 2:27

1 Sm 2:27

Rom 15:15

Mt 27:1

2 Chr 10:6

Mt 9:21

Lk 9:3

Lk 9:23; Mt 16:24

Gn 30:25

Phil 3:14

Chapter XI
HOW HE TOLD A PARABLE IN THE PRESENCE OF THE LORD POPE

[16]When he presented himself and his followers before Pope Inno- 1C 32-33; //LJS 2
cent to request a rule for his life,[c] it seemed to the pope that their proposal for a way of life was beyond their strength. A man of great
discernment, he said to Francis: "My son, pray to Christ that through
you he may show us his will, so that, once we know it, we may confidently approve your holy desire." The saint accepted the command of
the supreme shepherd and hurried to Christ. He prayed intently, and
devoutly exhorted his companions to appeal to God.

---

a. Cf. FA:ED I 203 d.

b. The AP 10, L3C 28 describe two men going with Francis to consult the Gospels, Bernard and Peter.
   In this text, Thomas mentions only Bernard that underscores his role as the first-born and the
   exemplar of the brothers.

c. The Latin text, *ad petendam regulam* [to seek a rule], refers to seeking recognition or approval of his
   proposal. *Regula* [rule] in this context does not refer to either the *Earlier Rule* or the *Later Rule*.
   Furthermore, Francis is not asking for a rule as much as a ruling on his proposal.

What next? In praying, the answer came to him and he told his sons the *news of salvation*. Thus, Christ's familiar speaking *in parables* is recognizable.[a]

Acts 13:26; Mt 13:3

AP 35; //L3C 50

"Francis," He said, "say this to the pope: 'Once upon a time there was a poor but lovely woman who lived in a desert. A king fell in love with her because of her great beauty; he gladly betrothed her and with her had lovely children. When they had grown up, having been nobly raised, their mother said: "Dear children, do not be ashamed because you are poor, for you are all children of a great king. Go joyfully to his court, and ask him for what you need." Hearing this they were amazed and overjoyed. At the thought of being royalty, their spirits were lifted. Knowing they would be the king's heirs, *they reckoned* all their poverty *riches*. They presented themselves boldly to the king: they were not afraid to look at him since they bore his very image. When the king saw his likeness in them, he was surprised, and asked whose sons they might be. When they said they were the children of the poor woman who lived in the desert, the king embraced them. "You are my *heirs*," he said, *"and my sons; have no fear!* If strangers are fed at my table, it is only right that I feed you; for by law my whole inheritance belongs to you." The king then sent orders to the woman to send all his sons to be fed at his court."' This parable made the saint happy, and he promptly reported this holy message to the pope.[b]

Tb 5:25

Rom 8:17; Mt 14:27; 17:7

[17]Francis himself was this woman, not because he was soft in his deeds,[c] but because he was fruitful and bore many children. The desert was the world, which was then wild and sterile, with no teaching of virtue. The many beautiful children were the large number of brothers, *clothed with* every *virtue*. The king was the Son of God, whom they resemble by their holy poverty. They were fed *from the king's table*, refusing to be ashamed of their lowliness, when, in imita-

1C 36, 37

2 Mc 3:26

Dn 1:8

---

a. The story or "exemplum" of Odo of Cheriton in 1219 is similar to this story, as it is to AP 34. Each instance, however, has its own nuances, prompting scholars to suggest that the story was passed by word of mouth and adapted to fit the circumstances in which it is told. Cf. FA:ED I 590-591; AP 34, infra p. 50; Jacques Dalarun, *La Malavventura di Francesco d'Assisi* (Milano: Edizioni Biblioteca Francescana, 1996), 61-63.

b. Cf. AP 35.

c. The Latin reads: *non factorum mollitie* [not soft in deeds]. Isidore of Seville (+636) taught in *Etymologies*, XI:2,18, *Mulier a mollitie, tamquam mollier, detracta littera . . . appellatur est* [Woman is taken from the word softness, as she is called soft]; and *Etymologies* X, 180 *Mollis . . . quasi mulier molliatur* [Woman as if a woman were softened]. In light of this, Thomas does a word play: *mulier . . . mollitie*.

tion of Christ,[a] they were content to live on alms and realized that because of the world's contempt they would be blessed.

The lord pope was amazed at *the parable presented* to him, and recognized without a doubt that Christ *had spoken in* this *man*. He remembered a vision he had seen only a *few days earlier*, and *instructed by the Holy Spirit*, he now believed it would come true in this man. *He saw in a dream* the Lateran basilica almost ready to fall down. A religious man, *small and scorned*, was propping it up with his own bent back so it would not fall.[b] "I'm sure," he said, "he is the one who will hold up Christ's Church by what he does and what he teaches!" Because of this the lord pope easily bowed to his request; from then on, filled with devotion to God, he always loved *Christ's servant* with a special love.[c] He quickly granted what was asked and promised even more.

Visiting *towns and villages,*
Francis began, with the authority now granted him,
to preach passionately
and to scatter the seeds of virtue.

Chapter XII
SAINT MARY OF THE PORTIUNCULA
HOW THE SAINT LOVED THIS PLACE,
HOW THE BROTHERS LIVED THERE, AND HOW THE BLESSED VIRGIN LOVED IT

[18]Francis, *the servant of God,*
was *small* in stature,
humble in attitude,
and *lesser* by profession.
While living in the world
he *chose* a little portion *of the world*

Side references: Mt 13:24; Acts 23:9; Acts 25:13; Lk 12:12; Gn 28:12; Is 16:14; 53:3; Rom 1:1; Jas 8:31; Mt 9:35; 2 Chr 29:9; Is 16:14; Mt 11:29; Lk 9:48; Jn 15:19; L3C 51; 1C 33; L3C 49; 1C 62; 1C 83; 1C 38; AC 56

a. The Latin text reads: *in imitatione Christi*, the only reference to this theme of spirituality found in the writings of Thomas of Celano. In 1C 25, Francis is described as "an imitator of those whom the Jewish leaders considered ignorant and without learning." In 2C 109 Sylvester becomes "a perfect imitator of the man of God," i.e. Francis. For its importance, see Alfonso Marini, " '*Vestigia Christi Sequi*' or '*Imitatio Christi*': Two Different Ways of Understanding Francis of Assisi's Gospel Life," GR 11:3 (1997), 331-358. For development of this Christological theme in Thomas, see Duane Lapsanski, *Evangelical Perfection: An Historical Examination of the Concept in the Early Franciscan Sources* (St. Bonaventure, NY: Franciscan Institute Publications, 1977), 103-105; 135-138.

b. The Latin text, *proprio dorso submisso, ne caderet, sustentabat* [propping it up with his own bent back so it would not fall], includes the notion of submission in order to hold up. In the next sentence, the pope bows to Francis's request. Compare 1C 33 where Thomas writes that Innocent, "a very high and lofty tree in the world, bent himself so kindly to his wish and request."

c. See L3C 51. The Quaracchi editors note that in Thomas's text, there is an addition to the Dominican text that Francis is "small and scorned" and will hold up the Church "by what he does and by what he teaches." Cf. AF X 141, note 8.

for himself and his followers,
since he could not serve Christ
unless he had something of this world.

1C 21,22; LJS 14 Since ancient times, prophetically,
this place was called "the Little Portion,"[a]
since it was the *lot ceded*   Jos 17:8
to those who wished to hold nothing of this world.
In this place
there was a church built for the Virgin Mother,
who by her unique *humility*   Lk 1:48
deserved, after her Son, to be the head of all the saints.
1C 44, 57 It is here the Order of Lesser Ones
had its beginning.
As their numbers increased,
there "a noble structure arose
1C 38 *upon* their solid *foundation."*   Eph 2:20-21
The saint loved this place more than any other.[b]
1C 106; LJS 68 He commanded his brothers
to venerate it with special reverence.
He wanted it, like a mirror of the Order,[c]
always preserved in humility and *highest poverty*,   2 Cor 8:2
and therefore kept its ownership in the hands of others,
keeping for himself and his brothers only the use of it.[d]

1C 39-41; 51-54 [19]There the most rigid discipline was kept in all things: as much in silence and in labor as in other religious observances.[e] The entrance there was not open except to specially selected brothers, gathered from every region, whom the saint wanted to be truly devoted to God and perfect in every respect. Similarly, entrance was completely

---

a. Cf. FA:ED I 201b; AC 56.

b. This description of the Portiuncula is first found in L3C 13, "this is the place which the glorious Virgin loved more than any other church in the world." A similar passage is also found in AC 56. In this passage, however, it is Francis, not the Virgin, who loves the church more than any other.

c. The use of *speculum* [mirror] is significant. Medieval authors saw the mirror as signifying a tableau, a portrait, or a description upon which a bystander could gaze and receive information or norms for everyday life. In 1C 90, it is Francis who is identified as a mirror for those who wish to "learn all perfection." In this passage it is the Portiuncula that is placed as the mirror of the Gospel life. See Margo Schmidt, "Miroir," *Dictionnaire de spiritualité ascétique et mystique, doctrine et histoire* XII (Paris: Beauchesne, 1986), 1290-1303; Ritamary Bradley, "Backgrounds of the Title *Speculum* in Medieval Literature," *Speculum* (1954): 100-115.

d. This paragraph reflects the later juridical vocabulary used by Pope Gregory IX in *Quo elongati* in 1230, which introduced the juridical distinction between "ownership" and "use," cf. FA:ED I 570-575. In another papal bull, *Ordinem Vestrum* (1245) of Innocent IV (1243-1254), the Pope assumed ownership of all movable and immovable goods of the Order, except in those cases where the donors reserved the right of ownership explicitly to themselves.

e. This text focuses on rigorous discipline and, as such, introduces a theme more reflective of the tensions of the fraternity of the 1240's than that of 1210.

forbidden to any secular person. He did not want the brothers dwelling there—always kept below a certain number—to have their *ears
itching* for worldly news and, interrupting their contemplation of
heavenly things, to be dragged down to dealing with lower things by
the talk of gossips. No one was allowed to speak *idle words* there, nor
to repeat those spoken by others. And, if anyone happened to do this,
punishment taught him to avoid *further harm* and not to repeat this *in
the future. Day and night, without interruption,* those living in the place
were engaged in the praises of God and, scented with a wonderful
fragrance, they led the life of angels.[a] This was only right! According
to the stories of the old neighbors, that church used to be called *by another name,* "Saint Mary of the Angels." As the blessed Father used to
say, God revealed to him, that among all other churches built in her
honor throughout the world, the blessed Virgin cherished that
church *with special affection.* For that reason the saint also *loved it more
than all others.*

2 Tm 4:3

Mt 12:36

1 Sm 27:4; Eccl 4:13

*Acts 12:5;
1 Thes 2:13; 5:17*

Gn 48:7

L3C 56

*1 Pt 1:22
2 Cor 12:13; Gn 37:4*

Chapter XIII
A VISION

[20]Before his conversion, a brother dedicated to God had a vision
about this church which is worth telling. He saw countless people
sadly *stricken with blindness, on their knees* in a circle around this
church, with their faces raised to heaven. All of them, with sobbing
voices and *upraised hands,* were *crying out to God* begging for mercy and
light. Then a great light came down from heaven and, diffusing itself
through them, gave each the sight and health they desired.

L3C 56

Gn 19:11; 2 Chr 6:13

2 Mc 14:34; Ps 55:17

1C 106

THE WAY OF LIFE OF SAINT FRANCIS AND THE BROTHERS

Chapter XIV
THEIR STRICT DISCIPLINE

[21]The resolute *knight of Christ* never spared his body. As if it were a
stranger to him, he exposed it to every kind of injury, whether in
word or deed. If anyone tried to enumerate everything this man un-
derwent, the list would be longer than that passage where the apostle recounts the tribulations of the saints.

2 Tm 2:3

AC 50

*2 Cor 11:23-29;
Hb 11:33-38*

---

a. For reference to "angelic life," cf. FA:ED I 273 a.

Those enrolled in that first school also subjected themselves to every discomfort. It was even considered criminal to seek any *consolation* except that *of the spirit*. Wearing iron belts and breastplates they grew weak from constant *fasting* and *frequent vigils*. They would have collapsed many times, were it not for their devoted shepherd's constant warnings that made them relax the rigors of their self-denial.

Acts 9:31
2 Cor 11:27

1C 40

Chapter XV
THE DISCERNMENT OF SAINT FRANCIS[a]

AC 50

²²**One night** while all were sleeping, **one** of his flock **cried out:** "Brothers! I'm dying! I'm dying of hunger!" At once that extraordinary shepherd got up, and hurried to treat the sick lamb with the right medicine. He ordered them to set the table, although filled with everyday fare. Since there was no wine—as often happened—they made do with water. Francis started eating first. Then, he invited the rest of the brothers to do the same, for charity's sake, so their brother would not be embarrassed.

Once *they had taken their food in the fear of the Lord*, so that nothing would be lacking in this act of charity, the father wove for his sons a long parable about the virtue of discernment. He ordered them to *season with salt every sacrifice to God*. With concern he reminded them that in offering *service to God each one should consider his own strength*.

Acts 2:46, 9:31
Lv 2:13
Jn 16:12

He insisted that it was just as much a sin to deprive the body without discernment of what it really needed as, prompted by gluttony, to offer it too much. And he added: "Dear brothers, realize that, what I just did by eating was not my own choice, but an exception,[b] demanded by fraternal charity. Let the charity, not the food, be an example for you, for the latter feeds the belly while the former feeds the spirit."

---

a. The Latin word *discretio* is translated as discernment. Benedicta Ward notes: "Since the eighteenth century, 'discretion' has been increasingly used in connection with good behavior, especially in speech, but earlier it was synonymous with 'discernment', both coming from *'discretio'* the Latin form of *'diakresis.'* " Cf. Benedicta Ward, "Discernment: A Rare Bird," in *The Way Supplement* 64 (1989): 10-18.

b. The Latin word *dispensatio* [*exception*] is used in a sense close to *epikeia*, exceptions to a rule that in itself is good.

Chapter XVI
HOW HE FORESAW THE FUTURE
AND HOW HE COMMENDED THE ORDER TO THE ROMAN CHURCH
AND OF A VISION HE HAD

²³As the holy father advanced in virtue and merit of life
his large crop of children
increased everywhere in number and grace.
With an amazing abundance of fruit,
their *branches extended to the farthest ends of the earth*.

1C 37, 89, 100

Ez 17:6,7; Ps 19:5

But he often worried about those *new plants*, how they could be
cared for and helped to grow, tied together in a *bond of unity*. He saw
that many people howled *like wolves* at that *little flock. Those grown old
in wickedness* would take every opportunity to hurt it just because it
was new. He could foresee that even his sons might do things opposed to holy peace and unity. He feared that some might turn into
rebels, as often happens among the chosen, *puffed up by their
self-importance*, ready for battle and prone to scandals.

Ps 144:12
Eph 4:3
Mt 7:15; Lk 12:32; Dn 13:52
Col 2:18
1C 74

²⁴Mulling over these things, the *man of God saw this vision*. As he
slept one night, he saw a small black *hen*, similar to a common
dove, with feathered legs and feet. She had countless *chicks*, and
they kept running around her frantically, but she could not *gather* all
of them *under her wings*. The *man of God woke up*, remembering his
concerns, *interpreted* his own *vision*. "I am the hen," he said, "small in
size and dark by nature, whose innocence of life should serve
dove-like simplicity, which is as rare in this world as it is swift in
flight to heaven. The chicks are the brothers, multiplied in number
and grace. The strength of Francis is not enough to defend them
from *human plotting* and *contradicting tongues*.

1 Kgs 13:1; Dn 10:7
Mt 23:37; Lk 13:34
1 Kgs 13:1; Mt 1:24
Dn 8:27
Ps 31:21
L3C 63

"Therefore, I will go and entrust them to the holy Roman Church.
The evil-minded will be struck down by the rod of her power. The *sons
of God* will enjoy *complete freedom*, which will help to increase eternal
salvation everywhere. From now on, let the children acknowledge
their mother's sweet favor, and always follow her holy footprints
with special devotion. With her protection, *nothing evil* will happen to
the Order, and no *son of Belial* will trample the *vineyard of the Lord* unpunished. She, that holy one, will emulate the glory of our poverty
and will prevent the praises of humility from being obscured by

Mt 5-9
Col 2:19; Gal 4:31
1 Kgs 5:4
Dt 13:13; 1 Sm 2:12; 25:17; Is 5:17
L3C 63

clouds of pride. She will *preserve* intact among us the *bonds of charity and peace,* striking dissidents with harsh punishments. In her sight the sacred observance of the purity of the Gospel will constantly flourish and she will not allow the *sweet fragrance of* their *life* to vanish even *for an hour."*

This was the saint's full intent in embracing this submission; this is precious proof of the man of God's foreknowledge of the need for this protection in the future.

Chapter XVII
HOW HE ASKED FOR THE LORD OF OSTIA
TO BE HIS OWN POPE

[25]When the *man of God* came to Rome, the Lord Pope Honorius and all the cardinals received him with great respect. For what his reputation proclaimed shone forth in his life and resounded in his speech and, when he was present, there was no room for anything but devotion. With conviction and passion he preached before the pope and the cardinals, letting whatever the Spirit moved him to say *pour out* from the *fullness* of his heart. Those *mountains were moved*[a] at his words and, sighing *from the depths* they washed their *inner selves* with tears.

When he had finished preaching, he exchanged a few brief and friendly words with the lord pope. Finally he made this request: "As you know, my lord, it is not easy for poor and unimportant men to gain access to such majesty. You hold the world in your hands, and the pressure of important business does not allow you time to look after little things. For this reason, my lord," he said," I beg your holiness to give us the lord of Ostia as pope. That way, while always saving your preeminent dignity, the brothers can turn to him *in their hour of need,* to benefit from his protection and direction."

The pope *looked with pleasure* on this holy request. He immediately set Lord Hugo, then bishop of Ostia, over the religion, as the *man of God had requested.* That holy cardinal embraced the flock entrusted to

Col 3:14; Eph 4:3

2 Cor 2:15

Sir 33:9; 2 Cor 7:8

Jdgs 13:6

1C 73; L3C 64

Ps 45:2; Ps 18:8; Is 54:10
Ps 130:1; Rom 7:22; Eph 3:16

L3C 65

Sir 8:12

1C 100; AP 45   2 Kgs 10:30

Jdgs 13:6

AP 43

---

a. Medieval exegesis often interpreted the "mountains" as symbols of the apostles, e.g. Augustine, " . . . we understand the mountains to represent certain illustrious people, great spiritual men in the Church, people who are great because of their massive worth; they are the prophets, the evangelists, the good teachers." Augustine, *Exposition of Psalm 39,* 6; see also, *Exposition on Psalm 35, 9; Exposition on Psalm 45,* 6. Augustine, *Exposition on The Psalms,* translated by Maria Boulding (Hyde Park: New City Press, 2000).

him. He became its diligent foster father and, to the day of his blessed passing,[a] he remained both its shepherd and its foster child.

Because of this unique submission, the holy Roman Church never ceases to show its preferential love and concern for the Order of Lesser Ones.

Here ends the first book.

---

a. Cardinal Hugolino, Pope Gregory IX, died on August 22, 1241.

The Second Book

²⁶To preserve the great deeds of ancestors for the remembrance of their children, gives honor to the former, and shows love in the latter. The ancestors, separated by the passage of time, offer their children a memorable witness. Those who did not know them in their bodily presence are at least spurred to do good by their deeds and encouraged to do better. The first benefit we receive—and a great one—is knowledge of our own smallness. We see their merits abound while ours can hardly be found.

1C 90

I consider blessed Francis the holiest *mirror* of the holiness of the Lord,[b] the *image of his* perfection. I think everything about him, both his words and deeds, is fragrant with God's presence. Anyone who studies them humbly and diligently, will quickly be filled with the teaching of salvation, ready for the saint's highest philosophy.

Wis 7:26

1C 91

1C Prol

I will recount a few things about him in a brief and simple style. I think it may be appropriate to mention a few of the many things that will honor the saint and rouse our dozing hearts.

Chapter I
THE SPIRIT OF PROPHECY
WHICH BLESSED FRANCIS POSSESSED

²⁷Elevated above what is of the world, our blessed father,
with a wonderful power,
had everything on earth subject to him.
His mind's eye was always fixed
on the highest Light.

1C 26-27

He not only knew by divine revelation what was going to happen
and foretold many things
in the spirit of prophecy;

Rv 19:10

1C 48

he even probed *the secrets of the heart,*
knew events from afar,

1 Cor 14:25

---

a. See 2C 3, supra, 241 a.
b. Cf. 2C 18, footnote on mirror, supra, 175 c.

foresaw, and foretold things to come.[a]
These examples will prove what we say.   1C 30,49-50

Chapter II
HOW HE KNEW SOMEONE CONSIDERED HOLY WAS A FRAUD

[28]There was a brother who, to all appearances, led a life of extraor-   AC 116
dinary holiness, but who stood out for his singular ways.[b] He *spent all*
his time in prayer, and kept such strict silence that he used to make his
confession by gestures instead of words. He took in the words of
Scripture with such great fervor that on hearing them he gave signs
of feeling great sweetness. What more shall I say? Everyone considered him holy three times over.

It happened that the blessed father came to that place to see and
hear this holy brother. While *everyone* was commending and *praising*
the man, our father replied: "Brothers, stop! Don't sing me the
praises of his devilish illusions. *You should know the truth.* **This is dia-**
bolical temptation, deception and fraud. I am sure about this. And
the fact that he won't go to confession proves it."

The brothers *took this very hard,* especially the saint's vicar.[c] "How
can this be true?" they asked. "How can lies and such deception be
disguised under all these signs of perfection?" "Tell him to go to confession twice or even once a week," the father said. "If he doesn't do
it, **you will know what I said is true.**"

The vicar *took* the brother *aside.* He first chatted pleasantly with
him, finally telling him to go to confession. He spat back, put his *fin-*
ger to his mouth, and shook his head, showing he would never make
his confession. The brothers were speechless, fearing the scandal of a
false saint. **A few days later** he left religion on his own, turned back
to the world and *returned to his vomit.* Finally, after doing even worse
things, he was deprived of both repentance and life.

Left margin references:
1 Cor 7:5
Lk 4:15
Mt 22:16
Gn 21:11
Jn 5:32
Lk 9:10
Jb 21:5, 29:9
Prv 26:11, 2 Pt 2:22

---

a. The first section of this Second Book, The Spirit of Prophecy (27-54), greatly expands on 1C 26-28.
   While the prophet may more generally be defined as any "inspired person who believes that he has
   been sent by God with a message to tell," the medieval Christian tradition understood that person
   differently, as "one who foretells the future, or the one who seeks to correct a present situation in the
   light of an ideal past or glorious future." In the apocalyptic milieu of his times, it is understandable
   that Thomas presents Francis in this light. Cf. Bernard McGinn, *Visions of the End: Apocalyptic*
   Traditions in the Middle Ages (New York: Columbia University Press, 1979), esp. 1-36.

b. Cf. 2C 14, supra, 171 a.

c. The "saint's vicar" is Elias who is named ten times in 1C and not once in 2C or 3C. Since these two
   works were written after Elias had fallen out of the brothers' favor and was subsequently deposed as
   General Minister in 1239, it is understandable that Thomas would not place him in a prominent
   position in his later writings. Cf. Rosalind B. Brooke, *Early Franciscan Government: From Elias to*
   Bonaventure (Cambridge: Cambridge University Press, 1959).

Beware of singularity:
it is nothing but a beautiful abyss.[a]
Experience shows that many who seem so unique
rise up to the heavens,
and then fall into the depths.   Ps 107:26
Realize the power of a good confession.
It is both a cause and sign of holiness.

Chapter III
AGAINST SINGULARITY
A SIMILAR CASE

[29]Something similar happened with another brother named Thomas of Spoleto. Everyone had a good opinion of him, firmly convinced of his holiness. Our holy father considered him wicked; and his later apostasy confirmed this. He did not remain long, for no false show of virtue can last. He left religion, and when he died outside it, he must have realized then what he had done.

Chapter IV
HOW HE FORETOLD THE MASSACRE OF CHRISTIANS AT DAMIETTA

[30] When the Christian army was besieging Damietta,[b] the *holy man of God* was there with his companions,[c] since they had crossed the sea in their fervor for martyrdom. When the holy man heard that our forces *were preparing* for war, *on the day of battle* he grieved deeply. He said to his companion: "If the battle happens on this day *the Lord has shown me* that *it will not go well* for the Christians. But *if I say* this, they will take me for a fool, and *if I keep silent* my conscience won't leave me alone. What do you think I should do?" His companion *replied:* "Father, don't give *the least* thought *to how people judge you.* This wouldn't be the first time people took you for a fool. Unburden your conscience, and *fear God rather than men.*"

The saint leapt to his feet, and rushed to the Christians crying out warnings to save them, forbidding war and threatening disaster. But they took the truth *as a joke.* They *hardened* their *hearts* and refused to

Margin references: 1C 57; LJS 36; 2 Kgs 2:4; Prv 21:31; 2 Kgs 8:10; Nm 14:41; Jb 16:7; Lk 3:16; 1 Cor 4:3; 1C 11; Lk 12:4-5; Acts 5:29; Tb 3:4; Ex 4:21; Jn 12:40

---

a. 2C 14, supra, 171 a.

b. The siege took place on August 29, 1219 during the Fifth Crusade. Francis had left for the Orient in early June, arriving there before August 29. See 1C 57, FA:ED I 231.

c. Jordan of Giano identifies the companions as Elias, Peter of Catanio, and Caesar of Speyer among his companions, cf. infra ChrJG 11, 12 14; Bonaventure also identifies Illuminato as one of these companions, LMj IX 8.

turn back. They charged, they attacked, they fought, and then the enemy struck back.

Nm 22:20-1 In that moment of battle, filled with suspense, the holy man made his companion *get up to look.* The first and the second time he got up, he saw nothing, so Francis told him to look a third time. What Jer 49:24 a sight! The whole Christian army was in *retreat fleeing* from the battle carrying not triumph but shame. The massacre was so great that between the dead and the captives the number of our forces was diminished by six thousand. Compassion for them drove the holy man, no less than regret, for what they had done overwhelmed them. He wept especially for the Spaniards: he could see their boldness in battle had left only a few of them alive.[a]

1 Chr 28:21; Ps 19:5   *Let the princes of the whole world take note* of this,
                             and let them know:
Sir 46:8   *it is not easy to fight against God,*
2 Cor 8:5   that is, against *the will of the Lord.*
                 Stubborn insolence usually ends in disaster.
                             It relies on its own strength,
                       thus forfeiting the help of heaven.
                  If victory is to be expected from on high,
          then battles must be entrusted to the divine Spirit.

Chapter V
HOW HE KNEW SECRETS OF A BROTHER'S HEART

[31]As the holy man was returning from overseas, with Brother   AC 72
Leonard of Assisi as his companion, he rode on a donkey for a while,
Jn 4:6 because he was weak and *tired from his journey.* His companion
Rom 6:19 walked behind, and was also quite tired. *Thinking in human terms,* he
Lk 7:39 *began to say to himself:* "His parents and mine did not socialize as

---

a. The bull, *Supplicasti nobis,* Honorius III of March 15, 1219, to the Archbishop of Toledo, identifies the role of the Spaniards in this Crusade. "Since many of those who throughout Spain had taken upon themselves the sign of the Cross in support of the Holy Land, could be of no or little help there in comparison to the help that they would lend in Spain fighting against the Moors; you asked us that you be allowed to relieve such persons of their apostolic obligations. Consequently, by the authority of the present document, we allow you to relieve such persons freely of their vows concerning the aforesaid undertaking, however, with the exception of the lords and knights whom we, until a certain point in time, do not want to be relieved of the vows that they have made in support of the Holy Land, unless perhaps some unless frail or poor that their journey to the Holy Land would seem useless: whom you can nevertheless relieve of their vows, provided that they designate some of their goods, in accordance with your judgment and advice, as well as according to their own capacities, for the purpose of supporting the Holy Land. Given at the Lateran on the Ides of March, in the third year of our Pontificate." Cf. AFH 16 (1923): 245-246.

equals[a], and here he is riding while I am on foot leading this donkey." *As he was thinking this,* the holy man immediately got off the donkey. "No, brother," he said. "It is not right that I should ride while you go on foot, for in the world you were more noble and influential than I." The brother was *completely astonished,* and *overcome with embarrassment:* he knew the saint had caught him. He fell down at his feet and, *bathed* in tears, he exposed his naked thought and begged forgiveness.[b]

Mt 1:20

Est 7:6; Nm 12:14

Est 8:3

Lk 7:38, 44

Chapter VI
HOW HE SAW A DEVIL OVER A BROTHER,
AND AGAINST THOSE WHO DRAW AWAY FROM UNITY

[32]There was another brother esteemed by the people for his good reputation. Because of his holiness, he was even more esteemed before God. The father of all *envy* was jealous of his virtue. He planned to *cut down this tree* which already *touched the heavens* and to snatch the crown from his hands. He scavaged, searched, shredded, and sifted everything about that brother, looking for the right way to make him stumble. He stirred up in him, under the appearance of greater perfection, a yearning to isolate himself. Then that jealous one could swoop down on him while he was alone and quickly make him fall. And *if someone falls while alone, there is no one to lift him up.*

What happened?

Separating himself from the religion of the brothers, he went about the world *as a guest and a pilgrim.* He wore a short tunic made from his habit and a hood not sown to the tunic; and, in this way, he wandered the countryside, despising himself in all things. *As he went about* in this way, *it came to pass,* that all divine comfort was taken from him. Soon he was awash in the waves of temptation. *The waters climbed up into his soul.* Desolate in body and spirit, he marched on *like a bird that hurries toward a snare.* Already near the abyss he was driven to the brink. Then *for his own good, the eye* of fatherly Providence *looked* mercifully on this miserable man. *In his panic* he regained

Wis 2:24

Dn 4:11; Gn 28:12

Eccl 4:10

SC 11

LR VI 2; Test 24

Heb 11:13

Lk 8:42

Lk 2:1

Ps 69:2

Prv 7:23

Sir 11:13

Is 28:19

---

a. The Latin text reads: *Non ludebat de pare parentes huius et mei* [His parents and mine did not socialize as equals]. Thomas's allusion seems to be to Horace's *Satires* Book II, satire 3, line 248, where children are said to play *par impar,* which seems to refer to a game called "odds and evens," but which could also be rendered "equal with unequal." Leonard obviously must have come from the kind of family that would not have let its children play with such as Francis's social class, mere merchants.

b. In light of AC 73, the story may have been given as testimony to the pope and cardinals during a canonical process on the holiness of Francis. In AC 73, the narration of this story concludes: "Indeed when the brothers in Assisi petitioned the Lord Pope Gregory and the cardinal to canonize blessed Francis, the brothers gave witness to this incident before the Lord Pope and the cardinals."

Acts 12:11
Ps 35:3

understanding. Coming to his senses, he said: "Oh, miserable one! Go back to religion! That's where *your salvation* is." Immediately he jumped up and ran to his mother's lap.

Phil 2:23
Mk 14:52

³³He went to the brothers' place in Siena, and Saint Francis was staying there. *As soon as* he *saw* that brother—and this is extraordinary—the saint *ran away from him* and quickly closed himself in a cell. The brothers were thrown into confusion and wondered why he ran away. "Why are you surprised that I ran away?" the saint asked. "Didn't you see the cause? I fled to the protection of prayer to set free the one who strayed. I saw in my son something that displeased me, and rightly so. But now, by the grace of my Christ, the whole delusion has vanished."

Prv 18:24

The brother fell on his knees and declared with shame that he was guilty. "May God be kind to you, brother," the saint said to him. "But I warn you: Never again separate yourself from religion and your brothers, under some pretext of holiness." From then on that brother became a *friend of company* and camaraderie. He was especially devoted to those groups where regular observance flourished.[a]

Ps 111:1-2

Wis 3:5; Ps 145:14

Prv 27:17

Prv 18:19

Lk 19:3

Rv 2:10

> *Great are the works of the Lord*
> *in the gathering and the assembly of the just!*
> There *the shaken* are held,
> *the fallen are lifted*
> and the lukewarm are roused;
> there *iron sharpens iron*
> and a *brother helped by his brother,*
> stands *like a strong city.*
> And even if you cannot see Jesus because of
> *the* worldly *crowds,*
> the heavenly crowd of angels[b]
> will never block your view.
> Just do not run away!
> *Be faithful unto death*
> *and you will receive the crown of life.*

---

a. Thomas does not write of *regularis observantia* [regular observance] except in this passage. The phrase connotes the exact and conscientious observance of the *regula* [rule]. It was frequently used in the context of the Cistercian reform in which the authentic or regular observance of the *Rule of Saint Benedict* was a burning issue. Cf. Louis J. Lekai, *The Cistercians: Ideals and Reality* (Kent State: Kent State University Press, 1977).

b. Cf. Easter Proclamation: *Exultet iam angelica turba caelorum* [Let the angelic crowd of heaven now rejoice]. References to the Easter Proclamation are also found in 1C 85, 119, 126.

[34] A little time later something similar happened to someone else. One of the brothers would not submit to the saint's vicar, but followed a different brother as his master. The saint was there at the time, and sent him a warning by means of a messenger. The brother at once cast himself at the feet of the vicar and, rejecting his earlier master, obeyed the one whom the saint had made his prelate.[a] The saint took a deep breath and said to the companion who had been sent as his messenger: "Brother, I saw the devil perched on the back of that disobedient brother holding him tightly by the neck. With a rider like that on him, he spit out the bit of obedience, and gave free rein to his own will. But when *I prayed to the Lord* for that brother, suddenly all confused the devil retreated."

This man was full of insight. His eyesight for physical things was weak, for spiritual things it was very sharp. Is it any wonder that one who refused to carry the *Lord of majesty* was burdened by this filthy baggage?

2 Cor 12:8

Is 3:8

> I tell you: there is no middle ground.
> Either carry the *burden that is light*
> —which rather carries you—
> or *evil will sit upon you like a lead weight,*
> like *a millstone*[b] *hung around your neck.*

Mt 11:30

Zec 5:7-8

Mt 18:6

Chapter VII
HOW HE FREED THE PEOPLE OF GRECCIO
FROM ATTACKS BY WOLVES AND FROM HAILSTORMS

[35] The saint used to enjoy staying in the brothers' place at Greccio. He found it rich in poverty and there, in a remote little cell on a cliff, he could give himself freely to heavenly things. This is the place where he had earlier recalled the birth of the *Child of Bethlehem*, becoming a child with the Child.

1C 84-86

1 Sm 16:18

Now, it happened that the people there had been stricken by multiple disasters. A pack of raging wolves devoured not only animals, but even people. And every year hailstorms destroyed their wheat

AC 74

---

a. The term *praelatus* [prelate] is used more extensively in 2C where it appears seventeen times. In 1C, the term appears only four times. Cf. FA:ED I 130 a.

b. The Latin reads: *molla asinaria* [millstone] and refers to the stone of a mill turned by the labor of an ass.

fields and **vineyards.** One day, while preaching to them, blessed

Wis 7:25

Francis said: **"To the praise and honor** of *Almighty* **God,** listen to the

Ps 30:10; 1 Jn 1:9

truth which I *proclaim* to you. If each of you *will confess your sins,* and

Lk 3:8

bear worthy fruit of genuine repentance, I swear to you that all these di-

Ex 14:24; Ps 11:4

sasters will cease, and *the Lord looking down upon you, will multiply your*

Jer 28:17; Acts 17:3

earthly goods. But also hear this," he said. *"I tell you* again, if you are un-

Prv 26:11; 2 Pt 2:22

grateful for these gifts, and *return to your vomit,* the disasters will re-

Jos 22:18

turn, the punishment will double, and greater *wrath* will *rage* against you."

³⁶**And so it happened: at that very hour** the disasters **ceased,** and through the merits and prayers of our holy father, all dangers van-

Dn 3:50

ished.[a] The wolves and hailstorms *caused no more harm.* And even more remarkable, whenever the hail, falling on neighboring fields, reached the boundaries of Greccio, either it would stop or move off in a different direction.

AC 74

Wis 11:4; Ps 107:38; Tb 12:3

So they *received relief, increased greatly,* and *overflowed* with earthly

Jb 15:27; 21:24

goods. But prosperity had its usual effect: either *their faces grew bloated,*

Tb 2:10

or *the dung* of earthly riches *blinded them* even more. They fell back to

Ps 106:21

ways worse than before, *forgetting the God who had saved them.* But they did not go unpunished. Divine justice punishes one who falls less se-

Sir 36:6

verely than one who repeats an earlier fall. *The wrath* of God *flared up* against them. The evils which had departed returned. The sword of human violence was now added, and a decree of death from heaven

Rv 8:7

devoured them. In the end the whole town *was burned to the ground* by flames of vengeance.

It is only just
that those who turned their backs on such gifts
should come to destruction.

Chapter VIII
HOW HE FORETOLD CIVIL WAR AMONG THE PEOPLE OF PERUGIA
WHEN HE PREACHED TO THEM,
AND HOW HE RECOMMENDED UNITY

³⁷Some days later, as our blessed father was coming down from that cell, he complained to the brothers who were with him: "The people of Perugia have done many evil things to their neighbors, and

AC 75

Jer 8:11; Ez 28:2-6

to their disgrace their *heart has grown proud.* But now there comes the

Jer 46:10; Jer 15:2

vengeance of God, whose hand is already *upon the sword."*

---

a. Thomas repeats part of Responsory VIII of *The Rhymed Office of Saint Anthony* by Julian of Speyer: *"Pereunt pericula, cessat et necessitas"* [Dangers vanish and necessity ceases].

After a few days had passed, with his soul on fire, he got up and set out for the city of Perugia.

The brothers clearly thought that he had seen some vision in his cell. Arriving in Perugia he began to preach to *the people gathered* there. But **the knights,** as usual, **racing their horses** and **jousting with their weapons,** drowned out *the word of God.* The saint *turned to them* and *groaned.* "Oh, the miserable madness of miserable men!" he said. "You neither consider nor fear the *judgment of God!* Hear what the Lord *tells you* through me, a little *poor man. The Lord has exalted* you above all *around you.* Because of this you should be kinder to your neighbors and more grateful to God. But you are ungrateful for these gifts, and fully armed you attack your neighbors: you kill and pillage. **I tell you,** *this will not go unavenged.* God will punish you severely: you will destroy yourselves in a civil war; in a general uprising one will rise up against the other. Wrath will teach you what kindness did not."

Not many days passed before **a** *scandal* **arose among them,** they took up arms against their neighbors. The common people attacked knights, and nobles drew their swords on the lower classes.[a] Things at last turned to such cruelty and slaughter that even the neighboring towns they had oppressed were moved to piety.

> Judgment worthy of praise!
> Since they had moved away from
> the One, the Most High,
> it followed that they lost their own oneness.
> A state can have no stronger bond
> than a devout love for God
> with a true and *sincere faith.*

Chapter IX

HOW HE PREDICTED TO A WOMAN
HER EVIL HUSBAND WOULD BECOME A GOOD ONE

[38]In those days, *the man of God* **was traveling to "Le Celle"** of **Cortona.** A noble woman from a village called Volusiano heard of this and hurried to see him. Exhausted from the long journey since *she was very refined and delicate,* she finally reached the saint. Our holy father was moved with compassion on seeing her exhausted and gasping for breath. "**What pleases you, my lady?**" he asked. "**Father,**

---

a. See AC 75.

Dt 31:12

Lk 11:28; Lk 9:55;
Mk 7:34

Rom 2:3

Jn 16:13; Is 66:2;
Ps 37:34
Ez 5:7, 11:12

Mt 23:38; Jb 24:12

Lk 15:13; Acts 1:5

1 Tm 1:5

AC 69

1 Sm 2:27

Dt 28:56

Gn 27:38

please bless me," she said. The saint asked: "Are you married or sin-
Jn 4:17 gle?" She replied: "Father, I have a husband, a very cruel man, an
antagonist to my service of Jesus Christ. He stops me from putting
2 Cor 5:8 into action the good will the Lord has inspired in me; and this is my
greatest sorrow. So I beg you, holy man, pray for him, that divine
Dn 5:22 mercy will *humble his heart*." The father was amazed at virility in a female, an aging spirit in a child.[a] Moved by piety, he said to her: "Go,
Jdt 12:32 *blessed daughter*, and, regarding your husband, know that you will
soon have consolation." And he added: "You may tell him for God
Sir 4:28, 40:7; 2 Cor 6:2 and for me, that *now is the time of salvation*, and later it will be the time
for justice."

After receiving his blessing, the lady returned home, found her
Acts 10:44; Eph 4:2 husband and relayed the message. Suddenly *the Holy Spirit came upon
him*, and he was changed from the old to the new man, prompting
Jos 22:27; Gn 19:19 him to reply *very meekly*: "My lady, *let us serve the Lord* and *save our souls*
in our own house."[b] And his wife replied: "It seems to me that conti-
Eph 2:20 nence should be placed in the soul as its *foundation*, and the other virtues *built upon it*." "This," he said, "pleases me as it pleases you."
They lived a celibate life for many years until, on the same day, both
departed happily—one as a *morning holocaust*, and the other as an *eve-
2 Kgs 16:15; Ps 141:2 ning sacrifice*.

What a fortunate woman!
She softened her lord for the sake of life![c]
In her was fulfilled that text from the Apostle:
1 Cor 7:14 *The unbelieving husband will be saved by his believing wife.*
But today
—to use a common saying—
you can count people like that on your fingers.[d]

a. Three Latin words are used in this paragraph: *mulier* [woman], *domina* [lady], and *femina* [female], all of which impact on Thomas of Celano's descriptions of Francis's attitudes toward women. Cf. 2C 112-114, infra, 239-41.

b. For background information on the "domestic" living of the Franciscan ideals by seculars, see Raoul Manselli, "Francis of Assisi and Lay People Living in the World: Beginnings of the Third Order?" GR 11 (1997): 41-48.

c. Another instance in which Thomas plays with the words: *mulier, mollitia* [woman, softness], cf. 2C 17, supra 173 c.

d. Pliny, *Natural History*, XXXIV:19, 38.

Chapter X
HOW HE KNEW THROUGH THE SPIRIT
THAT ONE BROTHER SCANDALIZED ANOTHER,
AND FORETOLD THAT THE FORMER WOULD LEAVE RELIGION

[39]Once two brothers were traveling from Terra di Lavoro, and the older one had seriously scandalized the younger one. I would say he was not a companion but a tyrant. The younger brother, because of God, endured all of this in remarkable silence. When they reached Assisi the younger one went to see Saint Francis, for he knew him well, and among other things the saint asked: "How did your companion behave toward you during the trip?" "Well enough, really, dear father," the brother answered. But the saint said to him: "Be careful, brother: don't lie under the pretext of humility! I know how he behaved toward you; but just wait a bit and you'll see." The brother was quite amazed that he knew, *through the Spirit,* such far away events. *Just a few days later* the one who *had scandalized his brother,* having turned against religion, was cast out.

Acts 21:4

Lk 15:13;
Rom 14:13; Mt 5:22

Without a doubt,
to share the same road with a good companion
and not to share his good will,
shows a *lack of understanding*
and is a mark of wickedness.

Sir 19:21

Chapter XI
HOW HE KNEW THAT A YOUNG MAN WHO ENTERED RELIGION
WAS NOT LED THERE BY THE SPIRIT OF GOD

AC 70

[40]About the same time **a noble boy from Lucca** came to Assisi, wishing **to enter religion.** When he was presented to Saint Francis, he *fell on his knees* and *with tears begged* the saint to receive him. The *man of God, looking intently at him,* knew at once *through the Spirit* that the boy was not *led by the Spirit,* and said to him: "**Wretched and carnal** as you are, why do you think you can lie to me and the Holy Spirit? Your tears come from the flesh, and *your heart is not* with *God. Get out! You have no taste for things of the spirit!*" **As he was saying this,** word came that the boy's **relatives** *were at the door,* **looking to seize** their son, and **take him back home.** He *went out to them,* and in the end agreed to return home. The brothers were amazed and *praised the Lord* in his saint.

2 Chr 6:13; Heb 5:7

1 Sm 2:27; Acts 3:4

Acts 21:4; Rom 8:14

Acts 5:3-4

Acts 8:21

Mk 8:33

Jn 18:16; Lk 11:54

Jn 18:29

Ps 150:1

1C 99; AC 95

Chapter XII
HOW HE HEALED A CLERIC
AND FORETOLD THAT BECAUSE OF HIS SINS
HE WOULD SUFFER EVEN WORSE THINGS

[41]While our holy father lay sick in the bishop's palace in Rieti, a canon named Gedeone—a lustful, worldly man—was seized by a painful illness.[a] And, with pains throughout his body, he was bedridden. He had himself carried to Saint Francis, and tearfully begged him to mark him with the sign of the cross. But the saint said to him: "How can I sign you with the cross, when you once lived according to the *desires of the flesh* and with no fear of the *judgments of God?*" But he made the sign of the cross on him, saying: "I will sign you in the name of *Christ*; but you must know you will suffer worse things if once set free you *return to your vomit.*" And he added: "The sin of ingratitude always brings on new ills *worse than the first.*"

When he made the sign of the cross over him, immediately the man who was lying crippled got up restored to health, and bursting with praise cried: "I am free!" Many people there heard the bones of his hips cracking, as when someone snaps dry twigs with his hands. But after a short time the canon, *forgetting God,* turned his body back to its unchaste ways. One evening he dined at the house of one of his fellow canons, and slept there that night. Suddenly the roof of the house collapsed on all of them. Others who were there escaped with their lives, and only that wretch was trapped and killed.

It is no wonder that,
as the saint told him,
worse evils follow *the first ones.*
Gratitude must be shown for forgiveness received,
and a crime repeated doubles displeasure.

Chapter XIII
A BROTHER WHO WAS TEMPTED

[42]While the saint *was staying in that same place,* a brother, a spiritual man, from the custody of Marsico, tormented by serious temptations, *said in his heart:* "Oh, if only I had something from Saint Francis, even the fingernail parings, I believe this whole storm of temptations would break up, and by the grace of God calm would return!" After receiving permission, he went to the place where Francis

Gal 5:16 · Sir 17:24 · Acts 4:10 · Prv 26:11 · Mt 12:45; Lk 11:26 · Jgs 3:7 · Mt 12:45 · Jn 11:6 · Ps 14:1

---

a. See AC 95.

was, and explained his purpose to one of our holy father's companions. But this brother answered him: "I'm afraid it won't be possible for me to give you his nail parings, for even though we do sometimes trim his nails, he commands us to throw the parings away, and forbids us to save them."

At that very moment the brother was called away and told to go to the saint, who was looking for him. "Would you look for some scissors for me, son," said the saint, "so you can *cut* my *nails* right away." The brother brought out the scissors which he had already picked up for that very purpose, and saving the clippings, gave them to the brother who had asked for them. He received them with devotion and preserved them even more devoutly, and was immediately set free from all his struggle.

Dt 12:12

Chapter XIV
A MAN WHO OFFERED A PIECE OF CLOTH
WHICH THE SAINT HAD EARLIER REQUESTED

1C 76

[43]While living at this same place, the *father of the poor* was dressed in an old tunic. One day he said to one of his companions, whom he had made his guardian: "Brother, if possible, I wish you would find me material for a tunic." On hearing this, the brother started turning over in his mind how he could get the necessary cloth so humbly requested. The next day at the break of dawn he went to the door, on his way to town for the cloth. There he found a man sitting on the doorstep and wishing to speak to him. This man said to the brother: "For the love of God, please accept this cloth, enough for six tunics; keep one for yourself and distribute the rest as you please for the good of my soul."

Jb 29:16

The brother was exhilarated, and returned to Brother Francis, announcing to him the gift sent from heaven. And our father said: "Accept the tunics, for this man was sent to care for my need in this way." And he added: "Thanks be to him who seems to be the only one *concerned for us!*"

1 Sm 9:5; Ps 40:18

Chapter XV
HOW HE INVITED HIS DOCTOR TO LUNCH
WHEN THE BROTHERS LACKED EVERYTHING,
AND HOW THE LORD SUDDENLY PROVIDED FOR THEM IN ABUNDANCE;
AND GOD'S PROVIDENCE FOR HIS OWN

[44]While the holy man was staying in a hermitage **near Rieti, a** AC 68
doctor used to visit him every day to treat his eyes. One day the saint
said to his brothers: "Invite the doctor, and **give him the best to eat.**"
Lk 14:9 The guardian **answered him: "Father,** *we're embarrassed* to say this,
but we're ashamed to invite him, because right now **we're so poor.**"
Mt 20:32; Jn 9:27 But the saint answered: *"Do you want me to tell you again?"* And **the**
doctor, who was nearby, **said:** "Dear brothers, I would consider it a
treat to share in your poverty."

The brothers hurried to place the whole contents of their store-
2 Chr 18:20 room on the table: **a little bread,** and not much wine, and, to make
the meal more lavish, the kitchen provided a few beans. Meanwhile,
Mal 1:7; Lk 13:25 *the table of the Lord* took pity on the table of his servants. *Someone* Test 22
knocked at the door, and they answered immediately. **There was a** 1C 34
woman offering a basket filled with beautiful bread, loaded with
fish and crabcakes, and with **honey and grapes** heaped on top. The
table of the poor rejoices at this sight, the cheap food is put away, and
the delicacies are eaten immediately.

The doctor heaved a sigh and spoke to them: "**Neither you,** brothers, as you should, nor we lay people, realize the holiness of this
man." They would not have been sufficiently filled if the miracle
had not fed them even more than the food.

Prv 30:17
A father's eye
never looks down on his own,
but rather feeds beggars with greater care
the needier they are.
The poor enjoy a more generous meal than a prince's,
as God is more generous than humans.

HOW HE SET BROTHER RICCERIO FREE FROM A TEMPTATION[a]

[44a]There was a brother called Riccerio, noble in birth and behav- 1C 49, 50; LJS 31
ior. He placed such trust in the merits of blessed Francis that he believed that anyone who enjoyed the gift of the saint's affection would

---

a. This paragraph is missing from a number of manuscripts, possibly because of its similarity with 1C
49 and 50. Nevertheless editors of the critical edition found in AF X published it as part of this text,
see AF X, 158 n. 13.

be worthy of divine grace; any without it would deserve God's wrath. He therefore anxiously longed to obtain the benefit of his intimacy, but *he was very fearful* that the saint might discover in him some hidden fault and then he would actually be further away from the saint's good will.

Jdt 8:8

These deep fears tormented that brother every day, and he did not reveal his thoughts to anyone. One day, worried as usual, he approached the cell where Saint Francis was praying. The *man of God* knew of both his coming and his state of mind and called him kindly to himself. "My son," he said, "let no fear or temptation disturb you any more, for you are very dear to me, and among all those who are dearest to me I love you with a special love. Come to me confidently whenever you want, and leave me freely whenever you want." The brother was extremely shocked and overjoyed at the words of the holy father. From that time on, knowing he was loved, he grew—as he believed—in *the grace of the Savior.*

1 Sm 13:1

Ti 2:11

Chapter XVI
How He Left His Cell to Bless Two Brothers, Knowing Through the Spirit What They Desired

AC 73

[45] Saint Francis usually passed the whole day in an isolated cell, returning to the brothers only when pressed by necessity to take some food. He did not leave it for dinner at the assigned time because his hunger for contemplation was even more consuming, and often completely overpowered him.

Now it happened one time that two brothers, with a way of life worthy of God, came to the place at Greccio from far away.[a] The only reason was to see the saint and to receive his blessing, which they had long desired. When they arrived, they *did not find him,* for he had already left the common area for a cell. They were greatly saddened. Since an uncertain outcome demanded a long stay, they left completely discouraged, believing their failure was caused by their faults.

Lk 2:45

Blessed Francis's companions accompanied them, comforting them in their discouragement. But when they had walked *about a stone's throw away* from the place, the saint suddenly called after them, and said to one of his companions: "Tell my brothers who came here to look back toward me." And when those brothers turned their faces to him, he made the sign of the Cross over them and affectionately blessed them. They became so joyful at receiving

Lk 22:41

---

a. AC 73 tells of one brother coming to see the saint. Thomas, however, writes of two. In both instances the brothers are not identified.

Lk 24:53   both their wish and even a miracle, that they returned home *praising and blessing the Lord.*

Chapter XVII
HOW HE BROUGHT FORTH WATER FROM THE ROCK BY PRAYER AND GAVE IT TO A THIRSTY PEASANT

[46]Once blessed Francis wanted to travel to a certain hermitage so that he could more freely spend time in contemplation. Because he was very weak, he got a donkey to ride from a poor man. It was sum-

Jos 2:16;
1 Kgs 13:14, 21   mer, and as the peasant *went up the mountain* following the *man of*
Jn 4:6   *God,* he was *worn out from the journey* over such a rough and long road. And before they came to the place, he was exhausted, fainting with a
Dt 13:17   burning thirst. He urgently cried out after the saint, begging him *to have pity on him.* He swore he would die if he was not revived by some-
Lk 4:34   thing to drink. *The holy one of God,* always compassionate to the distressed, immediately leaped down from the donkey, knelt down on
Col 1:9   the ground, and raised his hands to heaven, *praying unceasingly* until he sensed he had been heard. "Hurry now," he said to the peasant,
Is 48:21   "and over there you will find living *water* which at this very hour Christ *has* mercifully *brought forth from the rock for you to drink."* How amazingly kind God is, so easily bowing to his servants! By the power
Ps 78:16   of prayer a peasant drinks *water from the rock* and draws refreshment
Dt 32:13; Ps 1:3   *from the hard flint.*[a] There was no *flow of water* there before this; and even after a careful search, none was found there afterwards.

Why should we be surprised
that this one,
Lk 4:1   so *filled with the Holy Spirit,*
re-enacts the marvelous deeds of all the just!
If one is joined to Christ
by a gift of special grace,
is it not wonderful that he,
like other saints,
Mk 7:13   should do *similar things?*

---

a. Gregory the Great describes a similar incident in the life of Saint Benedict. Cf. Gregory the Great, *Dialogue* II 5, PL 66:144. See Saint Gregory the Great, *Dialogues,* translated by Odo John Zimmerman (New York: Fathers of the Church, Inc., 1959), 67-68.

Chapter XVIII
THE LITTLE BIRDS HE FED, ONE OF WHICH DIED BECAUSE OF ITS GREED

[47]One day when blessed Francis was sitting at table with the brothers, little birds, a male and a female, came over and took some *crumbs from* the saint's *table* as they pleased. They did this every day, anxious to feed their newly hatched chicks. The saint rejoiced over them, and caressed them, as was his custom, and offered them a reward for their efforts. One day the father and mother offered their children to the brothers, as if they had been raised at their expense; and once they entrusted their fledglings to the brothers, they were never seen again in that place. The chicks grew tame with the brothers and used to perch on their hands. They stayed in the house, not as guests but as members of the family. They hid at the sight of people of the world, showing they were the foster children of the brothers alone.

Mt 15:27; Mk 7:28

The saint noticed this, surprised, and invited the brothers to rejoice: "See," he said, "what our brothers the robins[a] have done, as if they were endowed with reason! They have said to us: 'Brothers, we present to you our babies, who have been fed by your crumbs. Do with them as you please; we will go off to another home.'"

The young birds became completely tame with the brothers, and all ate together peacefully. But greed broke up this harmony, for a bigger one grew arrogant and harassed the smaller ones. When the big one had already eaten his fill, he still pushed the others away from the food. "Look now," said the father, "at what this greedy one is doing! He's full to bursting, but he's still jealous of his hungry brothers. He will die an evil death." The punishment followed soon after the saint's word. The one who disturbed his brothers climbed on the edge of a water pitcher to take a drink, and suddenly fell into it and drowned; not a cat or any other animal was found that dared touch that one cursed by the saint.

When so punished in birds,
is not avarice an evil to be feared
when found in mortals!
And is not the judgment of the saint to be feared
when punishment ensues with such ease!

a. *Pectusrubei*, literally redbreasts; *pettirosso* is still the Italian for "robin."

Chapter XIX
HOW ALL THE THINGS WHICH HE FORETOLD ABOUT BROTHER BERNARD
WERE FULFILLED

[48]Another time he spoke prophetically about Brother Bernard,   1C 24; AC 12
who was the second brother in the Order, saying: "I tell you, Brother
Mt 12:45 **Bernard has been given the most cunning devils to test him,** *the*
worst among all the other evil spirits. They constantly strive to make this
Rv 6:13, 9:1;   *star fall from heaven*, but the *outcome* will be something else. He will be
Ru 3:18; 2 Mc 13:13   troubled, tormented, and harassed, but in the end he will triumph
over all." And he added: "Near the time of his death, with every
storm calmed, every temptation overcome, he will enjoy wonderful
Acts 20:24; 2 Tm 4:7   tranquillity and peace. *The race finished* he will pass over happily to
Christ."

And in fact it happened just like that: his death was lit up with
1 Kgs 13:31-32   miracles, and everything happened exactly as the *man of God foretold*.
Gn 42:8   That is why the brothers said when he died: "This brother *was not* really *recognized* while he lived!" But we leave to others the task of telling Bernard's praises.

Chapter XX
A BROTHER WHO WAS TEMPTED
AND WANTED TO HAVE SOMETHING WRITTEN BY THE HAND OF THE SAINT

[49]While the saint was secluded in a cell on Mount La Verna, one of
his companions was yearning with great desire to have something encouraging from the words of our Lord, commented on briefly by Saint
Francis and written with his own hand. He believed that by this means
he would be set free from, or at least could bear more easily, a serious
temptation which oppressed him, not in the flesh but in the spirit.
Though growing weary with this desire, he feared to express it to the
1 Cor 2:10   most holy father. But what man did not tell him, *the Spirit revealed*. One
2 Jn 12   day Saint Francis called this brother and said: "Bring me *paper and ink*,
because I want to write down the words of the Lord and his praises
Ps 77:7   upon which *I have meditated in my heart*." What he had asked for was
quickly brought to him. He then wrote down with his own hand the   PrsG
Praises of God and the words he wanted and, at the end, a blessing for   BlL
Gn 28:2   that brother, saying: "*Take* this paper *for yourself* and keep it carefully to
your dying day." The whole temptation disappeared immediately. The
letter was preserved; and later it worked wonders.[a]

---

a. The inscription of *The Praises of God*, cf. FA:ED I 108-112, indicates it is the text written by Francis
    on this occasion. The companion was Leo.

Chapter XXI
HOW HE GAVE HIS TUNIC TO THE SAME BROTHER WHO WANTED IT

1C 108

[50]Another wonder of our holy father was manifested for that same brother. When the saint lay sick in the palace at Assisi, that brother *thought to himself:* "Now our father is close to death, and *my soul would be comforted* so much if I could have the tunic of my father after his death." As if that *desire of the heart* had been spoken with his lips, Saint Francis called him shortly after and said: "I am giving you this tunic. Take it. From now on it is yours. Even though I wear it while I still live, at my death it should be returned to you." Amazed at his father's insight, the brother was consoled and accepted the tunic. Out of holy devotion, this tunic was carried to France.

Wis 2:1, Mt 16:7, Lk 12:17; Ps 77:3

2 Kgs 2:13

Ps 21:3

Chapter XXII
THE PARSLEY FOUND AT HIS COMMAND AMONG WILD HERBS AT NIGHT

[51]At the time of his last illness, and in the dark of night, he wanted to eat some parsley and humbly asked for it.[a] The cook was called so he could bring it, but he replied that he could not pick any in the garden at that time. "I've been picking parsley every day," he said, "and I've cut off so much of it that even in broad daylight I can hardly find any. Even more so now that darkness has fallen, I won't be able to distinguish it from the other herbs." "Brother" the saint replied, "don't worry, bring me the first herbs your hand touches." The brother went into the garden, unable to see anything, and tore up the first wild herbs he came upon, and brought them back into the house. The brothers looked at the wild herbs, and sorting through them carefully, they found a leafy, tender stock of parsley in the middle of them. The saint then ate a bit of it and felt much better. Then the father said to the brothers: *"Dear brothers,* do what you're commanded the first time you're told, and don't wait for it to be repeated. Don't pretend that something is impossible; for even if what I command is beyond your strength, obedience will find the strength." Thus to a high degree the Spirit entrusted to him the *spirit of prophecy.*

Phil 4:1

Rv 19:10

---

a. Parsley was used to give new strength to the dying, a belief that sprang from the ancient myth in which a snake bit Opheltes, the child of Hypsipyle, Queen of Lemmos. Since the boy, buried with the name "Archemorous," the forerunner of death, had been sitting on a parsley-bed when bitten, the herb became associated with dying. Cf. Michael Grant and John Hazel, "Hypsipyle," *Gods and Mortals in Classical Mythology* (Springfield, MA: G.&C. Merriam Company, Publishers: 1973), 240.

Chapter XXIII

THE FAMINE WHICH HE FORETOLD WOULD COME AFTER HIS DEATH

2 Sm 3:7

1 Cor 14:3

Jn 19:20

1 Mc 15:32

Gn 1:11; Gn 26:1;
Jos 22:18; Jer 14:5

1 Cor 13:5; Ps 45:2

Jn 3:11

Am 8:11

2 Tm 2:15

Mt 23:27-28

2 Cor 11:13-15

Lk 21:9

[52]Holy men are sometimes forced by the prompting of the Holy Spirit to say some remarkable things about themselves. Either the glory of God demands that they *reveal the word* or else the order of charity calls for it for the *edification* of their neighbor. This was why the blessed Father one day turned to a brother *he loved very much, and spoke this word, which* he had brought from the audience hall of God's majesty, which he knew so well. "Today there is a servant of God *upon this earth*," he said, "and for his sake the Lord will not allow *hunger to rage* against people as long as he is alive."

There was no vanity here but rather a holy pronouncement spoken by that *charity which is not self-seeking*, in modest and holy *words* for our edification. Neither should this favor of such a special love of Christ for his servant have been concealed by useless silence. All of us *who saw* these days *know well* how quietly and peacefully those times passed, as long as the servant of Christ was alive, and what rich abundance there was of all good things. There was no *famine of the word of God*, for the word of preachers in those days was especially full of power, and the hearts of all their listeners were *worthy of God's approval*. Examples of holiness were shining brightly in religious life, and the hypocrisy of *whitened sepulchers* had not yet infected so many holy people, nor had the teaching of *those who disguise themselves* excited so much curiosity. No wonder material goods were so abundant, when eternal goods were so truly loved by all!

[53]But once he had been taken away, the order of things was completely reversed and everything changed. *Wars and insurrections* sprang up everywhere, and the carnage of death in many forms suddenly spread through many regions.[a] A frightful famine spread far and wide, and many indeed were devoured by its cruelty, painful beyond anything else.[b] Sheer necessity turned all things into food, and

---

a. Thomas's description applies primarily to central Italy where, between 1227 and 1230, there was strife between Pope Gregory IX and Emperor Frederick II. In 1227 Gregory excommunicated him for postponing too long his departure for the Crusade. As Frederick was finally leaving for the Holy Land, in 1228, some of his imperial forces attacked the Marches of Ancona and the Duchy of Spoleto, under papal control. In retaliation the papal forces, in 1229, invaded the imperial territory of the Kingdom of Naples, and hostilities continued to spread. Cf. Riccardo di S. Germano, "Chronicon," in *Monumenta Germaniae Historica* XIX, 349 ff. See AF X,163, n.15.

b. This famine is described in contemporary chronicles, e.g. the *Chronicon Parmense*, 1138-1338: "In that year [1227] there was a great famine in all of Italy. From the month of May, a six-measure of grain cost 20 imperial soldi and spelt was six soldi. And in the city of Bologna a basket of grain cost 20 imperial soldi," in Muratori, *Rerum Italicarum Scriptores*, IX, 765; so also the *Corpus Chronicarum Bononiensium*, "In that year [1227] there was a great famine in Bologna and various regions," in Muratori, XVIII (2nd ed.) II, 92; and Riccardo di S. Germano, "1227, in the month of January there was such a famine in the city of Rome that the senate could hardly get a ruble of wheat for 20 soldi," in *Monumenta Germaniae Historica* XIX, 347.

human teeth bit into what animals would normally reject. Bread was made from nut shells and tree bark. Hunger became so compelling that parental piety was unmoved—to put it gently—by the death of their own children, as one of them admitted.

The blessed father Francis clearly revealed to that same brother, to whom, while he was yet living, he had foretold the future disasters, that he himself was that servant of God. He did this so that we would clearly know who that *faithful servant* was, for whose love the divine punishment held back its hand from vengeance, only a few days after his death. For one night as the brother was sleeping, he *called him* in a loud voice, *saying:* "Brother, *a famine* is now coming which, while I was living, the Lord did not allow to come *upon the earth.*" The brother woke up when he heard the voice, and later recounted it all from beginning to end. On the third night after this, the saint appeared to him again and repeated the same words.

Mt 24:45

Jn 11:28; Ps 105:16

Chapter XXIV
THE SAINT'S CLEAR SIGHT AND OUR IGNORANCE

[54]It should not seem strange to anyone that this prophet of our own time should shine with such great privileges. Truly freed from the darkness of earthly things and not subjected to the lusts of the flesh, free, his understanding flew up to the heights; pure, it stepped into the light.

Thus,
illumined by the flashes of light eternal,[a]
he drew from the Word what echoed in words.
Ah, how different we are today!
Wrapped in darkness
we are ignorant even of what we need to know.
And what do you think is the reason for this?
Are we not also friends of the flesh,
wallowing in the dust of worldly things?
Surely,
if we would only *raise our hearts as well as our hands to heaven,*
if we would choose to depend on the eternal,
maybe we would know what we do not know:
God and ourselves.
Mired in mud, we see only mud.

Wis 7:26

Jb 37:19

Lam 3:41

---

a. Cf. *Easter Proclamation: tellus . . . irradiata fulgoribus et aeterni regis splendore illustrata* [illumined by flashes of the eternal king].

For the eye fixed on heaven,
it is impossible not to see heavenly things.

POVERTY

Chapter XXV
THE PRAISE OF POVERTY

Ps 84:6-7   [55] *Placed in a vale of tears*
the blessed father scorned
Ps 31:20   the usual riches of the *children of men* as no riches at all[a]
and, eager for higher status,
Sir 47:10   *with all his heart,* he coveted poverty.
Realizing that she was a close friend[b]
Heb 7:3   of the *Son of God,*
Est 9:28   but nowadays an outcast throughout *the whole world,*
Jer 31:3   he was eager to espouse her *in an everlasting love.*
Wis 8:2   He *became the lover of her beauty*
Gn 2:24; Mt 19:5;   and not only *left his father and his mother*
Mk 10:7; Eph 2:18   but gave up everything he owned
so that he might *cling to his wife* more closely,
and *the two might be in one spirit.*
He held her close in chaste embraces
and could not bear to cease being her husband
Gal 2:5   *and even for an hour.*
He told his sons that she is the way of perfection.
She is the pledge and guarantee of eternal wealth.
No one coveted gold as avidly as he coveted poverty;
no one was as careful to guard a treasure
Mt 13:45-46   as he was to watch over this *pearl* of the Gospel.
In this especially would his sight be offended:
if he saw in the brothers
—whether at home or away from it—

---

a. Thomas again plays on words; in this instance *opes* [riches] *inopes* [no riches], which, in the Latin text, immediately strikes the ear since the two words are placed next to one another.

b. Cf. 1C 35, 39, 51. In contrast to the allegorical references on poverty found in 1C, this reflection on poverty develops the explicit spousal imagery found in earlier texts such as SC 3-5, 7-22. Its origins are clearly within the psycho-historical circumstances of the twelfth century during which spirituality struggled with the "difficult and dangerous discussion of love," as Origen described it. Cf. Ann W. Astell, *The Song of Songs in the Middle Ages* (Ithaca and London: Cornell University Press, 1990), 2. For a thorough study of this image, cf. Dominique Gagnon, "Typologie de la pauvreté chez saint François d'Assise: l'espouse, la dame, la mère," *Laurentianum* 19 (1977): 462-552.

anything that was contrary to poverty.
Truly, from the beginning of his religious life until his death,

Test 16-17

his entire wealth was a single tunic,
cord and breeches;
he had nothing else.
His poor clothing showed
where he stored his riches.
This was the reason he was happy;
he was carefree.
He was ready for the race.
He was glad to exchange perishable treasure
for the *hundredfold.*   Mt 19:29

POVERTY OF HOUSES

Chapter XXVI

AC 23

[56]He taught his own to build poor little dwellings out of wood, and not stone, and how to build these according to a crude sketch. Often, when he spoke to the brothers about poverty, he would insist on that saying of the Gospel: *"The foxes have holes and the birds of the air*   Mt 8:20; Lk 9:58 *have nests, but the Son of God has no place on which to rest his head."*

Chapter XXVII
THE HOUSE NEXT TO THE PORTIUNCULA THAT HE BEGAN TO PULL DOWN

[57]Once, there was going to be a chapter at Saint Mary of the Portiuncula. *The time was* already *close at hand,* and the people of Assisi   2 Tm 4:6 could see that there was no house there. So in a great rush they built a house for the chapter, while the *man of God* was away and unaware   2 Kgs 4:42 of this. When the father finally returned, he saw the house and was annoyed. He complained, and not gently. Immediately, wanting to dismantle the building, he was the first to get up; he *climbed up to the*   Lk 5:19 *roof* and started tearing out slates and *tiles with a mighty hand.* He or-   Ez 20:34 dered the brothers also to climb up and to tear down completely that monstrosity against poverty. He said that this would quickly spread throughout the Order, and everyone would take for an example any sign of pretension they saw in that place. He would have destroyed that house right to the foundations, but some knights standing

nearby dampened his fiery spirit. They told him that the building belonged to the town, not to the brothers.

Chapter XXVIII
THE HOUSE IN BOLOGNA WHERE HE THREW OUT THE SICK

[58]At another time, when he was returning from Verona and
wished to pass through Bologna, he heard that a new house of the
brothers had been built there. And just because he heard the words
"house of the brothers," he changed course and went by another
route, avoiding Bologna. Furthermore, he commanded the brothers
to leave the house quickly. For this reason the house was abandoned;
and even the sick could not stay, but were thrown out with the rest of
them. And they did not get permission to return there until Lord
Hugo, who was then Bishop of Ostia and Legate in Lombardy, declared while preaching in public that this house was his. And *he who*
writes this and bears witness to it was at that time thrown out from that
house while he was sick.[a]

Jn 21:24; 19:35

Chapter XXIX
HOW HE REFUSED TO ENTER A CELL BECAUSE IT WAS CALLED HIS

[59]He did not want the brothers to live in any place unless it had a
definite owner who held the property rights. He always wanted the
laws of pilgrims for his sons: to be sheltered under someone else's
roof, to travel in peace, and to thirst for their homeland.[b] Once at the
hermitage of Sarteano, one brother asked another brother where he
was coming from. "I'm coming from Brother Francis's cell," he answered. The saint heard this and replied: "Since you have put the
name 'Francis' on the cell making it my property, go and look for
someone else to live in it. From now on I will not stay there. When
the Lord stayed in a cell[c] where he prayed and *fasted for forty days*, he

AC 23

AC 57

Mt 4:1-2; Mk1:12-13;
Lk 4:2

---

a. This event occurred between 1219 and 1221. It is not clear if Hugolino was present in Bologna at the
time the house was abandoned. The one thrown out in this story is most probably not Thomas, but
rather one of his informants, who would have given him the story in writing and mentioned that he
was one of the sick.

b. For comment on the "laws of pilgrims," see AC 23.

c. The Latin reads *stetit in carcere* [stayed in a cell], but the context is clearly Christ in the desert. While
carcer means literally prison, it took on the sense of voluntary but temporary incarceration. Thus the
Franciscan hermitage on Subasio in Assisi, the Carceri, takes its name from the eremitical breaking
away or separation from the world, an incarceration. Cf. Marcella Gatti, "A Historical Look at the
Carceri in the Pre-Franciscan and Early Franciscan Period," *Franciscan Solitude*, ed. Andre Cirino
and Josef Raischl (St. Bonaventure: Franciscan Institute Publications, 1995), 128-138. Information
on the meaning of *carcer* can be found in Octavian Schmucki, "Place of Solitude: An Essay on the
External Circumstances of the Prayer Life of Francis of Assisi," GR 2 (1988): 103-106.

did not have a cell made for him or any kind of house, but stayed beneath a rock on the mountainside. We can follow him in the way prescribed: holding nothing as our own property, even though we cannot live without the use of houses."

.R VI 1; Test 24

Chapter XXX
POVERTY OF FURNISHINGS

AC 24

[60]This man not only hated pretense in houses; he also abhorred having many or fine furnishings in them. He disliked anything, in tables or dishes, that recalled the ways of the world. He wanted everything to sing of exile and pilgrimage.

Chapter XXXI
AN EXAMPLE OF THE TABLE SET ON EASTER DAY AT GRECCIO,
HOW HE PRESENTED HIMSELF AS A PILGRIM AFTER THE EXAMPLE OF CHRIST

[61]On a certain Easter Day[a] the brothers in the hermitage of Greccio set the table more carefully than usual, with white clothes and glassware. The Father came down from his cell and went to the table. He saw that it was elevated and elaborately decorated, but he did not smile at all at that smiling table. He secretly tiptoed away, put on his head the hat of a poor man who was there at the time, and with a staff in hand, *went outside.* He waited *outside, at the door,* until the brothers had started eating. They were accustomed not to wait for him when he did not come at the usual signal.

AC 74

Ps 41:7; Jn 18:16

As they began to eat, that true *poor man cried out* at the door: "For the love of the Lord God, *give alms* to this poor, sick pilgrim!" And the brothers replied: "Come in, man, for the love of Him you invoked." He quickly came in, and showed himself to those dining. You can imagine the surprise the pilgrim provoked in those homebodies! The beggar was given a bowl and, sitting on the ground by himself, placed his dish on the ashes. "Now," he said, "I am sitting like a Lesser Brother!" And he said to the brothers: "The *examples of the Son of God's* poverty should move us more than other religious. I saw here a table all prepared and decorated, and recognized it as not the table of poor men who go door to door."

Ps 34:7;
Mt 6:2

IX 1,4; LR VI 3;
LtOrd 29

Jn 5:25; 13:15

The chain of events proves that he was
like that other *pilgrim*

Lk 24:18

---

a. Thomas changes the text of AC 74 in which this event takes place on Christmas Day, not Easter.

who was alone in Jerusalem on that same day.
And he certainly made
the hearts of his disciples *burn as he spoke.*

Lk 24:32

Chapter XXXII
AGAINST EAGERNESS FOR BOOKS

Ps 19:8

[62] He taught that in books *the testimony of the Lord,* not value,   AC 25
should be sought, and edification rather than elegance. Nevertheless, he wanted few books kept, and these were to be available to
the brothers who needed them. And so, when a Minister asked him   1C 189; AC 102
for permission to keep some elegant and very expensive books, he
got this reply: "I refuse to lose the Book of the Gospel that I promised
for these books of yours! *Do as you please,* but don't use my permission
for a trap."

2 Sm 24:12

POVERTY OF BEDS

Chapter XXXIII
THE EXAMPLE OF THE LORD OF OSTIA AND IN PRAISE OF HIM

[63] Finally, beds and coverings abounded in such plentiful pov-   AC 26
erty that, if a brother had a ragged sheet over some straw he considered it a bridal couch.

It happened that the Lord of Ostia, with a great crowd of clerics   AC 74
and knights, came to visit the brothers at the time they were holding
a chapter at Saint Mary of the Portiuncula. When he saw how the
brothers *lay on the ground,* and had a good look at their beds, which
you might think were animals' dens, he began to weep loudly, and
said in front of everyone: "Look where the brothers sleep! *What will
become of us,* who are wasteful with our surplus?" And all those present were moved to tears, and left the place greatly edified.

Jdt 14:15

Mt 19:27

This was that man of Ostia   1C 99-101
who eventually became *the great door* of the Church,
a door which always held hostile powers at bay
until his blessed soul returned to heaven as a sacred offering.[a]
Oh, holy soul and heart of charity!

1 Cor 16:9

---

a. Thomas plays on the name of Hugolino's diocese of Ostia, connecting it with *ostium* [door], *hostibus*
[enemies] and *hostia* [sacrificial victim, or host].

Placed in an exalted position,
he grieved at not having exalted merits.
In fact, he was loftier in virtue than by status.

Chapter XXXIV
WHAT HAPPENED TO HIM ONE NIGHT BECAUSE OF A FEATHER PILLOW

AC 119

[64]Since we have mentioned beds, an incident comes to mind which may be useful to retell. From the time when this holy man *had turned to Christ* and *cast the things of this world into oblivion,* he never wanted to lie on a mattress or place his head on a feather pillow. He never broke this strict resolution, even when he was sick or receiving the hospitality of strangers. But it happened that while he was staying at the hermitage of Greccio his eye disease became worse than usual, and he was forced against his will to use a small pillow. The first night, during the morning vigil, the saint called his companion and said to him: "Brother, I couldn't sleep this whole night, or remain upright and pray. My head was spinning, my knees were giving way, and the whole framework of my body was shaking as if I had eaten bread made from ryegrass.[a] I believe," he added, "there's a devil in this pillow I have for my head. Take it away, because I don't want the devil by my head any more."

Acts 11:21; Lam 2:6; 1 Cor 7:33-34

The brother, sympathizing with the father's complaint, caught the pillow thrown at him to take away. But as he was leaving, he suddenly lost the power of speech. Struck by terror and paralyzed, he could not move his feet from where he stood nor could he move his arms. After a moment, the saint recognized this and called him. He was set free, came back in and told him what he *had suffered.* The saint said to him: "Last night as I was saying compline I knew for certain that the devil had come into my cell. Our enemy," he added, "is very cunning and subtle; when he can't harm you inside, in your soul, he at least gives you cause for complaint in your body."

Heb 5:8

Let those listen
who prepare *little pillows on every side*
so that wherever they fall
they will land on something soft!
The devil gladly follows luxury;

Ez 13:18

---

a. The Latin text reads: *uti comedissem panem de lolio* [as if I had eaten bread made from ryegrass]. *Lolium* [darnel or ryegrass] is a wheat-like weed (the "cockle" of Mt 13:25) which is particularly susceptible to ergot, a fungus which can cause convulsions and altered states of consciousness in those who eat bread made from flour infected by it.

he delights in standing by elegant beds,
especially where necessity does not demand them
and profession forbids them.
On the other hand

Rv 12:9

the *ancient serpent* flees from a naked man,
either because he despises the company of the poor
or because he fears the heights of poverty.
If a brother realizes
that the devil is underneath feathers
he will be satisfied with straw under his head.

EXAMPLES AGAINST MONEY

Chapter XXXV
THE SEVERE CORRECTION OF A BROTHER
WHO TOUCHED MONEY WITH HIS HANDS

1 Cor 7:33-34

[65]While this true friend of God completely despised all *worldly things* he detested money above all. From the beginning of his conversion, he despised money particularly and encouraged his followers to flee from it always as from the devil himself. He gave his followers this observation: money and manure[a] are equally worthy of love.

1C 9; L3C 45; A

ER VIII 6; LR IV

Gn 39:11

Now, *it happened one day* that a layman came to pray in the church of Saint Mary of the Portiuncula, and placed some money by the cross as an offering. When he left, one of the brothers simply picked it up with his hand and threw it on the windowsill.[b] What the brother had done reached the saint, and he, seeing he had been caught ran to ask forgiveness, threw himself to the ground and offered himself to be whipped. The saint rebuked him and reprimanded him severely for touching coins. He ordered him to pick up the money from the windowsill with his own mouth, take it outside the fence of that place, and with his mouth to put it on the donkey's manure pile. While that brother was gladly carrying out this command, fear filled the hearts of all of those who heard it. From then on, all of them held in even greater contempt what had been so equated with manure and were encouraged to despise it by new examples every day.

a. In 1C 9, Thomas uses the image of money as dust. In this text, money is even more despicable.
b. Cf. 1C 9 where Francis does the same after the priest at San Damiano refuses his money.

Chapter XXXVI
THE PUNISHMENT OF A BROTHER WHO ONCE PICKED UP A COIN

ER VIII 6

[66]Once two brothers were walking together and as they approached a hospital for lepers, they noticed a coin on the roadway. They stopped and began to discuss what to do with that manure. One of them laughed at the scruples of his brother and went to pick the coin up to give it to those responsible for the expenses of lepers. Seeing he was deceived by false piety, his companion told him to stop. He reminded his reckless brother of a passage in the *Rule*, which clearly teaches that when a coin is found it should be trampled underfoot like dirt. But that brother, who had always been *stiff-necked*, hardened his heart against these warnings. In contempt of the *Rule* he bent down and picked up the coin, but he did not escape the judgment of God. He immediately lost the power of speech; he *gnashed his teeth*, but could not manage to speak. Thus the punishment showed his insanity; and vengeance taught the proud man to obey the laws of the father. At last, he threw away the stinking thing, and his *unclean lips*[a] now washed by the waters of repentance were set free to give praise. There is an old proverb: "Correct a fool and he will be your friend."

Ex 32:9; 33:3

Ps 35:16

Is 6:5

Prv 28:23; Eccl 20:17

Chapter XXXVII
THE REBUKE OF A BROTHER WHO WANTED TO KEEP MONEY UNDER THE PRETEXT OF NECESSITY

[67]Brother Peter of Catanio,[b] the saint's vicar, saw that great crowds of brothers from other places visited Saint Mary of the Portiuncula, and that the alms received were not sufficient to provide for their needs. He told Saint Francis: "Brother, *I don't know what to do*; I don't have enough to provide for all the crowds of brothers pouring in from all over. I beg you, please allow some of the goods of those entering as novices to be kept so that we can have recourse to these for expenses *in due season.*" But the saint replied: "May that piety be elsewhere, my dear brother, which treats the *Rule* with impiety for the sake of anyone." "Then, what should I do?" asked Peter. "Strip the Virgin's altar and take its adornments when you can't care for the needy in any other way. Believe me, she would be happier to

Jn 15:15

Ps 145:15

---

a. See the hymn of Second Vespers for the feast of the Nativity of Saint John the Baptist written by Paul the Deacon. It prompted Guido of Arezzo to name the notes of the scale: . . . *solve polluti labii reatum, Sancte Ioannes.* [Loosen the bonds that hold our unclean lips, blessed John].

b. Information on Peter of Catanio can be found in FA:ED I 204 a.

have her altar stripped and the Gospel of her Son kept than have her altar decorated and her Son despised. The Lord will send someone to return to his Mother what He has loaned to us."

Chapter XXXVIII
THE MONEY THAT TURNED INTO A SNAKE

[68]Once traveling with a companion through Apulia near Bari, the *man of God* found a large bag lying on the road. It was the kind merchants call a "fonda" or sling, and it was bursting with coins. The saint's companion alerted him, and strongly urged him to pick the purse up from the ground and distribute the money to the poor. While he praised piety for the needy and extolled the mercy shown in giving them alms, the saint flatly refused to do it. He declared it was a trick of the devil. "My son," he said, "it isn't right to take what belongs to someone else. Giving away someone else's property deserves punishment as sin, not honor as a good deed."

They left that place and hurried to finish the *journey* they had *begun*. But that brother, deluded by empty piety, was not yet at peace; he kept insisting on the misdeed. The saint agreed to return to the place, not to *fulfill the* brother's *desire* but to *reveal divine mystery* to the fool. He called over a young man who happened to be *sitting on a wall* along the road, so that *by word of two or three witnesses* the sacrament of the Trinity might be evident. When the three of them had returned to the "fonda," they saw it was bursting with money, but the saint forbade either of them to approach it that by the power of prayer the devil's deceit might be revealed.

He withdrew *about a stone's throw* from there, and concentrated on holy prayer. He returned from praying, and ordered the brother to pick up the bag, which, after his prayer, now contained not money but a snake. The brother trembled. He was stunned. I don't know what he sensed, but something out of the ordinary was going through his mind. The fear of holy obedience made him cast all hesitation from his heart, and he grasped the bag in his hands. A large snake slid out of the bag, and showed him the diabolical deceit. Then the saint said to him: "Brother, to God's servants money is nothing but a devil and a poisonous snake."

Jgs 13:6, 8

Jgs 19:14

Nm 15:18; Dn 2:29

Jn 4:6

Mt 18:16

Lk 22:41

POVERTY IN CLOTHING

Chapter XXXIX
HOW THE SAINT REBUKED BY WORD AND EXAMPLE THOSE WHO WEAR FINE SOFT CLOTHES

AC 28

[69] Clothed with power from on high,
this man was warmed more by divine fire on the inside
than by what covered his body on the outside.

Lk 24:49

AC 29

He detested those in the Order who *dressed* in three layers of *clothing* or who wore soft clothes without necessity. As for "necessity" not based on reason but on pleasure, he declared that it was a sign of a *spirit* that was *extinguished*.

Mt 11:8

1 Thes 5:19

"When the spirit is lukewarm," he said, "and gradually growing cold as it moves from grace, flesh and blood inevitably *seek their own interests*. When the soul finds no delight, what is left except for the flesh to look for some? Then the base instinct covers itself with the excuse of necessity, and the *mind of the flesh* forms the conscience." And he added: "Let's say one of my brothers encounters a real necessity: he is affected by some need. If he rushes to satisfy it, *what reward will he get?* He found an occasion for merit, but clearly showed that he did not like it." With these and similar words he pierced those who would not tolerate necessity. He taught that not bearing patiently with need is the same as *returning to Egypt*.

Phil 2:21

Col 2:18

AC 30

Gn 29:15

Nm 14:2-4

ER II 13-14; LR II 14-15

He did not want the brothers to have more than two tunics under any circumstances, and these he allowed to be mended with patches sewn on them. He ordered the brothers to shun fine fabrics, and those who acted to the contrary he rebuked publicly with biting words. To confound them by his example he *sewed sackcloth* on his own rough tunic and at his death he asked that the tunic for his funeral be covered in cheap sackcloth.

Jb 16:16

But he allowed brothers pressed by illness or other necessity to wear a soft tunic next to the skin, as long as rough and cheap clothing was kept on the outside. For, he said: "A time will come when strictness will be relaxed, and lukewarmness will hold such sway, that sons of a poor father will not be the least ashamed to wear even velvet cloth, just changing the color."[a]

---

a. Cf. AC 30.

Father!

We are *children who are strangers*

and, it is not you whom we *deceive,*

but our own *iniquity deceives itself!*

This is obvious, clear as day,

and increases day by day.

Ps 18:46
Ps 27:12

Chapter XL

HE DECLARES THAT THOSE WHO WITHDRAW FROM POVERTY WILL BE
CORRECTED BY WANT

[70]The holy man would often repeat this: "As far as the brothers
will withdraw from poverty, that far the world will withdraw from
them; *they will seek,*" he said, *"but will not find.* But if they would only
embrace my Lady Poverty, the world would nourish them, for they
are given to the world *for its salvation."* He would also say: "There is an
exchange[a] between the brothers and the world: they owe the world
good example, and the world owes them the supply of necessities of
life. When they break faith and withdraw their good example, the
world withdraws its helping hand, a just judgment."

Concerned about poverty, the *man of God* feared large numbers:
they give the appearance, if not the reality, of wealth. Because of this
he used to say: "Oh, *if it were possible,* I wish the world would only
rarely get to see Lesser Brothers, and should be surprised at their
small number!" Joined by an unbreakable bond to Lady Poverty, he
expected her dowry in the future, not in the present. He also sang
with warmer feeling and livelier joy the psalms that praise poverty,
such as, *"The patience of the poor will not perish in the end"* and, *"Let the
poor see this and rejoice."*

Rv 9:6; Mt 7:8;
Lk 11:10; Jn 7:34

Phil 1:19

2 Kgs 1:9

Mk 14:35; Gal 4:15

Ps 9:19; Ps 69:33

---

a. The Latin text reads: *Commercium est inter mundum et fratres* [there is an exchange between the
brothers and the world]. See FA:ED I, 214 b. The concept of *commercium* is incorporated into the
title of the *Sacrum Commercium Sancti Francisci cum Domina Paupertate* [The Sacred Exchange of
Saint Francis with Lady Poverty]. In addition to this text, it is found only twice more in Thomas's
writings, 1C 35, 2C 19, always in the sense of an exchange but evoking ideas of contract and
covenant.

SEEKING ALMS

Chapter XLI
HIS RECOMMENDING THE SEEKING OF ALMS

ER IX 3-8; 2-3

[71]The holy Father was much happier to use alms begged from door to door rather than offerings. He used to say that being ashamed to beg was an enemy of salvation, asserting that shame while begging, which does not hang back, was holy. He praised the blush spreading over a sensitive face, but not the kind that means being overcome by embarrassment. *Using these words,* he would often exhort his followers to seek alms: "Go, for in *this last hour* the Lesser Brothers *have been given* to the world so that the elect may carry out for them what the divine Judge will praise: What *you did for one of my lesser brothers, you did for me.*" Because of this he used to say that this religion was privileged by the *Great Prophet,* who had so clearly expressed the *title of its name.*[a] He therefore wanted the brothers to dwell not only in cities, but also in the hermitages, so that people everywhere might be given the opportunity for merit, and the dishonest might be stripped of *the veil of an excuse.*

Sir 20:8
1 Jn 2:18
1 Sm 1:28
Mt 25:40

Lk 7:16
2 Sm 18:18

Jn 15:22; 2 Cor 2:16

Chapter XLII
THE SAINT IS AN EXAMPLE IN SEEKING ALMS

[72]So that he might never offend his holy bride even a single time, this *servant of the Most High God* would do as follows: whenever he was invited by some lord and was to be honored by a more lavish dinner, he would first beg *some pieces of bread* at the neighboring houses, and then, *enriched by poverty* he would hurry to the table. Sometimes people asked why he did this, and his answer was that he would not give up a permanent inheritance for a fief granted for an hour.[b] "Poverty," he said, "not your false riches, makes us *heirs* and kings *of the kingdom of Heaven.*"

Acts 16:17
Mt 15:36-37
2 Cor 8:9
Jas 2:5; Rom 8:17; Mt 13:24

LR VI 4

a. Thomas places these comments on poverty in an eschatological context, introduced by the apocalyptic phrase of "this last hour." It continues with the more feudal concepts of "privilege" and "title," implying notions of exemption as well as inheritance. The canonical "title" of poverty entitled one to a claim to God's care, cf. FA:ED I 198 c.

b. A lord granted a vassal land in "fief," i.e. in *fidelitas* [fidelity] for as long as he fulfilled the obligations prescribed. Feudalism, the political and economic system of medieval western Europe, was based on the institutions of vassalage and fief-holding; that is, the humble sought out a powerful lord and agreed to render services in return for protection and a piece of land. In this case, Francis understands poverty as a permanent inheritance, in contrast to land held under a conditional arrangement. These feudal allusions are continued in 2C 73 with its references to "a royal dignity and an outstanding nobility," and 2C 74 with its mention of "the down payment of a heavenly inheritance."

Chapter XLIII
THE EXAMPLE HE GAVE AT THE COURT OF THE LORD OF OSTIA, AND HIS RESPONSE TO THAT BISHOP

[73]Saint Francis once visited Pope Gregory of venerable memory, at that time holding a lesser office. When it was time for dinner, **he went out for alms,** and on his return he placed some crusts of black bread on the bishop's table. When the bishop saw this he was rather embarrassed, especially since there were dinner guests he had invited for the first time. The father, however, with a smile on his face, distributed the alms he had received to the knights and chaplains who were his table companions, and **they all accepted them with** remarkable **devotion.** Some ate the crusts, while others saved them out of reverence.

AC 97

When the meal was over **the bishop got up** from the table and, taking the man of God aside to a private place, **lifting up his arms he** *embraced* him "My brother," he said, "why did you **shame me in a house, which is yours and your brothers',** by going out for alms?" The saint replied: "**I showed you honor** instead, while I honored a greater Lord. For *the Lord is pleased by* poverty, and especially when one freely chooses to go begging. As for me, I consider it a royal dignity and an outstanding nobility *to follow* that *Lord* who, *though he was rich, became poor for our sake."* And he added: "I get greater delight from a poor table, set with some little alms, than from a great table with so many dishes that they *can* hardly *be numbered."*

Gn 33:4

Ps 68:17

Mt 19:21; Lk 18:22; 2 Cor 8:9

Ps 40:13

The bishop, greatly edified, said to the saint: "**Son,** *do what seems good in your eyes, for the Lord is with you."*

1 Sm 3:18; Jos 1:9

Chapter XLIV
HOW HE ENCOURAGED BY WORD AND EXAMPLE THE SEEKING OF ALMS

[74]At first he often used to go for alms by himself, both to train himself and to spare embarrassment for his brothers. But seeing that many of them were not giving due regard to their calling, he once **said:** "My *dearest brothers,* the Son of God was more noble than we are, and yet *for our sake he made himself poor in this world.* For love of him we have *chosen the way of* poverty. So we should not be ashamed to go for alms. The heirs of the kingdom should not at all be embarrassed by the down payment of a heavenly inheritance![a] *I say to you that many noble and*

AC 51

Phil 4:1; Mt 4:3 2 Cor 8:9
Ps 119:30

LR VI 3

Jas 2:5

Mt 5:22; 1 Cor 1:26

---

a. The Latin text reads: *Arrham caelestis hereditatis* [the down payment of a heavenly inheritance]. The word, *arrha,* is difficult to translate. In English, the word means "earnest money," and refers to a pledge of an eventual fuller gift or payment. The *arrha* gives the recipient an actual right to this fuller gift. By the time of Thomas of Celano it had come to designate those gifts that were given at the time of a betrothal. For a fuller discussion of the word, see Kevin Herbert, "Introduction," in Hugh of St. Victor, *Soliloquy on the Earnest Money of the Soul,* translated from the Latin with an introduction by Kevin Herbert (Milwaukee: Marquette University Press, 1956), 11.

learned men will join our company and will consider it an honor to go begging for **alms**. You, who are the *first fruits* of such men: *rejoice and be glad*! Do not refuse to do what you must hand on to those holy men." 1 Cor 15:16; Ps 32:11; Mt 5:12

Chapter XLV
THE REBUKE OF A BROTHER WHO REFUSED TO BEG

[75]Blessed Francis would often say that a true Lesser Brother should not go for long periods without seeking alms. "And the more noble my son is," he said, "the more eager he should be to go, because in that way merits for him are increased."

AC 97   In a certain place there was a brother who was no "one" for begging, but was "many" for eating. The saint observed this friend of the belly, who shared in the fruits but not in the labor, and said to him once: "**Go on your way, Brother Fly, because you want to feed on the sweat of your brothers but wish to be idle in the** *work of God.*[a]   1 Cor 15:58 You are just like Brother Drone, who wants to be the first to eat the honey without doing the work of the bees." This *man of the flesh* realized that his gluttony had been discovered, and he went back to the   1 Cor 3:3 world, which he had never left. He left religion. And he who was no "one" for begging, now was no brother; he who was many "ones" for eating, became even more for the devil.

Chapter XLVI
HOW HE RAN TO MEET A BROTHER CARRYING ALMS
AND KISSED HIM ON THE SHOULDER

AC 98   [76]Another time at the Portiuncula a certain brother was returning from Assisi with alms, and as he approached the place he broke into song, and began in a loud voice to *praise the Lord.* When the saint   Ps 135:1 heard him, he suddenly jumped up and ran outside. He kissed the brother on the shoulder, and took the sack on his own shoulder, saying: "Blessed be my brother who goes willingly, begs humbly, and *re-*   Lk 10:17 *turns joyfully!*"

Chapter XLVII
HOW HE GOT SOME SECULAR KNIGHTS TO GO SEEKING ALMS

AC 96   [77]When blessed Francis, suffering every kind of illness, was already close to his end, the people of Assisi through their formally

---

a. In the *Rule of Saint Benedict*, *Opus Dei* [the work of God] refers to the celebration of the Divine Office or Liturgy of the Hours. In this instance, the meaning includes the sacred work of begging for alms.

appointed representatives sought him out in the place at Nocera, so
as *not to give their glory to others*, that is, the body of the *man of God*. As
knights carried him reverently on horseback, they came to a very
poor village called Satriano.[a] Their hunger and the time of day called
for food, but they went through the whole place and *found nothing* for
sale. So the knights came back to blessed Francis and said: "**You
must give us some of your alms, because we can find nothing** here
to buy." The saint *replied and said:* "**You didn't find anything because
you trust your flies** more than in God." He used to call coins "flies."
"**But go back,**" he said, "**to the houses** you have visited, offering the
love of God instead of money, and humbly beg for alms! Don't be
embarrassed. After sin everything is bestowed as alms, for the Great
Almsgiver gives to the worthy and the unworthy with kind piety."
The knights overcame their embarrassment and promptly went begging alms, and they bought more with the love of God than with
money. In fact everyone eagerly gave with good humor, and hunger
could not have its way where lavish poverty held sway.

Is 42:8, 48:11; 1 Kgs 13:29

Mt 21:19

Jn 4:13

ER IX 8

Chapter XLVIII
A PIECE OF A CAPON TURNED INTO FISH AT ALESSANDRIA

[78]In almsgiving he sought profit for souls
rather than support for the body,
and *he made himself an example* for others
no less in *giving*
than in *receiving* alms.

Sir 4:36

Na 3:6

Once he came to Alessandria in Lombardy *to preach the word of God*,
and was devoutly welcomed as a guest by a *godfearing man* of praiseworthy reputation. This man asked him to *eat* of everything *set before
him,* in observance of the holy Gospel. Overcome by the graciousness
of his host, he graciously agreed. The host then hurried off and prepared a fat, seven-year-old capon for the *man of God* to eat.[b] As the Patriarch of the Poor[c] was sitting at table with the joyful family, a *son of*

Acts 13:5

Jb 2:3

Lk 10:8

ER III 13; LR III

2 Kgs 1:10

1 Sm 25:17

JLS 45

---

a. Fortini maintains that Satriano was a castello northeast of Assisi, in a valley beyond Mount Subasio. It is mentioned in the records of the Commune of Assisi in 1030 in which property in Satriano was given to the abbot of the monastery of Farfa. See Fortini, *Francis* 591j.

b. A belief existed that certain precious stones could be found in the entrails of a capon that had reached seven years, cf. Philippe de Thaon, *Les Lapidaires Francais au Môyen Age*, ed. L. Pannier (Paris, 1882). A French proverb maintained: Capon of eight months, a feast for a king, cf. Le Roux de Lincy, *Le Livres de Proverbs Francais*, t. I (Paris, 1842), 155.

c. This is only instance of Thomas's use of this title.

Belial[a] suddenly appeared at the door, poor in grace, but pretending to be poor in necessities of life. He cleverly invoked the love of God as he begged for alms, and in a tearful voice requested help for God's sake. The saint acknowledged the *Name which is blessed above all* and which was to him *sweeter than honey.* He gladly took a piece of the bird that was being served, put it on a piece of bread,[b] and gave it to the beggar.

What else? The wretch saved the gift so as to discredit the saint!

[79]*The next day* the people gathered and, as usual, the holy man was *proclaiming the word of God,* when that wicked man suddenly *cried out,*[c] trying to show the piece of capon to *all the people.* "Look," he yelled, "see what kind of man this Francis is. He preaches; you revere him as a holy man! Look at the meat he gave me, which he was eating last night!" They all turned on that wicked man, and accused him of being possessed by the devil, for what he insisted was a piece of capon appeared to all of them as a fish. The wretched man himself was astounded at the miracle, and he was compelled to admit what the others said. Finally, his *crime discovered,* blushing with shame, the miserable man wiped it away by penance. He begged the saint's forgiveness in front of everyone, confessing his evil intention. After *the rebel turned back* to his senses, the meat returned to its original nature.

THOSE WHO RENOUNCE THE WORLD

Chapter XLIX
THE EXAMPLE OF A MAN WHO GAVE TO HIS RELATIVES
RATHER THAN TO THE POOR
AND HOW THE SAINT REBUKED HIM

[80]The saint taught those coming to the Order
that, before giving to the world a *bill of divorce*
they should first offer what was theirs outwardly
and then *offer themselves* inwardly *to God.*

---

a. The term, "son of Belial," (cf. 2C 24) refers to one taken over by evil. In this case, it probably refers to a Cathar heretic, since the Cathars condemned the eating of flesh meat. For background information on the Cathars, see Herbert Grundmann, *Religious Movements in the Middle Ages,* translated by Steven Rowan with an introduction by Robert E. Lerner (Notre Dame, London: University of Notre Dame Press, 1995).

b. Slices or flat rolls of bread were often used instead of plates in the Middle Ages. Since the beggar could take the "plate" home and not have to return it, this custom would fit well in these circumstances.

c. The word *irrugit,* [cried out] appears only once in the Vulgate version of the Bible, i.e. in this passage of Gn 27:34, the plea of the frustrated Esau, the first born son, after Isaac bestowed his blessing on the younger son, Jacob.

Marginal references:
7, 19; Rom 9:5
14:18; Ps 19:11
Jn 1:43; 12:12
13:5; Gn 27:34
Acts 4:10
Jos 7:15
Is 46:8
Mt 5:31; Is 50:1; Jer 3:8
Heb 9:14

He would admit to the Order
only those who had given up everything
and kept nothing,

Mt 19:21   both because of the words of the holy Gospel   ER II 4; LR II 5
and because they should not cause scandal

Jn 12:6   by keeping *a money bag*.   ER VIII 7; Adm

[81]It happened once in the March of Ancona after the saint had   AC 62
been preaching, that a man came to him humbly requesting to enter

Jas 2:5   the Order. And the holy man said to him: "If you want to join *God's*

1 Cor 13:3   *poor*, first *distribute* what you have to the *poor* of the world." When he

Ps 112:9   heard this, the man went off and, led by the love of the flesh, *distrib-*
uted his goods to his relatives and not to the *poor*. When he came
back and told the saint about his open-handed generosity, the father
laughed at him: "Go on your way, Brother Fly," he said, "for you

Gn 12:1; Acts 7:3   have not yet *left your home* and *family*. You gave what you had to your

Sir 34:24-25   relatives and *cheated the poor*. You are not worthy of the holy poor. You

Wis 4:3   began with flesh, and *laid down* a crumbling *foundation* for a spiritual

1 Cor 2:14; Lk 6:30   building!" And so this *carnal man* returned to his own, and *demanded
back his goods*: refusing to leave them to the poor; he soon left his proposal of virtue.

Today, this kind of stingy distribution fools
many setting out on a blessed life with a worldly beginning.

Jgs 16:17   Nobody *consecrates* himself *to God*

Prov 10:22   to *make* his relatives *rich*,

Rom 2:7; Phil 1:22   but to *acquire life by the fruit of good work*,
redeeming his sins

Ex 13:13   *by the price* of piety.

He often taught that if the brothers were in want, it was better to
have recourse to others than to those who were entering the Order,
primarily for the sake of example and also to avoid any appearance of
base interests.

A VISION ABOUT POVERTY

Chapter L

[82]At this point I would like to tell about a memorable vision the saint had.

One night, after praying for a long time, he gradually grew drowsy and fell asleep. Then his holy soul was brought into *the sanctuary of God*, and, among other things, he saw *in a dream* a lady who looked like this: *Her head* seemed to be *of gold, her breast and arms of silver, her belly* was crystal, and her lower parts of *iron. She was tall in stature, slim and harmonious in form. But that very beautiful* lady was covered by a filthy mantle. When the blessed Father *got up the next morning* he told this vision to the holy man, Brother Pacifico, but without explaining what it meant.

Many have interpreted it as they please, but I do not think it out of place to keep to the interpretation of Pacifico, which *the Holy Spirit suggested* to him as he was hearing it. "This very beautiful lady," he said, "is the beautiful soul of Saint Francis. Her golden head is his contemplation and wisdom about things of eternity; her silver breast and arms are *the words of the Lord meditated in the heart* and *carried out in deeds.* The hardness of the *crystal* is his sobriety, its *sparkle* is his chastity, and iron is his steadfast perseverance. Finally, consider the filthy mantle as the little and despised body covering his *precious soul.*"

However, many others who also *have the Spirit of God* understand this Lady, as the father's bride, Poverty. "The reward of glory made her golden," they say, "the praise of fame made her silver; profession made her crystal, because she was internally and externally the same, without a money-pouch; and perseverance until the end made her iron. But the opinion of *carnal men* has woven a filthy garment for this exceptional lady."

Many also apply this vision to the Order, following the successive periods of Daniel.[a] But it is evident that the vision is principally about the father, since to avoid vanity he absolutely refused to interpret it. Surely if it had touched on the Order, he would not have passed over it in total silence.

Ps 73:17
Gn 20:3
Dn 2:31-33
Ez 23:23
Gn 24:54

Jn 14:26

Ps 11:7; Ps 118:11; Gn 11:6
Sir 43:22; Rv 4:6; Rv 22:1

Prv 6:26

Dn 4:5; 1 Cor 7:40

1 Cor 2:14

Dn 2:36-45

---

a. Daniel's interpretation of King Nebuchadnezzar's dream of the golden, silver, brass, and iron statue was considered a prophetic announcement of the course of the history. Cf. Bernard McGinn, *Visions of the End: Apocalyptic Traditions in the Middle Ages* (New York: Columbia University Press, 1979), 94-116.

SAINT FRANCIS'S COMPASSSION TOWARD THE POOR

Chapter LI
HIS COMPASSION TOWARD THE POOR
AND HOW HE ENVIED THOSE POORER THAN HIMSELF

[83]What tongue could
tell of this man's compassion for the poor?
He certainly had an inborn kindness,
doubled by the piety poured out on him.
Therefore,

Sg 5:6   Francis's *soul melted* for the poor,
and to those to whom he could not extend a hand,
he extended his affection.
Any need,   Off 1 V
any lack he noticed in anyone,
with a rapid change of thought, he turned back to Christ.
In that way
he read the Son of our Poor Lady in every poor person.
As she held Him naked in her hands
so he carried Him naked in his heart.

1 Pt 2:1   Although he had driven away *all envy* from himself,
he could not give up his envy of poverty.
If he saw people poorer than himself,   1C 76
he immediately envied them and,
contending with a rival for poverty
was afraid he would be overcome.

Gn 39:11;1 Sm 2:27   [84]*It happened* one day when the *man of God* was going about   AC 113
preaching he met a poor man on the road. Seeing the man's naked-
ness, he was deeply moved and, turning to his companion, said:
"This man's need brings great shame on us; it passes a harsh judgment on our poverty." "How so, brother?" his companion replied.
The saint answered in a sad voice: "I chose Poverty for my riches and
for my Lady, but look: She shines brighter in this man. Don't you
know that the whole world has heard that we are the poorest of all
for Christ? But this poor man proves it is otherwise!"

Oh enviable envy!
Oh rivalry to be rivaled by his children!
This is not the envy
that is distressed by the good fortune of others;

nor that which grows dim in the sun's rays,
opposed to piety and tormented by spite.
Do you think that Gospel poverty
has nothing worth envying?
She has Christ himself,
and through him has *all in all.*   1 Cor 12:6
Why do you pant after stipends,
clerics of today?
Tomorrow you will know Francis was rich
when you find in your hand
the stipend of torments.

Chapter LII

HOW HE CORRECTED A BROTHER WHO CRITICIZED A POOR MAN

AC 114

[85] Another day, when he was preaching, a sick poor man came to the place. Taking pity on the man's double misfortune—that is, his need and his illness—he began to speak about poverty with his companion. And since suffering with the suffering, he had moved beyond *to the depths of his heart,* when the saint's companion said to him: "My brother, it is true that he is poor, but it could be that in the whole province there is no one who desires riches more!" At once the saint rebuked him, and as the companion acknowledged his fault, said to him: *"Quickly now, strip off* your tunic; throw yourself down at the poor man's feet and confess your fault! And, don't just ask his pardon, but also beg for his prayers!" The brother obeyed, made his amends and returned. The saint said to him: "Brother, whenever you see a poor person, a mirror of the Lord and his poor Mother is placed before you. Likewise in the sick, look closely for the *infirmities* which He accepted *for our sake."*

Ps 73: 7

Is 5:19; Bar 5:1

5; 2LtF 5; 2C 83

Mt 8:17; Is 53:4

Ah!

Always *a bundle of myrrh* abided in Francis.[a]   Sg 1:13

Always *he gazed upon the face of* his *Christ.*   Ps 84:10, Vg

Always he caressed the *Man of Sorrows, familiar with suffering.*[b]   Is 53:3

---

a. Because myrrh was a bitter spice used in embalming, the verse, *My beloved is to me as a bundle of myrrh which rests on my bosom* (Sg 1:13), was interpreted mystically as meaning that the Passion of Christ should always be in the Christian's heart. See William of St-Thierry, *Commentary on the Song of Songs,* 80-83, and Bernard, *Homilies on the Song of Songs,* 43:3-5.

b. Francis's embrace of the Suffering Christ is developed in 1C 84, 92-93, 97-98, 102, 103. For the impact of Francis's continued gaze on Christ, see Octavian Schmucki, "The Passion of Christ in the Life of St. Francis of Assisi: A Comparative Study of the Sources in the Light of Devotion to the Passion Practiced in His Time," GR 4 (1990): 61-85.

Chapter LIII
THE MANTLE GIVEN TO AN OLD WOMAN IN CELANO

[86] In Celano at winter time Saint Francis was wearing a piece of folded cloth as a cloak, which a man from Tivoli, a friend of the brothers, had lent him. While he was at the palace of the bishop of the Marsi,[a] an old woman came up to him *begging for alms*. He quickly unfastened the cloth from his neck, and, although it belonged to someone else, he gave it to the poor old woman, saying: "Go and make yourself a tunic; you really need it." The old woman laughed; she was stunned—I don't know if it was out of fear or joy —and took the piece of cloth from his hands. She ran off quickly, so that delay might not bring the danger of having to give it back, and cut it with scissors. But when she saw that the cut cloth would not be enough for a tunic, she returned to the saint, knowing his earlier kindness, and showed him that the material was not enough. The saint turned his eyes on his companion, who had just the same cloth covering his back. "Brother," he said, "do you hear what this old woman is saying? For the love of God, let us bear with the cold! Give the poor woman the cloth so she can finish her tunic." He gave his, the companion offered his as well, and both were left naked so the old woman could be clothed.

AC 31

Acts 3:2

Chapter LIV
ANOTHER POOR PERSON TO WHOM HE GAVE ANOTHER MANTLE

[87] Another time when he was coming back from Siena he met a poor man, and the saint said to his companion: "Brother, we must give back to this poor man the mantle that is his. *We accepted* it *on loan* until we should happen to find someone poorer than we are." The companion, seeing the need of his pious father, stubbornly objected that he should not provide for someone else by neglecting himself. But the saint said to him: "I do not want to *be a thief*; we will be accused of theft if we do not give to someone in greater need." So his companion gave in, and he gave up the mantle.

AC 32

Lk 6:34; Prv 22:7

Jn 12:6

---

a. See AC 31.

Chapter LV
HE DOES THE SAME WITH ANOTHER POOR MAN

AC 33

[88]A similiar thing happened at "Le Celle" of Cortona. Blessed Francis was wearing a new mantle which the brothers had gone to some trouble to find for him. A poor man came to the place weeping for his dead wife and his poor little family which was *left desolate*. The saint said to him: "I'm giving you this cloak for the love of God, but on the condition that you do not hand it over to anyone unless they pay well for it." The brothers immediately came running to take the mantle away and prevent this donation. But the poor man, *taking courage* from the father's look, clutched it with both hands and defended it as his own. *In the end* the brothers had to redeem the mantle, and the poor man left after getting his price.

Ps 10:14

2 Chr 17:6

2 Mc 5:5

Chapter LVI
HOW HE GAVE HIS MANTLE TO A CERTAIN MAN
SO THAT HE WOULD NOT HATE HIS LORD

AC 34

[89]Once when he was at Colle in the county of Perugia Saint Francis met a poor man whom he had known before *in the world*. He asked him: "Brother, how are you doing?" The man malevolently began to *heap curses* on his lord, who had taken away everything he had. "Thanks to my lord, *may the Almighty Lord curse* him, I'm very bad off!" Blessed Francis felt more pity for the man's soul, rooted in mortal hatred, than for his body. He said to him: "Brother, forgive your lord for the love of God, so you may *set your soul free*, and it may be that he will *return* to you *what he has taken*. Otherwise you will *lose* not only your property but also your *soul*." He replied: "I can't entirely forgive him unless he first gives back what he took." Blessed Francis had a mantle on his back, and said to him: "Here, I'll give you this cloak, and beg you to forgive your lord for the love of *the Lord God*." The man's mood sweetened, and, moved by this kindness, he took the gift and forgave the wrongs.

Ti 2:12

Nm 5:19, 23

Rv 1:8, Gn 5:29

Est 4:13

Ex 22:12

Lk 9:24

Is 42:5

Chapter LVII
HOW HE GAVE THE HEM OF HIS TUNIC TO A POOR MAN

[90]Once, when a poor man asked him for something, he had nothing at hand, so he unstitched the hem of his tunic and gave it to the poor man. More than once in the same situation he took off his trousers.

Col 3:12

With such *depths of piety*
he knew no bounds for the poor;
with such depths of feeling he followed

1 Pt 2:21

the *footprints of* the poor *Christ.*

Chapter LVIII
HOW HE HAD THE FIRST NEW TESTAMENT IN THE ORDER
GIVEN TO THE POOR MOTHER OF TWO OF THE BROTHERS

[91]The mother of two of the brothers once came to the saint, confi- *AC 93*

Acts 3:2 dently *asking for alms.* Sharing her pain the holy father said to Brother
Peter of Catanio: "Can we give some alms to our mother?" He used
to call the mother of any brother his mother and the mother of all

Lk 11:41 the brothers. Brother Peter replied: "There is *nothing left* in the house
which we could *give* her." Then he added: "We do have one New
Testament, for reading the lessons at matins, since we don't have a
breviary." Blessed Francis said to him: "Give our mother the New
Testament so she can sell it to care for her needs, for through it we
are reminded to help the poor. I believe that God will be pleased
more by the giving than by the reading."[a] So the book was given to
the woman, and the first Testament in the Order was given away
through this sacred piety.

Chapter LIX
HOW HE GAVE HIS MANTLE TO A POOR WOMAN WITH AN EYE DISEASE

[92]At the time when Saint Francis was staying at the palace of the *AC 89*
bishop of Rieti to be treated for his eye disease, a poor woman from
Machilone who had the same disease as the saint came to see the
doctor.[b]

Then the saint, speaking familiarly to his guardian,[c] nudged him
a bit: "Brother Guardian, we have to give back what belongs to
someone else." And he answered: "Father, if there's such a thing
with us, let it be returned." And he said: "Yes, there is this mantle,

Lk 6:34 which we *received as a loan* from that poor woman; we should give it
back to her, because she has nothing in her purse for her expenses."

---

a. A similar incident occurs in the tradition of the desert when the monk Serapion sells his copy of the
   Gospels to help the poor, and says: "I have sold the book which told me to sell all that I had and give
   to the poor." Cf. Thomas Merton, *The Wisdom of the Desert: Sayings from the Desert Fathers* (New
   York: New Directions, 1960), 37.

b. Cf. Octavian Schmucki, "The Illnesses of Saint Francis of Assisi before His Stigmatization," GR 4
   (1990): 31-61.

c. Cf. FA:ED I 98 a.

The guardian replied: "Brother, this mantle is mine, and nobody lent it to me! Use it as long as you like, and when you don't want to use it any longer, return it to me." In fact the guardian had recently bought it because Saint Francis needed it. The saint then said to him: "Brother Guardian, you have always been courteous to me; now, I beg you, show your courtesy." And the guardian answered him: "Do as you please, father, as the *Spirit suggests* to you!" The saint called a very devout layman and told him: "**Take this mantle and twelve loaves of bread,** and *go say* to that poor woman **'The poor man to whom you lent this mantle thanks you for the loan,** but now **take what is yours!'**" The man went and said what he was told, but the woman thought *she was being mocked,* and **replied to him,** *all embarrassed: "Leave me in peace,* you and your mantle! *I don't know what you're talking about!"* The man insisted, and put it all in her hands. She saw that this was in fact no deception, but fearing that such an easy gain would be taken away from her, she left the place by night and returned home with the mantle, not caring about caring for her eyes.

Jn 14:26

Ez 3:1

Mt 20:14

Gn 27:12; Lk 14:9

1 Sm 20:13; Mt 26:70

Chapter LX
HOW THREE WOMEN APPEARED TO HIM ON THE ROAD,
AND HOW THEY DISAPPEARED AFTER A NOVEL GREETING

[93]I will tell in a few words something marvelous, doubtful in interpretation, most certain in truth. When Francis, the poor man of Christ, was traveling from Rieti to Siena for the treatment of his eyes, he passed through the plain near Rocca Campiglia, taking as a *companion on the journey* a doctor who was very devoted to the Order. Three poor women appeared by the road as Saint Francis was passing. They were so similar in stature, age, and face that you would think they were a three-part piece of matter, modeled by one form.[a] As Saint Francis approached, they reverently bowed their heads, and hailed him with a new greeting, saying: "Welcome, Lady Poverty!" At once the saint was *filled with* unspeakable *joy,* for he had in himself nothing that he would so gladly have people hail as what these women had chosen. And since he thought at first that they really were poor women, he turned to the doctor who was accompanying him, and said: "I beg you, for God's sake, give, so that I can give something to these poor women." The doctor immediately took out

Gn 33:12

Ps 126:2

---

a. Thomas is using a comparison from Aristotelian physics, according to which "matter" by itself is amorphous, but takes its shape and characteristics from the "substantial form" which is impressed on it.

some coins, and leaping from his horse he gave some to each of them.
They then went on for a short way, and suddenly the doctor and the
brothers glanced back and saw no women at all on that whole plain.

Ps 107: 8, 15   They were utterly amazed and counted the event *as a marvel of the*
Wis 5:11   *Lord,* knowing these were not women who had *flown away* faster *than*
birds.

SAINT FRANCIS'S DEDICATION TO PRAYER

Chapter LXI
THE TIME, PLACE AND THE INTENSITY OF HIS PRAYING

2 Cor 5:6   [94]*A pilgrim* while *in the body, away from the Lord,*
2 Kgs 5:8   Francis, the *man of God,*
1 Cor 5:3   strove to keep himself *present in spirit* to heaven,
and, being already made a fellow-citizen of the angels,
he was separated from them
only by the wall of the flesh.
Ps 63:2   With all his *soul* he *thirsted for* his Christ:
to him he dedicated not only his whole heart
but also his whole body.
We will tell only a few things, to be imitated by posterity
1 Cor 2:9   —to the extent that they can be told *to human ears*—
Sir 17:11   about the *wonders* of his prayer,
things we have *seen* with our own eyes.

He turned all his time into a holy leisure[a]
Sir 45:31   in which to engrave *wisdom on his heart,*
so that, if he did not always advance,
he would not seem to give up.
If visits from people of the world   1C 96
or any kind of business intruded,

a. This is Thomas's only use of the rich monastic phrase *otium sanctum* [holy leisure]. *Otium* is an
ambivalent word that could mean the post-Classical *otiositas* [laziness] and was seen as the
antithesis of *negotium* [employment]. Medieval monasticism saw *otium sanctum* as the field for
contemplation and frequently saw it in conjunction with *vacatio, quies or sabbatum,* all signifying
rest. Bernard of Clairvaux maintained that wisdom is the product of leisure and lamented that the
time of "holy leisure is not of sufficient length," cf. Bernard of Clairvaux, Sermon 85, *On the Song of
Songs,* translated by Irene M. Edmonds, introduction by Jean Leclercq (Kalamazoo, MI: Cistercian
Publications, 1980), 203; Sermon 58:1, *On the Song of Songs,* translated by Kilian Walsh and Irene
M. Edmonds, introduction by Emero Stiegman (Kalamazoo, MI: Cistercian Publication, 1979), 108.
See Hermann Josef Sieben, "Quies" et "Ōtium," *Dictionnaire de la Spiritualité Ascetique et Mystique*
XI (Paris: Beauchesne, 1982), 2746-2756; Jean Leclercq, *Otia Monastica: Études sur La
Vocabulaire de La Contemplation au Moyen Âge* (Rome: Herder, 1963), 26-41.

he would cut them short
rather than finish them,
and hurry back to the things that are within.
The world had no flavor to him,
fed on the sweetness of heaven,
and divine delicacies had spoiled him
for crude human fare.
He always sought out a *hidden place*   Mt 6:4
where he could join to God
not only his spirit
but every member of his body.
When it happened that he was suddenly overcome in public
by a *visitation of the Lord*   Lk 1:68
so as not to be without a cell,
he would make a little cell out of his mantle.
Sometimes, when he had no mantle,
he would cover his face with his sleeve
to avoid revealing the *hidden manna*.   Rv 2:17
He would always place something between himself and bystanders
so they would not notice *the Bridegroom's touch*.   Sg 5:4
Even when crowded in the confines of a ship,[a]
he could pray unseen.
Finally, when none of these things was possible,
he made a temple out of his breast.
Forgetful of himself
he did not cough or groan;
and being absorbed in God
took away any hard breathing or external movement.

[95]Thus it was at home.
But when praying in the woods or solitary places
he would fill the forest with groans,
water the places with tears,
strike his breast with his hand,
and, as if finding a more secret hiding place,
he often conversed out loud with his Lord.
There he replied to the Judge,
there he entreated the Father;
there he conversed with the Friend,
there he played with the Bridegroom.

C 6, 71, 91, 103

1C 55; 2C 30

---

a. The Latin text *navis plurimis insertus* [crowded in the confines of a ship] may have more than one meaning. *Navis* is translated here as ship. It could also be translated as the nave of a church.

Indeed, in order to make

Ps 66:15 all the marrow of his heart a holocaust in manifold ways,

Ps 101:3 he would place *before his eyes*

Wis 7:22 *the One who is manifold and supremely simple.*

Sg 7:9 He would often *ruminate* inwardly with unmoving *lips,*

and, drawing outward things inward,

he raised his spirit to the heights.

Thus he would direct all his attention and affection

Ps 27:4 toward the *one thing* he *asked of the Lord,*

not so much praying as becoming totally prayer.

How deeply would you think he was pervaded with sweetness,

as he grew accustomed to such things?

Jb 28:23 *He knows.*

I can only wonder.

Those with experience

will be given this knowledge;

but it is not granted to those with no experience.

Jb 41:22; Wis 7:22 His *spirit kindled,* with *boiling heat,*

his whole expression,

Sg 5:6 and his whole *soul melting.*

He was already dwelling in the highest homeland,

2 Tm 4:18 the *heavenly kingdom.*

The blessed Father usually

neglected no visitation of the Spirit,

but, whenever offered,

he would follow it;

1 Cor 16:7 and for as long as *the Lord allowed,*

he enjoyed the sweetness thus offered him.

When he was pressed by some business

or occupied with travel,

as he began to feel the touch of grace

he would enjoy brief tastes,

of the sweetest manna here and there.

Even on the road,

with his companions going on ahead,

he would stop in his tracks,

as he turned

a new inspiration into something useful.

2 Cor 6:1 *He did not receive grace in vain.*

Chapter LXII
HOW THE LITURGY OF THE HOURS SHOULD BE DEVOUTLY FULFILLED

96 He celebrated the canonical hours with no less awe than devotion. Although he was suffering from diseases of the eyes, stomach, spleen, and liver,[a] he did not want to lean against a wall or partition when he was chanting the psalms. He always fulfilled his hours standing up straight[b] and without a hood, without letting his eyes wander and without dropping syllables.

When he was travelling the world on foot, he always would stop walking in order to say the Hours, and when he was on horseback he would dismount to be on the ground. So, one day when he was returning from Rome and it was raining constantly, he got off his horse to say the Office, and, standing for quite a while, he became completely soaked. He would sometimes say: "If the body calmly eats its food, which along with itself will be food for worms, the soul should receive its food, which is its God, in great peace and tranquillity."

Chapter LXIII
HOW HE WOULD CHASE AWAY THE HEART'S IMAGININGS WHILE PRAYING

97 He thought he committed a serious offense if he was disturbed by empty imaginings while he was at prayer. When such a thing would happen, he did not fail to confess it and immediately make amends. He had made such a habit of this carefulness that he was rarely bothered by this kind of "flies."

One Lent he had been making a small cup, so as not to waste any spare time. But one day as he was devoutly saying terce, his eyes casually fell on the cup and he began to look at it, and he felt his *inner self* was being hindered in its devotion. He grieved that the cry of his heart to the divine ears had been interrupted, and when terce ended he said, so the brothers could hear: "Alas, that such a trifle had such power over me as to bend my soul to itself! I will sacrifice it to the Lord, whose sacrifice it had interrupted!" Saying this he grabbed the cup and *burned it in the fire*. "Let us be ashamed," he said, "to be seized by petty distractions when we are speaking with the *Great King* at the time of prayer."

---

a. For other references to Francis's specific illnesses, see AC 4.

b. In the Eastern and Western Churches it was the custom to chant the psalms standing, and listen to the readings while sitting down. Medieval choir stalls had a small projection or shelf called a "misericord," which would allow the singer some support while standing up. Francis did not even take advantage of the misericord.

Chapter LXIV
AN ECSTASY

[98]Many times he was often suspended in such sweetness of contemplation that he was carried away above himself and experienced things beyond human understanding, which he would not reveal to anyone.

However, one incident that did become known shows us how frequently he was absorbed in heavenly sweetness. One time he was riding on a donkey and had to pass through Borgo San Sepolcro, and when he stopped to rest at the dwelling of some lepers, many found out about the visit of the *man of God*. Men and women came running from every direction to see him, and with their usual devotion wanting to touch him. What then? They touched and pulled him, cut off bits of his tunic, but the man seemed not to feel any of this. He noticed as much of what was happening as if he were a lifeless corpse. They finally came to the place, and were long past Borgo, when that contemplator of heaven, as returning from somewhere else, *anxiously inquired* when they would be reaching Borgo.

2 Kgs 5:14

Dt 13:14

Chapter LXV
HOW HE ACTED AFTER PRAYING

[99]When he returned from his private prayers, in which he was *changed* almost *into a different man*, he tried his best to resemble the others; lest, if he appeared glowing, the breeze of favor might cancel what he had gained.

Often he would say to those close to him: "When a *servant of God* is praying, and is *visited by the Lord* in some new consolation, he should *lift his eyes up to heaven* before he comes away from prayer, fold his hands and say to the Lord: 'Lord, you have *sent* this sweetness and consolation *from heaven* to *me, an* unworthy *sinner*, and I send it back to you so you may *save it for me*, because I am a thief of your treasure.' And also, 'Lord, take away your gift from me *in this world,* and keep it for me *in the next*.' This is the way it should be," he said. "When one comes away from prayer he should appear to others a poor sinner, who had not obtained any new grace." He also used to say: "It happens that one loses something priceless for the sake of a small reward, and may easily provoke the giver not to give again."

1 Sm 10:6

2 Chr 24:9

Lk 1:68

Jn 6:5; Lk 18:13

1 Pt 1:12

Lk 18:13

Gn 27:36

Eph 1:21

Adm XXI, XXVII

Finally, his custom was to be so secret and quiet in rising for prayer that none of his companions would notice his rising or praying. But in the evening he made a good loud noise in going to bed, so that everyone would hear him as he went to rest.

Chapter LXVI
HOW A BISHOP FOUND HIM PRAYING AND WAS DEPRIVED OF SPEECH

AC 54

[100]Once when Saint Francis was praying in the place at the Portiuncula, the bishop of Assisi happened to come for a friendly visit, as he often did. As soon as he entered the place, he went rather boldly to the saint's cell without being invited, knocked on the little door and was about to barge in. But when he stuck his head inside, he saw the saint praying, and suddenly he was *struck with trembling,* his limbs froze, and he lost his voice. *By the Lord's will,* he was quickly pushed outside by force and dragged backwards a long way. I believe he was either unworthy of seeing something so secret, or that Francis was worthy of holding longer onto what he had. The bishop, stunned, returned to the brothers, and, at the first word confessing his fault, he regained his speech.

Jb 21:6

Acts 21:14; Ps 51:20

Chapter LXVII
HOW AN ABBOT FELT THE POWER OF HIS PRAYER

AC 76

[101]Another time the abbot of the monastery of San Giustino in the diocese of Perugia happened to meet Saint Francis, and quickly dismounting from his horse, conversed for a short time with him about the salvation of his soul. Finally, as he left him, he humbly asked him to pray for him, and Saint Francis replied: "My Lord, I will willingly pray." Now, when the abbot had ridden away a short distance, the saint said to his companion: "Wait for me a little while, brother, for I want to pay that debt I promised." For this was always his custom, that when he had a request for prayer he never did *toss* it *behind his back,* but rather *fulfilled his promise* quickly. As the saint entreated God, the abbot suddenly *felt in spirit* unusual warmth and sweetness like nothing he felt before, and carried *into ecstasy,* he seemed to faint away. This lasted for a short time, and then he *returned to his senses* and realized the power of Saint Francis's prayer. From that time on he always burned with ever greater love for the Order, and told many about this miraculous event.

Is 38:17

Prv 25:14

Rom 8:5

Acts 11:5

Lk 15:17

These small gifts are the kind
that servants of God should give each other;
among them,

Phil 4:15

this is the proper *communion* of *giving* and *receiving*.
This holy love, sometimes called "spiritual,"
is content with the fruit of prayer:
charity holds earthly gifts in low esteem.
To help and be helped in spiritual warfare,
to commend and be commended

2 Cor 5:10

before Christ's judgement seat,
that is what I believe is characteristic of holy love.
How far do you think Francis rose in prayer,
if he could raise up someone else this way by his merits?

THE SAINT'S UNDERSTANDING OF SACRED SCRIPTURE
AND THE POWER OF HIS WORDS

Chapter LXVIII
HIS KNOWLEDGE AND MEMORY

[102]Although this blessed man
was not educated in scholarly disciplines,

Col 3:1-3; Jas 1:17

still he learned from God *wisdom from above*
and, enlightened by the splendors of eternal light,
he understood Scripture deeply.
His genius, pure and unstained,

Col 1:26

penetrated *hidden mysteries.*
Where the knowledge of teachers is outside,
the passion of the lover entered.
He sometimes read the Sacred Books,
and whatever he once put into his mind,

Rom 2:15; 2 Cor 3:2

he *wrote* indelibly *in his heart.*
His memory took the place of books,[a]
Because, if he heard something once,
it was not wasted,
as his heart would mull it over with constant devotion.
He said this was the fruitful way to read and learn,
rather than to wander through a thousand treatises.
He considered a true philosopher
the person who never set anything ahead

---

a. Athanasius writes of Anthony: "For he paid such close attention to what was read that nothing from Scripture did he fail to take in, rather he grasped everything, and in him the memory took the place of books." Cf. Athanasius, *The Life of Antony* 3, in *Athanasius: The Life of Antony and The Letter to Marcellinus,* translation and introduction by Robert C. Gregg, preface by William A. Clebsch (New York, Ramsey, Toronto, Paulist Press, 1980), 31-32. For an in-depth study on the importance of the memory for a medieval person, see Mary J. Carruthers, *The Book of Memory: A Study of Memory in Medieval Culture* (New York: Cambridge University Press, 1990).

of the desire for eternal life.
He affirmed that it was easy to move
from self-knowledge to *knowledge of God*   Prv 2:5
for someone who searches Scripture intently
with humility and not with presumption.
He often untangled the ambiguities of questions.
Unskilled in words,   2 Cor 11:6
he spoke splendidly with understanding and power.

Chapter LXIX
HOW HE EXPLAINED A PROPHET'S WORDS
AT THE REQUEST OF A BROTHER PREACHER

AC 35   [103]While he was staying in Siena someone from the Order of
Preachers happened to arrive; he was a *spiritual man* and a Doctor   Hos 9:7
of Sacred Theology. He visited blessed Francis, and he and the holy
man enjoyed a long and sweet conversation about the *words of the*   Jn 3:34
AC36   *Lord.* This teacher asked him about the words of Ezekiel: *If you do*   Ez 3:18-20; 33: 7-9
not warn the wicked man about his wickedness, I will hold you responsible
for his soul. "I'm acquainted with many people, good Father, who
live in mortal sin, as I'm aware. But I don't always *warn them* about
their *wickedness.* Will I then be held *responsible for their souls*?"   Ez 3:18
Test 19   Blessed Francis then said that he was an unlettered man, and it
would be better for him to be taught by the other rather than to answer a question about Scripture. But that humble teacher replied:
"Brother, it's true I have heard these words explained by some
wise men, still, I'd be glad to hear how you understand it." So
blessed Francis said to him: "If that passage is supposed to be understood in a universal sense, then I understand it to mean that a
servant of God should be burning with life and holiness so brightly,   Dn 6:20
that by the *light* of *example* and the tongue of his *conduct,* he will re-   Jn 5:35; 1 Tm 4:12
buke all the wicked. In that way, I say, the brightness of his life and
the fragrance of his reputation will *proclaim their wickedness* to all of   Ez 3:19
them." That man went away greatly edified, and said to the companions of blessed Francis: "My brothers, the theology of this
man, held aloft by purity and contemplation, is a *soaring eagle,*[a]   Jb 9:26
while our learning *crawls on its belly on the ground.*"   Gn 3:14

---

a. An allusion to the well-known characteristics attributed to the eagle in the medieval bestiaries. The
eagle could soar close to the sun, and its eyes were not blinded by looking directly upon it, but were
rather fed and strengthened by it. Cf. *The Book of Beasts: A Translation from a Latin Bestiary of the
Twelfth Century,* trans. and ed. T.H. White (New York: G.P. Putnam, 1954), 105-106.

Chapter LXX
THINGS HE EXPLAINED WHEN ASKED BY A CARDINAL

[104]Another time, when he was in Rome at the home of a cardinal, he was asked about some obscure passages, and he *brought* to light their depths in such a way that you would think he was constantly studying the Scriptures. The Lord Cardinal said to him: "I'm not asking you as a scholar, but as a person who *has the Spirit of God*, and so I gladly accept the meaning in your answer, because I know it *comes from God alone.*"

Wls 6:24

1 Cor 7:40

Jn 15:26; Mt 4:4

Chapter LXXI
WHAT HE TOLD A BROTHER HE KNEW
WHEN URGED TO CONCENTRATE ON SOME READINGS

[105]Once when he was sick and full of pain all over, his companion said to him: "Father, you have always taken refuge in the Scriptures, and they always have offered you relief from pain. Please, have something from the prophets also read to you now, and maybe your *spirit will rejoice in the Lord.*" The saint said to him: "It is good to read the testimonies of Scripture, and it is good to seek the Lord our God in them. But I have already taken in so much of Scripture that I have more than enough for meditating and reflecting. I do not need more, son; *I know Christ,* poor and *crucified.*"

AC 79

Lk 1:47

1 Cor 2:2

Chapter LXXII
THE SWORDS THAT BROTHER PACIFICO
SAW GLEAMING FROM THE SAINT'S MOUTH

[106]In the March of Ancona there was a man of the world who had forgotten himself and did not know God, and who had prostituted himself entirely to vanity. He was known as the "King of Verses," because he was prince of bawdy singers and creator of worldly ballads.[a] To be brief I will just say worldly glory had raised the man so high that he had been pompously crowned by the Emperor himself.[b] While in this way, he was *walking in darkness* and *in the harness of vanity*

Jn 8:12; Is 9:1; Is 5:18

---

a. This is a reference to Brother Pacifico, cf. AC 65.

b. In the belief that this had been the custom in classical Rome, thirteenth-century custom introduced the formal crowning of poets with laurel by the hand of a civil authority. It is difficult to know which Emperor is referred to in the text, since there is no certain knowledge of the poet's age at the time of his conversion, or how long he had been an outstanding poet. Henry VI (1190-97) is known to have written love songs in German, Otto IV (1198-1214) may have known some Aquitanian troubadors in the court of Richard the Lion Hearted, who was his uncle, and Frederick II (King of Sicily in 1198, Emperor in 1215) was a patron of poets and writers; all three spent much time in Italy.

pulling iniquity, the divine piety had pity on him and *decided to call back*   2 Sm 14:14
the miserable man, *so the outcast would not perish.* By God's providence
blessed Francis and this man met each other at a monastery of poor
enclosed women;[a] the blessed father had come there with his companions to visit his daughters, while that man had come with many
of his comrades to see one of his women relatives.

Then *the hand of the Lord came upon* him, and, with his bodily eyes,   Ps 80:18
he saw Saint Francis marked with two bright shining swords inter-
secting in the shape of a cross. One of them stretched from his head
to his feet, and the other across his chest from one hand to the other.

He did not know blessed Francis, but once when he had been
pointed out by such a miracle, he recognized him immediately.
Struck at once by what he saw, he began to promise to live better at
some future date. But although the blessed Father at first preached
generally to everyone there, he pointed the *sword of God's word* on that   Heb 4:12
man. He took him aside and gently reminded him about the vanity of
society and contempt of the world, and then pierced his heart warning him about divine judgement. At once the man replied: "What's
the point of piling up any more words? Let's move on to deeds! Take
me away from people, and give me back to the Great Emperor!" The
next day the saint invested him, and, since he had been brought back
to the *peace of the Lord,* named him Brother Pacifico. His conversion   Is 26:12, Ps 85:9
was all the more edifying to many because the crowd of his vain com-
rades had been so widespread.

Enjoying the company of the blessed father, Brother Pacifico began to experience anointings he had never felt before. Repeatedly he
was allowed to see what was veiled to others. For, shortly after that,
he saw the great *sign of the Tau*[b] *on the forehead* of blessed Francis,   Ez 9:4,6
which displayed its beauty with the multi-colored circles of a pea-
cock.

---

a. Possibly the monastery of San Salvatore di Copersito in the city of San Severino in the March of
Ancona. See 1C 78 and Fortini, *Francis*, 389-392.

b. The *Tau* (ת) is a letter of the Hebrew and Greek alphabet. The origin of its use as a sign is found in Ez
9:4: "Pass through the city [through Jerusalem] and mark a ת on the foreheads of those who moan and
groan over all the abominations that are practiced within it." When Pope Innocent III opened the IV
Lateran Council on November 11, 1215, he preached on this text. The pope set forth the Tau as the
sign of penance and renewal in Christ. Francis embraced this sign as an expression of Christ's cross.
He drew it on walls and he signed his name with it. An example of Francis's signature as a ת is found
on the original parchment containing *The Praises of God and the Blessing.* For further information,
see Damien Vorreux, *A Franciscan Symbol: The Tau,* translated by Marilyn Archer and Paul
Lachance (Chicago: Franciscan Herald Press, 1977); and Octavian Schmucki, "The Passion of
Christ in the Life of St. Francis of Assisi: A Comparative Study of the Sources in the Light of Devotion
to the Passion Practiced in His Time," GR 4 (1990) Supplement: 13-21.

Chapter LXXIII
THE POWER OF HIS WORDS,
AND THE WITNESS GIVEN TO THIS BY A PHYSICIAN

[107]Although the evangelist Francis
preached to the simple,
in simple, concrete terms,
since he knew that virtue
is more necessary than words,
still, when he was among spiritual people
with greater abilities
he gave birth to life-giving and profound words.
With few words he would suggest
what was inexpressible,
and, weaving movement with fiery gestures,
he carried away all his hearers toward the things of heaven.
He did not use the keys of distinctions,[a]
for he did not preach about things he had not himself discovered.

1 Cor 2:1-2, 4-5   *Christ,* true *Power and Wisdom,*

Ps 68:34   *made his voice a voice of power.*

A physician, a learned and eloquent man, once said: "I remember the sermons of other preachers word for word, only what the saint, Francis, says eludes me. Even if I memorize some of his words, they

Sg 4:11   don't seem to me like those that originally *poured from his lips."*

Chapter LXXIV
HOW THE POWER OF HIS WORD CHASED THE DEVILS
OUT OF AREZZO THROUGH BROTHER SYLVESTER

[108]The words of Francis were powerful not only when he was

Is 55:11   present; but even when they were transmitted by others *they did not return to him empty.*

Once when he happened to come to the city of **Arezzo, the whole**   AC 108
city was shaken by a civil war which threatened its imminent de-
1 Sm 9:7   struction. Thus the *man of God* **received hospitality in a neighborhood outside the city walls.** He saw demons above that land leaping
for joy, fanning the flames of mutual destruction among its citizens.

---

a. At the time of Thomas, distinctions, techniques used in art of logic for clarifying and developing an argument, were in vogue in medieval scholastic theology. Since the human person was endowed with a special faculty for making distinctions, that ability became the trait defining the human being and enabling one to unlock the mysteries of creation. Thus medieval preaching was frequently characterized by a plethora of logical distinctions.

Calling **Brother Sylvester** by name, a *man of God,* of admirable sim- 1 Sm 9:7
plicity, *he gave him this command*: **"Go in front of the city gate** and on Gn 28:1
behalf of *Almighty God* **command the devils to leave the city** at once!" Wis 7:25

Devout simplicity hurried to carry out the obedience, and *caught* Ps 95:2
up in praise before the face of the Lord, he *boldly cried out* in front of the Dn 3:4
gate: "On behalf of God, and by the command of our father Francis,
get away from here, all you demons!" Shortly afterwards, the city returned to peace, and the people in it safeguarded civil law in great
tranquility.

Because of this, when blessed Francis was later preaching to
them, he said as he began to preach: **"I speak to you** as people once
subjugated to the devil **in demons' chains,** but now, I know, you
have been liberated through the prayers of a poor man."

Chapter LXXV
THE CONVERSION OF THAT SAME BROTHER SYLVESTER AND A VISION HE HAD

P 12; L3C 30-31 [109] I do not think it would be out of place to link to the preceding
story the conversion of that same Brother Sylvester, how the Holy
Spirit moved him to enter the Order. This Sylvester was a secular
priest of the city of Assisi. The *man of God* once bought from him some 2 Kgs 1:10
stones for repairing a church. At that time, this man Sylvester, inflamed with consuming greed, saw Brother Bernard—who was the
first small sprout of the Order of Lesser Ones after the *holy one of God,* Lk 4:34
perfectly giving up what he had, *and giving it to the poor.* He lodged a com- Mt 19:21, 29
plaint with the *man of God* that the price of stones he once sold to him 2 Kgs 1:10
had not been paid in full. Francis smiled when he saw that the
priest's mind was infected with the poison of avarice. Wishing to offer something to cool that man's cursed heat, he filled his hands with
money, without even counting it. The priest Sylvester rejoiced at this
gift, but even more he was amazed at the generosity of the giver.
When he returned home, he kept thinking about what happened.
Under his breath he grumbled a contented complaint that, although
he was already getting old, he still *loved this world;* it was amazing that 1 Jn 2:15
that younger man despised it all. At last, he was filled with a *pleasant* 2 Cor 2:15
fragrance, and Christ opened the bosom of His mercy.

He showed him *in a vision* how much the deeds of Francis were Acts 18:9
worth; how eminently they shone in His presence; how magnificently they filled the frame of the whole world. *He saw in a dream* a
golden cross coming out from Francis's mouth. *"Its top touched the* Gn 28:12
heavens,"[a] its outstretched arms circled the world on every side with

---

a. Matins for *Dedication of a Church,* 2nd nocturn, 2nd antiphon: *Vidit Jacob scalam summitas eius*
caelos tangebat . . . [Jacob saw a ladder, its top touched the heavens . . .].

their embrace. Struck to the heart by what he saw, the priest cast off
harmful delay, left the world and became a perfect imitator of the
man of God. He began perfectly his life in the Order, and by the grace
of Christ completed it more perfectly.[a]

Is it surprising
that Francis appeared crucified
when he was always so much with the cross?
Is it any wonder
that the wondrous cross,
taking root inside him,
and sprouting in such *good soil*
should bear remarkable flowers, leaves, and fruit?[b]
Nothing of a different kind
could come to be produced by such soil,
which that wonderful cross from the beginning claimed
entirely for itself.

But now we must return to our subject.

Chapter LXXVI
A BROTHER FREED FROM THE ATTACK OF A DEMON

[110]A certain brother happened to be vexed for a long time by a
temptation of the spirit, which is worse and more subtle than
prompting of the flesh. At last he came to Saint Francis, and humbly
threw himself at his feet; overflowing with bitter tears, he could say
nothing, prevented by deep sobs. The father was moved with piety
for him, realizing that he was tormented by wicked impulses, *"I command you,"* he said,*"by the power of God,* from this moment demons,
stop attacking my brother, as you have dared to do up to now." At
once the *gloom of darkness* scattered and the brother rose up free, no
more bothered than if it had never happened.

---

a. Brother Sylvester had already died in 1240 before the writing of this text.

b. See the third verse of the hymn by Venantius Fortunato (530-609), *Lustra sex qui iam peregit,* Lauds
during the season of Lent: *Crux fidelis, inter omnes/Arbor una nobilis:/Silva talem nulla
profert/Fronde, flore, germine:/Dulce ferrum, dulce lignum,/dulce pondus sustinent* [Faithful Cross!
above all other,/One and only noble Tree!/None in foliage, none in blossom,/None in fruit thy peers
may be;/Sweetest Wood and sweetest Iron!/Sweetest Weight is hung on thee]. *The Hymns of the
Breviary and Missal,* edited with introduction by Matthew Britt, preface by Hugh T. Henry (New
York, Cincinnati, Chicago: Benziger Brothers, 1922), 53.

Chapter LXXVII
THE VICIOUS SOW THAT DEVOURED A LAMB

1C 58-61   [111]His word had marvelous power even on brute beasts, as shown clearly elsewhere. I will touch on one instance that I have at hand. One night, when the *servant of the Most High* was a guest at the monas-   Acts 16:17 tery of San Verecondo in the diocese of Gubbio, a little sheep gave birth to a baby lamb.[a] There was a cruel sow there, which did not spare the life of the innocent but killed it with a ravenous bite. *In the*   Mk 16:9 *morning*, when the people were *rising*, they found the little lamb dead, and they *knew surely* that the sow was guilty of that vicious   Jn 17:8 deed. When the pious father heard this, he was moved to remarkable compassion, and, remembering that other Lamb, lamented for the 1C 77-79   dead baby lamb, *saying in front of everyone*: "Alas, brother lamb, inno-   Gal 2:14 cent animal, always displaying to people what is useful! *Cursed be* the   Jb 24:18 pitiless one who killed you, and neither man nor beast shall eat of   Gn 3:17 her!" It is amazing to tell. Immediately the vicious sow began to get sick and, after paying the punishment of torments for three days, fi- nally suffered an avenging death. She was thrown in the monas- tery's ditch, and laying there for a long time, dried up like a board, and did not become food for any hungry creature.

AGAINST FAMILIARITY WITH WOMEN

Chapter LXXVIII
AVOIDING FAMILIARITY WITH WOMEN
AND HOW HE SPOKE WITH THEM

    [112]He ordered avoiding completely honeyed poison, that is, famil- iarities with women, by which *even* holy men *are led astray*.[b] He feared   Mt 24:24 that in this the weak spirit would quickly be broken, and the strong *spirit often be weakened*. He said that avoiding contagion when   Ez 21:7

---

a. An allusion to this same event is found in the *Passion of San Verecondo*.

b. This narrative of 2C 112, unlike many other narratives in Book Two, is not found in any earlier source. Notice the contrast between the harshness of this number with the earlier story in 2C 38, also found in AC 69, that highlights Francis's warmth upon "seeing" the "very refined and delicate" noble lady from Volusiano. For other examples of Francis's response to women, see 2C 53, 59, 60, 86, 92, 95,132, 155, 157. It seems that in 2C 112 issues of the 1240's are attributed to Francis. Although echoing monastic encouragement of caution and respect regarding relationships with women, this negative attitude is not evident in his writings or in other earlier texts. For one who in his writings never even mentions Eve in his accounts of the Fall, the above narrative of 2C 112 is not consistent.

Jas 1:12; Prv 6:28
conversing with them,[a] except for *the most well-tested*, was as easy as *walking on live coals without burning his soles,* as Scripture has it. But in
Ti 2:7
order to speak by action, *he showed himself an exemplar of virtue.*

Indeed the female even troubled him so much that you would believe this was neither caution nor good example,[b] but fear or terror. When their inappropriate chattering made for competition in speaking,
Dn 10:15; Rom 9:28
with face lowered with a humble and *brief word*, he called for silence. Sometimes, with his eyes *looking up to heaven,* he seemed to
Acts 7:55
Is 29:4
draw from there what he replied to those who *were muttering from the ground.* Women in whose minds the urging of holy devotion had made a home for Wisdom, he taught in wonderful but brief conversations.

LR IX 3

When he spoke with a woman, he would speak out in a loud voice so that all could hear. He once said to his companion: "I'll tell you the truth, dear brother, I would not recognize any woman if I looked at her face, except for two.[c] I know the face of this one and that one, but any other, I do not know."

Well done, father! For looking on them makes no one holy. Well done, I say, for that brings no gain, but rather, much loss, at least of time. They are an obstacle to those who want to undertake the hard
Est 15:17
journey, and look on the *face full of grace.*[d]

Chapter LXXIX
A PARABLE ABOUT LOOKING AT WOMEN

Ps 119:120;
1Cor 13:12
[113] However, he used to *pierce* eyes that are not chaste *with this parable*: "A powerful king sent two messengers to his queen, one after the other. The first returned and simply reported her words verbatim. Truly *the eyes of the wise man* stayed *in his head* and did not
Eccl 2:14
dart elsewhere. The other returned and, after reporting in brief words, launched into a long story about the lady's beauty. 'Truly, my lord, I saw a lovely woman; happy is he who enjoys her!' And
Mt 18:32
the king said, '*Evil servant*, you cast your shameless eyes on my

AC 37

---

a. The Latin is: *harum contagionem evadere conversantem cum eis* [avoiding contagion when conversing with them].

b. The Latin text uses *femina* [female] instead of *mulier* [woman] in expressing this negative attitude. While Thomas uses femina in 1C 36, 62, 138, he does so in 2C 9, 38, 47, 93, 112, 207. In two instances of 2C, he uses the word to contrast the masculine and feminine (2C 38, 47); in two other instances, he uses the word in a negative sense (2C 9, 112). For further development on this issue see, Jacques Dalarun, *Francesco: un passaggio—Donna e donne negli scritti e nelle leggende di Francesco d'Assisi* (Roma: Viella Libreria Editrice, 1994), 88-93.

c. The originator of this story had to allow two exceptions. Francis's relationships with Clare and Jacopa di Settesoli was well known.

d. This is an allusion to King Ahasuerus who looked upon Esther with a glance of gracious kindness. It is here used allegorically to refer to the countenance of Christ.

wife? It is clear that you would like to buy what you inspected so carefully!' He then called back the first messenger and asked: 'What did you think of the queen?' And he answered: 'I thought very highly of her, for she listened in silence and then replied wisely.' 'And don't you think she's beautiful?' the king said. 'My lord,' he said, 'this is for you to see; my job was simply to deliver messages.' And the king then pronounced his sentence: 'You, chaste of eyes, even more chaste in body, stay in my chamber. Let that other man leave my house, so he does not defile my marriage bed!'"

The blessed father used to say: "When one is too secure, one is less wary of the enemy. If the devil can hold on to one hair of a person, he will soon make it grow into a plank. And if for many years he cannot pull down the one he's tempting, he doesn't complain about the delay, as long as that one gives in to him in the end. This is his work, day and night. He isn't concerned about anything else."

Chapter LXXX
THE SAINT'S EXAMPLE AGAINST EXCESSIVE FAMILIARITY

[114] Once as Saint Francis was going to Bevagna he was so weak from fasting that he could not reach the village. His companion sent a messenger to a certain spiritual lady to ask humbly for some bread and wine for the saint. When she heard this, she hastened to the saint with her daughter, a virgin dedicated to God,[a] carrying what was needed. When the saint had eaten and regained some strength, he in turn fed the mother and daughter with the word of God. But while he was preaching to them, he *looked* at neither of them *in the face*. When they left, his companion said to him: "Brother, why didn't you look at the holy virgin, who came to you with such devotion?" The father answered: "**Who would not fear to look at the bride of Christ?** And if preaching is done with the eyes and the face, she may look at me, but I do not look at her."

Ps 84:10

AC 37

Many times, when he spoke about this matter, he declared that all conversation with women was unnecessary except for confession, or as often happens, offering very brief words of counsel. And he used to say: "What business does a Lesser Brother have with a woman, except when she religiously makes a request of holy penance or advice about a better life?"

ER XII 3-4

---

a. The Latin text reads: *virgo Deo devota* [a virgin dedicated to God]. This implies she lived at home under a private vow of chastity, most probably as a lay woman penitent. See 2C 34.

THE TEMPTATIONS HE ENDURED

Chapter LXXXI
THE SAINT'S TEMPTATIONS AND HOW HE OVERCAME ONE TEMPTATION

[115]As the merits of Saint Francis increased,
his quarrel with the *ancient serpent* also increased.
The *greater his gift*,
the more subtle the serpent's attempts,
and the more violent his attacks on him.
Although he had often shown himself to be
a mighty warrior
who had not *yielded* in the struggle even for an hour,
still the serpent tried to attack
the one who always won.

Rv 12:9
1 Cor 12:31
Is 3:2
Gal 2:5

At one time a very serious temptation of spirit came upon the holy father, surely to embellish his crown. Because of it he was *filled with anguish and sorrow*; he *afflicted* and chastised his body, he prayed and wept bitterly. He was under attack in this way for several years, until one day while praying at Saint Mary of the Portiuncula, he heard in spirit a voice: "Francis, **if you had faith like a mustard seed, you would tell the mountain to move from here, and it would move.**" The saint replied: "Lord, **what is the mountain** that I could move?" And again he heard: "The **mountain is your temptation.**" And he said, sobbing: "*Lord,* **be it done to me as you have said!**" At once the whole **temptation** was driven away. He was set free and inwardly became completely calm.

AC 63
Heb 11:37
Mt 17:19
Lk 1:38

Chapter LXXXII
HOW THE DEVIL CALLED HIM AND TEMPTED HIM TO LUST AND HOW THE SAINT OVERCAME IT

[116]In the brothers' hermitage at Sarteano that evil one who always envies the progress of *God's children* dared to attempt something against the saint. Seeing that *the holy man was becoming even holier,* and not overlooking *today's profit* because of *yesterday's,* as the saint *gave himself one night to prayer* in his cell, the evil one *called* him *three times*: "Francis! Francis! Francis!" And he *replied saying*: "*What do you want?*" The reply was: "There is no sinner in the world whom the Lord will not forgive *if he is converted.* But if anyone kills himself by hard penance, for all eternity *he will find* no *mercy.*" At once *by a revelation,* the

Rom 5:2
Rv 22:11
Jas 4:13; 1 Cor 7:5
1 Sm 3:8
Mk 9:37; Mt 20:21
Ez 33:9
Dn 3:39;
Gal 1:12; Sir 1:6

saint *recognized* the enemy's *cunning*, how he was trying to call him back to being lukewarm. What then? The enemy did not give up. He tried a new line of attack. Seeing that he had not been able to hide this *snare*, he prepared a different one, namely, an urge of the flesh. But to no use, since the one who detected a clever trick of the spirit could not be fooled by the flesh. The devil sent into him a violent temptation to lust, but as soon as the blessed father felt it, he took off his clothes and lashed himself furiously with the cord, saying: "Come on, Brother Ass, that's the way you should stay under the whip! The tunic belongs to religion: no stealing allowed! If you *want to leave, leave!*"

Ps 140:6

Is 40:4; 1 Sm 30:13

[117]However, when he saw that the temptation did not leave even after the discipline, though he painted welts all over his limbs black and blue, he opened the cell, *went out* to the garden, and threw himself naked into the deep snow. Taking snow by the handful he packed it together into balls and *made seven piles*. Showing them to himself, he began to address his body: "Here, this large one is your wife, and those four over there are your two sons and your two daughters; the other two are your servant and your maid who are needed to serve them. So hurry" he said, "get all of them some clothes, because they're freezing to death! But if complicated care of them is annoying, then take care to *serve one Master!*" At that the devil went away in confusion, and the saint *returned* to his cell *praising God*.

Mk 14:68

Jb 38:38

Mt 4:10
Lk 2:20

A certain spiritual brother was *giving himself to prayer at that time, and he saw it all in the bright moonlight*. When the saint later learned that the brother had seen him that night, he was very disturbed, and ordered him not to reveal it to anyone *as long as he lived in the world*.

1 Cor 7:5
Jb 31:36

Ti 2:12

Chapter LXXXIII
HOW HE FREED A BROTHER FROM TEMPTATION
AND THE BENEFITS OF TEMPTATION

[118]Once a brother who was tempted was sitting alone with the saint and said to him: "*Pray for me*, kind father, for I firmly believe if you should be good enough to pray for me, I'll be freed from *my temptation* immediately. I really am tormented beyond my strength, and I know this is not hidden from you." Saint Francis said to him: "*Believe me*, son, I believe you are even more a *servant of God* because of this. And you should know the more you're tempted, the more I will love you." He added: "I tell you the truth, no one should consider himself a servant of God until he has *passed through temptations and tribulations*. A temptation overcome is like a ring with which the Lord betroths

1 Kgs 13:6;
1 Thes 5:25
Lk 22:28

Jn 4:21
Acts 16:17

Jdt 8:23

Ps 86:4   the *soul of his servant*. Many flatter themselves over their many years
of merit and rejoice at never having suffered any temptations. But
sheer fright would knock them out before a battle even started. So
they should know that the Lord has kept in mind their weakness of
spirit. Hard fights are rarely fought except by those with the greatest
strength."

HOW DEMONS STRUCK HIM

Chapter LXXXIV
HOW DEVILS BEAT HIM AND THAT COURTS ARE TO BE AVOIDED

Lk 22:31   [119]Not only was this man *attacked by Satan* with temptations, he   AC 117
even had to struggle with him hand to hand. On one occasion Lord
Leo, the Cardinal of Santa Croce,[a] invited him to stay with him for a
little while in Rome. He chose to stay in a detached tower, which offered nine vaulted chambers like the little rooms of hermits. The first
2 Chr 6:19   night, when he had *poured out his prayer to God* and wanted to go to
Lk 4:34   sleep, demons came and fiercely attacked the *holy one of God*. They
Lk 10:30   beat him long and hard, and finally *left him half dead*. When they left
and he had caught his breath, the saint called his companion who
was sleeping under another vault of the roof. When he came over he
said to him: "Brother, I want you to stay by me, because I'm afraid to
be alone. A moment ago demons were beating me." The saint was
trembling and quaking in every limb, as if he had a high fever.

[120]They spent a sleepless night, and Saint Francis said to his com-   AC 119
panion: "Demons are the police[b] of our Lord, whom he assigns to
punish excesses. It is a sign of special grace that he does not leave
anything in his servant unpunished while he still lives in the world. I
Rom 12:1   do not recall my offense which, *through God's mercy*, I have not
washed away by reparation. For He has always acted toward me with
such fatherly kindness, that in my prayer and meditation He shows
me what pleases or displeases Him. But it could be that He allowed
His police to burst in on me because my staying at the courts of the
great doesn't offer good example to others. When my brothers who
stay in poor little places hear that I'm staying with cardinals, they
Lk 7:25   might suspect that I am *living in luxury*. And so, brother, I think that
Jb 17:6; Prv 28:27   one who is *set up as an example* is better off avoiding courts,

---

a. For information on the identity of Leo, Cardinal of Santa Croce, see AC 117.
b. The Latin *castaldus* [police] or *gastaldus* designates in the Lombard dialect a *praefectum* [prefect]
with authority to police and, if necessary, punish citizens.

strengthening those who suffer want by putting up with the same things." So *in the morning they went* to the cardinal, told him the whole story, and said goodbye to him.   Mk 16:2

Let those in palaces[a] be aware of this,
and let them know that they are *aborted,*   1 Cor 15:8
torn *from their mother's womb.*   Mk 16:2
I do not condemn obedience;
but ambition, idleness, and luxuries
I denounce.
Finally, I put Francis
ahead of all obediences.
We have to endure what *displeases God,*   Eccl 5:3; Ps 53:6
seeing that it *pleases men.*[b]

Chapter LXXXV
A RELEVANT EXAMPLE

[121]Something now comes to mind which I don't think should be overlooked. There was a brother who, seeing some other brothers dwelling in a certain court, was seduced by I don't know what vanity. He longed to become a palace man along with them. When he was inquiring about the court, one night he *saw in a dream* those brothers   Gn 31:4
put outside the place of the brothers and cut off from their company. He saw besides that they were eating out of a filthy and disgusting trough for pigs, where they ate chickpeas mixed with human excrement. The brother was stunned by what he saw, and when he *rose at*   Mk 1:35
dawn he had lost all interest in court.

Chapter LXXXVI
THE TEMPTATIONS HE SUFFERED IN A SOLITARY PLACE
AND A BROTHER'S VISION

AC 65

[122]The saint once arrived with a companion at a church located far from any inhabited area. He wanted *to offer* solitary *prayer,* and so he   Tb 12:12
notified his companion: "Brother, I would like to spend the night

---

a. At the time of the composition of this text, 1247, some brothers were serving as chaplains, counselors or clerks in the households of nobles or important prelates.
b. There is a sense of deep irony in this passage directed at those who enjoy the hospitality of royal courts because it pleases their hosts. All the while it displeases God.

here alone. Go to the hospice[a] **and come back to me at dawn."** When

Ps 142:3; Mt 23:14

he was alone, he *poured out long* and devout *prayers to the Lord.* Finally

Mt 8:20

he looked around for a *place to lay his head* so he could sleep. Suddenly

Jn 13:21; Mk 14:33

he was *disturbed in spirit* and *began to feel fear and loathing,* and to shake in every part of his body. He clearly felt diabolical attacks against him and heard packs of devils running across the roof of the house with a

Mt 26:75

great clatter. He quickly got up, *went outside,* traced the sign of the cross on his forehead and said: **"On behalf of Almighty God I tell you, demons,** do to my body **whatever** is permitted to you: I will

Sal V 14

gladly bear it. I have no **greater enemy** than the body, **so you will be**

Lk 18:3; Nm 33:4

avenging me on my opponent when you *exercise vengeance* on it in my place." And so those who had gathered to terrify his spirit discovered

Mt 26:41; Ps 71:13

a *willing spirit in weak flesh* and quickly vanished in *shame and confusion.*

Jn 21:4

[123]**When** *morning came* his companion returned to him, and find-

AC 65

1 Kgs 8:31

ing the saint lying prostrate *before the altar,* **waited for him outside the choir,** praying fervently before the cross. He passed **into an ec-**

Rv 4:1-2

stasy! He saw many *thrones in heaven,* **and one of them was** more no-

Est 15:9

ble than the rest, **adorned with** *precious stones* and glittering with

Dn 4:16

great glory. He wondered *within himself* about that noble throne, and

Acts 9:4

silently thought about whose it might be. Then *he heard a voice saying to*

Is 14:9-15

him: **"This throne** belonged to one of those who fell, and now it is re-

Acts 12:11

served **for the humble Francis."** Finally the brother *came back to himself,* and saw the blessed Francis coming away from prayer. Immediately he prostrated himself **in the form of a cross** and spoke to him as if he were already reigning in heaven, not still living in the

Ps 32:2;

world: "Father, pray for me to the Son of God, that he may *not consider*

Mt 14:31; 1 Kgs 13:4;
Acts 3:7

my sins!" Extending his hand the man of God lifted him up, realizing that something must have been shown him in prayer. As they were leaving the brother asked blessed Francis: "Father, what is your own opinion about yourself?" And he replied: "I see myself as the greatest of sinners. For if God had pursued any criminal with so much mercy, he would be ten times more spiritual than I am." At this point the

Dn 8:26

Spirit said within that brother's heart: "Now you know that *the* vision was true. Humility will lift the humblest one to the seat that was lost by pride."

---

a. The Latin *hospitale* refers to a hospice or asylum where travelers and the poor could lodge. Here it refers to the hospice for lepers at Trevi.

Chapter LXXXVII
A BROTHER FREED FROM TEMPTATION

AC 55

[124]A certain brother, a spiritual man, an elder in religion, was afflicted with a great *tribulation of the flesh*, and seemed to be *swallowed into the depth* of despair. His sorrow doubled daily, as his conscience, more delicate than discerning, made him go to confession over nothing. Certainly there is no need to confess having a temptation, but only giving in to it, even a little. But he was so shamed that he was afraid to reveal the whole thing, even though it was nothing, to a single priest. Instead, dividing up these thoughts, he confided different pieces to different priests. One day as he was walking with blessed Francis, the saint said to him: "Brother, I tell you that from now on you do not have to confess your tribulation to anyone. *Do not be afraid.* Whatever happens to you that is not your doing will not be to your blame, but to your credit. Whenever *you are troubled,* I give you my permission just to say seven *Our Fathers.*" The brother wondered how the saint could have known about this; *smiling and overjoyed,* he got over the temptation in a short time.

1 Cor 7:28; Ps 69:16

Gn 15:1; Mt 1:20

Ps 107:6

Prv 15:13

TRUE SPIRITUAL JOY

Chapter LXXXVIII
SPIRITUAL JOY AND ITS PRAISE
AND THE EVILS OF ACEDIA[a]

AC 120

[125]This holy man insisted that spiritual joy was an infallible remedy against a thousand *snares* and *tricks* of the enemy. He used to say: "The devil is most delighted when he can steal the *joy of spirit* from a servant of God. He carries dust which he tries to throw into the tiniest openings of the conscience, to dirty a clear mind and a clean life. But if spiritual joy fills the heart, the serpent *casts its poison in vain.* The devils cannot harm a servant of Christ when they see him *filled* with holy *cheerfulness.* But when the spirit is teary-eyed, feeling abandoned and sad, it will easily be *swallowed up in sorrow,* or else be carried away toward empty enjoyment." The saint therefore always strove to keep a joyful heart, to preserve the anointing of the spirit and the *oil of gladness.*

Eph 6:11; 2 Cor 11:3

Gal 5:22

Prv 23:32

Acts 2:28; Ps 16:11

2 Cor 2:7

Ps 45:8

---

a. *Acedia* is one of the capital sins, described by monastic authors as one of the most enervating in the spiritual life. A type of spiritual discouragement that saddens the soul, it causes a loss of interest in the spiritual life. For an overview of considerations of *acedia,* see G. Bardy, "Acedia," *Dictionnaire de Spiritualité Ascétique e Mystique, Doctrine et Histoire* I (Paris: Beauchenes, 1936), 166-169.

He avoided very carefully the dangerous disease of *acedia,* so that when he felt even a little of it slipping into his heart, he quickly rushed to prayer. For he used to say: "When a servant of God gets disturbed about something, as often happens, he must get up at once to pray and remain before the most High Father until he *gives back to him the joy of* his *salvation.* But *if he delays,* staying in sadness, that Babylonian sickness will grow and, unless scrubbed with tears, it will produce in the heart permanent rust."[a]

Ps 51:14

Hab 2:3

Chapter LXXXIX
THE ANGELIC LUTE HE HEARD

[126]In the days when he was staying at Rieti[b] for the treatment of his eyes, he called one of the companions, who in the world had been a lute player, and said to him: "Brother, *the children of this world* do not understand *the divine* sacraments.[c] Human lust has turned musical instruments, once assigned to the divine praises, into enjoyment for their ears. But I would like you, brother, to borrow a lute secretly and bring it here and to play some decent song to give some consolation to Brother Body, which is filled with pain." But the brother answered: "I would be quite embarrassed to do this, father, for I fear people will suspect me of being tempted to my old levity." And the saint said to him: "Then, brother, let's let it go! It is good to let go of many things to avoid offending people's opinion."

The following night, as the holy man was keeping vigil and meditating on God, suddenly a lute was playing with wonderful harmony an extraordinarily *sweet melody.* He could see no one, but the *changes in his hearing* suggested that the lute player was moving back and forth from one place to another. At last, with his *spirit turned to God,* he enjoyed such delight in that sweet-sounding song that he thought he had exchanged this world for the other.

When he *arose in the morning,* the saint called the brother in question and told him *everything from beginning to end,* adding: "The Lord, who *consoles* the afflicted, has never left me without *consolation.* See, since I could not hear the lutes of humans, I have heard a more delightful lute."

AC 66

Lk 16:8

Wis 2:22

Sir 40:21; Ez 10:13

Jb 34:14

Gn 28:18

Est 15:9

2 Cor 1:4

---

a. An allusion to Ezechiel's allegory of the destruction of Jerusalem in 588 B.C., cf. Ez 24:3-14. Written during the siege of the city, the prophet describes the fate of remaining in Jerusalem in terms of a pot in which the best cuts of meat are placed to be boiled. Eventually everything, the pot and its contents, will be consumed. Thomas places this unique reference on the lips of Francis describing the similar fate of the one who broods in sadness, the rust of the heart.

b. This event took place when the Roman Curia was residing in Rieti. See 1C 99.

c. Thomas employs a broad notion of *sacramentum* [sacrament]. Cf. supra 2C 9, supra, 166 a.

Chapter XC
HOW THE SAINT USED TO SING IN FRENCH WHEN EXHILARATED IN SPIRIT

AC 38

[127]Sometimes he used to do this: a sweet melody of the spirit bubbling up inside him would become a French tune on the outside; the *thread of a divine whisper* which *his ears heard secretly* would break out in a French song of joy. Other times—as I saw with my own eyes[a] —he would pick up a stick from the ground and put it over his left arm, while holding a bow bent with a string in his right hand, drawing it over the stick as if it were a viola, performing all the right movements, and in French *would sing* about the Lord. All this dancing often ended in tears, and the song of joy dissolved into compassion for Christ's suffering. Then the saint would sigh without stopping, and sob without ceasing. Forgetful of lower things he had in hand, he was caught up to heaven.

Jb 4:12

Ps 13:6

Chapter XCI
HOW HE REBUKED A SAD BROTHER AND TOLD HIM HOW TO BEHAVE

AC 120

[128]Once he saw a companion with a sad and depressed face and, not taking it kindly, said to him: "It is not right for a *servant of God* to show himself to others *sad and upset*, but always pleasant. Deal with your offenses *in your room,* and weep and moan *before* your *God.* But when you come back to your brothers, put away your sorrow and conform to the others." A little later he added: "Those who envy the salvation of humankind bear a grudge against me, and when they cannot disturb me, they try to do it among my companions."

Is 42:2

Eccl 10:20; Gn 6:8

ER VII 16

He so loved the man filled with spiritual joy, that at one chapter he had these words written down as a general admonition: "Let them be careful not to appear outwardly as sad and gloomy hypocrites but show themselves *joyful,* cheerful, and consistently gracious *in the Lord.*"

Is 61:6

Chapter XCII
HOW THE BODY SHOULD BE TREATED THAT IT WILL NOT COMPLAIN

AC 120

[129]The saint also said on one occasion: "Brother Body should be cared for with discernment, so that it won't raise the storm of *acedia.* We must take away from it the occasions for complaining, so it won't get weary keeping vigil and *staying* reverently *at prayer.* Otherwise it

Lam 2:19

---

a. The narrator here is not Thomas, but the one who submitted the story.

will say: *'I'm dying of hunger.* I can't hold up the load of your exercises.' Now, if it grumbles that way after it has gobbled down a sufficient ration, then you will know that lazy ass needs a good kick, and
the reluctant donkey is waiting for the stick."

This was the only teaching in which the most holy father's actions
were not in harmony with his words. For he tamed his innocent body
with flogging and privation, covering it with *wounds for no reason.* For
the burning of his spirit had already refined his body so much that
his most holy *flesh thirsted for God in many ways, just as did his soul.*

2C 116

Prv 23:29

1C 97

Ps 63:2

FALSE JOY

Chapter XCIII
AGAINST VAINGLORY AND HYPOCRISY

[130]While he embraced spiritual joy, he carefully avoided the false
kind, knowing that what perfects should fervently be loved, but
what corrupts should be carefully avoided. He strove to uproot *empty
boasting* as it sprouted, not allowing anything *that would displease the
eyes of his Lord* to survive even for a moment. Many times it happened,
as he was being highly praised, he felt pain and grief, instantly turning the feeling into sadness.

One winter his holy little body was covered with only a single tunic. It was mended with cheap patches. His guardian, who was also
his companion, acquired a piece of fox fur and brought it to him,
saying: "Father, you're suffering illness in your spleen and stomach; so I'm begging your charity in the Lord to allow this skin to be
sewn inside your tunic. And if you don't want the whole skin, at least
take some of it to cover your stomach." The blessed Francis answered him: "If you want me to put up with this under my tunic,
have another piece of the same size sewn on the outside, telling people that a piece of fur is hidden underneath." The brother heard, but
did not agree; he insisted, but got nowhere. At last his guardian gave
in, and one piece was sewn on top of the other, so that Francis should
not appear differently on the outside than he was on the inside.

Oh, the same in word and life!
The same outside and inside!
The same as subject and as prelate!
You, who would always *boast in the Lord,*
loved nothing of outward glory,

Gal 5:26

1 Sm 29:7

AC 81; ER II 14;
LR II 16; Test 16

1 Cor 1:31

nothing of personal glory!
But, please I do not wish to offend
those covered in furs,
if I say: *"skin for skin!"* Jb 2:4
After all,
we know those stripped of innocence
needed *tunics made of skins!* Gn 3:21

Chapter XCIV
HOW HE ACCUSED HIMSELF OF HYPOCRISY

AC 81

¹³¹Once at the hermitage of Poggio about the time of the Lord's nativity a large crowd assembled for the sermon, which he began with this opening: "You all believe me to be a holy man, and that is why you came to me with great devotion. But I declare to you that this whole Lent I have eaten food flavored with lard." In this way he often blamed pleasure for what was, in fact, a concession to illness.

Chapter XCV
HOW HE ACCUSED HIMSELF OF VAINGLORY

AC 82

¹³²With the same fervor, whenever his spirit was moved to vanity, he displayed it naked before everyone with a confession. Once as he was going through the city of Assisi, an old woman met him and *asked him for something*. As *he had nothing* except his mantle, he offered Mt 20:20; 2 Cor 6:10
it with quick generosity. But then he felt an impulse of empty con-
1C 52
gratulations, and at once he confessed before everyone that he felt vainglory.

Chapter XCVI
HIS WORDS AGAINST THOSE WHO PRAISE THEMSELVES

AC 10

¹³³He strove to hide the *good things of the Lord* in the secrecy of his Ps 27:13
heart, not wanting to display for his own glory what could be the cause of ruin. Often, when many were calling him blessed, he would reply *with these words*: "Don't praise me as if I were safe; I can still Gn 39:10
have sons and daughters! No one should be praised as long as his end is uncertain. Whenever something is on loan and the lender wants it back, all that's left is body and soul—and even non-believers have that much!" This he would say to those who praised him. But he would say to himself: "If the Most High had

given so much to a thief, he would be more grateful than you, Francis!"[a]

Chapter XCVII
FURTHER WORDS AGAINST THOSE WHO PRAISE THEMSELVES

[134]He would often say to the brothers: "No one should flatter himself with big applause for doing something a sinner can do. A sinner can fast," he said, "he can pray, he can weep, he can mortify his flesh. But this he cannot do: remain faithful to his Lord. So this is the only reason for boasting: if we *return to God the glory* that is his; if we serve him faithfully and credit him for what he has given us.

Sir 35:10; Jn 9:24

Adm V

"A person's worst enemy is the flesh; it does not know how to remember what it should regret and it doesn't know how to foresee what it should fear. All its concern is how to squander the present. What is worse," he said, "it claims for itself and takes credit for what was given not to it, but given to the soul. It grabs the praise for virtues and outsiders' applause for vigils and prayers. It leaves nothing for the soul, and even expects to be paid for its tears."

THE HIDING OF THE STIGMATA

Chapter XCVIII
HOW HE ANSWERED THOSE WHO ASKED ABOUT THEM AND THE CARE WITH WHICH HE HID THEM

[135]It would not be right to pass over in silence
the marks of the Crucified,
worthy of the reverence of the highest spirits.
How thickly he covered them!
How carefully he concealed them!
From the *very first,*
when true love of Christ
transformed the lover *into his very image,*[b]

1C 95-96

Is 8:23

2 Cor 3:18

---

a. This is an echo of the sentiment found in 2C 123, cf. supra 246.

b. See Augustine, tenth treatise *On the First Epistle of John,* ch. 4, n. 9 (PL 35, 2051) and Hugh of St. Victor, *Ea vis amoris est, ut talem esse necesse sit, quae illus est quod amas, et qui per affectum conjungeris, in ipsius similitudinem ipsa quodammodo dilectionis societate transformaris* [This is the force of love, that it is necessary for you to be such as the one you cherish. Somehow by the association of love you are transformed to the likeness of the very one to whom you are joined by affection]. Hugh of St. Victor, *De arrha animae,* PL 176, 954; *Soliloquy on the Earnest Money of the Soul,* translated with introduction by Kevin Herbert (Marquette: Marquette University Press, 1956), 16.

he began to hide and conceal the treasure with such care
that, for quite *a long time,*   Wis 4:13
even those closest to him were not aware of them.
But Divine Providence did not want them to be forever hidden,
never meeting the eyes of those dear to him.
In fact, they were on parts of the body that were plainly visible
and could not be hidden.

One time a companion saw the marks on his feet, and said to him:
"What is this, good brother?" But he replied: *"Mind your own busi-*   Sir 41:15; Jas 1:25
ness!"

[136]Another time the same brother asked him for his tunic in order
to clean it, and noted the blood. When he returned it, he said to the
saint: "Whose blood is this that has stained your habit?" The saint
put a finger to his eye and said to him: "Ask what this is, if you don't
know it's an eye!"

He rarely washed his hands completely; he would only wash his
fingers, so as not to allow those standing nearby to see the wounds.
He washed his feet very infrequently, and no less secretly than rarely.
When someone would ask to kiss his hand, he offered it halfway,
putting out only his fingers; sometimes instead of the hand he offered his sleeve.

He began to wear woolen socks so his feet could not be seen, placing a piece of leather over the wounds to soften the wool's roughness. And while the holy Father was not able to hide completely the
stigmata on his hands and feet from his companions, he was vexed if
someone stared at them. So even his close companions, filled with
prudence of spirit, would *avert their eyes* when he had to uncover his   Ex 28:3; Ps 119:37
hands or feet for any reason.

Chapter XCIX
HOW SOMEONE SAW THEM BY A PIOUS RUSE

[137]When the *man of God* was staying at Siena,[a] a brother from   Jdg 13:6
Brescia happened to come there. He was very anxious to see the stigmata of our holy Father, and insistently asked Brother Pacifico for a
chance to do so. He answered: "When I take my leave, I'll ask to kiss
his hands, and when he offers them, I'll signal to you with *a wink,*   Prv 10:10
and you will get a look." When they were ready to leave, the two of
them went to the saint and Brother Pacifico *on bended knee* said to   Eph 3:14

---

a. In April or May of 1226.

Saint Francis: "Give us your blessing, my dearest mother,[a] and give me your hand to kiss!" He kissed the hand, offered reluctantly, and signaled the brother to look. Then he asked for the other hand too, kissed it and showed it to the other. After they had left, the father suspected a holy trick had been played on him, and judging that pious curiosity to be impious, he at once called Brother Pacifico back and said to him: "The Lord forgive you, brother. You sometimes make *a lot of trouble* for me!" Pacifico immediately *prostrated himself* and humbly asked: "What trouble have I caused you, dear mother?" But blessed Francis made no answer, and the incident ended in silence.

2 Cor 2:4; Jdt 9:1

Chapter C
HOW SOMEONE LOOKED AT THE WOUND IN HIS SIDE

[138]Although the very location of the wounds on the hands and feet in such exposed parts of the body allowed some to see them, no one was worthy to see the wound in his side while he still lived, with only one exception, and he saw it only once.

Whenever he had his tunic shaken out, he covered the wound on the side with his right arm, though occasionally he would conceal that blessed cut by applying his left hand to his pierced side.

When a companion was rubbing him, his hand fell on the wound, causing him acute pain. Another brother was straining with eager curiosity to see what was hidden from the others, and one day said to the holy father: "Father, would you like us to shake out your habit?" And the saint replied: *"The Lord reward you* brother, because it really does need it." As Francis stripped, that brother spied him with *watchful eyes*, and he saw the wound plainly marked on his side. He alone saw it during his life. None of the others did until after his death.

Ps 18:21, 25

Lam 4:17

1C 95

Chapter CI
HIDING VIRTUES

[139]In this way this man rejected any glory
which did not *recall* Christ:
in this way he inflicted everlasting anathema on human favor.

Phil 3:19

---

a. For an understanding of the title "mother," see RH, FA:ED I 61-62. Carolyn Walker Bynum also notes the practice of addressing abbots in a similar way among the Cistercians. See Carolyn Walker Bynum, *Jesus as Mother: Studies in the Spirituality of the High Middle Ages* (Berkeley, Los Angeles, London: University of California Press, 1982), 110-116.

He realized that the price of fame
is to lose privacy of conscience,
and that misusing virtues is much more harmful
than not having them.
He knew that protecting what you have
is as virtuous as seeking what you lack.[a]
Ah! Vanity inspires us more than charity;
and the world's approval prevails over the love of Christ.
We do not discern initiatives;
we do not *test the spirits*. 1 Jn 4:1
And so, when vanity drives us to do something
we imagine it was prompted by charity.
Furthermore, if we do even a little good,
we *cannot bear its weight*, Jb 31:23
while we are living we keep unloading it,
and let it slip away as we approach the final shore.
We can patiently accept not being good.
What we cannot bear
is not being considered good, not appearing good.
And so we live only for *human praise*, Rom 2:29
since *we are* only *human*. Mt 8:9

HUMILITY

Chapter CII
SAINT FRANCIS'S HUMILITY IN MANNER, OPINION AND CONDUCT
AND AGAINST HOLDING ONTO OPINIONS

[140]Humility is
the guardian and embellishment
of all virtues.
Any spiritual building without this foundation
may appear to rise higher
but is headed for ruin.
So that this man,
adorned with so many gifts,
should lack nothing,
this gift *filled* him more *abundantly*. Ps 65:12
In his own opinion

---

a. A paraphrase of Ovid's *Ars Amatoria* II:213. *Nec minor est virtus quam quaerere parte tueri* [No less is it a virtue to see what parts are to be protected].

he was nothing but a sinner,
though he was the beauty and splendor
of every kind of holiness.

It was on this
that he strove to build himself,
Heb 6:1   to *lay the foundation*
Mt 11:29   as he had learned from Christ.
Mt 25:16,17   Forgetting what *he had gained,*
Ps 101:3   he *kept before his eyes* only what he lacked,
considering that more was lacking in him than present.
Not satisfied with his first virtues,
his only ambition was to become better
and to add new ones.
Humble in manner,
he was more humble in opinion,
and most humble in his own estimation.
Gn 23:6   This *prince of God*
could not be identified as a prelate,
except by this sparkling gem:
he was the least among the lesser.
This virtue, this title, this badge pointed him out
as general minister.
There was no arrogance in his mouth,
no pomp in his gestures,
no conceit in his actions.
Sir 16:24; Wis 9:18   He *learned* by revelation
the meaning of many things,
but when he was conversing among others
he put the opinions of others ahead of his own.
He considered the opinions of his companions safer than his own
and the views of others better than his own.
He would say
Mt 19:27   that a man had not yet *given up everything* for God
as long as he held on to the moneybag
of his own opinions.
Ps 31:14   He would rather *hear himself blamed* than praised,
since the former moved him to change
while the latter pushed him to fall.

Chapter CIII
HIS HUMILITY TO THE BISHOP OF TERNI AND A PEASANT

AC 10

[141]Once, when he was preaching to the people of Terni, the bishop[a] of that city commended him to everyone at the end of the sermon, saying: *"In this last hour* God has honored his Church by means of this *little, poor, and* looked down upon *man,* simple and unlettered. And because of this we should always *praise the Lord,* realizing that *he has not done this for every nation."*

1 Jn 2:18

Is 53:3, 66:2

Ps 147:1

Ps 147:20

When the saint heard this, he accepted it with deep feeling, for the bishop had so expressly referred to him as a contemptible man. Entering the church,[b] *he fell down at* the bishop's *feet,* saying: "My Lord Bishop, *in truth* you have done me great honor, for you alone have kept safe for me what is my own, while others take it away. *You have distinguished between what is precious from what is vile,* like a discerning man, *giving God the glory* and me the scorn."

Mk 5:22

Ps 111:8

Jer 15:19

Lk 18:43

[142]The *man of God* not only showed himself humble to the great, but also to his peers and to the lowly, more willing to be admonished and corrected than to admonish others. For example, one day he was riding a donkey, since he was too weak and sickly to walk, and he passed through the field of a peasant who was working there. The peasant ran to him and asked anxiously if he were Brother Francis. When the *man of God* humbly answered that he was, the peasant said: "Try hard to be as good as everyone says you are, because many people put their *trust in you.* So I'm warning you; don't ever be different from what people expect!" When the *man of God,* Francis, heard this, he got down from the donkey on to the ground, and *prostrate* before the peasant, humbly *kissed his feet, thanking him* for being so kind to admonish him.

Jdg 13:6

Jdg 13:6

Heb 6:9

Jdg 13:6

Lk 7:38

Tb 11:7

Although so famous that many considered him a saint, he thought himself vile *in the sight of God and people.* He did not feel proud of his great fame or the holiness attributed to him: not even of the many holy brothers and *sons* given *to him* as the down payment of a *reward* for his merits.

Rom 12:17

2 Cor 6:13,18

---

a. Terni had been without a bishop for almost five hundred years. In 1218 Honorius III nominated bishop Rainerio (+1253).

b. It seems the bishop's sermon was preached outside in the open piazza, as often happened when the church could not hold the crowds. The bishop may have spoken from a balcony or loggia on the church's façade.

Chapter CIV
HOW HE RESIGNED AS PRELATE AT A CHAPTER,
AND HIS PRAYER

[143]In order to preserve the virtue of holy humility, a few years af-   AC 39; AC 11, █
ter his conversion, at a chapter,[a] he resigned the office of prelate before all the brothers of the religion, saying: "From now on, I am dead
to you. But here you have Brother Peter of Catanio; let us all, you and
I, obey him." And bowing down immediately, he promised him   ER Pr 3; LR I 2
"obedience and reverence." The brothers were weeping, and sorrow
drew deep groans from them, as they saw themselves orphaned of
such a father.

Jn 17:1   As blessed Francis got up, he joined his hands and, lifting his *eyes
to heaven*, said: "Lord, I give back to you the family which until now
you have entrusted to me. Now, sweetest Lord, because of my infir-
Lk 10:35   mities, which you know, I can no longer *take care of them* and I entrust
them to the ministers. If any brother should perish because of their   ER IV 6
negligence, or example, or even harsh correction, let them be bound
Mt 12:36   *to render an account* for it before You, Lord, on the *Day of Judgment*."

From that time on, he remained subject until his death, behav-   Test 27-29
ing more humbly than any of the others.

Chapter CV
HOW HE GAVE UP COMPANIONS

[144]Another time he consigned all his companions to his vicar,   AC 40
saying: "I don't want to seem singular because of this privilege of
freedom; any brothers can go with me from place to place 'as the   LR II:7
Lord inspires them.' " And he added: "Why, I have seen a blind
man who had no guide for his journey except one little dog." This
indeed was his glory: he gave up any appearance of being singular
2 Cor 12:9   or important, so that *the power of Christ might dwell in him*.

Chapter CVI
HIS WORDS AGAINST THOSE WHO LOVED BEING PRELATES
AND THE DESCRIPTION OF A LESSER BROTHER

[145]Seeing how some were panting for prelacies, an ambition   AC 109
which even by itself made them unworthy of presiding, he said that
Gal 5:4   they were not Lesser Brothers, but that *they had fallen away from glory*

---

a. Cf. AC 39.

by forgetting *the vocation to which they were called.* He criticized the wretched few who were upset when removed from office; they were looking for honors, not burdens.

Eph 4:1

He once said to his companion: "I would not consider myself a Lesser Brother unless I had the attitude which I will describe to you." And he said: "Here I am, a prelate of the brothers, and I go to the chapter. I preach to the brothers and admonish them, and, in the end, they speak against me: 'An uneducated and despicable man is not right for us; *we do not want you to rule over us.* You cannot speak; you are *simple and ignorant.*' So in the end I'm thrown out in disgrace, looked down upon by everyone. I tell you, unless I hear these words with the same expression on my *face,* with the same *joy* in my heart, and with the same resolution for holiness, then I am in no sense a Lesser Brother." And he would add: "In a prelacy there is a fall; in praise, a precipice; in the humility of a subject, profit for the soul. Why, then, do we pay attention to danger more than profits, while we have time for making profit?"

TPJ 11

Lk 19:14

Acts 4:13

Ps 16:9

Chapter CVII
THE SUBMISSION HE WANTED HIS BROTHERS TO SHOW TO CLERICS, AND WHY

AC 19

146 Although he wanted his sons *to keep peace with all,* and to behave as little ones toward everyone, he taught them to be particularly humble toward clerics by his word and showed them by his example. He used to say: "We have been sent to help clerics for the *salvation of souls*[a] so that we may make up whatever may be lacking in them. *Each shall receive a reward,* not *on account of* authority, but because of the *work* done. Know then, brothers, that the *good of souls* is what pleases God most, and this is more easily obtained through peace with the clergy than fighting with them. If they should stand in the way of the people's salvation, *revenge is* for God, *and he will repay* them *in due time.* So, be subject to prelates so that as much as *possible on your part* no jealousy arises. *If you are children of peace,* you will win over both clergy and people for the Lord, and *the Lord* will judge that more *acceptable* than only winning over the people while scandalizing the clergy. Cover up their failings, make up for their many defects, and *when you have done* this, be even more humble."

Rom 12:18

1 Pt 1:9

1 Cor 3:8

Wis 3:13

Dt 32:35

Rom 12:18; Lk 10:6

1 Pt 2:5

Lk 17:10

---

a. Cf. AC 19.

Chapter CVIII
THE RESPECT HE SHOWED TO THE BISHOP OF IMOLA

LR IX 1

[147]When Saint Francis came to Imola, a city of Romagna, he presented himself to the bishop of that region[a] and asked him for permission to preach. But the bishop said: "Brother, I preach to my people and that is enough."[b] Saint Francis bowed his head and humbly *went outside*, but less than an hour later he *came back in*. "What do you want now, brother?" the bishop asked. "What else do you want?" Blessed Francis replied: "My Lord, if a father throws his son out by one door, he should come back in by another!" The bishop, overcome by his humility, embraced him with a smile, saying: "From now on you and your brothers have my general permission to preach in my diocese. Holy humility earned it!"

Mt 26:75, 58

Chapter CIX
HIS HUMILITY TO SAINT DOMINIC, AND VICE VERSA,
AND THEIR MUTUAL CHARITY

Gn 1:16

[148] Those two *bright lights* of the world, Saint Dominic and Saint Francis, were once in the City with the Lord of Ostia, who later became Supreme Pontiff. As they took turns pouring out honey-sweet words about the Lord, the bishop finally said to them: "In the early Church the Church's shepherds were poor, and men of charity, not on fire with greed. Why don't we make bishops and prelates of your brothers who excel more than others *in teaching* and *example?*"

Ti 2:7

There *arose a disagreement* between the saints about answering —neither wishing to go first, but rather each deferring to the other. Each urged the other to reply. Each seemed superior to the other, since each was devoted to the other. At last humility conquered Francis as he did not speak first, but it also conquered Dominic, since in speaking first, he humbly obeyed.

Lk 22:24

Blessed Dominic therefore answered the bishop: "My Lord, my brothers are already raised to a good level, if they will only realize it, and as much as possible I would not allow them to obtain any other mark of dignity."

As this brief response ended, Blessed Francis bowed to the bishop and said: "My Lord, my brothers are called 'lesser' precisely

AC 49

---

a. Mainardo Aldigheri was bishop of Imola from 1207 to 1249.

b. The bishop was the "ordinary minister" for preaching in his own diocese or city. This early tradition had recently been reiterated at the Fourth Lateran Council in 1215.

so they will not presume to *become 'greater.'* They have been called this to teach them to stay down to earth, and to *follow the footprints of Christ's* humility, which in the end will exalt them above others *in the sight of the saints.* If you want them *to bear fruit in the Church of God,* keep them in the status in which they *were called* and hold them to it. Bring them back down to ground level even against their will. And so I beg you, Father, never allow them to rise to become prelates, otherwise they will just be prouder because they're poorer, and treat the others arrogantly." These were the replies of those blessed men. Mt 20:26
1 Pt 2:21
Wis 3:13
Jn 15:2,8; Phil 3:6
1 Cor 7:20

[149]What do you say, *sons of the saints? Your jealousy and envy* show you are degenerates, and your ambition for honors proves you are illegitimate. *You bite and devour each other,* and these *conflicts and disputes* arise only because of *your cravings. Your struggles* must be *against* the forces *of darkness,* a *hard struggle* against armies of demons—and instead you turn your weapons against each other! Tb 4:12; 1 Mc 8:16
Gal 5:15; Jas 4:1
Eph 6:12
Wis 10:12

Your fathers, *full of knowledge, look at each other* as friends, *their faces turned to the Mercy Seat,*[a] but their sons are *full of envy,* and find it *hard even to see* each other! What will the body do, if its *heart* is *divided?* Surely the teaching of piety would flourish more *throughout the whole world* if the *ministers of God's word* were more closely joined by the *bond of charity!* What we say or teach becomes suspect especially because *evident signs* show the leaven of hatred in us. I know this is not about the good men on both sides, but about the bad ones who, I believe, should be rooted out so they will not infect the holy ones. Rom 15:14; Ex 25:20
Rom 1:29; Wis 2:15
Hos 10:2
2 Mc 3:12
Acts 6:4; Col 3:14

2 Mc 14:15

Finally, what should I say about those concerned with higher matters? It was by way of humility, not by haughtiness, that the fathers *reached the Kingdom;* but their sons *walk in circles* of ambition and *do not ask the way to an inhabited town.* What should we expect? If we do not follow their way, we will not reach their glory! *Far be it from us, Lord!* Make the disciples humble under the wings of their humble masters. Make those who are brothers in spirit kind to each other, and *may you see your children's children. Peace upon Israel!*[b] Lk 23:42; Ps 12:9
Ps 107:4
Jos 24:16

Ps 128:6

---

a. In this context, Exodus 25:20, Francis and Dominic are portrayed as the two golden cherubim placed on the ark of the covenant. The Mercy Seat is as a symbol of Christ.

b. This encouragement to peace and harmony reflects an encyclical letter of John the German, O.P., Prior General between 1241-1252, sent to the followers of Saint Dominic in 1246. "Show kindness above all to the Lesser Brothers. Show yourselves affable and kind to them, for the Church conceived twins in her womb and, at almost the same time, gave them birth in the light of the nations. Beware more diligently of every offensive gesture, take away any cause of anger, and should anything be annoying, while safeguarding the laws of our Order, be careful to remove it. "Litterae Encylicae Magistrum Generalium," *Monumenta Ordinis Fratrum Praedicatorum Historica* V (Rome: 1900), 7-9.

Chapter CX
How each entrusted himself to the other

[150]When the servants of God finished their replies, narrated   AC 49
above, the Lord of Ostia was greatly edified by the words of both,
and gave unbounded *thanks to God*. And as they left that place,
blessed Dominic asked Saint Francis to be kind enough to give
him the cord he had tied around him. Francis was slow to do this,
refusing out of humility what the other was requesting out of charity. At last the happy devotion of the petitioner won out, and he devoutly put on the gift under his inner tunic. Finally they clasped
hands, and commended themselves to each other with great
sweetness. And so one saint said to the other: "Brother Francis, I
wish your Order and mine might become one, so we could share
the same form of life in the Church." At last, when they had *parted
from each other*, Saint Dominic said to the many bystanders: *"In
truth I tell you,* the other religious should follow this holy man Francis, as his holiness is so perfect."

Acts 27:35

Acts 15:39
Lk 4:25

OBEDIENCE

Chapter CXI
How he always had a guardian for the sake of true obedience

[151]In order to make a profit in every possible way,
and *melt down* all the present time into merit,
this very shrewd businessman chose to do everything
under the harness of obedience
and to submit himself to the rule of another.

Jer 6:29

He not only resigned the office of general, but also, for the greater
good of obedience, he asked for a special guardian to honor as his
personal prelate. And so he said to Brother Peter of Catanio, to whom
he had earlier promised obedience: "I beg you for God's sake to entrust me to one of my companions, to take your place in my regard
and I will obey him as devoutly as you. I know the fruit of obedience,
and that no time passes without profit for one who *bends his neck to the
yoke* of another." His request was granted, and *until death* he remained a subject wherever he was, always submitting to his own
guardian with reverence.

One time he said to his companions: "Among the many things
which God's mercy has granted me, he has given me this grace, that I

Sir 51:26
Phil 2:8

Test 27-29

AC 11

would readily obey a novice of one hour, if he were given to me as my guardian, as carefully as I would obey the oldest and most discerning. For a subject should not consider his prelate a human being, but rather the One for love of whom he is subject. And the more contemptibly he presides, the more pleasing is the humility of the one who obeys."

Chapter CXII
HOW HE DESCRIBES ONE WHO TRULY OBEYS,
AND THREE SORTS OF OBEDIENCE

[152]Another time, when he was sitting with his companions, blessed Francis let out a sigh: "There is hardly a single religious in the whole world who obeys his prelate perfectly!" His companions, disturbed, said to him: "Tell us, father, what is the perfect and highest obedience?" And he replied, describing someone truly obedient using the image of a dead body:[a] "Take a lifeless corpse and place it wherever you want. You will see that it does not resist being moved, does not complain about the location, or protest if left. Sit it on a throne, and it will look down, not up; dress it in purple and it will look twice as pale. This," said he, "is someone who really obeys: he doesn't argue about why he's being moved; he doesn't care where he's placed; he doesn't pester you to transfer him. When he's raised to an office, he keeps his usual humility, and the more he's honored, the more he considers himself unworthy."

On another occasion, speaking about this same matter, he said that things granted because of a request were really "permissions," but things that are ordered and not requested he called "holy obediences." He said that both were good, but the latter was safer. But he believed that the best of all, in which *flesh and blood* had no part, was the one by which one goes "among the non-believers, by divine inspiration" either for the good of one's neighbor or from a desire for martyrdom. He considered this request very *acceptable to God.*

Mt 16:17

R XV 3; LR XII 1

Phil 4:18

---

a. The concept of obedience as a form of death may well have its origin in the thought of John Cassian who saw death to the world as a form of obedience, cf. John Cassian, *De coenobiorum institutionum* XII 32 (PL 47, 475). Although Thomas places this saying on his lips, Francis's writings convey a different impression of "loving obedience," cf. SalV 14, that is re-inforced by his concept of prelate as a "minister and servant" of his brothers. To see the contrasts between Francis's theology of obedience and that of others, see Jean-Marie R. Tillard, "Obéissance," *Dictionnaire de Spiritualité Ascetique et Mystique, Doctrine et Histoire* XI (Paris: Beauchesne, 1982), 535-563.

Chapter CXIII
THAT COMMANDS UNDER OBEDIENCE SHOULD NOT BE GIVEN LIGHTLY

[153] His opinion was that only rarely should something be com-   AC 1
manded under obedience, for the weapon of last resort should not
be the first one used. As he said, "The hand should not reach
quickly for the sword." He who does not hurry to obey what is
commanded under obedience neither *fears God nor respects man.*   Lk 18:4
Nothing could be truer. For, what is command in a rash leader, but
a sword in the hands of a madman? And what could be more hopeless than a religious who despises obedience?

Chapter CXIV
A BROTHER WHOSE HOOD HE CAST INTO THE FIRE
BECAUSE, THOUGH DRAWN BY DEVOTION, HE CAME WITHOUT AN OBEDIENCE

[154]On a certain occasion he took off the hood from a brother who
had come alone and without an obedience,[a] and ordered that it be
cast into a great bonfire. No one kicked the hood out of the fire, for
they were scared by the upset expression on the father's face, and the
saint ordered it to be pulled out of the flames, and it was unharmed.

Of course this may have been caused by the merits of the saint.
But possibly that brother also was not without merit, for he had been
overcome by his dedication to seeing the most holy father, even
though he had been lacking in discernment, which is the only charioteer of the virtues.[b]

---

a. An "obedience" is a formal directive expressed by one in authority and, in many cases, could be
communicated in writing.

b. A reminiscence of Plato's analogy of the soul as the charioteer who must control the two horses of
emotion and desire (*Phaedrus*, 246, 253-6), Aristotle's doctrine that prudence must regulate all the
other virtues (*Nicomachean Ethics*, VI:13), and Bernard of Clairvaux, Sermon 49:5, *On the Song of
Songs*, translated by Kilian Walsh and Irene M. Edmonds, introduction by Emero Stiegman
(Kalamazoo, MI: Cistercian Publications), 1979) 25. For a thorough study, cf. André Cabassut,
"Discrétion," *Dictionnaire de Spiritualité Ascetique et Mystique, Doctrine et Histoire* III (Paris:
Beauchesne, 1957), 1311-1330.

THOSE WHO GIVE GOOD OR BAD EXAMPLE

Chapter CXV
THE GOOD EXAMPLE OF ONE OF THE BROTHERS
AND A CUSTOM OF THE EARLY BROTHERS

1C 36-37; AC 41

[155] He used to affirm that the Lesser Brothers had been *sent from the Lord* in *these last times* to show forth examples of light to those wrapped *in the darkness* of sins.[a] He would say that he was filled with the sweetest fragrance and anointed with strength from *precious ointment* whenever he *heard of the great deeds* of holy brothers in faraway lands.

Jn 1:6

Jude 18
Mt 5:15-16; Eph 5:8
Prv 7:9

Ex 29:18; Jn 12:3
Mt 26:7
Acts 2:11

It happened that a brother named Barbaro once *threw out* an insulting *word* at another brother in the presence of a nobleman of the island of Cyprus.[b] But, when he saw that his brother was rather hurt by the impact of that word, he took some donkey manure, and, burning with rage against himself, put it into his mouth to chew, saying: "Let the tongue which *spat the poison* of anger upon my brother now chew manure!" The knight was thunderstruck at seeing this, and went away greatly edified; from that time on, he freely put himself and all he had at the disposal of the brothers.

Jb 18:2

Prv 23:32

All the brothers observed this custom without fail: if any of them spoke an upsetting word to another, he would immediately *fall to the ground* and embrace the feet of the one he had offended, even if unwilling, with holy kisses.

2 Mc 10:4

The saint rejoiced over such behavior, when he heard the examples of holiness which his sons themselves produced, and he would heap blessings *worthy of full acceptance* on those brothers, who, by *word or deed*, led sinners to the love of Christ. *Zeal* for souls, which *filled him* completely, made him want his sons to resemble him as a true likeness.

1 Tm 1:15

Col 3:17; Acts 5:17

---

a. This passage echoes that of Gregory the Great: *"cum per bona opera proximis lucis exempla monstramus* [since we show by good deeds done for our neighbors examples of light]" which was used in Third Nocturn of the Common of Confessors. Cf. Gregory the Great, *Homilia in Evangelium* XIII 1 (PL 76: 1124).

b. At that time Cyprus was under the Latin dynasty of the Lusignans, who had been kings of Jerusalem, and still claimed that title. Others propose the reading "island of Scipio," or Limisiano (Limigiano), near Assisi.

Chapter CXVI
SOME WHO HAVE BAD EXAMPLE,
THE SAINT'S CURSE ON THEM,
AND HOW PAINFUL THIS WAS TO THEM

2 Pt 2:8

[156]So also, anyone who violated sacred religion by *evil deeds* or bad example incurred the heavy penalty of his curse.

One day he was told how the bishop of Fondi[a] had told two brothers who came to him who, under the pretext of greater self-contempt, let their beards grow longer: "Watch out that the beauty of your religion is not disfigured by this bold search for novelties." At

2 Mc 14:34

this the saint immediately got up, *stretched out his hands to heaven,* his face streaming with tears, broke out into words of prayer, or rather a curse:

"Lord Jesus Christ, you chose twelve Apostles, though one fell,

Eph 2:18

the rest clung to you, and filled with *one Spirit,* preached the Holy Gospel.

1 Jn 2:18; Ps 89:50

"You, Lord, in this *last hour, remembering your ancient mercies,* have planted the religion of the brothers as a support for your faith, and that the mystery of your Gospel through them might be fulfilled. Who, then, will make satisfaction for them before you, if they not

Rom 13:12

only fail to show examples of Light to all, but, rather, display *works of darkness?*

"By you, most holy Lord, and by the whole court of Heaven, and by me, your little one, may they be cursed who break up and destroy by their bad example what you earlier built up, and do not cease to build up, through holy brothers of this religion!"

Where are they now, those who proclaim themselves happy because of his blessing, and boast about having been as close to him as they wished? If, God forbid, they should be found without repen-

Rom 13:12

tance showing in themselves *works of darkness* endangering others,

Jude 11

woe to them! Woe of eternal damnation!"[b]

Lam 5:7

[157]He used to say: "The best brothers are confounded by the deeds of the bad ones; they *bear* being judged by the example of the wicked, although they themselves have not *sinned.* They are stabbing me with a sharp sword, twisting it in my bowels all day long." It was principally because of this that he withdrew from the company of the

---

a. Fondi is a city near Gaeta, near what was the border between the Papal States and the Kingdom of Naples; its bishop at the time was Robert (1210-1217), a Cistercian monk.

b. This may be an allusion to Brother Elias, who had been an intimate friend of Francis and had received a personal blessing from the dying saint (Cf. 1C 107). At the time of this writing Elias had already been deposed (1239) by Pope Gregory XI and had fled to Pisa to the court of the excommunicated emperor Frederick II, thus incurring the same penalty.

brothers, so that he would not happen to hear some evil report about any of them, and so renew his pain.

AC 2   He also said: "A *time will come* when the religion loved by God will have such a bad reputation because of bad examples that it will be embarrassing to go out in public. Whoever comes to enter the Order at that time will be led only by the working of the Holy Spirit; *flesh and blood* will put no *blot* on them; they will be truly *blessed by the Lord.* Although they will not do works of merit, the *love* which makes saints work fervently *will have grown cold,* still they will undergo temptations; and whoever passes the tests of that time will be better than those who came before. But woe to those who congratulate themselves over the appearance of a religious way of living, those numbed by idleness, those who do not firmly resist the temptations which are permitted to test the chosen! Only those who are *tested will receive the crown of life,* those who, in the meantime, are disturbed by the malice of the wicked."

Ez 7:12

Mt 16:17; Sir 11:23

Ps 114:5

Jas 1:12

Chapter CXVII
A REVELATION MADE TO HIM BY GOD ABOUT THE STATE OF THE ORDER AND THAT THE ORDER WILL NEVER DIE OUT

AC 112   [158]He was greatly consoled, however, by *God's visitations* which re-assured him that the foundations of the religion would always remain unshaken. He was also promised that the number of those being lost would undoubtedly be replaced by those being chosen. One time he was disturbed by some bad examples. In his disturbance he turned to prayer and received a scolding from the Lord: "Why are you so upset, little man? Have I set you up as shepherd over my religion so that you can forget that I am its main protector? I have entrusted this to you, a simple man, so that the things that I work in you for others to imitate may be followed by those who want to follow. *I have called; I will preserve, and I will pasture;* and I will raise up others to make up for the fall of some, so that, even if they *have not been born,* I will have them born! So do not be upset, but *work out your salvation,* for even if the religion should come to number only three, by my gift it will still remain forever unshaken."

1 Pt 5:6

Is 48:15; Rv 10:3

Mt 26:24

Phil 2:12

    From that time on he used to say that the virtue of a single holy person overwhelms a great crowd of the imperfect, just as the deepest darkness disappears at a single ray of light.

AGAINST IDLENESS AND THE IDLE

Chapter CXVIII
A REVELATION HE RECEIVED ABOUT WHEN HE WAS A SERVANT OF GOD AND WHEN HE WAS NOT

^{Zec 13:7}
^{Dn 1:2}

^{Rom 9:11}

[159]From the time in which this man gave up transitory things and began to *cling to the Lord,* he allowed hardly a second of time to be wasted. Although he had brought *into the treasury of the Lord* a great abundance of merits he remained always new, always ready for spiritual exercise. He thought it a grave offense not *to be doing something good,* and he considered not going forward going backward.

^{2 Cor 12:8}
^{Ps 119:125}

Once, when he was staying in a cell near Siena, he called his companions one night while they were sleeping and said to them: "Brothers, *I prayed to the Lord* that he might deign to show me when *I am his servant* and when I am not, for I want to be nothing except his servant. And now the gracious Lord himself in his mercy is giving me this answer: 'Know that you are in truth my servant when you think, speak, or do things that are holy.' And so I have called you brothers, because I want to be shamed in front of you if ever I am not doing any of those three."

^{AC 3}

Chapter CXIX
THE PENANCE AGAINST IDLE WORDS AT THE PORTIUNCULA

^{2 Tm 3:17}
^{Mt 12:35}

^{Mt 12:35, 36}

[160]Another time, at **Saint Mary's of the Portiuncula,** the *man of God* began to consider how the benefit of prayer is lost through *idle words.* And so **he** established the following remedy: "Whenever a brother *utters a useless* or idle *word,* he must admit his fault at once, and for each idle word he must say one *Our Father.* Further, if he accuses himself of what he did, let him say the *Our Father* for his own soul, but if someone else corrected him first, let him say it for the soul of the one who corrected him."

^{AC 107}

Chapter CXX
HOW, WORKING HIMSELF, HE DESPISED THE IDLE

^{Rv 3:16}

[161]He used to say that the *lukewarm,* who do not apply themselves constantly to some work, would be quickly *vomited out of the Lord's mouth.* No idler could appear in his presence without feeling the sharp bite of his criticism. This exemplar of every perfection al-

^{AC 48}

Test 20-21

ways worked, and *worked with his hands,* not allowing the great gift of time to go to waste. And so he would often say: "I want all my brothers to work and keep busy, and those who have no skills to learn some." And he gave this reason: "That we may be less of a burden to people, and that in idleness the heart and tongue may not stray into what is forbidden." But he would not have profit or payment for work left to the whim of the worker, but entrusted it to the guardian or the family.[a]

1 Cor 4:12
1 Thes 4:11

Chapter CXXI
A COMPLAINT TO HIM ABOUT THE IDLE AND GLUTTONS

[162]Allow me today, holy father, to raise a complaint up to heaven about those who claim to be yours! The exercises of virtues have become hateful to many who want to rest before they work, proving they are sons of Lucifer, not of Francis.

We have a more abundant supply of invalids than soldiers, even though they were *born to work* and should consider *life warfare.* They do not like to contribute through action, and are incapable of doing so through contemplation. They upset everyone by their singularity, and work more with their jaws than with their hands. *They hate him who corrects them at the gate,* and will not allow themselves to be touched even with a fingertip.

I am even more amazed at their lack of shame, to use the words of blessed Francis: if they had stayed home they would have lived only *by their own sweat,* but now, without working, they feed themselves on the sweat of the poor. How clever! They do nothing, but you'd think they're always busy. They know the time for meals, and if they ever feel hungry, they complain that the sun fell asleep. Can I believe, good father, that these monsters of men are worthy of your glory? They're not worth your tunic!

You always taught that in this slippery, fleeting time we should seek the riches of merit so that in the future age we should not have to beg. But these men are not now enjoying the heavenly fatherland, and in the future life will have to go into exile. This sickness spreads in the subjects because the prelates ignore it, as if it were possible for them to put up with their vice and not earn their painful punishment.

Jb 5:7; Jb 7:1

Am 5:10

Gn 3:19

---

a. This is the only instance in which *familia* [family] is applied to a local fraternity. Elsewhere the word is used to indicate the entire Order, 1C 73, 100; 2C 143, 184, 192; AC 48.

THE MINISTERS OF GOD'S WORD

Chapter CXXII
WHAT A PREACHER SHOULD BE LIKE

[Acts 6:14; 17:13] [163]He wanted *ministers of the word of God* to be intent on spiritual study and not hindered by other duties. He said that these men were heralds chosen by a great king to deliver to the people the decrees received from his mouth. For he used to say: "The preacher must first secretly draw in by prayer what he later pours out in sacred preaching; he must first of all grow warm on the inside, or he will speak frozen words on the outside." He said that this office was worthy of reverence and that those who exercised it should be revered by all. As he said, "They are the life of the body, the opponents of demons, the [Mt 5:14] *lamp of the world.*"

He considered doctors of sacred theology to be worthy of even greater honor. Indeed he once had it written as a general rule that "we should honor and revere all theologians and those who minister [Test 13] [Jn 6:64] to us the words of God, as those who minister to us *spirit and life.*" And once, when writing to blessed Anthony, he had this written at the beginning of the letter: "To brother Anthony, my bishop." [LtAnt 1]

Chapter CXXIII
AGAINST THOSE LONGING FOR EMPTY PRAISES,
AND AN EXPLANATION OF A PROPHETIC SAYING

[164]He felt deeply sorry for those preachers who often sell what [AC 103] they do for the price of some empty praise. He would sometimes treat the swelling of such people with this antidote: "Why do you boast about people being converted? My simple brothers converted them [1 Sm 2:5] by their prayers!" And then he would explain the saying *while the barren one has given birth to many children* in this sense: *"the barren one* is my poor little brother who does not have the duty of producing children in the Church. At the Judgement he will *give birth to many children,* for then the Judge will credit to his glory those he is converting now by [1 Sm 2:5] his secret prayers. But *the mother of many will languish,* because the preacher who rejoices over many as if they were born through his power will then discover that he has nothing of his own in them."

He had little love for those who would rather be praised as orators than as preachers or for those who speak with elegance rather than feeling. He said that they divided things badly, putting everything in

preaching and nothing in devotion. But he would praise that
preacher who takes time to taste and eat a bit himself.

THE CONTEMPLATION OF THE CREATOR IN CREATURES,
ANIMATE AND INANIMATE

Chapter CXXIV
THE SAINT'S LOVE FOR CREATURES
ANIMATE AND INANIMATE

[165]This happy traveler,
hurrying to leave the world
as the exile of pilgrimage,
was helped, and not just a little,
by what *is in the world.*   Jn 17:11, 16
Toward *the princes of darkness,*   Eph 6:12
he certainly used it as a field of battle.
Toward God, however, he used it
as the clearest *mirror of goodness.*   Wis 7:26
In art
he praises the Artist;
Off 1 V   whatever he discovers in creatures
he guides to the Creator.
He rejoices in all the works of the Lord's hands,   Ps 92:5
and through their delightful display
he gazes on their life-giving reason and cause.
1C 80, 81   In beautiful things he discerns Beauty Itself;
all good things cry out to him: Gn 1:31
"*The One who made us* is the Best."   Ps 100:3
Following the *footprints* imprinted on creatures,
he *follows his Beloved* everywhere;   Jb 23:11; Sg 5:17; Mt 12:18
out of them all he makes for himself a *ladder*   Gn 28:12-13
by which he might reach the Throne.   Jb 23:3

He embraces all things
with an intensity of unheard devotion,
speaking to them about the Lord
1C 58-61; 77-79   and exhorting them to praise Him.

He spares lanterns, lamps, and candles unwilling to use his hand
to put out their brightness which is a sign of the *eternal light.*

1C 58-61, 77-7⁴
AC 88

He walked reverently over rocks, out of respect for Him **who is**
1 Cor 10:4; Ps 61:3 **called** *the Rock*. When he came to the verse "You have set me high
upon the rock," in order to express it more respectfully, he would
Ps 18:39 say: "You have set me high *under the feet* of the Rock."

When the brothers are cutting wood he forbids them to cut down
the whole tree, so that it might have hope of sprouting again.

He commands the gardener to leave the edges of the garden un-
disturbed, so that in their season the green of herbs and the beauty of
Eph 4:6 flowers may proclaim the beautiful *Father of all*. He even orders that
within the garden a smaller garden should be set aside for aromatic
and flowering herbs so that those who see them may recall the memory of eternal savor.

He picks up little worms from the road so they will not be tram- 1C 80
pled underfoot.

That the bees not perish of hunger in the icy winter, he commands
that honey and the finest wine should be set out for them.

He calls all animals by a fraternal name, although, among all
kinds of beasts, he especially loves the meek. 1C 77

Sir 18:2   *Who is capable of describing* all of this?
                    Truly, that fountain-like goodness,[a]
1 Cor 12:6   which will be *all in all*,
                    already shone clearly in all for this saint.

Chapter CXXV
HOW CREATURES RETURNED HIS LOVE
AND THE FIRE THAT DID HIM NO HARM

[166]All creatures, therefore, 1C 58-61
strive to return the saint's love,
and to respond to his kindness with their gratitude.
They smile at his caress,
his requests they grant,
they obey his commands.

It may be good to tell of a few cases. At the time of an eye disease,
he is forced to let himself be treated by a physician. A surgeon is 1C 98, 101
called to the place, and when he comes he is carrying an iron instrument for cauterizing. He ordered it to be placed in the fire until it became red hot. But the blessed Father, to comfort the body, which was

---

a. Cf. Pseudo Dionysius, *Celestial Hierarchy* IV:1 and *Divine Names* IV:1, 20.

AC 86 struck with panic, spoke to the fire: "**My brother Fire**, your beauty is the envy of all creatures, the *Most High created* you strong, beautiful and useful. *Be gracious to me* in this hour; be courteous! For a long time I have loved you in the Lord. I pray the *Great Lord* who created you to temper now your heat that I may bear your gentle burning." Sir 1:8, 9
Gn 33:10
Ps 48:2; Dt 32:6

When the prayer is finished, he makes the sign of the cross over the fire and then remains in place unshaken. The surgeon takes in his hands the red-hot glowing iron. The brothers, overcome by human feeling, run away. The saint joyfully and eagerly offered himself to the iron. The hissing iron sinks into tender flesh, and the burn is extended slowly straight from the ear to the eyebrow. How much pain that burning caused can best be known by the witness of the saint's words, since it was he that felt it. For when the brothers who had fled return, the father says with a smile: "Oh, you *weak souls of little* heart; why did you run away? *Truly I say to you,* I did not feel the fire's heat, **nor any pain** in my flesh." And turning to the doctor, he says: "If the flesh isn't well cooked, try again!" The doctor had experienced quite a different reaction in similar situations, exalts this as a divine miracle, saying: "I tell you, brothers; *today I have seen wonderful things!*" I believe he had returned to primeval innocence, for when he wished, the harshest things grew gentle. 1 Thes 5:14; Mt 14:31
Lk 4:25

Lk 5:26

Chapter CXXVI
A LITTLE BIRD NESTLING IN HIS HANDS

[167]Heading to the hermitage of Greccio, blessed Francis was crossing the lake of Rieti in a small boat. A fisherman offered him a little water-bird so he might rejoice in the Lord over it. The blessed Father received it gladly, and with open hands, gently invited it to fly away freely. But the bird did not want to leave: instead it settled down in his hands as in a nest, and the saint, his eyes lifted up, remained in prayer. *Returning to himself* as if after a long stay in another place, he sweetly told the little bird to return to its original freedom. And so the bird, having received permission with a blessing, flew away expressing its joy with the movement of its body. Acts 12:11

Chapter CXXVII
A FALCON

[168]When blessed Francis, fleeing, as was his custom, from the sight of human company, came to stay in a certain hermitage place, a falcon nesting there bound itself to him in a great covenant of

Lk 4:34

friendship. At nighttime with its calling and noise, it anticipated the hour when the saint would usually rise for the divine praises. The *holy one of God* was very grateful for this because the falcon's great concern for him shook him out of any sleeping-in. But when the saint was burdened more than usual by some illness, the falcon

2 Tm 3:17

would spare him, and would not announce such early vigils. As if *instructed by God*, it would ring the bell of its voice with a light touch about dawn.

It is no wonder that other creatures revere
the greatest lover of the Creator.[a]

Chapter CXXVIII
BEES

Dn 14:36

[169]Once a little cell was made on a certain mountain. In it the *servant of God* did penance rigorously for a period of forty days. After that span of time was over he left that place, and the cell remained in its lonely location without anyone taking his place. The small clay cup from which the saint used to drink was left there. Now, some people one time went to that place out of reverence for the saint, and they found that cup full of bees. With wonderful skill they had constructed the little cells of their honeycomb in the cup itself, certainly

Mk 1:24

symbolizing the sweetness of the contemplation which the *holy one of God* drank in at that place.

Chapter CXXIX
A PHEASANT

[170]A nobleman from the area of Siena sent a pheasant to blessed Francis while he was sick. He received it gladly, not with the desire to eat it, but because it was his custom to rejoice in such creatures out of love for their Creator. He said to the pheasant: "Praised be our Creator, Brother Pheasant!" And to the brothers he said: "Let's make a test now to see if Brother Pheasant wants to remain with us, or if he'd rather return to his usual places, which are more fit for him." At the saint's command a brother carried the pheasant away and put

---

a. "For if a man faithfully and wholeheartedly serves the maker of all created things, it is no wonder though all creation should minister to his commands and wishes." Cf. Bede, *Vita S. Cuthberti* XXI, in *Two Lives of Saint Cuthbert: A Life by an Anonymous Monk of Lindisfarne and Bede's Prose Life*, texts, translation, and notes by Bertram Colgrave, (New York: Greenwood Press, Publishers, 1969), 224-225.

him down in a vineyard far away. Immediately the pheasant returned at a brisk pace to the father's cell.

The saint ordered it to be carried out again, and even further away, but with great stubbornness it returned to the door of the cell, and as if forcing its way, it entered under the tunics of the brothers who were in the doorway. And so the saint commanded that it should be lovingly cared for, caressing and stroking it with gentle words. A doctor who was very devoted to the *holy one of God* saw this, and asked the brothers to give it to him, not because he wanted to eat it, but wanting rather to care for it out of reverence for the saint. What else? The doctor took it home with him, but when separated from the saint it seemed hurt, and while away from his presence it absolutely refused to eat. The doctor was amazed, and at once carried the pheasant back to the saint, telling him in order all that happened. As soon as it was placed on the ground, and saw its father, it threw off its sadness and began to eat with joy.

Mk 1:24

Chapter CXXX
A CRICKET

AC 110

[171]A cricket lived in a fig tree by the cell of *the holy one of God* at the Portiuncula, and it would sing frequently with its usual sweetness. Once the blessed father stretched out his hand to it and gently called it to him: "My **Sister Cricket, come to me!**" And the cricket, as if it had reason, **immediately climbed onto his hand.** He said to it: "**Sing, my sister cricket,** and with joyful song praise the Lord your Creator!" The cricket, obeying without delay, **began to chirp,** and did not stop singing until the *man of God*, mixing his own songs with its praise, told it to return to its usual place. There it remained **constantly for eight days,** as if tied to the spot. Whenever the saint would come down from the cell he would always touch it with his hands and command it to sing, and it was always eager to obey his commands. **And the saint said to his companions: "Let us give permission to our sister cricket** to leave, who has up to now made us so happy with her praises, so that our *flesh may not boast* vainly *in any way."* And **as soon as it had received permission,** the cricket went away and **never appeared there again. On seeing all this, the broth**ers were quite amazed.

Mk 1:24

2 Kgs 4:9

1 Cor 1:29

CHARITY

Chapter CXXXI
HIS CHARITY
AND HOW HE SHOWED HIMSELF AN EXAMPLE OF PERFECTION FOR THE
SALVATION OF SOULS

[172]The power of love
had made him
a brother to other creatures;
no wonder *the charity of Christ*
made him even more a brother to those marked
with the image of the Creator.

2 Cor 5:14

1 Pt 1:9   He would say that nothing should be placed ahead of the *salvation of souls* and would often demonstrate this with the fact that the
Jn 3:18   *Only-begotten Son of God* saw fit to hang on the cross for the sake of souls. From this arose his effort in prayer, his frequent travel in preaching and his extraordinary behavior in giving example.

Jn 15:14-15; 1 Jn 4:21   He would not consider himself a *friend of Christ* unless he *loved* the souls which *He loved*. For him this was the principal cause for revering
Rom 16:9   the doctors of theology: they are the *helpers of Christ*, who carry out
Ez 25:6   with Christ this office. With all the *unbounded affection* of the depths of his heart, he embraced the brothers themselves as fellow members
Gal 6:10; Heb 9:15   in *the household of the* same *faith*, united by a share in an *eternal inheritance*.

Dt 32:11   [173]Whenever somebody criticized him for the austerity of his life, he would reply that he was given to the Order as an example, *as an eagle that prompts her young to fly*. His innocent flesh, which already submitted freely to the spirit, had no need of the whip because of any
Ps 17:4   offense. Still he renewed its punishments because of example, *staying on hard paths* only *for the sake* of others. And he was right.

Sir 28:19, 20; Jdt 13:7   In prelates what *the hand* does is *noticed* more than what *the tongue* says. By your deeds, Father, you convinced more gently; you per-
1 Cor 13:1-3   suaded more easily, you proved things more certainly. For *if* they *were to speak in the tongues of men and angels, but without* showing examples of *charity*, it *profits* little; they *profit nothing*. For if the one who gives correction is not feared, and gives his will as the reason to act,[a] will

---

a. An allusion to a verse of Juvenal, *Sic volo, sic iubeo, sit pro ratione voluntas* [Thus I will, thus I command; the fact that I will, it is argument enough!] *(Satires*, VI: 223).

the trappings of power suffice for salvation?[a] Still, what they thunder about should be done: as water flows to the gardens in empty canals. Meanwhile, let the rose be gathered from thorns, that *the greater may serve the lesser.*

Gn 25:23; Rom 9:12

Chapter CXXXII
HIS CONCERN FOR SUBJECTS

[174]But who now takes on himself Francis's concern for subjects? He always *raised his hands to heaven* for the *true Israelites,* attending first to his brothers' health and often forgetting his own. Casting himself at the feet of Majesty he offered *sacrifice of spirit* for his sons, urging God to give generous gifts.

Ex 17:11-13; Jn 1:47

Ps 51:19

For the *little flock* which he drew behind him he felt compassion and love filled with fear, that after losing the world, they would also come to lose heaven. He thought he would be without future glory unless he could make those entrusted to him glorious along with him. His *spirit* had *given birth* to them *with greater labor pains* than a mother feels within herself.

Lk 12:32

Gal 4:19

Chapter CXXXIII
HIS COMPASSION FOR THE SICK

[175]Great was his compassion towards the sick and great his concern for their needs. If lay people's piety sent him tonics he would give it to the others who were sick even though he had greater need of them. He had sympathy for all who were ill and when he could not alleviate their pain he offered words of compassion. He would eat on fast days so the weak would not be ashamed of eating, and he was not embarrassed to go through the city's public places to find some meat for a sick brother.

AC 45

However, he also advised the sick to be patient when things were lacking and not stir up a scandal if everything was not done to their satisfaction. Because of this he had these words written in one of the rules: "I beg all my sick brothers that in their illness they do not become angry or upset at God or the brothers. They should not anxiously seek medicine, or desire too eagerly to free the flesh, that is soon to die and is an enemy of the soul. *Let them give thanks*

ER X 4

1 Thes 5:18

---

a. The Latin text reads: . . . *satis ad salutem sigilla sufficiunt* [will the trappings of power suffice for salvation?] *Sigilla* refers to the seals or official stamps to make an order or a document official and binding. It can also refer to the symbols to express authority of an office.

for all things and let them desire, however, to be as God wills them
to be. For God teaches with the rod of punishment and sicknesses

Acts 13:48
those whom *he has destined to eternal life* as he himself has said:

Rv 3:19
'Those I love, I correct and chastise.'"

[176]He once realized that a sick brother had a craving to eat grapes,   AC 53

1 Mc 4:4
so he took him into the vineyard and, *sitting under a vine,* in order to
encourage him to eat, began to eat first himself.

Chapter CXXXIV
THE COMPASSION HE SHOWED TO THOSE WHO WERE SICK IN SPIRIT,
AND THOSE WHO DO THINGS CONTRARY TO THIS

[177]With even greater mercy and patience he would bear with and

Eph 4:14
comfort those sick brothers whom he knew were like *wavering chil-*

Ps 77:4
dren, agitated with temptations and *faint in spirit.* Avoiding harsh cor-

Prv 13:24; 1 Mc 13:5
rections when he saw no danger he *spared the rod* so as to *spare the soul.*
He would say that it was proper for a prelate, who is a father, not a tyrant, to prevent occasion for failure and not allow one to fall who,

Ps 145:14
once *fallen* can be *lifted up* only with difficulty.

> Woe to the pitiful madness of our age!
> Not only do we not lift up or even hold the tottering,
> but often enough we push them to fall!
> We consider it nothing
> to take away from that greatest shepherd,
> one little lamb
> for whose sake

Heb 5:7
> *he offered loud cries and tears* on the cross.

On the contrary you, holy father, preferred to correct the strays
rather than lose them. We know that in some the disease of self-will
is so deeply rooted that they need cauterizing, not salve. It is clear

Ps 2:9
that for many it is healthier to be *broken with a rod of iron than to be*

Eccl 3:1; Lk 10:34
rubbed down with hands. Still, *to every thing there is a season; oil and wine;*

Ps 23:4
rod and staff; zeal and pity, burning and salving, prison and womb. All

Ps 94:1; 2 Cor 1:3
of these are demanded by *the God of vengeance,* and *Father of mercies,*

Mt 9:13
who desires *mercy* more *than sacrifice.*

Chapter CXXXV
THE BROTHERS IN SPAIN

[178]This most holy man sometimes *went out of the mind to God* in a
wondrous manner, and was overflowed with joy in the spirit, whenever the *sweet fragrance* of his sons reached him.

Once a Spaniard, a devout cleric, happened to enjoy some time
seeing and talking with Saint Francis. Among other news about the
brothers in Spain, he made the saint happy with this report: "Your
brothers in our country stay in a poor hermitage. They have set up the
following way of life for themselves: half of them take care of the
household chores and half remain free for contemplation. In this
manner each week the active half moves to the contemplative, and
the repose of those contemplating returns to the toils of labor.[a] One
day, the table was set and a signal called those who were away. All
the brothers came together except one, who was among those contemplating. They waited a while, and then went to his cell to call him
to table, but he was being fed by the Lord at a more abundant table.
For they saw him *lying on his face* on the ground, stretched out in the
form of a cross, and showing no signs of life; not a breath or a motion.
At his head and at his feet there flamed twin candelabra, which lit up
the cell with a wonderful golden light. *They left* him *in peace* so as not
to disturb his anointing[b] or *awaken the beloved until she wished.* The
brothers peeked through the openings in the cell, *standing behind the
wall and peering through the lattice.* What else? *While the friends listened for
her who waited in the gardens,* suddenly the light disappeared and the
brother returned to his human self. He got up at once, came to the table, and confessed his fault for being late. That's the kind of thing,"
said the Spaniard, "that happens in our country."

Saint Francis could not restrain himself for joy; he was so pervaded by *the fragrance of his sons.* He suddenly rose up to give praise, as
if his only glory was this: hearing good things about the brothers. He
burst out from the depths of his heart: "*I give you thanks* Lord,
Sanctifier and Guide of the poor, you who have gladdened me with
this report about the brothers! Bless those brothers, I beg you, with a
most generous blessing, and sanctify with a special gift all those who
make their profession fragrant through good example!"

Margin notes: 2 Cor 5:13; 2 Cor 2:15; RH 10; Tb 12:16; Lk 2:29; Sg 2:7; Sg 2:9; Sg 8:13; Gn 27:27; Lk 18:11

---

a. See Kajetan Esser, "The *Regula Pro Eremitoriis Data* of St. Francis of Assisi," in *Franciscan Solitude,* ed. André Cirino and Josef Raischl (St. Bonaventure, NY: Franciscan Institute Publications, 1995)147-205; Octavian Schmucki, "Place of Solitude: An Essay on the External Circumstances of the Prayer Life of St. Francis of Assisi," GR 2 (1988): 77-132.

b. *Unctioni* [anointing] indicates an elevated state of contemplation.

Chapter CXXXVI
AGAINST THOSE WHO LIVE INCORRECTLY IN HERMITAGES,
AND HOW HE WANTED ALL THINGS TO BE IN COMMON

[179]Although we learn from these things the love which made the saint rejoice in the successes of those he loved, we believe this is also a great criticism of those who live in hermitages in a very different way.

Many turn the place for contemplation into a place for laziness, and turn the way of life in the hermitage, established for perfection of souls, into a cesspool of pleasure. This is the norm of those modern anchorites for each one to live as he pleases.[a] This does not apply to all; we know saints *living in the flesh* who live as hermits by the best of rules. We also know that the fathers who went before us stood out as solitary flowers.

Gal 2:20

> May the hermits of our times not fall away
> from that earliest beauty:
> may the praise of its justice remain forever!

[180]As Saint Francis exhorted all to charity, he encouraged them to show a friendly manner and a family's closeness. "I want my broth-   ER IX 11; LR V
ers," he said, "to show they are sons of the same mother, and that if one should ask another for a tunic or cord or anything else, the other should give it generously. They should share books and any pleasant thing; even more, one should urge the other to take them."

> And so that, even in this,
> he might not speak of anything
> that Christ has done through him,
> he was the first to do all these things.

Chapter CXXXVII
TWO FRENCH BROTHERS TO WHOM HE GAVE HIS TUNIC

[181]Two French brothers, men of great holiness, happened to meet   AC 90
Saint Francis. This made them incredibly happy, and their joy was doubled because they had carried this desire a long time. After ex-

---

a. Cf. Jerome, *Letter to Eustochium*, XXII, 34 (PL 22,419); in *The Letters of St. Jerome*, translated by Charles Christopher Mierow, introduction and notes by Thomas Comerford Lawler (Westminster, MD: The Newman Press, 1963), 169-170; John Cassian, *The Conferences*, Eighteenth Conference VII-VIII, translated and annotated by Boniface Ramsey (New York, Mahwah: Paulist Press, 1997), 640-643.

changing affectionate gestures and pleasant words, their ardent devotion led them to ask Saint Francis for his tunic. He quickly took off the tunic and remaining naked gave it to them devoutly; in a pious exchange, he put on the poorer tunic he received from one of them.[a]

> He was ready to give not only things like this,
> but even himself,
> and whatever he was asked for
> he gave away with gladness.

SLANDER

Chapter CXXXVIII
HOW HE WANTED SLANDERERS TO BE PUNISHED

[182]Finally, since a spirit filled with charity will hate those *hateful to God*, this was upheld in Saint Francis. He had a horrible loathing for slanderers, more than any other kind of vicious people, and used to say that they had *poison* in their *tongues*, with which they infect others. And so he avoided rumormongers like biting fleas, and when they spoke he turned away his ears—as we ourselves have seen—so they would not be contaminated by hearing them.

Rom 1:30

Jas 3:8

One time, when he heard one brother blackening the reputation of another, he turned to brother Peter of Catanio, his vicar, and threw out these terrifying words: "Danger threatens religion if it doesn't stop slanderers. Unless the *mouths* of stinking men *are closed*, soon enough the *sweet smell* of many *will stink*. Get up! Get up! Search thoroughly; and if you find the accused brother innocent, make the accuser known publicly by a severe punishment. If you can't punish him yourself, throw him to the Florentine boxer!" (Brother John of Florence was a man of great height and tremendous strength, and so he used to call him "the boxer.") "I want you and all the ministers," he said, "to take extreme care that this foul disease does not spread."

Est 13:14

Lev 1:13; Ex 5:21

More than once he decided that a brother should be stripped of his tunic if he had stripped his brother of his good reputation, and that he could not *raise his eyes* up to God until he had given back what he had stolen. Because of this the brothers of those days had a special abhorrence for this vice, and set up a firm rule among themselves carefully to avoid anything that might take away the honor of another. That was right and good! For what is a slanderer? If not the

Lk 18:13

---

a. This brother may have been Lawrence of Beauvais, one of the first to go to England. Cf. ChrTE 1.

bile of humanity, the yeast of wickedness, the shame of the earth!
What is a backbiter? If not the scandal of the Order, the poison of the
cloister, a breaker of unity! Ah, the *surface of the earth* is crawling with
these poisonous animals, and it is impossible for the righteous to
avoid the fangs of the envious! Rewards are offered to informers, and
after innocence is undermined, the palm of victory often enough
goes to falsehood. Where a man cannot make a living by reputable
means, he can always earn his food and clothing by devastating the
reputation of others.

[183]About this Saint Francis often used to say: "These are the
words of the slanderer: 'My life is far from perfect, and I don't have at
my disposal any supply of learning or special grace, and so I cannot
find a position with God or men. *I know what I will do: let me put a stain
on the chosen,* and so I'll win the favor of the great. I know my prelate
is human; he sometimes uses my same method: cut down the *cedars*
so only the *buckthorn* can be seen in the forest.'

"You wretch! Go ahead and feed on human flesh; since you can't
survive otherwise, gnaw at your brothers' entrails! That type strives
to appear good, not to become good; they point out vices; they do not
give up vices. They only praise people whose authority they want for
protection. Their praises go silent if they think they will not be reported to the person they praised. They sell for the price of pernicious
praise the pallor of their *fasting faces, that they may appear to be spiritual
men who can judge all, and may be judged by none.* They rejoice in the reputation, not the works of holiness, in the name, not in the virtue of
'angels.' "

A DESCRIPTION OF THE GENERAL MINISTER
AND OF THE OTHER MINISTERS

Chapter CXXXIX
HOW HE SHOULD BEHAVE WITH HIS COMPANIONS

[184] As he neared the end of his call to the Lord, a brother who
was always concerned about the things of God, asked him a question
out of piety for the Order. "Father, you will pass on, and the family
of your followers will be left behind *in this vale of tears.* Point out
someone in the Order, if you know one, on whom your spirit may
rest, and on whom the weight of the general ministry may safely be
laid."

Ex 10:5 · Lk 16:4; Sir 11:33 · Jgs 9:15 · Mt 6:16; 1 Cor 14:37 · 1 Cor 2:15 · AC 42 · Ps 84:7

Saint Francis, drawing a sigh with every word, replied as follows: "Son, I find no one adequate to be the leader of such a varied army, or the shepherd of such a widespread flock. But I would like to paint one for you, or make one by hand, as the phrase goes, to show clearly what kind of person the father of this family should be.

185"He must be a very dignified person, of great discernment, and of praiseworthy reputation. He must be without personal favorites, lest by loving some more than others, he create scandal for all. He must be a committed friend of holy prayer, who can distribute some hours for his soul and others for the flock entrusted to him. *Early in the morning*, he must put first the sacrament of the Mass, and with prolonged devotion commend himself and his flock to divine protection. After prayer, he must make himself available for all to pick at him, and he should respond to all and provide for all with meekness. He must be someone who does not create sordid *favoritism toward persons*, but will take as much care of the lesser and simple brothers as of the learned and greater ones. Even if he should be allowed to excel in gifts of learning, he should all the more bear in his behavior the image of holy simplicity, and nourish this virtue.

Mt 20:1

Rom 2:11

"He should loathe money, the principal corrupter of our profession and perfection; as the head of a poor religion, offering himself to others as someone to be imitated, he must never engage in the abuse of using any money pouch. For with his needs," he said, "a habit and a little book should be enough, and, for the brothers' needs, he should have a pen case and seal. He should not be a book collector, or too intent on reading, so he does not take away from his duties what he spends on his studies.

AC 43

"Let him be someone who comforts the afflicted, and *the final refuge of the distressed*, so that the sickness of despair does not overcome the sick because he did not offer healing remedies. In order to bend rebels to meekness, let him lower himself, let go of some of his rights *that he may gain a soul for Christ*. As for runaways from the Order, let him not *close a heart of mercy* to them, for they are like *lost sheep*; and he knows how overpowering the temptations can be which can push someone to such a fall.

Ps 32:7; 46:2

Phil 3:8; Mt 16:26
1 Jn 3:17; Lk 15:4, 6

AC 43

186"I want all to honor him as standing in Christ's place, and I wish that all his needs be provided for with every kindness. He should not enjoy honors, or delight in approval more than insults. If he should need more substantial food when he is sick or tired, he should not eat it in secret but in a public place, so that others may be freed from embarrassment at having to provide for their weak bodies. It especially pertains to him to discern what is hidden in consciences and to draw out the truth from its hidden veins, not lending an ear to gossips. Finally, he must be one who would never allow the desire for preserving honor to weaken the strong figure of justice, and he must feel such a great office more a burden than an honor. And yet, excessive meekness should not give birth to slackness, nor loose indulgence to a breaking down of discipline, so that, loved by all, he is feared, nonetheless, by *those who work evil.*

Prv 10:29

"I would like him to have companions endowed with honesty, who, like him, *show themselves an example of all good works*: stern against pleasures, strong against difficulties, and yet friendly in the right way, so that they receive all who come to them with holy cheerfulness. There," he concluded, "that is the kind of person the general minister of the Order should be."

Ti 2:7

Chapter CXL
THE PROVINCIAL MINISTERS

[187]The blessed Father also demanded all these things in provincial ministers, though each ought to stand out even more in the general minister. He wanted them to be friendly to the lesser ones, and peaceful and kind so that those who committed faults would not be afraid to entrust themselves to their affection. He wanted them to be moderate in commanding, gracious when offended, more willing to bear injuries than to inflict them; enemies of vice but healers of the vice-ridden. In short, he wanted them to be men whose life would be a mirror of discipline for others. He would have them honored and loved in every way, as those who bear the burden of cares and labor. He said they deserved the highest rewards before God if they rule the souls committed to them according to this model and this law.

Chapter CXLI
THE ANSWER THAT THE SAINT GAVE WHEN HE
WAS ASKED ABOUT THE MINISTERS

[188] Once a brother asked him why he had renounced the care of all the brothers and turned them over into the hands of others as if they did not belong to him. He replied: "Son, I love the brothers as I can, but if they would *follow my footsteps* I would surely love them more, and would not make myself a stranger to them. For there are some among the prelates who draw them in a different direction,

AC 44

1 Pt 2:21

placing before them the examples of the ancients[a] and paying little attention to my warnings. But what they are doing will be seen in the end."

A short time later, when he was suffering a serious illness, he raised himself up in bed in *an angry spirit*: "Who are these people? They *have snatched out of my hands* my religion and that of the brothers. If I go to the general chapter, then I'll show them what my will is!" And that brother asked him: "Won't you also change those provincial ministers who for a long time have abused their freedom?" And our father answered, sobbing, with this terrible word: "Let them live any way they want, for there is less harm in the damnation of a few than in the damnation of many!"

Ps 48:8

Jn 10:28

He did not say this about all, but because of some who had been prelates for such a long time that they seemed to have laid claim to their positions by right of property. He always commended this in all kinds of religious prelates: not to change behavior except for the better; not to beg to win favors; not to exercise power, but fulfill a duty.

HOLY SIMPLICITY

Chapter CXLII
THE NATURE OF TRUE SIMPLICITY

[189]Holy *Simplicity,*
the daughter of grace,
the sister of wisdom,
the mother of justice,
with careful attention he showed in himself
and *loved* in others.
It was not just any kind of simplicity that he approved,
but only that
which, content with her God
scorns everything else.[b]
This is she
who *glories in the fear of God,*
who does not know how to do evil

Wis 1:1

Sir 9:16

---

a. That is, Saints Benedict, Augustine, or Bernard. Cf. AC 18.

b. Traditionally simplicity is seen as one of the most salient virtues of the spiritual life, cf. "Simplicité," *Dictionnaire de Spiritualité Ascétique et Mystique* (Paris: Beauchesne, 1990), 892-921; in particular, Vincent Desprez, "II Monchisme Ancien et Médiéval," 903-910.

or speak it.
This is she
who examines herself
and *condemns no one* by her judgment;
who grants due authority to her betters
and seeks no authority for herself.
This is she
who does not
consider the best glories of the Greeks
and would rather *do,*
than *teach* or learn.
This is she
who, when dealing with all the divine laws,
leaves all wordy wanderings,
fanciful decorations,
shiny trappings,
showy displays and odd curiosities,
who seeks not the rind but the marrow,
not the shell but the kernel,
not the many, but the much,
supreme and enduring good.

Jn 8:16

2 Mc 4:15

Acts 1:1

She was what the most holy father demanded in the brothers, learned and lay; not believing she was the contrary of wisdom but rather, her true sister, though easier to acquire for those poor in knowledge and more quickly to put into use. Therefore, in the *Praises of the Virtues* which he composed, he says: "Hail, Queen Wisdom! May the Lord protect you, with Your Sister holy pure Simplicity!"

SalV 1

Chapter CXLIII
BROTHER JOHN THE SIMPLE

[190] Once, when Saint Francis was passing by a village near Assisi, a certain John, a very simple man, was plowing in the field. He ran to him, saying: "I want you to make me a brother, *for a long time* now I have wanted *to serve God.*" The saint rejoiced noticing the man's simplicity, and responded to his intention: "Brother, if you want to be our companion, *give to the poor* if you have anything, and once rid of your property, I will receive you." He immediately unyoked the oxen and offered one to Saint Francis saying: "Let's give this ox to the poor! I am sure I deserve to get this much as my *share of my father's things.*" The saint smiled, but he heartily approved his sense of sim-

AC 61

Acts 14:3; Mt 6:24

Mt 19:21

ER I 2; II 4; LR

Lk 15:12

plicity. Now, when the parents and younger brothers heard of this, they hurried over in tears, grieving more over losing the ox than the man. The saint said to them: *"Calm down!* Here, I'll give you back the ox and only take away the brother." And so he took the man with him, and, dressed in the clothing of the Order, he made him his special companion because of his gift of simplicity.

Bar 4:27

Whenever Saint Francis stayed in some place to meditate, simple John would immediately repeat and copy whatever gestures or movements the saint made. If he spat, John would spit too, if he coughed, he would cough as well, sighing or sobbing along with him. If the saint *lifted up his hands to heaven,* John would raise his too, and he watched him intently as a model, turning himself into a copy of all his actions. The saint noticed this, and once asked him why he did those things. He replied: **"I promised to do everything you do.** It is dangerous for me to leave anything out." The saint delighted in this pure simplicity, but gently told him not to do this anymore. Shortly after this the simple man departed to the Lord in this same purity. The saint often proposed his life as worth imitating and merrily **calling him not Brother John, but Saint John.**

Dt 32:40

Note that it is typical of holy simplicity
to live by the norms of the elders
and always to rely
on the example and teaching of the saints.
Who will allow human wisdom to follow him,
now reigning in heaven,
with as much care as holy simplicity
conformed herself to him on earth!
What more can I say?
She followed the saint in life,
and went before the saint to Life.

Jb 6:8; 1 Cor 2:4

Chapter CXLIV
HOW HE FOSTERED UNITY AMONG HIS SONS
AND SPOKE ABOUT IT IN A PARABLE

[191]His constant wish and watchful concern
was to foster among his sons *the bond of unity*
so that those *drawn by the same Spirit*
and *begotten by the* same *father*
should be held peacefully
on the lap of the same mother.

Eph 4:3
Jb 34:14
Prv 23:22

He wanted to unite the greater to the lesser,
to join the wise to the simple in brotherly affection,
and to hold together those far from each other
with the glue of love.

He once presented a moral parable, containing no little instruction. "Imagine," he said, "a general chapter of all the religious in the
Church. Because the literate are present along with those *who are un-*
lettered, the learned, as well as those who, without learning, have
learned *how to please God,* a sermon is assigned to one of the wise and
another to one of the simple. The wise man, because he is wise, *thinks*
to himself: 'This is not the place to show off my learning, since it is full
of understanding scholars. And it would not be proper to make myself stand out for originality, making subtle points to men who are
even more subtle. Speaking simply would be more fruitful.'

"*The appointed day* dawns, *the gathering of the saints gathers as one,*
thirsting to hear this sermon. The learned man comes forward *dressed*
in sackcloth, with *head sprinkled with ashes,* and to the amazement of
all, *he spoke briefly,* preaching more by his action. 'Great things have
we promised,' he said, 'greater things have been promised us; let us
observe the former and yearn for the latter. Pleasure is short and
punishment is eternal; suffering is slight and glory infinite. *Many are*
called; few are chosen, all are repaid.' The hearts of the listeners *were*
pierced, and they *burst into tears,* and revered this truly wise man as a
saint.

" 'What's this?' the simple man says *in his heart.* 'This wise man
has stolen everything I planned to do or say! But *I know what I will do.* I
know a few verses of the psalms; I'll use the style of the wise man,
since he used the style of the simple.' The next day's meeting arrives
and the simple brother gets up, and proposes a psalm as his theme.
Then, inspired with the divine Spirit, he preaches by the inspired gift
of God with such fire, subtlety and sweetness that all are *filled with*
amazement and say: 'Yes, *He speaks with the simple!'* "

^{192}The *man of God* would then explain the moral parable he told:
"Our religion is a very large gathering, like a general council gathered
together from every part of the world under a single form of life. In it
the learned can draw from the simple to their own advantage when
they see the unlettered seeking the things of heaven with fiery vigor
and those not taught by men knowing *spiritual things by the Spirit.* In it
even the simple turn to their advantage what belongs to the learned,
when they see outstanding men, who could live with great *honor*
anywhere *in the world,* humble themselves to the same level with
themselves. Here," he said, "is where the beauty of this blessed fam-

Marginal references:
Acts 4:13
Heb 11:6
Mt 16:17
Est 10:11; Est 8:11; Ps 11:1
Jn 3:5
Lam 2:10
Rom 9:28
Mt 20:16
Gn 43:30
Ps 14:1
Lk 16:4
Acts 3:10
Prv 3:32
1 Kgs 13:1
Acts 11:28; Mt 16:23
Sir 44:1, 2
Off 17 II

ily shines; a diverse beauty that gives great pleasure to the father of the family."

Chapter CXLV
HOW THE SAINT WANTED TO BE SHAVED

[193]Whenever Saint Francis was being shaved, he would always say to the one who shaved him: "Be careful: don't give me a big tonsure! I want my simple brothers to *have a share in* my head!"[a]

Really he wanted the Order to be held in common by the poor and illiterate and not just by the learned and rich. *"With God,"* he would say, *"there is no respecting of persons,* and the Holy Spirit, the general minister of the religion, rests equally upon the poor and simple." He really wanted to put these words in the *Rule*, but the papal seal already given to the rule precluded it.

Chapter CXLVI
HOW HE WANTED "EMINENT CLERICS" WHO ENTERED THE ORDER TO GIVE UP THEIR PROPERTY

[194]Once he said that if an "eminent cleric"[b] were to join the Order, he should in some way renounce even learning, so that having renounced even this possession, he might offer himself naked to the arms of the Crucified.[c] "Learning," he would say, "makes many hard to teach, not allowing them to bend something rigid in them to humble disciplines. And so I wish an educated man would first *offer* me this *prayer*: 'Look, Brother; I have *lived* for a long time *in the world* and have *not* really *known* my *God*. Grant me, I pray you, a place removed from the noise of the world, where *I may recall my years in* sorrow and where I may gather the *scattered bits of* my *heart* and turn my spirit to better things.' What do you think will become," he asked, "of someone who begins in this way? He will emerge an unchained lion, strong enough for anything, and the blessed sap which he tapped in the beginning will grow in him through constant progress. To him at last the true *ministry of the word* will be given safely, for he will pour out what bubbles up in his heart."

Jb 31:2

Rom 2:11

Heb 5:7

Ti 1:12

Jn 1:10

Is 38:15

Ps 147:2; Lk 1:51

Acts 6:4

---

a. The lay brothers at that time wore small tonsures, while the clerics wore large ones. Cf. AP 36 and L3C 51.

b. A *magnus clericus* [eminent cleric] is a person of great learning. Cf. Lothar Hardick, "Gedanken zu Sinn und Tragweite des Begriffes Clericus," AFH 50 (1957): 7-26.

c. For a study of this phrase, see FA:ED I 194 a.

What a holy teaching! What is more necessary, for someone returning from the land of unlikeness,[a] than to scrape and wash away, by humble exercises, worldly feelings stamped and ground in for a long time? Whoever enters the school of perfection will soon reach perfection.

Chapter CXLVII
HOW HE WANTED THE BROTHERS TO STUDY,
AND HOW HE APPEARED TO A COMPANION OF HIS
WHO WAS INTENT ON BEING A PREACHER

[195]It grieved him when brothers sought learning while neglecting virtue, especially if they did not *remain in that calling in which
they were* first *called.* He said: "Those brothers of mine who are led
by curiosity for knowledge will find themselves *empty-handed* on
the *day of reckoning.* I wish they would grow stronger in virtue, so
that when the *times of tribulation* arrive they may have the Lord with
them *in their distress.* For," he said, "a *tribulation is approaching,*
when books, useful for nothing, shall be thrown into cupboards
and into closets!" He did not say these things out of dislike for the
study of the Scriptures, but to draw all of them back from excessive
concern for learning, because he preferred that they be good
through charity, than dilettantes through curiosity.

Besides, he could smell in the air that a time was coming, and
not too far away, when he knew learning would be an occasion of
ruin, while dedication to spiritual things would serve as a support to
the spirit.

A lay brother who wanted to have a psalter asked him for permission: he offered him ashes instead of a psalter.

After his death he appeared in a vision to one of the companions
who was once tending toward preaching, and he forbade it, commanding him to walk on the way of simplicity. *As God is his witness,*
he felt such a sweetness after this vision that for many days it seemed
the dew of the father's words was still dropping into his ears.

Margin references: 1 Cor 7:20, 24; Sir 35:4; Hos 9:7; Ps 37:39; 2 Chr 15:4; Ps 22:12; Prv 1:27; Rom 1:9 — AC 47; AC 104; AC 47

---

a. The "land of unlikeness" is a very common image in the writings of St. Bernard and the Cistercian school of spirituality; its origin is in the thought of St. Augustine and ultimately in Plato's *topos tes anomoiotetos,* a land which is not the soul's true country. See Amédée Hallier, OCSO, *The Monastic Theology of Aelred of Rievaulx* (Spencer, Mass: Cistercian Publications, 1969), 12.

THE SAINT'S SPECIAL DEVOTIONS

Chapter CXLVIII
HOW HE WAS MOVED WHEN HE HEARD "THE LOVE OF GOD"

[196]Perhaps it would be useful and worthwhile to touch briefly on the special devotions of Saint Francis. Although this man was devout in all things, since he enjoyed the *anointing of the Spirit,* there were special things that moved him with special affection.

Lk 4:18

Among other expressions used in common speech, he could not hear "the love of God" without a change in himself. As soon as he heard "the love of God" he was excited, moved, and on fire, as if these words from the outside were a pick strumming the strings of his heart on the inside.

He used to say that it was a noble extravagance to offer such a treasure for alms, and that those who considered it less valuable than money were complete fools. As for himself, he kept until his death the resolution he made while still entangled in the things of this world: he would never refuse any poor person who asked something "for the love of God."

1C 17

Once a poor man begged something of him "for the love of God," and since he had nothing, he secretly picked up scissors and hurried to cut his small tunic in two. And he would have done just that, except that he was caught by the brothers and they had the poor man supplied with a different compensation.

AC 91

He said:
"The love of him who loved us greatly
is greatly to be loved!"

Chapter CXLIX
HIS DEVOTION TO THE ANGELS,
AND WHAT HE DID OUT OF LOVE FOR SAINT MICHAEL

[197]He venerated the angels with the greatest affection, for they are with us in battle, and *walk* with us *in the midst of the shadow of death.* He said that such companions should be revered everywhere, and invoked as protectors. He taught that their gaze should not be offended, and no one should presume to do in their sight what he would not do *in the sight of others.* And since in choir one *sings* the psalms *in the presence of the angels,* he wanted all who were able to gather in the oratory and *sing psalms wisely.*

Ps 23:4; Is 9:2

Rom 12:17; Ps 138:1

Ps 47:8

He often said that Blessed Michael should be especially honored because his duty is presenting souls to God.[a] In honor of Saint Michael he would fast with great devotion for forty days between the Feast of the Assumption and St. Michael's feast day. For he used to say: "Each person should *offer God* some special praise or *gift* in honor of such a great prince."

Mt 5:23-24

Chapter CL
HIS DEVOTION TO OUR LADY
TO WHOM HE ESPECIALLY ENTRUSTED THE ORDER

[198]He embraced the Mother of Jesus with inexpressible love, since she made *the Lord of Majesty* a brother to us. He honored her with his own *Praises*, poured out prayers to her, and offered her his love in a way that no human tongue can express. But what gives us greatest joy is that he appointed her the Advocate of the Order, and placed *under her wings* the sons to be left behind, that she might *protect* and cherish them to the end.

Ps 29:4; Is 2:10

SalBVM

Ps 17:8

Oh Advocate of the Poor!
Fulfill towards us your duty as *protectress*
until the time set by the Father!

Gal 4:2

Chapter CLI
HIS DEVOTION TO THE LORD'S NATIVITY
AND HOW HE THEN WANTED ALL TO RECEIVE ASSISTANCE

[199]He used to observe the Nativity of the Child Jesus with an immense eagerness above all other solemnities, affirming it was the Feast of Feasts, when God was made a little child and hung on human breasts. He would kiss the images of the baby's limbs thinking of hunger, and the melting compassion of his heart toward the child also made him stammer sweet words as babies do. This name was to him like *honey and honeycomb* in his mouth.

1C 84-86

Ps 19:11; Prv 16:24

When there was discussion about not eating meat, because it was on Friday, he replied to Brother Morico: "You sin, brother, when you call 'Friday' the day when *unto us a Child is born.* I want even the walls to eat meat on that day, and if they cannot, at least on the outside they be rubbed with grease!"

Is 9:6

---

a. Cf. *Roman Breviary*, third antiphon for Lauds on the feast of St. Michael: *Archangele Michael, constitui te principem super omnes animas suscipiendas* [Archangel Michael, I have set you as prince over all the souls who are to be presented to me].

AC 14

²⁰⁰He wanted the poor and *hungry to be filled* by the rich, and *oxen and asses* to be spoiled with extra feed and hay. "If ever I speak with the Emperor," he would say, "I will beg him to issue a general decree that all who can should throw wheat and grain along the roads, so that on the day of such a great solemnity the birds may have an abundance, especially our sisters the larks." 1 Sm 2:5

L3C 15

2C 83, 85

He could not recall without tears the great want surrounding the little, poor Virgin on that day. One day when he was sitting down to dinner a brother mentioned the poverty of the blessed Virgin, and reflected on the want of Christ her Son. No sooner had he heard this than he *got up from the table*, groaning with sobs of pain, and bathed in tears 1 Sm 20:34

BR IX 5; 2LtF 5

ate the rest of his bread on the naked ground. He used to say this must be a royal virtue, since it shone so remarkably in a King and Queen.

When the brothers were debating in a gathering about which of the virtues made one a greater friend to Christ, he replied, as if opening the secret of his heart: "My sons, know that poverty is the special *way to salvation;* its fruits are many, and known only to a few." Acts 16:17

Chapter CLII
HIS DEVOTION TO THE BODY OF THE LORD

²⁰¹Toward the sacrament of the Lord's Body
he burned with fervor to his very marrow,
and with unbounded wonder
of that loving condescension
and condescending love.
He considered it disrespectful
not to hear, if time allowed, at least one Mass a day.
He received Communion frequently
and so devoutly
that he made others devout.
Following that which is so venerable with all reverence
he offered the sacrifice of all his members,
and receiving *the Lamb that was slain* Rv 5:12; 1 Pt 1:19
he slew his own spirit
in the *fire* which *always burned* Lv6 6:5, 6
upon the altar of his heart.

Because of this he loved France as a friend of the Body of the Lord,[a]
and even wished to die there, because of its reverence for sacred things.

---

a. The Latin, *Francia*, would mean the *Ile de France* or northern France, including the Low Countries. This love for the Eucharist was in contrast to southern France where the Albigensian heresy was widespread. Francis could have been informed of this devotion by James of Vitry, later a cardinal, who was ordained bishop of Akon in Perugia on July 31, 1216. For the situation in *Francia*, see Miri Rubin, *Corpus Christi: The Eucharist in Late Medieval Culture* (Cambridge: Cambridge University Press, 1991).

Jn 3:16

He once **wanted to** *send* brothers *throughout the world* **with** pre-cious **pyxes,** so that **wherever** they should find the price of our re-demption in an unsuitable place they might put it away in the very best place.

He wanted great reverence shown to the hands of priests, since they have the divinely granted authority to bring about this mystery. He often used to say: "If I should happen at the same time to come

Jn 3:31; Gal 1:8

upon any saint *coming from heaven* and some little poor priest, I would

Rom 12:10

first show honor to the priest, and hurry more quickly to kiss his hands.

1 Jn 1:1

For I would say to the saint: 'Hey, Saint Lawrence,[a] wait! His *hands* may *handle the Word of Life,* and possess something more than hu-man!'"

AC 108

1LtCl 11; 2LtCl
1LtCus 4; Test

Chapter CLIII
HIS DEVOTION TO RELICS

Sir 45:1

[202]This *beloved one of God*
showed himself greatly devoted to divine worship

Mt 22:21

and left nothing *that is God's*
dishonored through carelessness.

When he was at Monte Casale in the province of Massa he com-manded the brothers to move with all reverence the holy relics from an abandoned church to the place of the brothers. He felt very bad that they had been robbed of the devotion due them for a long time. When, for an urgent reason, he had to go somewhere else, his sons, forgetting the command of their Father, disregarded the merit of obedience. But one day the brothers wanted to celebrate, and when as usual they removed the cloth cover from the altar they discovered some beautiful and very fragrant bones. They were stunned at this, since they had never seen them there before. Shortly afterwards the

Lk 4:34

holy one of God returned, and he took care to inquire if his orders about the relics had been carried out. The brothers humbly confessed their fault of neglecting obedience, and won pardon together with a pen-

Ps 18:47

ance. And the saint said: *"Blessed be the Lord my God,* who himself car-ried out what you were supposed to do!"

Consider carefully Francis's devotion,

Ps 69:14

pay attention to *God's good pleasure* towards our dust;

Ps 69:31

magnify the praise of holy obedience.

---

a. Saint Lawrence (+258) was a deacon and a Roman martyr.

For when humans did not heed his voice
God obeyed his prayers.

Chapter CLIV
HIS DEVOTION TO THE CROSS
AND A CERTAIN HIDDEN SACRAMENT

[203]Finally, who can express,
or who can understand,
how it was *far from him to glory*   Gal 6:14
except in the cross of the Lord?
To him alone is it given to know,
to whom alone it is given to experience.
Without a doubt, even if
we were to perceive it in some sense in ourselves,
words would be unable to express such marvels,
soiled as they are by cheap and everyday things.
For this reason perhaps
it had to appear in the flesh,   1 Tm 3:16
since it *could not be explained in words.*   Eccl 1:8
Therefore,
let silence speak, where *word falls short,*   Sir 43:29
for symbol cries out as well, where sign falls short.
This alone intimates to human ears
what is not yet entirely clear:
why that *sacrament appeared* in the saint.[a]   1 Tm 3:16
For what is revealed by him
draws understanding and purpose from the future.
It will be true and worthy of faith,
to which nature, *law* and *grace*   Jn 1:17
will be witnesses.

THE POOR LADIES

Chapter CLV
HOW HE WANTED THE BROTHERS TO HAVE DEALINGS WITH THEM

[204]It would not be right to pass over in silence
the memory of a spiritual building,

---

a. See 2C 9, supra, 166 a.

much nobler than that earthly one,
that the blessed father established in that place

Is 63:14 with the Holy *Spirit leading*
for the increase of the heavenly city,
after he had repaired the material church.
We should not believe
that for the sake of repairing a crumbling and perishable building,
that Christ spoke to him from the wood of the Cross
and in such an amazing way

2 Mc 12:22 that it *strikes fear* and inflicts pain
upon anyone who hears of it.
But, as earlier foretold by the Holy Spirit,
an Order of holy virgins was to be established there
to be brought one day

1 Pt 2:5 as a polished collection of *living stones*[a]
for the restoration of the heavenly house.
The virgins of Christ
had begun to gather in that place,
assembled from diverse regions of the world,
professing the greatest perfection

2 Cor 8:2 in the observance of the *highest poverty*
Jdt 10:4 and *the beauty of every virtue.*
Though the father gradually withdrew

2 Cor 10:10 his *bodily presence* from them,
Mt 3:11 he still offered *in the Holy Spirit,*
his affection to care for them.
The saint recognized that they were marked
with many signs of the highest perfection,
and that they were ready to bear any loss

Phil 1:29 and undergo any labor *for Christ*
Ps 119:21 and did not ever want to *turn aside*
from the holy *commandments.*
Therefore, he firmly promised them,
and others who professed poverty
in a similar way of life,
that he and his brothers
would perpetually offer them help and advice.
And he carried this out carefully
as long as he lived,

---

a. This line alludes to the hymn *Urbs beata Ierusalem*, from the Common of the Dedication of a Church: "Living stones are planed and polished / by the hammer's buffets / at the builder's hand, and fitted / to their proper places; / thus arranged, they stand forever / joined into one building."

and when he was close to death
he commanded it to be carried out without fail always,
saying that
one and the same Spirit　　　　　　　　　　　1 Cor 12:11
had led the brothers and those little poor ladies
out of this world.　　　　　　　　　　　Gal 1:4

[205]The brothers were sometimes surprised that he did not often
visit such holy handmaids of Christ in his *bodily presence*, but he　　Col 2:5
would say: "Don't imagine, dear brothers, that I don't love them
fully. For if it were a crime to cherish them in Christ, wouldn't it be
even worse to have joined them to Christ? Not calling them would
not have been harmful, but not to care for them after calling them
would be the height of cruelty. But *I am giving you an example, that as I*　　Jn 13:15
do, so should you also do. I don't want one volunteering to visit them,
but rather command that those who are unwilling and very reluctant
should be assigned to their service, as long as they are *spiritual men*　　Hos 9:7
tested by a longstanding, worthy way of life."

Chapter CLVI
HOW HE REPROVED SOME OF THE BROTHERS
WHO WENT FREELY TO MONASTERIES

[206]On one occasion a brother who had two daughters of a very
holy life in a certain monastery said that he would gladly bring to
that place a poor little gift which the saint was sending. But the saint
scolded him harshly, indeed, using words which are best not repeated here, and sent the gift with someone else who had refused, although not to the point of obstinacy.

Another brother went to a monastery in winter, for reasons of
compassion, unaware of the saint's prohibition about going. When
the saint found out about this, he made him walk naked for many
miles in the snow and bitter cold.

Chapter CLVII
PREACHING MORE BY EXAMPLE THAN BY WORD

[207]While the holy father was staying at San Damiano, he was pes-
tered by his vicar with repeated requests that he should present the
word of God to his daughters, and he finally gave in to his insistence.
The Ladies gathered as usual to *hear the word of God,* but no less to see
their father, and he *raised his eyes to heaven,* where he always had his

Mt 6:21
1 Mc 3:47 *heart,* and began to pray to Christ. Then he had ashes brought and made a circle with them round himself on the floor, and then *put the rest on his own head.*

As they waited, the blessed father remained in silence within the circle of ashes, and real amazement grew in their hearts. Suddenly Ps 51:3 he got up, and to their great surprise, recited the *"Have mercy on me, God,"* instead of a sermon. As he finished it, he left quickly. The hand-maids of God were so filled with contrition by the power of this mime that they were flowing with tears, and could hardly restrain their hands from punishing themselves. By his action he taught them to consider themselves ashes, and that nothing else was close to his heart except what was in keeping with that view.

This was his way of behaving with holy women;
this was his way of visiting them
rare and constrained, but very useful!
This was his will for all the brothers,
whom he wanted to serve
Col 3:24 for the sake of *Christ, whom they serve*:
Prv 1:17; Ps 69:23 that they might always, like *winged* creatures,
beware of *the nets before them.*

EXTOLLING THE RULE OF THE BROTHERS

Chapter CLVIII
EXTOLLING THE RULE OF SAINT FRANCIS,
AND A BROTHER WHO ALWAYS CARRIED IT WITH HIM

²⁰⁸ He burned with great zeal for the common profession and *Rule,* and endowed those who were zealots about it with a special blessing. AC 46

Sir 24:32; Rv 3:5;
1 Thes 5:8
Gn 17:13 He called it their *Book of Life, the hope of salvation,* the marrow of the Gospel, the way of perfection, the key of Paradise, *the pact of an eternal covenant.* He wanted all to have it, all to know it, in all places 1C 32

ER XXIV; Test 3
Rom 7:22; Wis 8:9 to let it speak to the *inner man* as *encouragement in weariness* and as a reminder of a sworn oath.

He taught them to keep it always before their eyes as a reminder of the life they should lead and, what is more, that they should die with it.

This teaching was not forgotten by a certain lay brother whom we believe should be venerated among the martyrs, since he gained the palm of glorious victory.[a] When he was taken by the Saracens to his martyrdom, he held the *Rule* in his uplifted hands, and kneeling humbly, said to his companion: "Dear brother, I proclaim myself guilty before *the eyes of Majesty* of everything that I ever did against this holy *Rule!*" The stroke of the sword followed this short confession, and with this martyrdom he ended his life, and afterward shone with *signs and wonders*. This brother had entered the Order so young that he could hardly bear the *Rule's* fasting, yet even as a boy he wore a harness next to his skin. Oh happy child, who began happily, that he might finish more happily!

         Is 3:8

         2 Cor 12:12

Chapter CLIX
A VISION EXTOLLING THE RULE

[209]The most holy Father once saw by heavenly revelation a vision concerning the *Rule*. It was at the time when there was discussion among the brothers about confirming the *Rule*, and the saint was extremely anxious about this matter. This is what was shown to him *in a dream:* It seemed to him that he was gathering tiny bread crumbs from the ground, which he had to distribute to a crowd of hungry brothers who stood all around him. He was afraid to give out such little crumbs, fearing that such minute particles might slip between his fingers, when a *voice cried out* to him from above: "Francis, make one host out of all the crumbs, and give it to those who want to eat." He did this, and whoever did not receive it devoutly, or showed contempt for the gift received, soon appeared obviously infected with leprosy.

         Mt 1:20

         Dn 6:20

In the morning the saint recounted all this to his companions, regretting that he did not understand the *mystery of the vision*. But shortly afterward, as he *kept vigil in prayer*, this *voice came down* to him *from heaven:* "Francis, the crumbs you saw last night are the words of the Gospel; the host is the *Rule*, and the leprosy is wickedness."

         Dn 2:19

         Tb 3:11; 2 Pt 1:17-18

The brothers of those times
did not consider this promise which they had sworn
either hard or harsh;
they were always more than ready

---

a. This was Brother Electus, who was executed by the Muslims, probably at Tunis, before 1246, and quite possibly during the lifetime of Francis.

Lk 10:35 *to give more* than required in all things.[a]
For there is no room for apathy or laziness
where the goad of love is always urging to greater things.

THE ILLNESSES OF SAINT FRANCIS

Chapter CLX
HOW HE CONVERSED WITH A BROTHER ABOUT CARE OF THE BODY

[210]Francis, the herald of God,
Jos 3:13 *put* his *footprints* on the ways of Christ
through innumerable labors and serious diseases,
and he did not retreat
Lk 14:30 until he had more perfectly *completed*
what he had perfectly *begun.*
Jgs 16:16 When *he was exhausted*
and his whole body completely shattered,
he never stopped on the race of his perfection
and never allowed relaxing
the rigor of discipline.
For even when his body was already exhausted
he could not grant it even slight relief
without some grumbling of conscience.

So, when even against his will it was necessary to smear medical
remedies on his body, which exceeded his strength, he spoke kindly
one day with a brother whom he knew was ready to give him advice:
"What do you think of this, dear son? My conscience often grumbles
about the care of the body. It fears I am indulging it too much in this
illness, and that I'm eager for fine lotions to help it. Actually, none of
this gives it any pleasure, since it is worn out by long sickness, and
the urge for any savoring is gone."

[211]The son replied attentively to his father, realizing that the
words of his answer were given to him by the Lord. "Tell me, father, if
you please, how attentively did your body obey your commands
while it was able?" And he said:

---

a. *Supererogare* [to give more] is used only once in the Old and New Testaments, that is, in this passage
of Luke's Gospel treating of the Good Samaritan. It is also the only use of the word in Thomas's
writings suggesting an obvious connection in his thought, the promise of the Good Samaritan and that
of the brothers.

> "I will *bear witness* to it, my son,   <small>Jn 5:31</small>
> for it was *obedient in all things.*   <small>Col 3:20</small>
> It did not spare itself in anything,
> but almost rushed headlong
> to carry out every order.
> It evaded no labor,
> it turned down no discomfort,
> if only it could *carry out commands.*   <small>Jgs 9:54</small>
> In this it and I were in complete agreement:
> that *we should serve the Lord Christ*   <small>Col 3:24</small>
> without any objection."

The brother said: "Well, then, my father, where is your generosity? Where is your piety and your great discernment? Is this a repayment worthy of *faithful friends*: to accept favors gladly but then not <small>Sir 6:14-16</small> give anything in return in time of need? To this day, what service could you offer to Christ your Lord without the help of your body? Haven't you admitted that it exposed itself to every danger for this reason?"

"I admit, son," said the father, "this is nothing but the truth."

And the son replied: "Well, is it reasonable that you should desert a *faithful friend* in great need, who risked himself and all that he had <small>Gn 18:25</small> for you, even to the point of death? *Far be it from* you, father, you who <small>Gn 18:25</small> are the help and support of the afflicted; *far be it from you to sin against* <small>1 Sm 12:23</small> *the Lord in such a way!"*

"*Blessed are you* also, *son,*" he said, "you have wisely given me a <small>1 Sm 26:25</small> drink of healing medicine for my disquiet!" And he began to say jok-
<small>2C 116, 129</small> ingly to his body: "Cheer up Brother Body, and *forgive me*; for I will <small>Jb 7:16</small> now gladly do as you please, and gladly hurry to relieve your complaints!"

> But, what could delight this little body already so ruined?
> What could uphold it,
> already broken in every way?
> Francis *was* already *dead to the world,*   <small>Gal 2:19-20; 6:14</small>
> but *Christ lived in* him.
> The delights of the world were a cross to him,
> since he carried the *cross of Christ* rooted in his heart.   <small>Gal 6:14</small>
> And that is why the stigmata
> shone outwardly in his flesh,
> because inwardly that root was growing
> deep in his spirit.

Chapter CLXI
WHAT THE LORD PROMISED HIM FOR HIS SUFFERINGS

[212]Worn out with sufferings on all sides, it was amazing that his strength could bear it. But in fact he did not call these tribulations by the name of "pains," but rather "Sisters." There is no question that they came from many causes. Truly, in order that he might become more famous through victories, the Most High not only entrusted to him difficult tasks during his early training but also gave him occasions for triumph while he was a veteran.

In this too the followers have him for an example,
for he never slowed down because of age
or became more self-indulgent because of his illness.
And there was a reason that his purgation was complete
Ps 84:7 *in this vale of tears:*
Mt 5:25 so he might *repay up to the last penny,*
if there was anything to burn left in him,
so at the end completely cleansed
he could fly quickly to heaven.
But I believe the principal reason for his sufferings was,
as he affirmed about others,
Ps 19:11 that *in* bearing *them there is great reward.*

[213]One night, when he was more worn out than usual because of various serious discomforts from his illnesses, he began to feel sorry for himself in the depths of his heart. But, lest his *willing spirit* should
Mt 26:41 give in to the flesh in a fleshly way even for a moment, unmoving he held the shield of patience by praying to Christ.

And as he *prayed* in this *struggle,* he *received a promise of eternal life*
Lk 22:43;
Heb 10:36; Jn 6:68
Is 40:12 through this comparison: "If the whole *mass of the earth* and fabric of the universe were made of the most precious gold, and you with all pain gone were given as the reward for the hard suffering you're
Wis 7:9 bearing a treasure of such glory that all this *gold* would be as nothing *in comparison* to it,—not even worth mentioning—wouldn't you rejoice, and gladly bear what you're bearing at the moment?" "I'd be
2 Cor 4:17 happy to," said the saint, "I'd be *immeasurably happy.*"

"Rejoice, then," the Lord said to him, "for your illness is the
Wis 7:23 pledge of my Kingdom; by merit of your patience you can be *firm and*
Eph 5:5 *secure* in expecting the *inheritance of this Kingdom.*"

Can you imagine the joy felt by one
blessed with such a happy promise?

Can you believe the great patience,
and even the charity,
he showed in embracing bodily discomforts?
He now knows it perfectly,
but then it was impossible for him to express it.
However, as he could, he told a little to his companions.
TC; 1C 80; AC 83
It was then that he composed
the *Praises about Creatures*,
rousing them in any way
to praise of the Creator.

THE PASSING OF OUR HOLY FATHER OUT OF THIS WORLD

Chapter CLXII
HOW AT THE END HE ENCOURAGED AND BLESSED HIS BROTHERS

[214]*At a human's end,* says the wise man,   Sir 11:27-28
comes the disclosing of his works,
and we see this gloriously fulfilled in this saint.
Running eagerly *on the road of God's commandments,*   Ps 119:32
he scaled the steps of all the virtues
until he reached the very summit.
Like a malleable metal,
he was brought to perfection
under the hammering blows of many tribulations,
and *saw the end of all perfection.*[a]   Ps 119:96
Then his wonderful work shone all the brighter,
and it flared out in *the judgement of truth*   Ps 111:7
that everything he lived was divine.
He trampled on the allure of mortal life
and escaped free into the heights.
For he considered it dishonor to live for the world,
loved his own to the very end,   Jn 13:1
and welcomed Death singing.
When he approached his final days
—when *light eternal*[b] was replacing
the limited light that had been removed—

---

a. This refers to a medieval technique for purifying and strengthening metals by hammering. Therefore the blacksmith who worked with iron, but also gold-and-silver smiths.
b. Entrance Antiphon for the Requiem Mass, taken from the apocryphal book of 4 Ezra, 2:35.

he showed by his example of virtue
that he had nothing in common with the world.

As he was wasted by that grave illness which ended all his sufferings, he had himself placed naked on the naked ground, so that in 1C 110
that final hour, when the Enemy could still rage, he might wrestle naked with the naked.[a] The fearless man awaited triumph and, with
2 Tm 4:8; Jb 20:4 hands joined, held the *crown of justice.* Placed *on the ground* and
Jb 11:15 stripped of his sackcloth garment, he *lifted* up his *face to heaven* as
Acts 7:55 usual, and, totally *intent* upon that *glory*, he covered the wound on his right side with his left hand, so no one would see it. Then he said to
1 Kgs 19:20; Eph 4:21 his brothers: "I have done *what is mine; may Christ teach* you what is yours!"

215 Seeing this, his sons wept streams of tears, drawing sighs from deep within, overwhelmed by sorrow and compassion.

Meanwhile, as their sobs somewhat subsided, his guardian, who by divine inspiration better understood the saint's wish, quickly got up, took the tunic, underwear and sackcloth hood, and said to the father: "I command you under holy obedience to acknowledge that I am lending you this tunic, underwear and hood. And so that you know that they in no way belong to you, I take away all your author-
Sg 3:11 ity to give them to anyone." The saint rejoiced, and his *heart* leaped
Mt 10:22 for *joy* seeing that he had kept faith *until the end* with Lady Poverty. For he had done all of this out of zeal for poverty, not wanting to have at the end even a habit of his own, but one borrowed from another. He had been wearing a sackcloth cap on his head to cover the scars he had received in the treatment of his eyes; what was really needed for this was a smooth cap of the softest and most expensive wool.

2 Chr 6:13 216 After this the saint *raised his hands to heaven*
and glorified his Christ;
free now from all things, he was going to him free.

1 Cor 4:16 But in order to show himself in all things a true *imitator of Christ,* AC 22
Jn 13:1 his God, *he loved to the very end* the brothers and sons *he had loved* from the beginning. **He had them call to him** all the brothers present
Zec 1:13 there, and, comforting them about his death with *words of consolation,* he exhorted them to the love of God with fatherly affection. He spoke

a. See Gregory the Great, *Homilia in Evangelium,* 32:2. "All of us who come to the wrestling ground of Faith are to wrestle with the evil spirits. Now, the evil spirits possess nothing in this world, and therefore it behooves us to wrestle naked with naked adversaries. For if a clothed man should wrestle with a naked man, he will soon be thrown down, for his adversary will have something by which to take hold of him." This passage became a common quotation in medieval ascetical literature. See also FA:ED I 194 a.

at length about patience, about preserving poverty, and about placing the Holy Gospel ahead of all other observances.

As all the brothers sat around him *he stretched out his right hand over them* and, beginning with his vicar, *he placed it on* each of *their heads* saying:

Gn 48:14-22

1C 108

"Good-bye, my sons,
live in the *fear of the Lord*
and remain in it always!
A great trial and tribulation is at hand!
Happy are they who will persevere
in the things they have begun!
I am hurrying to God,
to whose grace I commend all of you!"

Acts 9:31

He then blessed in those who were there, all the other brothers who *were living* anywhere *in the world*, and those who *were to come after* them *unto the end of all ages.*

2 Cor 1:12; Jn 1:15

Dn 7:18

Let no one claim this blessing as his own
for he pronounced it for those absent through those present.
As written elsewhere
it sounded like something for an individual;[a]
instead it should be redirected to the office.

Chapter CLXIII
HIS DEATH AND WHAT HE DID BEFORE IT

AC 22

[217]As the brothers shed bitter tears and wept inconsolably, the holy father had *bread brought* to him. He *blessed and broke* it, and gave each of them a piece to eat.

Mt 14:17, 18; Mt 26:26

1C 110

He also ordered a Book of the Gospels to be brought and asked that the Gospel according to Saint John be read to him starting from that place which begins: *Before the feast of Passover.*[b] He was remembering that most sacred Supper, the last one the Lord celebrated *with his disciples.* In reverent memory of this, to show his brothers how much he loved them, he did all of this.

Jn 13:1

Mt 26:20

---

a. In 1C 108-109, the blessing could be interpreted as given to Brother Elias personally. Here the author interprets the blessing as designated for the one who holds the office of Vicar.
b. Here, in contrast to 1C 110, Thomas corrects the confusion about the starting point for the reading of the Gospel. See FA:ED I 278 a.

The few days that remained to him before his passing he spent in   1C 109
praise of God, teaching his beloved companions how to praise Christ
with him. As best he could, he broke out in this psalm, *With my voice I*   1C 108
cried to the Lord, With my voice I beseeched the Lord. He also invited all
creatures to the praise of God, and exhorted them to love by some
words which he had composed earlier.[a] Even death itself, terrible
and hateful everyone, he exhorted to praise, and *going to meet her joy-*
fully, invited her to be his guest, saying: "Welcome, my Sister Death!"
And to the doctor he said: "Be bold, Brother Doctor, foretell death is
near; for to me she will be the gate of Life!" But to the brothers he
said: "When you see I have come to my end put me out naked on the
ground as you saw me naked the day before yesterday,[b] and once I
am dead, allow me to lie there for as long as it takes to walk a lei-
surely mile."

Ps 142, 2-8

Jgs 19:3

The *hour came.*
All *the mysteries of Christ*
were fulfilled in him,
and he happily flew off to God.

Jn 4:21
Col 4:3

HOW A BROTHER SAW THE PASSING OF THE HOLY FATHER'S SOUL

[217a]One of his disciples, a brother of no small fame, saw the soul of   1C 110, 112, 11
the most holy father *like a star ascending to heaven,* having the immen-
sity of the moon and the brightness of the sun, extending *over many*
waters carried by *a little white cloud.*

Because of this *a great crowd of many peoples* gathered, *praising and*
glorifying the name of the Lord. The whole city of Assisi rushed down in
a body and the whole region hurried to see the *wonderful works of God,*
which the *Lord* had *displayed* in his servant. The sons lamented the
loss of such a father and displayed their hearts' tender affection by
tears and sighs.

But a new miracle turned their weeping into jubilation and their
mourning into cries of joy. They saw the body of their holy father
adorned with the wounds of Christ. Not the holes of the nails but the
nails themselves in the middle of his hands and feet, made from his
own flesh, in fact grown in the flesh itself retaining the dark color of
iron and his right side stained red with blood. His skin, naturally

Sir 50:6; Jos 8:20
Ps 29:3
Rv 14:14
Acts 21:30; Lk 2:20

Acts 2:11
Lk 2:15

---

a. This refers to the *Canticle of the Creatures,* see FA:ED I 113-114
b. Thomas does a word play here: *sicut me nudiustertius nudum vidistis.*

dark before, now shining bright white promised the rewards of the blessed resurrection.

Finally, his limbs had become soft and pliable; not rigid, as usual with the dead, but changed to be like those of a boy.

Chapter CLXIV
THE VISION BROTHER AUGUSTINE SAW AS HE WAS DYING

[218]At that time the minister of the brothers of Terra di Lavoro was Brother Augustine. He was in his last hour, and had already for some time lost his speech when, in the hearing of those *who were standing* by, *he suddenly cried out and said*: "Wait for me, father, wait! Look, I'm coming with you!" The amazed brothers asked him to whom he was speaking, and he responded boldly: "Don't you see our father Francis going to heaven?" And immediately his holy soul, released from the flesh, followed his most holy father.

Acts 23:4

Lk 9:39

Chapter CLXV
HOW THE HOLY FATHER APPEARED TO A BROTHER AFTER HIS PASSING

[219]At the very same hour that evening the glorious father appeared to another brother of praiseworthy life, who was at that moment absorbed in prayer. He appeared to him clothed in a purple dalmatic[a] and followed by an innumerable crowd of people. Several separated themselves from the crowd and said to that brother: *"Is this not Christ,* brother?" And he replied: *"It is he."* Others asked him again, saying: "Isn't this Saint Francis?" And the brother likewise replied that it was he. For it really seemed to that brother, and to the whole crowd, as if Christ and Saint Francis were one person.

Jn 7:26

Mt 26:48

And this will not seem at all like a rash statement to those who rightly understand it, for whoever *clings to God,* becomes *one spirit* with Him, and that *God* will be *all in all.*

1 Cor 6:17

1 Cor 12:6

Finally the blessed father and the crowd arrived at a very beautiful place, watered with the clearest waters, flourishing with the beauty of flowers and full of every delightful sort of tree. There, too, was a palace of amazing size and singular beauty. The new inhabitant of heaven entered it eagerly. He found inside many brothers sitting at a splendidly set table loaded with various delicacies and with them he delightfully began to feast.

---

a. The dalmatic is the liturgical vestment proper to deacons. The color of the dalmatic is probably meant to be a royal purple.

Chapter CLXVI
THE BISHOP OF ASSISI'S VISION OF THE HOLY FATHER'S PASSING

[220]At that time the bishop of Assisi[a] had been at the church of Saint Michael[b] because of a pilgrimage. He was returning from there, and was lodging at Benevento, when the blessed father Francis appeared to him in a vision on the night of his passing, and said to him:
Jn 16:28; Gn 24:54 "See, my father, *I am leaving the world and going to Christ!" When he rose in the morning,* the bishop told his companions what he had seen, and summoning a notary, had the day and hour of the passing noted. He was very saddened about this, and flowing with tears he regretted
Mt 2:12 having lost such an outstanding father. And so *he returned to his own*
Acts 27:35 *country* and told it all in order, giving unending *thanks to the Lord* because of his gifts.

THE CANONIZATION AND TRANSFER OF SAINT FRANCIS

1 Cor 6:11 [220a]*In the name of the Lord Jesus.* Amen.   1C 88, 119-126
In the twelfth hundredth twenty-sixth year of the Incarnation,
on the fourth day before the Nones of October,
the day he had foretold,
having completed twenty years
from the time he perfectly adhered to Christ,
1 Pt 2:21   *following in the footsteps*
and the life of the Apostles,
the apostolic man Francis,
freed from the fetters of mortal life,
departed happily to Christ.
He was buried in the city of Assisi
and began to shine with so many wonders
and with diverse miracles in every region,
that,
in a short time,
he had led most of the earth
to admire the new age.

Since in the new light of miracles, he was already shining in many parts of the world and those who rejoiced in being saved from disasters by his favor were hastening from everywhere, the Lord Pope

---

a. Bishop Guido, who was bishop of Assisi throughout the whole of Francis's religious life.
b. At Monte Gargano in southern Italy.

Gregory, who was then in Perugia with all the cardinals and other prelates of the Church, began to discuss with them the issue of his canonization. All of them, with one accord, gave the same opinion. They read and approved the miracles which the Lord had worked through his servant, and extolled the life and behavior of the blessed father with the highest praises.

The *princes of the earth* were called first to this great solemnity, and on the appointed day a great number of prelates along with an infinite multitude of people entered with the blessed Pope into the city of Assisi, for it was there that the canonization was to be held, for greater reverence of the saint.

And so, when all had come to the place which had been prepared for such a solemn gathering, Pope Gregory preached first to *all the people* and announced with honey-flowing affection *the wonderful works of God*. He also praised the holy father Francis with the most noble sermon, and as he spoke of the purity of his way of life he was wet with tears. Then, when his sermon was over, Pope Gregory *lifted his hands to heaven* and cried out with a loud voice . . . [a]

Ps 148:11

Heb 9:19

Sir 18:5

2 Mc 3:20

A PRAYER OF THE SAINT'S COMPANIONS TO HIM

Chapter CLXVII

[221]Behold, our blessed father, the efforts of our simple capacities have attempted to praise your wondrous deeds to the best of our ability, and to tell at least a few of the countless virtues of your holiness for your glory. We know that our words have much diminished the splendor of your outstanding deeds, since they have been found unequal to expressing the great deeds of such perfection.

We ask you, and also those who read this, to keep in mind our affection and our effort, and to rejoice that the heights of your life are beyond the best efforts of human pens. For who, oh outstanding saint, could be able to bring into himself the burning *ardor of your spirit* or to impress it on others? Who would be able to conceive those inexpressible feelings which flowed uninterruptedly between you and God? But we wrote these things delighting in your sweet memory which, while we still live, we try to express to others even if it is by stammering.

You who once were hungry, now *feed upon the finest wheat;* you who once were thirsty, now *drink of the torrent of delight.* But we do not believe that you are so far *inebriated with the abundance of God's house,* as to have *forgotten your own children* when he who is your very drink *keeps us in mind.*

Draw us, then, to *yourself,*
that we may run after the fragrance of your perfumes,
for, as you can see, we have become
lukewarm in apathy,
listless in laziness,
half-dead in negligence!
This *little flock* is stumbling
along in your footprints;
the weakness of our eyes cannot bear
the shining rays of your perfection.
Give us such days as we had of old,
oh mirror and exemplar of the perfect!
Do not allow that those
who are like you by profession
be unlike you in life.

Margin references:
Is 4:4
Ps 81:17
Ps 36:9
Ps 36:9
Hos 4:6; Ps 115:12
Sg 1:3
Lk 12:32
Lam 5:21

[222]At this point we *lay down* the prayer of our lowliness before the merciful kindness of the *eternal Majesty* for Christ's servant, our minister, the successor of your holy humility, and emulator of your true poverty, who, for *the love of your Christ,* shows diligent *care for* your *sheep* with gentle affection.

Dn 9:18

Ps 72:19

Rom 8:35; Gn 46:32

> We ask you, oh holy one,
> so to encourage and embrace him that,
> by constantly adhering to your footprints,
> he may attain forever *the praise and glory*
> which *you have achieved.*

Phil 1:11

1 Tm 4:6

[223]We also pray with all our heart's affection, oh kind father, for that son of yours who now and earlier has devoutly written your praises. He, together with us, offers and dedicates to you this little work which he put together, not in a manner worthy of your merit but at least devoutly, and as best he could.

> *From* every *evil*
> mercifully preserve
> and *deliver* him.
> Increase holy merit in him,
> and, by your prayers,
> join him forever to the company of the saints.

Mt 6:13

[224]Remember all your children, father.
You, most holy one, know perfectly how,
lost in a maze of mystifying perils,
they *follow your footprints*
from how great a distance.
Give them strength, that they may resist.
Purify them, that they may shine radiantly.
Fill them with joy, that they may delight.

Gn 33:14

> Pray that
> *the spirit of grace and of prayer may inundate them*
> that they may have the true humility you had;
> that they may cherish the poverty you embraced;
> that they may be filled with the love
> with which you always loved
> *Christ crucified.*
> Who with the Father and the Holy Spirit
> *lives and reigns forever and ever.*
> Amen.

Zec 12:10

1 Cor 1:23

Rv 11:15

THE TREATISE ON THE MIRACLES

OF SAINT FRANCIS

(1250–1252)

Introduction

In *The Life of Saint Francis, The Legend for Use in the Choir* based on it, and *The Remembrance of the Desire of a Soul*, Thomas of Celano wrote of the miracles of Francis of Assisi. In each of these works, Thomas saw these miracles as signs through which God had authenticated the holiness of his subject and, at the same time, as extraordinary deeds attesting to God's power working through him.[1] When John of Parma, the newly elected General Minister, approached the now aging writer to treat of them in one collection, he was implicitly asking for the completion of a trilogy in which each work had its own unique focus and its own contribution to the entire portrait.

Written between 1250 and 1252, *The Treatise on the Miracles of Saint Francis* is made up of 198 paragraphs. Fifty-four of these are taken from *The Life of Saint Francis*, one from *The Legend for Use in the Choir*, and nine from *The Remembrance of the Desire of a Soul*. In other words, for one third of his work, Thomas relies on his earlier portraits of Francis. The remaining paragraphs come from different sources. *The Assisi Compilation* is easily identifiable and suggests that "we who were with him," as Francis's companions write of themselves, contributed to Thomas's awareness of the miracles. Other paragraphs come from an unknown source, prompting speculation about the existence of a "process of canonization" in which an official or notary would have written down the testimonies of witnesses to these miracles. Throughout, however, the hand of Thomas is obvious as he orders, sculpts and refines the material given to him into the portrait of Francis the Thaumaturgist, the Miracle Worker.

Thomas divided his work into nineteen chapters. One manner of approaching these chapters is to see them simply in terms of those miracles performed while Francis lived, that is, the first six chapters, and those performed, through his intercession, after his death, that is, the final thirteen. However, the first six chapters deal with miracles that touch more on the inner dynamic of Francis himself or on that of his brothers: the founding and growth of the fraternity, the stigmata, the miraculous power he had over creatures, and the arrival of Lady Jacoba at his death. These far more reflective and theological chapters reveal Thomas at his inspirational best, never hesitating to add his own interpretation of an incident or to draw a moral from it. The remaining chapters, with the exception of the conclusion, i.e., chapter nineteen, are far more historical and ordered giving the impression that Thomas was following a predetermined order. From considerations of Francis's miraculous raising of the dead to his healing of broken bones, Thomas presents one hundred and fifty-seven miracles. In doing so, he deftly paints a portrait of this "new man," Francis, through whom the Creator makes all things new (3C 1).

The first printed edition of the Latin text of *The Treatise on the Miracles of Saint Francis* appeared only in 1899 when François van Ortroy published it in the *Acta Bollandiana*.[2] In his edition of the complete corpus of Thomas of Celano in 1906, Édouad d'Alençon also published it, as did the editors of the tenth volume of the *Analecta Franciscana*.[3] The latest publication of the text is that of the *Fontes Franciscani* in 1995.[4]

Translating this lengthy list of miracles, however, seems to have been a daunting enterprise, and, because of its repetitious nature, one that was tedious and tiring. That translators and publishers gave little attention to Thomas's last work is verified by the fact that there have been no complete translations of the work. The Spanish, French, and American editions either printed selected paragraphs or nothing at all.[5] Thus, little attention has been given to the work until the Italian *Fonti Francescane* published *The Treatise on the Miracles of Saint Francis* in its entirety, prompting six studies that began to shed light on its richness.[6] The authors of these essays examined aspects such as the sites of the miracles, the sociological backgrounds of the recipients, the information the incidents provide concerning the daily life of those involved, and Thomas's changing image of Francis.

Notes

1. For a thorough study of the medieval understanding and appreciation of miracles, see Benedicta Ward, *Miracles and the Medieval Mind: Theory, Record and Event, 1000-1215* (Philadelphia: University of Pennsylvania Press, 1982). For background information on Thomas of Celano's approach to miracles in *The Life of Saint Francis*, see Roberto Paciocco, "Miracles and Canonized Sanctity in the 'First Life of St. Francis,'" GR 5(1991): 251-274.

2. François van Ortroy, "Traité des miracles des François d'Assise par le b. Thomas de Celano," *Analecta Bollandiana* 18 (1899): 81-179.

3. Eduardus Alenconiensis, *Sancti Francisci Assiensis Vita et Miracula, additis opusculis liturgicis auctore Fr. Thoma de Celano*, (Romae, 1906), 341-432; "Tractatus de Miraculis," *Analecta Franciscana* X (Ad Claras Aquas, Quaracchi: Collegium S. Bonaventurae, 1926-1941), 269-331.

4. *Fontes Franciscani*, ed. Enrico Menestó, Stefano Brufani, Giuseppe Cremascoli, Emore Paoli, Luigi Pellegrini, and Stanislao da Campagno (Sta. Maria degli Angeli, Assisi: Edizioni Porziuncula, 1995).

5. The Spanish edition, *San Francisco de Asis. Sus escritos. Las Florecillas. Biografías del santo por Celano, san Buenaventura y los Tres Compañeros. Espejo de Perfección*. 5 ed. (Madrid: BAC, 1951), ignored the work completely. The French edition, *Saint François d'Assise: Documents, écrits et premières biographies*. (Paris: éditions Franciscaines, 1968), was limited to only the titles. The American edition, *Saint Francis of Assisi, Writings and Early Biographies: English Omnibus of The Sources for the Life of Saint Francis* (Chicago: Franciscan Herald Press, 1972), published only certain paragraphs, i.e., those that had already been translated.

6. *Fonti Francescane. Scritti e biografie di san Francesco d'Assisi. Cronache e altre testimonianze del primo secolo francescano. Scritti et biografie di santa Chiara*. 2 Volumes. (Assisi: Movimento Francescano, 1977).

Mariano D'Alatri, "Da Una Rilettura del 'Tratatto dei miracoli' di Fra Tommaso da Celano," *l'Italia Francescana* 53 (1978): 29-40; Jacques Paul, "L'Image de Saint François dans Le Traite 'De Miraculis' de Thomas de Celano," in *Francesco d'Assisi nella Storia, Secoli XIII-XV*, a cura di Servus Gieben (Roma, 1983): 251-274; Roberto Paciocco, *Da Francesco ai 'Catologi Sanctorum.' Livelli Istituzionali e Immagini Agiografiche nell'Ordine Francescano (Secoli XIII-XIV)* (Assisi: 1990); Maria Antonietta Romano, "Tractatus de Miraculis B. Francisci," *Hagiographica* 2 (1996): 187-221; and Jacques Dalarun, "Il Tractatus de Miraculis, Vertice dell'Opera Celaniana," in *La Malavventura di San Francesco: Per Un Uso Storico delle Leggende Francescane* (Milano: Edizioni Biblioteca Francescana, 1996), 97-119.

The Treatise on the Miracles of Saint Francis

Chapter I
THE BEGINNING OF HIS RELIGION WAS MIRACULOUS

[1]We have undertaken to write down
the miracles of our most holy father Francis;
and we have decided to note in first place in this account,
before all the others,
that sacred miracle by which the world was warned,
by which it was roused, and by which it was frightened.
That miracle was the beginning of the religion:
the sterile made fruitful,
giving birth to a varied people.
People observed
that the old world was growing *filthy* with a mange of vices,
that Orders were slipping away from the footprints of the apostles,
that *the night* of sinners had reached *mid-course in its journey,*
and *silence* had been imposed on sacred studies.

Just then, suddenly, there *leapt upon the earth*
a new man;
a new army quickly appeared;
and the peoples marveled *at the signs* of an apostolic newness.[a]
Quickly there *came to light*
the long-buried perfection of the primitive Church:
the world read of its marvels,
but did not see any examples of it.
Why, therefore, should *the last* not be called the *first,*
since now *the hearts of fathers are* wondrously *turned to their children*
and the hearts of children to their fathers?
Sould *the mission* of the two Orders,[b]
so well known and famous,

Margin references:
, 31, 36-7, 62, 89; LCh 9
1C 8 — Rv 22:11 — Wis 18:14-15
Eph 2:15
1C 89 — Ps 65:9; Mk 16:20 — Jb 28:11
Mt 19:30; 20:16 — Mal 4:6
1C 37-8, 18-20 — 2 Cor 5:20

---

a. Thomas returns to a theme found throughout his earlier works, that of newness. While it is most prominent in 1C in which *novus* [new] appears thirty-nine times, it is proportionately less so in 2C where it appears twenty-four times. In this work, it appears thirteen times. In this instance, the theme of the "newness" found in the "new man" appears to indicate the wonders brought by the saint and the "new Orders" founded by him. Cf. FA:ED I 196 c.

b. A reference to the Order of Friars Minor and that of Saint Damian, the Poor Ladies. *Solet annuere,* the papal decree of Pope Honorius III confirming the *Later Rule* with a papal seal (cf. FA:ED I 99-106), declared the Lesser Brothers an Order. In the papal document, *Cum omnis vera religio* (August 6, 1247), Pope Innocent IV called the Poor Ladies, the followers of Clare of Assisi (+1253), the "Order of Saint Damian." It was not called the Order of Saint Clare until the papal decree of Pope Urban IV in 1256. Thomas omits mention of the Third Order, the Order of Penitents.

be considered unimportant,
and not a portent of great things to come?
Never since the time of the apostles was there
such an outstanding, such an amazing warning to the world!

Wonderful, its sterile fruitfulness.
Sterile, I say, and dried out this poor little Religion:
the moisture of earthly things remains far from it.
Sterile indeed the one who *neither reaps nor gathers into barns,*
nor *carries a* bulging *wallet on the way of the Lord.*
And yet this saint *believed, hoping against hope,*
that *he would inherit the world,*
not thinking his own body as good as dead
and the womb of Sarah sterile.
God's power brought forth from her the Hebrew people.
He was not sustained
by full *cellars,*
by overflowing *storehouses,*
or bountiful possessions;
but the same poverty that makes him worthy of heaven
marvelously nourished him in the world.
O weak one of God, stronger than men,
you both bring glory to our cross
and also sustain our poverty with plenty!
We then saw that vine spreading, in the briefest time,
extending its fruitful branches from sea to sea.
People came running from everywhere,
the crowds swelled,
and were quickly joined *as living stones*

to the grand *structure of* this marvelous *temple.*
Not only do we see it multiply with children in a short time;
we also see it become famous,
for we know that many of those it bore
have obtained the palm of martyrdom,[a]
and we venerate many others enrolled in the catalog of saints[b]
as confessors of most perfect holiness.
But let us turn now to him who is the head of them all.

Marginal references:
Mt 6:26
Lk 9:3; 10:4
Acts 18:25
Rom 4:18
Rom 4:19
Jb 4:13; Gn 11:30
Lk 12:24; Is 39:2
1 Cor 1:25
Ez 17:6-7; 47:17; Ps 80:12
1 Pt 2:5
Mk 13:1
1C 36-7, 89

---

a. This is a reference to Brothers Berard, Otto, Peter, Adjutus, and Accursius, who were put to death in Morocco on January 16, 1220. Cf. AF III, 579-96; AF IV 322-3; Jordan, *Chronicle* 7-8. Thomas writes of another unnamed brother martyred by the Saracens, cf. 2C 208. Brother Daniel and seven companions were killed in Ceuta, Mauritania, present day Morocco, on October 10, 1227; cf. AF III 613-6; IV, 296f. Brothers John of Perugia and Peter of Sassoferrato were put to death by Moors in 1231 (certainly not before 1225); see AF III, 186-7; IV, 324.

b. Anthony of Lisbon, who died in Padua on June 13, 1231, was proclaimed a saint by Gregory IX with the papal decree, *Cum dicat Dominus,* June 12, 1232. Cf. *Bullarium Franciscanum* I (hereafter BFr), ed. Joannis H. Sbaraleae, 79-84; 1C 48; 2C 163. In the *Catalogo Sanctorum Fratrum Minorum* ed. Leonard Lemmens (Rome: 1903), 9; AF IV, 235.

Chapter II
THE MIRACLE OF THE STIGMATA
AND THE MANNER IN WHICH THE SERAPH APPEARED TO HIM

C 112, 114; 2C 11

²*The new man,* Francis,   Eph 4:24
became famous for a new and stupendous miracle.
By a singular privilege, not granted in previous ages,
he appeared marked,
adorned with the sacred stigmata,
and *conformed in this body of death*   Phil 3:10, 21;
to the body of the Crucified.   Rom 7:24

Whatever human speech can say about this will be less than the praise it deserves. No explanation should be demanded, because it was a wonder. No example should be sought, because it was unique.[a]

2C 109, 203; 1C 45, 115

All the striving of this *man of God,* whether in public or in private,   1 Sm 9:6
revolved around the cross of the Lord. From the earliest days when he began his knightly service for the Crucified, various mysteries of the cross shone around him. At the beginning of his conversion, when he had decided to take leave of the allurements of this life, Christ spoke to him from the wood of the cross while he prayed.

2C 10

From the mouth of Christ's image a voice declared: "Francis, go, re-build my house, which, as you see, it is all being destroyed." From that moment the memory of the Lord's passion was stamped on his heart with a deep brand-mark, and as conversion reached his deep-

1C 22

est self, his soul began *to melt, as his beloved spoke.* And he also enclosed   Sg 5:6
himself in the cross itself when he put on the habit of a penitent, bearing the image of the cross.

Though for him the more the habit reflected poverty,
the more appropriate it would be to his plan,
the saint approved in it even more the mystery of the cross,
because just as, internally, his mind *had put on* the crucified Lord,   Gal 3:27
so, externally, his whole body put on *the cross of Christ.*   Gal 6:14
And, in the sign
by which God had vanquished the powers of the air
his army would battle for God.

2C 109

³Brother Sylvester, one of his brothers, a man of the greatest discipline in everything, saw coming forth from the saint's mouth a

---

a. The prominence given to the stigmata at the beginning of this work reflects the hesitancy on the part of some within the Order, as well as some in the larger Christian community, to put credence in the miracle. Cf. infra, *An Umbrian Choir Legend,* (hereafter UChL).

golden cross whose extended arms wonderfully indicated the whole world. *It is written,* and verified by trustworthy report, that Brother Monaldo, who was famous for his life, behavior and deeds, saw, in bodily fashion, blessed Francis crucified, while blessed Anthony was preaching about the inscription on the cross. It was his custom, established by a holy decree also for his first sons, that wherever they saw the likeness of the cross they would give it honor and due reverence. He favored the sign of the Tau over all others.[a] With it alone he signed letters he sent, and painted it on the walls of cells everywhere. That *man of God,* Pacifico, seer of heavenly visions, saw with his bodily eyes a great sign of the Tau on the forehead of the blessed father. It was many-colored and flashed with the brightness of gold.

How worthy then of reasonable human conviction
and of catholic credence
that one who so wonderfully excelled in love of the cross
should also so wonderfully become a wonder in honor of the cross!
Nothing therefore is more appropriate to him
than what is preached about the stigmata of the cross.

[4]This was the manner of the apparition. Two years prior to the time that he returned his spirit to heaven, in the hermitage called LaVerna, which is in the province of Tuscany, he was wholly intent on heavenly glory in the recesses of devout contemplation.

He saw in a vision a Seraph upon a cross, having six wings, extended above him, arms and feet affixed to a cross. *Two of his wings were raised up over his head, two were stretched out as if for flight,* and *two covered his whole body.* Seeing this, he was filled with the greatest awe, but as he did not know what this vision meant for him, joy mixed with sorrow flooded his heart. He greatly rejoiced at the gracious look that he saw the Seraph give him, but the fact that it was fixed to the cross terrified him. With concern his mind pondered what this revelation could mean, and the search for some meaning made his spirit anxious. But understanding came from discovery: while he was searching outside himself, the meaning was shown to him in his very self.

At once signs of the nails began to appear on his hands and feet, just as he had seen them a little while earlier on the crucified man in the air over him. His hands and feet seemed to be pierced through the middle by nails, with the heads of the nails appearing on the inner part of his hands and on the upper part of his feet, and

a. Cf. 2C 106, supra, 235 b.

IC 113 — their points protruding on opposite sides. The heads of the nails in his hands and feet were round and black, while their points were oblong and flattened, rising from the flesh itself, and extended beyond the flesh around them. His right side was marked with an oblong red scar as if pierced by a lance, and, since this often dripped blood, his tunic and undergarments were stained with his holy blood.

LJS 63; 2C 138 — Rufino, that *man of God* of angelic purity, one time rubbed the holy father with the affection of a son; and his hand slipped and he physically touched the wound. The holy one of God felt great pain and pushed Rufino's hand away, crying out *for the Lord to spare him.*

1 Tm 3:17

Gn 19:16

2C 217a — [5]When, after two years' time, with a blessed ending, he at last exchanged the valley of misery for the blessed homeland, the amazing announcement of this extraordinary thing reached peoples' ears.

A crowd of people came together praising and glorifying the name of the Lord. The whole city of Assisi rushed down as a group and *the entire region* hurried, eager to see that new wonder that God newly displayed *in this world.* The novelty of the miracle changed their weeping to jubilation, and swept up their bodily sight toward amazement and ecstasy. They observed the blessed body adorned with the stigmata of Christ, not the holes of the nails, but the nails themselves, in the middle of his hands and feet, marvelously fashioned by divine power from his own flesh, in fact, grown in the flesh itself. From whatever point they were pressed, simultaneously, as if a single tendon, they pulsed at the opposite end. They also saw his side stained red with blood.

Acts 21:30; Mi 5:7, 8; Lk 2:13, 20; Ps 86:9
Mt 8:34; Mt 3:5

2 Cor 1:12

> We who say these things
> *have seen* these things;
> *we have touched with our hands*
> what we are writing by hand.
> With tears in our eyes,
> we have sketched what we profess with our lips,
> and what we once swore,
> while touching sacred things,
> we declare for all time.

1 Jn 1:1, 4; Jn 3:11

Ps 89:36

IC 113 — Many brothers besides us saw it[a] while the saint was alive; at his death, more than fifty of them with countless lay people venerated it.

---

a. It is not clear from this use of the first person plural whether Thomas is speaking for himself, or is speaking for other authors or eyewitnesses.

Let there be no room for ambiguity:
let no one doubt this outpouring of everlasting goodness!

1 Cor 12:12
If only *the many members* were joined

Eph 1:22
in that same seraphic love *to Christ their head!*

Eph 6:11
If only they were to be found worthy of such *armor* in a similar
battle,

Rv 1:9
and be raised to the same rank in the Kingdom!

Mk 5:15
Who *of sane mind* would not attribute this to the glory of Christ?
But let the punishments already inflicted on unbelievers repay the
irreverent
and make the reverent even more confident.

⁶In Potenza, a city in the kingdom of Apulia, there was a cleric
named Ruggero, an honorable man and a canon of its major church.
He was weakened by a long illness, and one day he entered a church
to pray for his health. In the church there was a painted image of
blessed Francis, showing the glorious stigmata. He approached,
knelt down before the image and prayed with sincere devotion.
However, as he fixed his eyes on the saint's stigmata, he turned his
thoughts to useless things, and did not repel by force of reason the
creeping sting of doubt. With the old enemy deceiving him, his heart
torn, he began to say to himself: "Could this be true, that this saint
could be singled out for such a miracle, or was this a pious fraud of
his followers? Was this," he asked, "a sham discovery, perhaps a deception invented by the brothers? This goes beyond common sense,
and is far from reasonable judgment."

The madness of the man! Fool! You should rather have humbly
venerated that divine work all the more, the less you could compre-
hend it. You should have known, if your reason was working, that it
is the easiest thing for God to renew the world always with new mir-

1 Cor 4:12
acles, always *to work in us* for His glory things He has not done in others.

What happened? A severe wound was inflicted by God on the one

Heb 5:8
thinking empty thoughts, so that he might *learn from the things he suf-
fers* not to blaspheme. He was instantly struck in the palm of his left
hand (he was left-handed) as he heard a noise like an arrow shot

1 Mc 14:45
from a bow. Instantly, as he was *injured by the wound* and stunned by
the noise, he took off the glove from his hand, since he was wearing
gloves. Though there had previously been no mark in his palm, he
now saw a wound in mid-hand, as if struck by an arrow. So much
heat was coming from it that he thought he would pass out. What a
wonder! There was no mark on the glove, so the pain of the hidden
wound corresponded to the hidden wound of his heart.

[7]He cried out and roared, afflicted with terrible pain for two days, and unveiled his unbelieving heart to all. He declared that he believed that the sacred stigmata were truly in Saint Francis, and swore to affirm that all shadow of doubt was gone. He humbly prayed *the holy one of God* to come to his aid through his sacred stigmata, and he seasoned his many prayers with the sacrifice of tears.

Mk 1:24

Amazing! His unbelief discarded, bodily healing followed the healing of the spirit: all the pain calmed, the fever cooled, and no sign of the wound remained. He became a man humble before God, devoted to the saint, and subject in lasting friendship to the brothers of the Order.

The miraculous nature of this incident was attested by a signed oath, fully corroborated by the bishop of the place. In all things, blessed be the wonderful potency of God, which in the city of Potenza He magnificently demonstrated![a]

[8]It is the custom of noble Roman matrons, whether widowed or married, especially those whose wealth preserves the privilege of generosity, and on whom Christ pours out his love, to have in their own homes small chambers or a bedroom set apart for prayer. There they would have some painted icon, and the image of the saint they especially venerated.

A certain lady[b] of upright life and noble family chose Saint Francis for her advocate. She had his image in *the secluded chamber,* where she *prayed to the Father in secret.* One day while she was praying devoutly, her eyes searched intently for those sacred signs, but could not find them at all: she was sad and very surprised. No wonder they were not in the painting: the painter left them out! For several days the woman kept this *in her heart* and told no one. Often she gazed at the image, and always with sadness. Suddenly, one day those wonderful signs appeared in the hands, just as they are usually painted in other images. Divine power supplied what human art had neglected.

Jdt 8:5
Mt 6:6

Lk 2:51

[9]The woman was shaken, astonished, and quickly called her daughter, who followed her mother in a holy way of life. The mother showed her what had happened, *inquiring diligently* whether she had seen the image before then without the stigmata. The daughter affirmed and swore that before it was without the stigmata, but now truly appeared with the stigmata.

Lk 15:8

But since the human mind sometimes stumbles over itself, and calls the truth into doubt, harmful doubts again entered the

a. Here Thomas engages again in word play, praising the wonderful potency or power (*potentia*) of God demonstrated in the city of Potenza (*potenza*).
b. She must be distinguished from two other (named) Roman ladies, Jacoba dei Settesoli and Prassede, mentioned below in 3C 37-39 and 3C 181.

woman's heart: perhaps the image had those marks from the beginning. So the *power of God* added a second miracle, so that the first
would not be denied. Suddenly the marks disappeared and the image remained denuded of those privileged signs. Thus the second
sign became proof of the first. (I met this married and virtuous
woman. I declare that I saw in secular clothing a spirit consecrated to
Christ the Lord.)[a]

[10]Still, human reason from the very moment of birth is ensnared
by the stirring of the senses and crass illusions. It is sometimes
driven by the waves of imagination to call into doubt anything that is
supposed to be believed. As a consequence, only with difficulty do we
believe the marvelous deeds of the saints, and frequently faith itself
struggles with many obstacles in matters of salvation.

A certain brother, Lesser by Order, preacher by office, religious by
life, was firmly convinced of the holy stigmata. But, either from force
of habit or from excessive marvel, he began to be irritated by a scru-
ple of doubt about the saint's miracle. Imagine the battle going on in
his spirit, with reason defending the side of truth, and fantasy always pushing on the opposing side! Reason posited, with many supporting arguments, that it was just as it was said to be, and when
other evidence was lacking, it relied on the truth believed by holy
church. On the opposing side the senses' shadows conspired against
the miracle: it seemed contrary to all of nature, and *unheard-of in all
the ages.*

One evening, worn out by this wrestling-match, he entered his
bedroom, carrying with him a weakened reason and a strengthened,
bold imagination. As he slept, Saint Francis appeared to him, with
muddy feet, humbly stern and patiently irritated. And he spoke:
"Why all these conflicting struggles in you? Why these filthy doubts?
See my hands and my feet!" He saw the pierced hands, but he did not
see the stigmata on the muddy feet. Francis said, "Remove the mud
from my feet and examine *the place of the nails.*" He took hold of the
saint's feet, and it seemed to him the mud washed away, and he
touched with his *hands the places of the nails.* Then suddenly, as the
brother awoke, he was flooded with tears, and he cleansed himself of
his earlier muddy feelings by public confession.

[11]Those sacred stigmata of the invincible *soldier of Christ* should
not be considered lacking in great power, besides being a sign of special grace and a privilege of supreme love which the whole world
does not cease to admire.

Marginal references:
Acts 8:10
1 Jn 9:32   2C 10
Jn 20:27
Jn 20:25
1 Jn 1:1
1 Tm 2:3

---

a. It must be Thomas of Celano himself who speaks here.

How those signs are also powerful weapons for God can be understood through a novelty and evident miracle that happened in Spain,
namely in the Kingdom of Castile. There were two men who for a
long time had been quarreling with each other with deep hostility.
There was no rest for their bitterness; there could be no enduring re-
lief for their violent enmity, nor for *even a moment* any cure for the an-   Gal 2:5
imosity they harbored, unless one were to die the cruelest death at
the hand of the other. So each of them, fully armed, with many comrades, set up frequent ambushes for his adversary, because the crime
could not be committed in public.

One evening, in the deepening dusk, a man of honest life and
praiseworthy reputation happened to pass by on the road where
there was concealed an ambush of one for the death of the other.
This man was hurrying on his way to pray, as he usually did, after the
hour of compline at the church of the brothers, for he had given him-
self with deep devotion to Saint Francis. The *sons of darkness* rose up   1 Thes 5:5
against the *son of light,* and they believed him to be that rival of theirs
whom they had long sought to kill. Stabbing him with deadly blows
from every side, they left him half-dead. But at the last moment the
cruelest enemy thrust a sword deeply into the man's throat, and, unable to remove it, left it in the wound.

[12]People rushed from everywhere, and with cries to heaven the
whole neighborhood wailed at the death of the innocent. Because *the
living spirit* was still in the man, the advice of doctors prevailed: that   Wis 15:11
the sword not be removed from his throat. (Perhaps they did this for
the sake of confession, so that he might be able to confess at least by
some sign.) The doctors worked the whole night until the hour of
matins to wipe away the blood and close the wounds, but because of
the multiple, deep stab wounds, they could do nothing and ceased
treatment. Some Lesser Brothers stood by the bed with the doctors,
filled with grief, awaiting the departure of their friend.

Then the brothers' bell rang for matins. The man's wife heard the
bell and, groaning, ran to the bed and cried: "My Lord, *rise quickly,* go   Acts 12:7
to matins, your bell is calling you!" Immediately, the one believed to
be dying, with a groaning rumble of the chest, struggled to stammer
some wheezing words. And raising his hand toward the sword stuck
in his throat, he seemed to be motioning for someone to remove it. A
miracle! The sword immediately sprang from its place, and in the
sight of them all it flew over to the door of the house as if launched by
the hand of a very strong man. The man got up, unharmed and in
perfect health, as if rising from sleep, and *recounted the wonderful deeds*   Ps 26:7
of the Lord.

Lk 5:9; Acts 1:24 [13] Such great amazement *seized the hearts of all* that they all seemed out of their minds. They thought they were seeing a fantastic vision. Lk 2:10 But the one who was healed said, *"Do not be afraid!* Do not believe that what you see is false, because Saint Francis, to whom I was always devoted, has just left this place and has cured me completely of every wound. He placed those most holy stigmata of his over each of my wounds, and he rubbed all of my wounds with their gentleness. By their touch, as you see, he wondrously knit together everything that was broken. When you heard the rattle of my rumbling chest, the other wounds were already healed with great gentleness. Then the most holy father seemed to be leaving, with the sword left in my throat. Since I could not speak, I signaled to him with my weak hand to extract the sword, the one threat of imminent death. Immediately he took hold of it, as you all saw, and threw it with a powerful hand. And thus, as before, with the sacred stigmata he stroked and rubbed my throat. He so perfectly healed it that the flesh that was cut and what was still intact both appear the same."

Who would not marvel at these things? Who would pretend anything different from what is preached about the stigmata as something wholly divine?

Chapter III
THE POWER FRANCIS HAD OVER INANIMATE CREATURES: FIRST, FIRE[a]

[14] At the time of an eye disease, he is forced to let himself be treated. A surgeon is called to the place, and when he comes he is carrying an iron instrument for cauterizing. He ordered it to be placed in the fire until it became red hot. But the blessed Father, to comfort the body, which was struck with panic, spoke to the fire: Sir 1:8, 9 "My brother Fire, your beauty is the envy of all creatures, the *Most* Gn 33:10 *High created* you strong, beautiful and useful. *Be gracious to me* in this hour; be courteous! For a long time I have loved you in the Ps 48:2; Dt 32:6 Lord. I pray the *Great Lord who created you* to temper now your heat that I may bear your gentle burning."

2C 166

When the prayer is finished, he makes the sign of the cross over the fire and then remains in place unshaken. The surgeon takes in his hands the red-hot, glowing iron. The brothers, overcome by human feeling, run away. The saint joyfully and eagerly offers himself to the iron. The hissing iron sinks into tender flesh, and

---

a. In the following paragraphs, passages taken verbatim from earlier works are identified by an emboldened font. In this instance, it is helpful to see how Thomas has edited the text of AC, that material submitted by "we who were with him," that is, Francis's companions.

the burn is extended slowly from the ear to the eyebrow. How much pain that burning caused can best be known by the witness of the saint's words, since it was he that felt it. For when the brothers who had fled return, the father says with a smile: "Oh, you *weak souls of little heart;* why did you run away? *Truly I say to you,* I did not feel the fire's heat, nor any pain in my flesh." And turning to the doctor, he says: "If the flesh isn't well cooked, try again!" The doctor, who had experienced quite a different reaction in similar situations, exalts this as a divine miracle, saying: "I tell you, brothers; *today I have seen wonderful things!"* Lk 5:26

I believe
he had returned to primeval innocence,
for when he wished the harshest things grew gentle.[a]

[1 Thes 5:14; Mt 14:31]
[Lk 4:25]

2C 46 [15]Once blessed Francis wanted to travel to a certain hermitage so that he could more freely spend time in contemplation. Because he was very weak he got a donkey to ride from a poor man. It was summer, and as the peasant *went up the mountain* following the *man of God,* he was *worn out from the journey* over such a rough and long road. And before they came to the place, he was exhausted, fainting with a burning thirst. He urgently cried out after the saint, begging him *to have pity on him.* He swore he would die if he was not revived by something to drink. *The holy one of God,* always compassionate to the distressed, immediately leaped down from the donkey, knelt down on the ground, and raised his hands to heaven, *praying unceasingly* until he understood he had been heard. "Hurry now," he said to the peasant, "and over there you will find living *water* which at this very hour Christ *has* mercifully *brought forth from the rock* for you to drink." How amazingly kind God is, so easily bowing to His servants! By the power of prayer a peasant drinks *water from the rock* and draws refreshment *from the hard flint.* There was no *flow of water* there before this; and even after a careful search, none was found there afterwards.

[Jos 2:16]
[1 Kgs 13:14, 21]
[Jn 4:6]
[Dt 13:17]
[Lk 4:34]
[Col 1:9]
[Is 48:21]
[Ps 78:16; Dt 32:13]
[Ps 1:3]

[16]Gagliano is a populous and noble town in the diocese of Valva.[b] A woman named Maria lived there who, through the difficult ways of this world, was *converted to God* and she subjected herself completely to the service of Saint Francis.

[Acts 14:15]

---

a. The place of this episode as the first example of Francis's power over inanimate creatures, found at the end of 2C, exemplifies Thomas's understanding of Francis as a new Adam. Thomas, therefore, places Francis in a new perspective, i.e., that of primeval innocence.
b. Now Gagliano-Aterno, a town east of Celano, in the diocese of Sulmona. In Monte Canale, above Gagliano-Aterno, the fountain mentioned is said to flow near the remains of a chapel of Saint Francis. Cf. A. Chiappini, *L'Abruzzo Francescano nel secolo XIII* (Rome, 1926), 23.

One day she went out to a mountain that was totally deprived of water to prune maple trees, and she forgot to take water along with her. The heat was unbearable and she began to faint from thirst. When she could no longer work and was lying nearly lifeless on the ground, she began intently to call upon her patron, Saint Francis. In her exhaustion she drifted off to sleep. And there was Saint Francis,

Is 40:26

who *called her by name.* "Get up," he said, "and drink the water that is provided by divine gift for you and for many!" At the sound the woman yawned but, overcome by drowsiness, fell back asleep. She was called again, but fell back on the ground in her weariness. But the third time, strengthened by a command of the saint, she got up. She grabbed a fern next to her and pulled it from the earth. When she saw that its root was all wet, she began to dig around it with her finger and a twig. Immediately the hole was filled with water and the

Est 10:6

little puddle *grew into a spring.* The woman drank, and when she had had enough, she washed her eyes. They were clouded by a long

Sm 14:27n

illness, and she could see nothing clearly. *Her eyes were enlightened,* their old roughness removed, and were flooded as if with new light.

The woman ran home and told everyone about the great miracle,

Mt 9:26

to the glory of Saint Francis. *News* of the miracle *spread* and reached

Mk 1:34; Jn 5:4

the ears of everyone, even in other regions. *Many troubled by various*

1 Pt 1:9

diseases came running from every direction, and putting the *health of their souls* first, through confession, they were then freed of their illnesses. The blind recovered their sight, the lame their walk, the swollen grew slim, and for various illnesses their appropriate remedy was offered. That clear spring still flows, and a chapel in honor of Saint Francis has been built there.

[17]At the hermitage of Sant'Urbano he was suffering from a severe illness, when with a weak voice he requested some wine. The response was that there was no wine there to give him. He ordered some water to be brought, and when it was brought he blessed it with the sign of the cross. Immediately the element was transformed to another use; it lost its own taste and took on another. What had been pure water became excellent wine. What poverty could not provide, holiness furnished. Once he tasted it, he recovered easily. That marvelous conversion was the cause of his marvelous healing, and the marvelous healing a proof of the marvelous conversion.

1C 61

[18]In the province of Rieti a serious plague broke out, destroying

Jb 1:1

cattle so cruelly that almost none remained.[a] A certain *God-fearing man* was instructed in a dream to go quickly to the hermitage of the

---

a. In this and the following paragraph, Thomas shifts his attention to the more "indirect" influence of Francis upon inanimate creatures. Thus, the water he once used, or the bread he blessed, the cord he wore, or the straw he used in Greccio.

brothers and to collect some water used to bathe the hands or feet of blessed Francis, who was then staying there. On getting it, he was to sprinkle all the cattle with it. *Rising early,* anxious for his own benefit, he came to the place, and unknown to the saint, he pilfered some of the wash water with the help of some brothers. With it he sprinkled all the cattle as he had been commanded. From that moment, *by the grace of God,* the contagious pestilence ceased and never again returned to that region.

Mk 16:9

Rom 5:15

1C 63

[19]In many places the fervent devotion of many people led them to offer bread and other food for Francis to bless. These they kept for a long time, preserved from spoiling by divine gift; when they were eaten bodily illnesses were healed. It has even been shown that such foods had the power to ward off violent thunderstorms and hailstorms.

1C 120; 63

Many claim that through the cord that he wore and patches from his clothes illnesses were put to flight, fevers ceased, and long-sought health returned.

1C 84-86

On the day of the Lord's Nativity when he celebrated the memory of the manger of the Child of Bethlehem, he mystically repeated all the events that once surrounded the child Jesus. God manifested

1C 87

many wonders there. Among them, the hay taken from the manger was for many a health remedy, especially for women with difficulties in childbearing, and for all infected animals. After offering these samples concerning insensible creatures, let us include a few words about the obedience of sensible creatures.

Chapter IV
HIS MASTERY OVER SENSIBLE CREATURES

2C 166

[20]Creatures themselves strove to repay Saint Francis for his love and to respond to his kindness with their gratitude.

1C 58

One time as he was passing through the Spoleto valley, he came upon a place near Bevagna, in which a great multitude of birds of various kinds had assembled. When *The holy one of God* saw them, because of the outstanding love of the Creator with which he loved all creatures, he ran swiftly to the place. He greeted them in his usual way, as if they shared in reason. As the birds did not take flight, he went to them, going to and fro among them, touching their heads and bodies with his tunic. Meanwhile his joy and wonder increased as he carefully admonished them to listen to the Word of God: "My brother birds, you should greatly praise your Creator and love Him always. He clothed you with feathers and gave you wings for flying. Among all His creatures He made you free and

Lk 4:34

Lk 12:4
gave you the purity of the air. You neither *sow nor reap*, He nevertheless governs you without your least care." At these words, the birds gestured a great deal, in their own way. They stretched their necks, spread their wings, opened their beaks and looked at him. They did not leave the place until, having made the sign of the cross, he blessed them and gave them permission. On returning to the brothers he began to accuse himself of negligence because he had not preached to the birds before. From that day on, he carefully exhorted birds and beasts and even insensible creatures to praise and love the Creator.

1C 59
²¹Once he went to a village called Alviano to preach. The people gathered and he called for silence. But some swallows nesting there were shrieking so much that he could not be heard at all. In the
Tb 12:20
hearing of all, he spoke to them: "My sister swallows, now *it is time*
Ez 6:3
for me also to speak, since you have already said enough. Hear the
1 Chr 36:21
word of God and stay quiet until *the word of the Lord is completed.*" As if capable of reason, they immediately fell silent, and did not leave from that place until the whole sermon was over. All who saw this
Acts 3:10; Mt 9:8
were *filled with amazement* and *gave glory to God.*

²²In the city of Parma there was a scholar who was so annoyed by the inconsiderate chattering of a swallow that he could not stay in the place he needed for meditation. Rather provoked, he began to say, "This swallow was one of those we read about,ᵃ who once would
Mt 22:34
not allow Saint Francis to preach until he *imposed silence* on them." And turning to the swallow he said, "In the name of Saint Francis I command you to let me catch you." Without hesitation the bird flew to his hands. The surprised scholar gave it back its original freedom, and never again heard its chattering.

²³Heading to the hermitage of Greccio, blessed Francis was crossing the lake of Rieti in a small boat. A fisherman offered him a little water-bird so he might rejoice in the Lord over it. The blessed Father received it gladly, and with open hands, gently invited it to fly away freely. But the bird did not want to leave: instead it settled down in his hands as in a nest, and the saint, his eyes lifted up to
Acts 12:11
heaven, remained in prayer. *Returning to himself* as if after a long stay in another place, he sweetly told the little bird to return to its original freedom. And so the bird, having received permission with a blessing, flew away expressing its joy with the movement of its body.

---

a. Doubtless in 1C 59 or LJS 38.

²⁴Another time he was travelling by boat on the same lake. When he arrived at the port, someone offered him a large fish that was still alive. Calling it "brother" in his usual way, he put it back next to the boat. The fish kept playing in the water in front of the saint, which made him very happy, and he praised Christ the Lord. The fish did not leave the spot until it was commanded by the saint.

²⁵When blessed Francis, fleeing, as was his custom, from the sight of human company, came to stay in a certain hermitage, a falcon nesting there bound itself to him in a great covenant of friendship. At nighttime with its calling and noise, it anticipated the hour when the saint would usually rise for the divine praises. The *holy one of God* was very grateful for this because the falcon's great concern for him shook him out of any lazy sleeping-in. But when the saint was burdened more than usual by some illness, the falcon would spare him, and would not announce such early vigils. As if *instructed by God*, it would ring the bell of its voice with a light touch about dawn.

It is no wonder that other creatures revered
the greatest lover of the Creator.

²⁶A nobleman from the area of Siena sent a pheasant to blessed Francis while he was sick. He received it gladly, not with the desire to eat it, but because it was his custom to rejoice in such creatures out of love for their Creator. He said to the pheasant: "Praised be our Creator, Brother Pheasant!" And to the brothers he said: "Let's make a test now to see if Brother Pheasant wants to remain with us, or if he'd rather return to his usual places, which are more fit for him." At the saint's command a brother carried the pheasant away and put him down in a vineyard far away. Immediately the pheasant returned at a brisk pace to the father's cell.

The saint ordered it to be carried out again, and even further away, but with great stubbornness it returned to the door of the cell, and as if forcing its way, it entered under the tunics of the brothers who were in the doorway. And so the saint commanded that it should be lovingly cared for, caressing and stroking it with gentle words.

A doctor who was very devoted to the *holy one of God* saw this, and asked the brothers to give it to him, not because he wanted to eat it, but wanting rather to care for it out of reverence for the saint.

What else? The doctor took it home with him, but when separated from the saint it seemed hurt, and while away from his presence it absolutely refused to eat. The doctor was amazed, and at

1C 61

2C 168

Lk 4:34

1 Tm 3:17

2C 170

Mk 1:24

once carried the pheasant back to the saint, telling him in order all that happened. As soon as it was placed on the ground, and saw its father, it threw off its sadness and began to eat with joy.

Mk 1:24 [27]A cricket lived in a fig tree by the cell of *the holy one of God* at the Portiuncula, and it would sing frequently with its usual sweetness. Once the blessed father stretched out his hand to it and gently called it to him: "My Sister Cricket, come to me!" And the cricket, as if it had reason, immediately climbed onto his hand. He said to it: "Sing, my sister cricket, and with joyful song praise the Lord your Creator!" The cricket, obeying without delay, began to 1 Kgs 4:9 chirp, and did not stop singing until *the man of God*, mixing his own songs with its praise, told it to return to its usual place. There it remained constantly for eight days, as if tied to the spot. Whenever the saint would come down from the cell he would always touch it with his hands and command it to sing, and it was always eager to obey his commands. And the saint said to his companions: "Let us give permission to our sister cricket to leave, who has up to now 1 Cor 1:29 made us so happy with her praises, so that our *flesh may not boast vainly in any way.*" And as soon as it had received permission, the cricket went away and never appeared there again. On seeing all this, the brothers were quite amazed.

2C 171

[28]While he was staying in a poor place the holy man used to drink from a clay cup. After his departure, with wonderful skill bees had constructed the little cells of their honeycomb in it, wonderfully indicating the divine contemplation he drank in at that place.

2C 169

[29]In Greccio a little hare, live and unharmed, was given to Saint Francis. When it was put down, free to run away where it pleased, at the saint's call it leapt quickly into his lap. The saint gently took it and kindly warned it not to let itself be caught again. He then gave it his blessing and ordered it to return to the woods.

1C 60

[30]Something similar happened with another little rabbit, a wild one, when he was on the island in the Lake of Perugia.

1C 60

[31]Once when the man of God was on a journey from Siena to the valley of Spoleto he passed a field where a sizeable flock of sheep were grazing. He greeted them kindly as he usually did, and they all Lk 21:28 ran to him, *raised* their *heads* and returned his friendly greeting with loud bleating. His vicar took careful note of what the sheep had done and, following at a slower pace with the other companions, said to Jb 1:1 the rest, "Did you see what these sheep did for the holy father? *He is* truly *great* whom the dumb animals revere as their father, and those lacking reason recognize as a friend of their Creator."

³²Larks are birds that are the friends of light and dread the shadows of dusk. But in the evening when Saint Francis passed from this world to Christ, when it was already twilight of nightfall, they gathered above the roof of the house, where they circled about noisily for a long while. Whether they were showing their joy or their sadness with their song, we do not know. They sang with tearful joy and joyful tears, either to mourn the orphaned children, or to indicate the father's approach to eternal glory. The city watchmen who were guarding the place with great care were amazed and called others to admire this.

Chapter V
DIVINE MERCY WAS
ALWAYS RESPONSIVE TO FRANCIS'S REQUESTS

³³ Not only did creatures offer this man their services at his wish, but even the providence of the Creator everywhere consented to do his pleasure. That fatherly mercy anticipated his wishes and ran, as it were, to foresee his needs. His lack and its filling were one, his wish and its fulfillment.

In the sixth year of his conversion, burning with the desire for holy martyrdom, he wished to take a ship to the region of Syria. But after he had boarded a ship to go there, contrary winds started blowing, and he found himself with his fellow travelers on the shores of Slavonia.

When he realized that he had been cheated of what he desired, after a while he begged some sailors going to Ancona to transport him with them. But the sailors stubbornly refused to do so since he could not pay them. The holy one of God, trusting God's goodness, secretly boarded the ship with his companion. Immediately, by divine providence, a man arrived—no one knew him—who brought the food needed. He called over a person from the ship, *a God-fearing man. "Take with you* all these things," he said, "and in their *time of need* faithfully give them to those poor men hiding in your ship."

A great storm arose and they had to spend many days *laboring at the oars*. They had used up all their food. Only the food of the poor Francis remained. Owing to divine grace and power, his food multiplied so much that, although there were still many days of sailing remaining, it fully supplied the needs of them all until they reached the port of Ancona. When the sailors realized that they had escaped the dangers of the sea through God's servant Francis, and that they received through him what they had denied to him, they

1C 55

Jb 1:1; Tb 11:4

Sir 8:12

Mk 6:48

Sir 50:19
gave thanks *to almighty God,* who is always revealed through his servants as awesome and loving.

[34] Saint Francis became gravely ill while returning from Spain after failing to reach Morocco as he had wished.[a] Suffering from want and weariness, he was expelled from his lodging by a rude host and lost his speech for three days. When he had recovered his strength a bit, while walking along the road he said to Brother Bernard that he would have eaten a bit of a bird if he had one. Just then a horseman came riding across the field carrying an exquisite bird. He said to blessed Francis, "Here, servant of God, take gladly what divine mercy sends you." He *accepted* this gift *with joy* and, seeing how Christ cared for him, *he blessed Him for everything.*

Tb 7:1
Tb 13:1; 1 Thes 5:23

Jb 29:16
[35] While he lay sick in the bishop's palace at Rieti, the *father of the poor* was dressed in an old tunic. One day he said to one of his companions, whom he had made his guardian: "Brother, if possible, I wish you would find me material for a tunic. "On hearing this, the brother started turning over in his mind how he could get the necessary cloth so humbly requested. *The next day* at the break of dawn he went to the door, on his way to town for the cloth. *There* he found *a man* sitting on the doorstep and wishing to speak to him. This man said to the brother: "For the love of the Lord, brother, please accept this cloth, enough for six tunics; keep one for yourself and distribute the rest as you please for the good of my soul." The brother was overjoyed, and returned to Brother Francis, announcing to him the gift sent from heaven. And our father said: "Accept the tunics, for this man was sent to care for my need in this way." And he added: "Thanks be to him who seems to be the only one *concerned for us.*"

2C 41; 2C 43

Jas 4:13
Lk 22:10

1 Sm 9:5; Ps 40:18

[36] While the holy man was staying in a hermitage near Rieti, a physician used to visit him every day to treat his eyes. One day the saint said to his brothers: "Invite the doctor, and give him a good meal." The guardian answered him: "Father, *we're embarrassed* to say this, but we're ashamed to invite him, because right now we're so poor." But the saint answered: *"Do you want me to tell you again?"* And the doctor, who was nearby, said: "Dear brothers, I would consider it a treat to share in your poverty." The brothers hurried to place the whole contents of their storeroom on the table: *a little bread,* and not much wine, and, to make the meal more lavish, the kitchen provided a few beans. Meanwhile, *the table of the Lord* took pity on the table of his servants. *Someone knocked at the door,* and

2C 44

Lk 14:9

Mt 20:32, Jn 9:27

1 Chr 18:20

Mal 1:7
Lk 13:25

Test 22

---

a. The failed attempt to reach Morocco and illness are mentioned in 1C 56, but the other events appear here for the first time.

they answered immediately. There was a woman offering a basket
filled with beautiful bread, loaded with fish and crabcakes, and
with honey and grapes heaped on top.

> The table of the poor rejoices at this sight,
> and, the cheap food is put away,
> the delicacies are eaten today.
> The doctor heaved a sigh and spoke to them:
> "Neither you, brothers,
> as you should,
> nor we lay people,
> realize the holiness of this man."
> They would not have been sufficiently filled
> if the miracle had not fed them even more than the food.
> A father's *eye*
> never *looks down on* his own,
> but rather feeds beggars with greater care
> the needier they are.

Prv 30:17

Chapter VI
LADY JACOBA DEI SETTESOLI [a]

AC 8

[37] Jacoba dei Settesoli, equal in fame and holiness in the city of
Rome, earned the privilege of special love from the saint. It is not for
me to repeat, in praise of her, her noble lineage, family honor, and
ample wealth, nor the great perfection of her virtues and long, chaste
widowhood.

The saint was bedridden with that illness by which, putting off all
his weariness, he was about to *complete* the *race* with a blessed ending. A few days before his death he decided to send for Lady Jacoba in
Rome, telling her that if she wanted to see the one whom she so loved
so warmly as an exile, she should come with all haste, because he
was about to return to his homeland. A letter was written; a messenger noted for his swiftness was sought and, once found, was outfitted for the journey. Just then there was heard at the door the sound
of horses, the commotion of knights, the crowd of an escort. One of
the companions, the one who had given instructions to the messenger, went to the door and found there present the one whom he
sought because absent. He was struck with wonder and ran very
quickly to the saint. Unable to restrain himself for joy, said, "I have

1 Tm 4:7

---

a. Although much of the material of this chapter can be found in AC 8, its last section, i.e., the outcome
of Lady Jacoba's pilgrimage, is new.

good news for you, father." Without a pause the saint immediately
replied, *"Blessed be God,* who has brought our Brother Lady Jacoba to
us! Open the doors and bring her in. The decree about women is not
to be observed for Brother Jacoba!"[a]

[Ps 66:20]

38There was great rejoicing among the noble guests, but their spiritual delight was mingled with flowing tears. To make the miracle
complete, it was discovered that the holy woman had brought with
her everything that the letter just written had requested for the father's burial. God had supplied everything that the spirit of this man
wanted: she brought some ash-colored cloth to cover the little body
of the one who was departing; many candles; a cloth for his face; a
cushion for his head; and a special dish[b] the saint had a longing for.

But I want to narrate the outcome of this pilgrimage, so that I do
not leave the noble pilgrim without consolation. A great crowd of
people, especially the devout inhabitants of the city, expected the
saint's birth through death very shortly. But he seemed to be
strengthened by the arrival of the devout Roman lady, and there was
a glimmer of hope that he would recover. So the lady gave orders that
the rest of her escort should leave: she alone with her children and a
few attendants would remain. But the saint said to her, "No, don't! I
will depart on Saturday, and on Sunday you and all the others will
return." And so it happened. At the predicted time, he who had
fought valiantly in the Church militant entered the Church trium-
phant. I omit here[c] the crowds of people, the shouts of rejoicing, the
ringing of bells, the streams of tears. Likewise I leave out the mourning of his sons, the sobbing of those dear to him, the lament of his
companions. I want to recount only how this pilgrim, deprived of the
solace of her father, was consoled.

39All wet with tears, she was brought in private and alone, and the
body of her friend was placed in her arms. "Here," said his vicar,
"hold, even in death, the one you loved when alive!" Her warm tears
bathed his body, and with sobs and sighs she kept hugging and kissing him, and pulled back the veil to see him unveiled. What did she
see? She gazed on that *precious vessel* that hid a precious treasure
adorned with five pearls.[d] She beheld those engravings that the hand
of the Almighty alone had produced for the whole world to admire.
Then she was refreshed with unusual joy over the death of her friend.

[Prv 20:15]

---

a. See the prohibitions about entry to the Portiuncula in 2C 19, supra, 175-6.
b. According to AC 8, the pastry called *mostacciolo,* made of almonds, sugar or honey, and other
   ingredients.
c. Cf. 1C 112, 113, 116-118.
d. Namely the stigmata. Cf. 1C 112-13.

Right then she counseled that such an unheard-of miracle should not be disguised or hidden any further. Rather, she wisely advised it should be displayed for all to see with their own eyes. All ran eagerly to see this sight.[a] They were able to verify for themselves that God *had not done thus for any other nation* and stood in awe.

Here I will put down my pen rather than stammer over something I cannot explain. Giovanni Frigia Pennate,[b] who was then a boy, and afterwards a Roman proconsul and count of the Sacred Palace, freely swears and declares, against all doubts, that at that time he was with his mother, and that he *saw with* his own *eyes* and *touched* it *with* his *hands.* The lady pilgrim may now return to her homeland,[c] comforted by this privilege of grace. Let us now turn to events after the saint's death.

Ps 147:20

Jb 13:1; Gen 27:12; 1 Jn 1:1

Chapter VII
THE DEAD RAISED THROUGH THE MERITS OF BLESSED FRANCIS[d]

[40]I turn now to those who were raised from the dead through the merits of the confessor of Christ. I ask the attention of listeners and readers alike. For the sake of brevity I will omit many of the circumstances, and will keep silent about the account of the amazed witnesses, recounting only the extraordinary events themselves.

There was a woman, noble by birth and nobler in virtue, in Monte Marano near Benevento. She clung to Saint Francis with special devotion and offered him her reverent service. She took sick and her end seemed near: she was going *the way of all flesh.* She died at sundown, but burial was delayed to the following day to allow her many dear ones to gather. The clergy came at night with their psalters to sing the wake and vigils. There was a gathering of *many of both sexes* for prayer. Suddenly, in the sight of all, the woman sat up in bed and

Jos 23:14

1 Chr 31:18

---

a. Cf. 1C 113.

b. His is another form of the family surname (also rendered *Frangipani*). Cf. AC 8, note. Giovanni was the eldest son of Lady Jacoba; in 1226 he would have been a young man, rather than a boy.

c. That is, to Rome, or possibly to heaven.

d. Although there are no miracles of resurrection described in Thomas's earlier works, the accounts given here reflect the tendencies of the late thirteenth and fourteenth centuries. André Vauchez explains: "This should probably be seen as a consequence of the development of the canonization procedure rather than of a change of attitude on the part of the faithful toward the saints. Aware that it was difficult to get a favorable decision out of the papacy and that the Curia was very demanding with regard to miracles, the promoters of a cause were tempted to raise the threshold of the miraculous to prove the sanctity of their candidates." Vauchez, *Sainthood in the Later Middle Ages,* translated by Jean Birrell (Cambridge, New York, Melbourne: Cambridge University Press, 1997), 467. A thorough study of the understanding of miraculous phenomena in the Middle Ages can be found in Benedicta Ward, *Miracles and the Medieval Mind: Theory, Record and Events, 1000-1215* (Philadelphia: University of Pennsylvania Press, 1982).

called to one of them, a priest who was her godfather, "I want to confess, Father, hear my sin! I have indeed died, and was destined for a harsh prison because I had never confessed the sin I will reveal to you. But Saint Francis prayed for me as I was always devoted to him. I have now been permitted to return to my body so that after confessing my sin I might *merit forgiveness.* So now, as all of you watch, after I reveal that to you I will hurry off to my promised rest." She then shakily confessed to the shaken priest, received absolution, composed herself peacefully on the bed and happily *fell asleep in the Lord.*

Gn 4:13

Acts 7:60

Who can adequately praise Christ's mercy? Who can sufficiently sing the praises of the power of confession and of the saint's merits?

[41]Confession is a marvelous gift of God which ought to be wholeheartedly embraced by all; and in Christ's presence this saint always enjoyed special merit. These things can be amply demonstrated by recounting events of his life on earth, and even more clearly proven by what his Christ did in his regard after death.

When the blessed father Francis once went to Celano to preach,[a] a knight invited him insistently, with humble devotion, to dine with him. After much refusing and declining, he finally gave in to the insistent pressure. He arrived at dinnertime and a splendid table was prepared. The devout host was overjoyed, and his whole family was delighted at the arrival of their poor guests. Blessed Francis stood and *raised his eyes to heaven,* then called his host aside privately. "Look," he said, "brother host, I was overcome by your requests, and *I have entered your home* to eat. Do quickly what I tell you, for you shall not eat here but elsewhere! *Confess* your *sins* with devotion and contrition; leave nothing within you unconfessed. The Lord will repay you today for receiving His poor with such devotion." The man *agreed to* the saint's *words* without delay. He called the companion of Saint Francis, who was a priest, and told all his sins in a good confession. *He put his house in order* and without any doubts waited for the saint's word to be fulfilled. Then they went to the table and began to eat. After marking his breast with the sign of the cross, the knight reached with his hand—it was shaking—for the bread. But before he could draw back his hand, he *bowed his head* and breathed forth his *spirit.*

Dn 4:31

Lk 7:44
1 Jn 7:44

1 Tm 6:3

Is 38:1

Jn 19:30

O, how the confession of sins should be cherished!
See how the dead are revived in order to confess.
And so that the living should not *perish forever*
they are set free by benefit of confession.

Jn 10:28

---

a. This is the author's birthplace, but he unfortunately did not reveal the name of the soldier. Celano is again mentioned as a place for miracles in 3C 51.

[42]A barely seven-year-old son of a notary of the city of Rome wanted in his childish way to follow his mother who was going to the church of San Marco[a] to hear a preacher. He was turned back by his mother and her refusal upset him. By some diabolical impulse—I do not know why—he threw himself from the window of the building and, shaking with a last tremor, he came to know the passing of death, the common lot of all. The mother had not gone far, and the sound of someone falling made her suspect the fall of her treasure. She quickly returned home and saw her son lifeless. She turned avenging hands on herself; her neighbors rushed out at her screams; and doctors were called to the dead boy. But could they *raise the dead?*   Acts 26:8
The time for prognoses and prescriptions was past. He was in the hands of God: that much the doctors could determine, but could not help. Since all warmth and life were gone, all feeling, movement and strength, the doctors determined he was dead.

Brother Rao, of the Order of Lesser Brothers and a well-known preacher in Rome, was on his way to preach there. He approached the boy and, full of faith, spoke to the father. "Do you believe that Francis, the saint of God, is able to raise your son *from the dead* be-   Acts 17:31; Acts 8:37; 11:17
cause of the love he always had for the *Son of God, the Lord Jesus Christ?*" The father replied, "I firmly believe and confess it. I will be his lasting servant, and I will regularly visit his holy place." That brother knelt with his companion in prayer and urged all those present to pray. With that the boy began to yawn a little, lift his arms and sit up. His mother ran and embraced her son; the father was beside himself for joy. All the people, filled with wonder, marveled and, shouting, praised Christ and His saint. In the sight of all the boy immediately began walking, restored to full life.

[43]The brothers of Nocera asked a man named Peter for a certain cart that they needed for a short time. He foolishly replied, "I would rather skin the two of you, and Saint Francis too, rather than loan you a cart." The man immediately regretted his blasphemous words, slapped his mouth, and asked forgiveness. He feared revenge, and it came soon after.

At night he *saw in a dream* his home full of men and women danc-   Gn 28:12
ing with loud jubilation. His son, named Gafaro, soon took sick and shortly afterwards gave up his spirit. The dances he had seen were turned into a funeral's mourning, and the jubilation to lament. He recalled the blasphemy he had uttered against Saint Francis. His punishment showed how serious was his fault. He rolled about on

---

a. Probably the very ancient church of San Marco in Via Lata. It was incorporated in 1477 into the Palazzo Veneto, on what is today the Piazza Venezia in the heart of Rome.

1 Sm 24:17

the ground and called out to Saint Francis again and again, saying, "*It is I who have sinned*; you were right to punish me. Give me back, dear saint, the one you took from this wicked blasphemer, for now I have repented. I surrender myself to you; I promise you lasting service, and will always offer you all the first fruits."

Amazing! At these words the boy arose, called for a halt to the wailing, and spoke about his experience of death. "When I had died," he said, "blessed Francis came and led me along a very dark and long road. Then he put me in a garden so beautiful and delightful that the whole world can't be compared to it. Then he led me back along the same road and said to me, 'Return to your mother and father; I do not want to keep you here any longer.' And, as he wished, I have returned."

Ps 46:5

[44]In the city of Capua a lad was playing carelessly with his friends on the bank of the river Volturno. From the bank of the river he fell into the deep. The *force of the river* quickly swallowed him up and buried him, dead, beneath the sand.

The children who had been playing near the river with him shouted, and many men and women ran quickly to the spot. When they learned what happened they cried out tearfully, "Saint Francis, return the boy to his father and grandfather: they are sweating in your service!" Indeed the boy's father and grandfather were working as hard as they could on building a church in honor of blessed Francis. All the people were humbly and devoutly invoking the merits of blessed Francis.

Acts 22:16

Some distance away a swimmer heard their cries and approached them. He learned that a good hour had passed since the boy fell into the river. He *invoked the name* of Christ and the merits of blessed Francis, then taking off his clothes flung himself naked into the river. Since he did not know where the boy had fallen in, he began to search back and forth along the banks and on the bottom. Finally by the will of God he found the place where mud had covered over the boy's cadaver like a tomb. He dug and dragged him out, and was saddened to find him dead. Though the crowd saw that the youth was dead, they nevertheless wept and cried out, "Saint Francis, give the father back his child!" The same phrase was also said by the Jews who had come, moved by natural piety: "Saint Francis, give the father back his child!" Blessed Francis, moved by the people's prayers and devotion (as is clear from what happened) quickly raised the dead boy. They all marveled and rejoiced. When the boy got up, he begged to be taken to the church of blessed Francis, swearing he had been revived thanks to him.

LCh 15

LCh 15 ⁴⁵In the city of Sessa, in the neighborhood called "Le Colonne," the devil, destroyer of souls and killer of bodies, destroyed and leveled a house. He tried to destroy many children who were playing their children's games near that house, but trapped only one youth who was instantly killed by the falling house. Men and women heard the crash of the house and came running from all around. Raising beams here and there, they succeeded in restoring the dead son to his poor mother. She tore at her face and hair, sobbed bitterly, shed rivers of tears, and cried out as best she could, "Saint Francis, Saint Francis, give me back my son!" She was not alone: all the men and women there wept bitterly and cried, "Saint Francis, give this poor mother back her son!" After an hour of this pain the mother caught her breath, recovered her senses, and made this vow: "O Saint Francis, give back to me in my misery my beloved son! I will wreathe your altar with silver thread; I will cover it with a new altar cloth; and I will encircle your whole church with candles!" Since it was night, they placed the cadaver on a bed, waiting to bury him the following day. But about midnight the young man began to yawn; warmth returned to his limbs; and before daybreak he was fully revived and burst into shouts of praise. When all the people and the clergy saw him healthy and unharmed, they too rendered thanks to blessed Francis.

⁴⁶In the village of Pomarico, in the mountains of Apulia, a mother and father had an only daughter, tender of age and tenderly loved. And since they did not expect any future offspring, she was the object of all their love, the motive for all their care. When she became deathly ill, the girl's mother and father considered themselves dead. Day and night they kept anxious watch over the child's care, but one morning they found her dead. Perhaps they had been negligent, overcome by sleep or the strain of their vigil. The mother, deprived of her daughter and with no hope of other offspring, seemed to die herself.

Friends and neighbors gathered for a very sad funeral and prepared to bury the lifeless body. The unhappy mother lay grief-stricken, and the depth of her sorrow kept her from noticing what was going on. In the meantime, Saint Francis with one companion visited the desolate woman and spoke these comforting words, *"Do not weep, I will rekindle the light of your quenched lamp!"* Lk 7:13; 2 Sm 21:17 The woman jumped up, told everyone what Saint Francis had told her, and would not allow the body of the deceased to be carried away. Then the mother turned to her daughter, invoked the saint's name, and lifted her up safe and sound. We leave it to others to describe the wonder that filled the hearts of the bystanders and the rare joy of the girl's parents.

[47]In Sicily, a young man named Gerlandino, from Ragusa, went out with his parents to the vineyard at harvest-time. He crawled into a wine vat beneath the press to fill some skins. The wooden supports shifted, and the huge stones used to press the grape skins[a] instantly struck his skull a deadly blow. The father hurried over to his son, but he could not help him; he left him under the weight where it had fallen. Other vineyard workers rushed to the scene when they heard the loud wail and cry. Pitying the pitiful father, they pulled his son from the ruin. They took the lifeless body aside and wrapped it, concerned only about his burial. But the father defiantly fell at the feet of Jesus Himself. He implored Him to give him back his only son through the merits of Saint Francis, whose feast day was coming soon. He groaned his prayers, he promised works of piety, and promised to visit the holy man's bones very soon. A little while later the boy's mother arrived and fell madly upon her dead son; her wailing moved the others also to wail. Then suddenly the boy stood up, told them to stop crying, and rejoiced that he had been brought back to life through the help of Saint Francis. All the people who had gathered raised their cries of praise on high, to the One who through His saint had freed the boy from the cords of death.

[48]He raised another dead person in Germany: the Lord Pope Gregory recounted this event in his apostolic letter on the occasion of the translation of blessed Francis.[b] Through it he informed and gladdened all the brothers who had gathered for the translation and the chapter. I did not write the account of this miracle because I did not know of it, believing that papal testimony is a proof that surpasses any other assertion.

Let us now go on to others whom he snatched from the jaws of death.

Chapter VIII
THOSE FRANCIS BROUGHT BACK
TO LIFE FROM THE JAWS OF DEATH

[49]A certain Roman nobleman named Rodolfo had a tower of considerable height, and, as is usual, had a guard in the tower. One night

LCh 15

LCh 15

---

a. That is, the *vinaccia* [pulp].

b. The "translation" is the official moving of a saint's body: here, the moving of Francis's body to the Basilica dedicated to him. The letter is the bull *Mirificans*, promulgated by Gregory IX on May 16, 1230, cf. BFr I, 64-65.

the guard was sleeping soundly at the very top of the tower. He lay upon a pile of wood on the top edge of the wall. Then the pulley either came loose or broke at its base and, in a flash, he fell along with the planks onto the roof of the palace, and from there to the ground. The loud crash awoke the whole family and, suspecting hostile action, the knight got up and went out armed. He shook his drawn sword over the prone man, intending to strike the sleeping man, since he did not recognize him as the guard. But the wife of the knight feared that this might be her brother—her husband hated him to death, so she stopped him from wounding the man, throwing herself upon the prostrate man in loyal defense. What an amazing sleeping potion! The sleeping man never woke, either at his double fall nor at the loud noise.

Finally he was shaken awake with a gentle hand, and as if deprived of pleasant rest he said to his lord, "Why are you disturbing my sleep now? I have never rested so easily; I was sleeping sweetly in the arms of blessed Francis."

When he learned from the others about his fall, and he saw himself on the ground, not up above where he was lying, he was amazed that he had not felt what had happened. He then promised publicly to do penance, and his master gave him permission to set out on a pilgrimage. The lady sent a beautiful priestly vestment to the brothers staying in her hometown outside the City, out of reverence and honor for the saint. The Scriptures promise a great reward for hospitality, and examples confirm it. For the lord in question had that night given hospitality to two Lesser Brothers, out of reverence for Saint Francis. They had also been among those who ran out when that servant fell.

[50]In the town of Pofi, located in Campagna, a priest named Tommaso went with many others to repair a mill belonging to his church. Below the mill was a deep gorge, and the raised channel flowed rapidly. The priest carelessly walked along the edge of the channel, and accidentally fell into it. In an instant he was thrust by force against the wooden blades that turned the mill. There he remained, pinned against the wood, unable to move at all. Because he was lying face down the flow of water pitiably muffled his voice and blocked his sight. But his heart, if not his tongue, was free to call plaintively on Saint Francis.

He remained there a long time, and his companions, rushing back to him, nearly despaired of his life. "Let's turn the mill by force in the opposite direction," said the miller, "so it will release the corpse." With a struggle they turned the mill in reverse, and they saw the trembling body thrown into the water.

The priest, still half-alive, was being rolled around in the pool, when suddenly there appeared a Lesser Brother in a white tunic bound with a cord.[a] With great gentleness he drew the unfortunate man by the arm out of the water, and said, "I am Francis, the one you called." The man was stunned to be freed in this way and began to run here and there saying, "Brother, Brother!" and asking the bystanders, "Where is he? Which way did he go?" But they were terrified: they *fell prostrate to the ground and gave glory to God* and to his saint.

Nm 14:5; Lk 2:20

[51] Some children from the town of Celano in the Capitanata region went out together to cut grass. In those fields there was an old well: its opening was covered with plant growth; and it held water with a depth of four paces. While the children ran about on their own, one accidentally fell into the well. But while he suffered earthly disaster, he invoked heavenly aid. "Saint Francis," he said as he fell, "help me!" The others *turned around this way and that,* and when they noticed that the other *boy was missing* they went in search of him, shouting and crying. Finally they came to the opening of the well. Seeing the grass just springing back from being stepped on, they realized that the boy had fallen in. They ran crying back to the village, gathered a crowd of people, and returned to the spot, though everyone thought it hopeless. A man was lowered by a rope into the well and he found the boy floating on the surface of the water totally unharmed. When the boy was lifted out of the well, the boy said to all who had gathered, "When I suddenly fell, I called for Saint Francis's protection, and he instantly arrived while I was still falling. He reached out his hand and gently held me and did not leave until, along with you, he pulled me from the well."

1 Kgs 18:45

Gn 37:30

[52] The treatment of a young girl of Ancona, worn out by a deadly illness, had been terminated, and for her passing funeral arrangements had already begun. Blessed Francis came to her when her last breath was near and said to her, *"Courage, daughter,* for through my favor you are completely healed. *Tell no one* until evening about your health, which I am restoring." *When evening came* she suddenly raised herself up in bed, stunning *the bystanders,* who fled. They thought that a demon had invaded the body of the dying girl: when her own soul had left, a perverse spirit had replaced it. The girl's mother dared to come closer, and breathing oaths against what she thought was a devil, she tried to get the girl to lie down on the bed. But the daughter said, "Mother, please don't think it's the devil. At the third hour

Mt 9:22

Mt 8:4

Mt 20:8

Mk 14:70

---

a. The apparition of Francis in this garb appears again in 3C 52. He is further described as "glorious," (3C 105, 106) is accompanied with one or more brothers, or on a most beautiful throne (3C 152), or together with the Blessed Virgin and the Apostles (3C 158). All of these images suggest new dimensions to the cult of the saint and accentuate his place as a "miracle worker."

blessed Francis healed me of all the sickness, and ordered me to tell no one until this hour." The name of Francis was cause for surprise and joy for them, just as the devil was cause for flight. They encouraged the girl right away to eat some chicken, but shaking her head she refused to eat because it was the Great Lent. *"Do not be afraid,"* she said. "Don't you see Saint Francis dressed in white? He is commanding me not to eat meat because it is Lent, and to offer the funeral tunic to a certain woman in prison. Look, you can see him leaving!" Mt 17:7

[53]In Nettuno, there were three women in a house. One of them was devoted to the brothers and most devoted to Saint Francis. A great *wind* shook *the house,* demolished it, and *crushed,* killed, and buried two of them. Blessed Francis quickly arrived at a silent request, and did not allow the one devoted to him to suffer any harm. For the wall to which she clung remained intact to her height; a beam fell on it from above in such a way that it bore all the weight of the falling debris. People heard the crash of the collapse and came running. For the two deceased there were tears; for the surviving friend of the brothers all gave thanks to Saint Francis. Jb 1:19

[54]Corneto[a] is a powerful and not an unimportant town in the diocese of Viterbo. There a bell of no small size was to be cast at the brothers' place, and many of the brothers' friends had gathered to contribute their help to the project. When the casting was completed, with great rejoicing a grand banquet began. Then an eight-year-old boy named Bartolomeo, whose father and uncle had worked devotedly on the casting, carried in a gift for those at the banquet. All of a sudden a *great wind came up and shook the house;* with great force it blew down the large, heavy door of the house onto the boy. It was feared that its weight pressing upon him had crushed him to death. He was so completely buried under its weight that nothing of him could be seen from the outside. The work of the foundry turned into confounding,[b] and the lament of mourners replaced the *festivity of the banquet.* Jb 1:19 Jude 12

Everyone rushed from the table; the uncle dashed with some others to the door, calling on Saint Francis. The father, however, could not move, his limbs frozen *from grief.* Vowing out loud, he offered his son to Saint Francis. The deadly weight was lifted off the boy, and there he was! The one they thought was dead appeared cheerful, like someone waking from sleep, with no sign of injury. After the Is 65:14

---

a. More recently named "Tarquinia."
b. Another of Thomas's play on words: *fusioni confusio* [the foundry turned into] ... *succedit* [confounding].

Lk 1:14; Gn 15:1 confusion, there was an infusion of joy,[a] and *great gladness* followed the interrupted banquet. The boy himself reported to me[b] that no feeling of life remained in him as he lay beneath that weight. When he reached the age of fourteen he became a Lesser Brother and later became a learned man and an eloquent preacher in the Order.

⁵⁵A little boy of the same town swallowed a silver buckle that his father had placed in his hand. It so blocked all the passages of his throat that he was completely unable to breathe. The father wept bitterly and *rolled on the ground* in a frenzy because he considered himself his son's murderer. His mother tore at her hair and her whole body, wailing at the sad news. All their friends shared their grief, that a healthy youth was snatched by such sudden death.

Mk 9:20

The father invoked the merits of Saint Francis and offered a vow to the saint to save his son. Then suddenly the boy spat the buckle from his mouth and joined the others in blessing the name of Saint Francis.

Jgs 15:18 ⁵⁶A man named Niccolò from the town of Ceprano one day *fell into the hands* of cruel enemies. With beastly rage they heaped blow upon blow on him, and did not stop their cruelty until they thought him Lk 10:30 dead or soon to die. They left him *half dead* and went away spattered with blood. When the first blows fell on him, Niccolò started calling out in a loud voice, "Help me, Saint Francis! Save me, Saint Francis!" Many heard his voice from far away but could not help him. When he had been carried home drenched with his own blood, he claimed that he was not about to die and did not feel any pain, because Saint Francis had come to his aid and begged the Lord that he be allowed *to* Mk 6:12 *do penance.* So, cleansed of blood and contrary to any human hope, he was rescued.

⁵⁷Some men of Lentini[c] cut a huge stone from a mountain. It was to be set over the altar of the church of blessed Francis which was soon to be consecrated. A good forty men strained to load the stone on a cart, but after several attempts the stone fell on one man and covered him like a tomb. In their mental confusion they did not know what to do: most of the men left in despair. The ten who remained plaintively invoked Saint Francis not to allow this man who was in his service to die so hopelessly. The man lay buried, half-dead, Wis 15:11 but *the living spirit* in him sighed for the help of Saint Francis. With renewed courage, those men then so easily removed the stone that no

---

a. Another play on words: *successit confusioni refusio* [after the confusion, there was an infusion].

b. No doubt Thomas himself.

c. In the Sicilian province of Siracusa where, at the time of Thomas, the brothers had built a convent. See AF IV, 533.

one doubted that the hand of Francis was involved. The man stood up unharmed; he who was almost *dead revived* completely. He recovered his eyesight as well, which earlier had been dimmed: further proof to all of the power of Francis in desperate cases.

Lk 15:24

⁵⁸A similar incident worth remembering happened at San Severino in the Marches. A huge stone from Constantinople was being transported to Assisi for the construction of a fountain in honor of Saint Francis. With the efforts of many it was being dragged along at a rapid pace when a man fell beneath it. He appeared to be not just dead, but totally crushed.

At once Saint Francis arrived, as it seemed to him and as it turned out to be true, lifting the stone and thrusting it aside without any injury to him. So it happened that what looked horrible turned into something astonishing to all.

⁵⁹Bartolomeo, a citizen of Gaeta,[a] was hard at work on the construction of the church of Blessed Francis. He was trying to position one of the building's beams, but the beam, poorly positioned, fell and crushed his neck severely. He was bleeding profusely, and with trembling breath he asked one of the brothers for Viaticum. The brother was not immediately able to find it, and thinking he would die at any moment, he quoted to him the words of blessed Augustine, "Believe, and you have eaten."[b]

That night blessed Francis appeared to him with eleven brothers; he carried a little lamb between his breasts. He approached the bed, *called him by name,* and said, "Do not fear, Bartolomeo, the enemy *will not prevail against you.* He wanted to keep you from my service, but you will arise in good health! Here is the lamb you asked for: you have received it because of your good desire. That brother gave you good advice!" Then drawing his hand across the wounds, he told him to return to the work he had begun.

Gn 4:17; Jer 1:19

The man got up very early the next morning, and the workers who had left him half-dead were shocked and amazed when he appeared, healthy and unharmed. Because there seemed to be no hope for his recovery, *they thought* they were seeing a *ghost,* neither man nor flesh, but a spirit. (Since there has been mention of the construction of buildings in honor of this saint, I thought it only right to include here another extraordinary miracle.)

Mk 6:49

⁶⁰Two Lesser Brothers once undertook to build a church in honor of the holy father Francis in the town of Peschici in the diocese of

---

a. On the Tyrrhenian Sea, between Rome and Naples. By this time the friars had also buit a friary in Gaeta, see AF IV, 529.

b. From his commentary on the Gospel of John: *In Joh. Evang.* 25: 12, in *PL* 35, 1602.

Siponto.[a] They had a very fatiguing task, and lacked the means necessary to complete the construction. One night when they had *risen from sleep* to offer lauds, they began to hear the sound of falling and crashing stones. Each encouraged the other to go look, and when *they went outside* they saw a great crowd of people competing to gather stones. They all came and went in silence, and all were dressed in white clothing. The great pile of stones gathered was proof that this was not an illusion: these did not run out until the work was finished. The suspicion that this was accomplished by men *living in the flesh* was removed when a diligent search turned up no one who would have planned such a thing.

Jgs 16:14

Mt 10:14

Gal 2:20

[61] The son of a nobleman of Castel San Gimigniano suffered from a severe illness; all hope was abandoned and he seemed near the end. A stream of blood trickled from his eyes, like the flow of blood from the severed vein of an arm. Other signs of death's approach appeared in the rest of his body, and he seemed already gone. His friends and family, as is usual, gathered for mourning and arranged the funeral. All that remained was the burial. Meanwhile, his father, surrounded by the crowd of mourners, remembered a vision he had previously heard of. He rushed off to the church of Saint Francis, which had been built in that same town.[b] With a cord hanging around his neck he humbly *threw himself on the ground. He made a vow* and *prayed repeatedly*. With sighs and groans, he gained Saint Francis as his patron with Christ. As the father returned quickly to his son and found him restored to health, his *mourning turned into joy*.

Jdt 10:23
1 Sm 1:11; Jb 4

Lam 5:15

[62] A certain young man of the village of Piazza in Sicily had already had his soul commended in the last rites of the church. He was brought back from the threshold of death through the holy father's intercession after his uncle made a vow to him.

[63] In the same neighborhood a young man called Alessandro was tugging a rope with some companions on a high cliff. The rope broke, and he fell from the cliff; he was carried away, presumed dead. His father, with tears and sobs vowed to the saint of Christ, and got him back safe and sound.

[64] A woman of the same town suffered from typhus and was nearing her end. The commendation of her soul had already been performed, but those around her invoked the most holy father and she was instantly *restored to health*.

Mt 12:13

---

a. Near Manfredonia in Apulia, Peschici is on the northern side of Monte Gargano. Concerning the church of Saint Francis, see AF IV, 531. This incident is recounted in *Dialogus de gesti sanctorum fratrum minorum*, ed. Frederick Delorme (Ad Claras Aquas, Quaracchi: Collegium S. Bonaventurae, 1923), 253.

b. Concerning the church there, see AF IV, 518.

⁶⁵In Rete of the diocese of Cosenza two boys of that town got into a brawl at school, and one wounded the other in the abdomen so severely that the stomach was torn and undigested food came out through the wound. He was unable to retain any nourishment and he could not digest food, nor hold it in. It all came out undigested through the wound. Doctors could offer him no help. He and his parents finally, at the suggestion of one of the brothers, first forgave the one who had inflicted the wound, then made a vow to blessed Francis. If he would snatch from the jaws of death the mortally wounded boy, who was given no hope by the doctors, they would send him to his church and ring it with candles. On making their vow, the boy was so completely and wonderfully healed that doctors from Salerno[a] called it no less a miracle than if he had been raised from the dead.

⁶⁶At Monte near Trapani[b] two men arrived together on business when one of them suddenly became ill *to the point of death.* Doctors were called and came quickly to help him, but they could do nothing to cure him. His healthy companion *made a vow* to Saint Francis. If the sick man should receive healing through the saint's merits, he would observe his feast every year with a solemn Mass. After making his vow, he returned to the house where he had left his companion speechless and motionless, thinking him already doomed to destruction. There he found him restored to his former health.

⁶⁷A boy from the city of Todi lay on his bed for eight days as if dead. His mouth was tightly shut, and there was no light in his eyes. The skin of his face, hands and feet turned black as a pot. No one held out hope for his recovery, but as a result of his mother's vow he recovered with amazing speed. Though he was just an infant and *could not speak* he said, lisping, that he was saved by blessed Francis.

⁶⁸A young man who had been up on a very high place fell from there and lost the use of all his limbs as well as his ability to speak. For *three days he neither ate nor drank* nor felt anything, so that they thought he was dead. His mother, without even seeking the aid of a doctor, asked blessed Francis to cure him. After she had made a vow the young man was restored to her, alive and sound, and she began to praise the all-powerful Creator.

⁶⁹A boy from Arezzo by the name of Gualtiero was suffering from prolonged fever and so tormented by multiple abscesses that

Margin notes:
Ps 68:21
Ps 132:2
1C 139 — Mt 9:2
Jer 1:6
1C 140 — Mt 11:18; Acts 9:9
1C 140

---

a. Doctors from the school at Salerno, near Naples, were considered outstanding at that time.
b. Now Monte San Giuliano. Probably the ancient Erycinum, in Sicily.

all the doctors gave up hope for him. But his parents made a vow to blessed Francis, and he recovered the health they so longed for.

Chapter IX
CASES OF DROPSY AND PARALYSIS

[70] In the city of Fano a man suffering from dropsy obtained a complete cure of his illness through the merits of blessed Francis.

[71] A woman in the city of Gubbio lay paralyzed in bed; after she invoked the name of blessed Francis three times for her healing she was freed from her infirmity and cured.

[72] A girl from Arpino in the diocese of Sora was beset by a paralytic illness. She was deprived of all human functions, and her limbs were so uncontrolled and twisted by nerves that she appeared more harassed by a demon than animated by a human spirit. She was so tormented by this infirmity that she seemed to have regressed to the cradle. Finally, her mother, by divine inspiration, took her to the church of blessed Francis in Vicalvi.[a] She carried her in a cradle, and after many tearful prayers the girl was freed from every danger of illness and was restored to her former age and health.

[73] A young man of the same town was bound by a paralysis that held his mouth shut and distorted his eyes. His mother took him to the church mentioned above. She prayed fervently for him, and whereas he had been completely unable to move, he recovered his original health before they reached their home.

[74] In Poggibonsi a girl named Ubertina suffered from falling sickness,[b] as severe as it was incurable. Her parents despaired of any human remedy, and strenuously demanded the help of blessed Francis. By common agreement they vowed to the saint that they would fast on the vigil of the most blessed father's feast and provide food for the poor on the day of his solemnity every year if he would free their daughter from such an unusual affliction. After making their vow, the girl totally recovered and never again suffered any harm from that hurtful illness.

[75] Pietro Mancanella, a citizen of Gaeta,[c] lost the use of an arm and hand to paralysis, and his mouth was twisted back to his ear. When he submitted to the advice of doctors, he lost both his sight and his hearing. Finally he humbly dedicated himself to blessed Francis, and

1C 141

1C 142

---

a. On this church, see AF IV, 529.

b. That is, epilepsy.

c. See 3C 59, supra, 347 a.

was thus completely freed from his affliction through the merits of that most blessed man.

⁷⁶A citizen of Todi suffered from such an acute arthritic condition that he could not lie down at all. It seemed he would become entirely helpless; and as he received no relief from doctors, in the presence of a priest he called on Saint Francis. Having made his vow, he regained his former health.

⁷⁷A man by the name of Bontadoso suffered such pain in his feet that he was absolutely unable to move about. He was losing both his sleep and his appetite. A woman encouraged him to vow himself humbly to Saint Francis but, beside himself with pain, he replied that he did not believe him to be a saint. The woman nevertheless stubbornly persisted, and finally he vowed himself in this way: "I vow myself to Saint Francis, and I believe he is a saint if he frees me from this illness in three days." He immediately got up, to his own surprise, with the health that had left him now fully restored.

⁷⁸A woman was confined to bed for many years by illness, unable to turn or move at all. She was healed by blessed Francis and resumed her usual duties.

⁷⁹A young man in the city of Narni was in the grip of a very serious illness for ten years; his whole body was so swollen no medicine could treat it. His mother vowed him to Saint Francis, and he immediately received from him the relief of health.

⁸⁰In the same city there was a woman who for eight years had a withered hand with which she could do no work. Blessed Francis appeared to her *in a vision,* and stretching her hand made it able to work as well as the other.

Chapter X
THOSE SAVED FROM SHIPWRECK

⁸¹Some sailors were placed in grave danger at sea when a fierce storm came up while they were ten miles out from the port of Barletta. Anxious for their lives, they let down the anchors. But the *stormy wind* swelled the sea more violently, breaking the ropes and releasing the anchors. They were tossed about the sea on an unsteady and uncertain course.

Finally at God's pleasure the sea was calmed, and they prepared with all their strength to recover their anchors, whose lines were floating on the surface. So they put their full effort into retrieving the

1C 141

1C 141

1C 141

1C 141

1C 141

Dn 4:10

Ps 11:6

anchors. They invoked the help of all the saints and were worn down by their exertion, but could not recover even one after a whole day.

One of the sailors was named Perfetto, though he was perfectly good for nothing. He despised everything *that belongs to God.* With malice he scoffed and said to his companions, "You have invoked the aid of all the saints, and as you see not one of them has helped. Let's call that Francis. He's a new saint; let him dive into the sea with his capuche and get our anchors back. We can give an ounce of gold to his church, which is just being built in Ortona, if we decide he helped." The others fearfully agreed with the scoffer, but they rebuked him by making a vow. At that very moment the anchors were suddenly floating on the water with no support, as if the nature of iron had been changed into the lightness of wood.

[82]A pilgrim, feeble in body, and not quite sound in mind because of a bout of madness he had suffered, was traveling with his wife by ship from regions overseas.[a] He was not completely free of his illness and was troubled by a burning thirst. As the water had run out, he began to shout loudly, "Go confidently, pour me a cup! Blessed Francis has filled my flask with water!" What a wonder! The flask they had left *void and empty* they now found filled with water.

Some days later a storm came up and the boat was being *swamped by the waves* and shaken by strong winds so that they feared they would be shipwrecked. That same sick man suddenly began to shout around the ship, "Get up, everyone, come to meet blessed Francis. He is here to save us!" And with a loud voice and tears he *bowed down to worship.* As soon as he had seen the saint the sick man recovered his full health; and, on *the sea, calm* ensued.

[83]Brother Giacomo of Rieti was a passenger on a small boat making a river crossing. At the shore, his companions disembarked first, and he prepared to get out last. But the boat's small raft accidentally overturned, and while the pilot could swim, the brother was plunged *into the depths.* The brothers on shore with tender cries called on blessed Francis and tearfully insisted that he save his son. The drowning brother too, in the belly of a great whirlpool, could not call with his mouth, but called out from his heart as well as he could. See! With the help of his father's presence he walked across the depths as if on dry land. He caught hold of the overturned little boat and reached the shore with it. More wonderful still, his clothes were not wet: not a drop of water clung to his tunic.

[84]Two men and two women with one child were travelling by boat across the Lake of Rieti. The little boat accidentally shifted to one side

Mt 22:21

Gn 1:2

Mt 8:24

Jn 9:38

Mt 8:26

Mt 18:6

---

a. The Holy Land, also called *Outremer,* "beyond the sea," i.e., the Mediterranean.

and was quickly filled with water; they seemed to be heading for death. All shouting, convinced they were going to die, one of the women cried out with very great trust, "Saint Francis, you favored me while still *living in the flesh* with the kindness of your friendship. Now from heaven give your help to us who are going to perish!" The saint was there as soon as he was called and carefully escorted the boat full of water to shore. Someone had brought a sword aboard the boat, and it miraculously floated among the waves following the boat.

Phil 1:22

⁸⁵Some sailors from Ancona were caught in a violent storm and knew they were in danger of sinking. In desperation for their lives they humbly invoked Saint Francis. A great light appeared on the sea, and with the light a heaven-sent calm. To fulfill their vow they offered a splendid curtain and countless expressions of thanks to their rescuer.

⁸⁶A brother named Bonaventure was crossing a lake with two men when a side of the boat split, and, with the force of the water rushing in, they sank. "From the deep lake"[a] they called on Saint Francis, and shortly the water-filled boat reached the shore with them in it.

Similarly a brother from Ascoli was saved by the merits of Saint Francis when he fell into a river.

⁸⁷A man from the parish of Saints Cosmas and Damian in Pisa confirmed by his testimony that he was at sea with many others when the ship was driven by a great storm toward collision with a mountain. The sailors saw this and built a sort of raft out of ropes and planks as a refuge for themselves and others on board. But the man from Pisa lost his balance on the raft, and a strong wave *threw him into the sea.* He did not know how to swim and could not be helped by the others, so he headed desperately toward the depths of the sea. He was unable to speak, but in his heart he devoutly commended himself to blessed Francis. He was quickly raised from the depths as if by some hand and carried back to the raft, and was saved from shipwreck with the others. The ship, though, hit the mountain and was completely demolished.

Mt 21:21

---

a. *De profundo lacu* [from the deep lake]: from the Offertory of the Mass for the dead.

Chapter XI
THE BOUND AND IMPRISONED

[88]In Romania[a] it happened that a Greek servant of a certain lord was falsely accused of theft. His lord ordered him to be shut in a narrow prison and heavily chained; after final sentencing he was to have a foot cut off. The wife of the lord was concerned to free the innocent man, but her husband remained firm and rejected her request. The lady turned humbly to Saint Francis and, by a vow, commended the innocent man to his compassion. Quickly the helper of the afflicted was present. He took the imprisoned man by the hand, loosened his chains, broke open the jail, and led the innocent man out. "I am the one to whom your mistress devoutly commended you," he said. The man shook with fear as he wandered at the edge of a precipice, looking for a way to descend from the very high cliff. Suddenly he found himself on level ground without knowing how.

He returned to his lady and told her his miraculous story. She immediately made a wax image because of her vow, and hung it before the saint's picture for all to see. The *unjust man* was upset, and when he struck his wife with his hand he fell gravely ill. He was not able to heal until he had confessed his fault and rendered sincere praise to the Saint of God, Francis.

Prv 16:29

[89]In Massa San Pietro a poor fellow owed a certain knight a sum of money. Since he had no means of paying the debt, the knight had him confined as a debtor. He humbly asked for mercy and, interjecting prayers, requested a deferral for love of Saint Francis. He thought the knight respected this famous saint. The knight haughtily scorned his prayers; he stupidly mocked the love of the saint as something stupid. He obstinately replied, "I will lock you up in such a place and *put you in* such a *prison* that neither Francis nor anyone else will be able to help you." And he attempted to do what he said. He found a dark prison and threw the chained man into it.

Gn 41:10

A short time later Saint Francis arrived and broke open the prison; he shattered the man's leg-irons and led him to his own home unharmed. Afterward the man brought his chains to the church of blessed Francis in Assisi. In them he had experienced the mercy of the father; now they would become a demonstration of his marvelous power. Thus the strength of Francis plundered the proud knight and *delivered from evil* the captive who had made himself his subject.

Mt 6:13; 2 Tm 4:18

---

a. That is, the Latin Empire of the East, "Roman" territory. There are two other miracles performed in Romania, 3C 118, 194, suggesting that devotion to Saint Francis had begun to spread to this part of Europe.

⁹⁰Five officials of a great prince were arrested under suspicion. They were not only sturdily chained together but also confined to a very narrow prison. When they heard that blessed Francis was shining through miracles everywhere, they devoutly entrusted themselves to him. One night Saint Francis appeared to one of them and promised them the favor of freedom. The one who saw the vision was overjoyed and told his fellow captives about the promised favor. Though still in the dark, they both wept and rejoiced. They *made their vows* and *prayed repeatedly.* One of them immediately began to scratch the thick wall of the tower with a bone; its mortar gave way so easily that it seemed a mixture of ashes. When the wall was breached he tried to pass through, and with their chains broken, one after the other they reached freedom. There was still a steep drop that blocked their escape. But Francis, their bold leader, gave them the boldness to climb down. So they went off unharmed and got away safely; they became great heralds of the mighty works of this saint.

⁹¹Alberto of Arezzo was being held tightly in chains for debts unjustly charged to him. He humbly placed his innocence before Saint Francis. He greatly loved the Order of the brothers and venerated Francis with special affection among all the saints. His creditor had made the blasphemous statement that neither God nor Francis would be *able to deliver him from his hands.*

On the vigil of the feast of Saint Francis the bound man had eaten nothing, but out of love for the saint had given his meal to someone in need. As night fell, Saint Francis appeared to him during his vigil. At the saint's entry, the *chains fell from his hands* and his feet. The doors *opened by themselves* and the boards on the roof fell down; the man got away free and returned to his home. From then on he kept his vow to fast on the vigil of Saint Francis and to make an annual offering of a candle, to which each year he added an extra ounce.

⁹²A young man from the region of Città di Castello[a] was accused of arson. As he lay shackled in a harsh prison, he humbly entrusted his case to Saint Francis. One night, as he was restrained by both chains and guards, *he heard a voice saying to him, "Get up quickly* and go where you like, for your chains are loosed!" He lost no time in obeying the command, and once outside the jail he took the road to Assisi to offer to his liberator a *sacrifice of praise.*

⁹³When the Lord Pope Gregory IX[b] was occupying the see of blessed Peter there arose an inevitable persecution of heretics. A

Margin notes:
1 Sm 1:11
Jb 40:27
Dn 3:17
Acts 12:7
Acts 12:10
Acts 9:4;12:7
Ps 50:14

---

a. See FA:ED I 242 a.
b. Pope from 1227 to 1241. See 1C 1 Prologue, FA:ED I 180 b.

certain Pietro from Alife[a] was among those accused of heresy, and he was arrested in Rome. The Lord Pope Gregory handed him over to the bishop of Tivoli for safekeeping. Fearing the threat of losing episcopal office, the bishop took him and bound him in leg irons. But because Pietro's simplicity indicated innocence, he was granted less careful watch.

Some nobles of the city, it is said, had a long-standing hatred of the bishop and were eager to see him incur the punishment decreed by the Pope. So they secretly advised Pietro to escape. He agreed with them; he escaped one night and soon fled far away.

When the bishop heard this, he took it seriously: he feared the expected punishment and he was no less pained to see his enemies' wish fulfilled. So he took every precaution and sent out searchers in every direction. When the poor fellow was found, considering him ungrateful, he put the man in the strictest custody for the future. He had a dark jail cell prepared, surrounded with thick walls. Inside he had the man confined between thick planks and fastened with iron

Ps 149:8   nails. He had him bound in *fetters of iron* weighing many pounds, and
Ez 4:16   provided him food *by weight* and drink *by measure.*

Because all other hope of freedom was now cut off, God, who does
Jb 4:7   not allow the *innocent to perish,* soon came with His mercy to help him. That poor man, with much weeping and praying, began to call on blessed Francis to take pity on him. He had heard that the vigil of his solemnity was near. The man had great faith in Saint Francis because, as he said, he had heard that heretics railed furiously against him.[b] On the night before his feast, around dusk, blessed Francis mercifully came down into the prison, called him by name, and or-
1 Chr 10:4 dered him to stand up. The man asked *in great fear* who was calling him, and heard that it was blessed Francis. He jumped up, called the
Gn 45:3   guard and said, "I am *very afraid,* someone is here ordering me to get up, and he says he is Saint Francis." "Lie down, wretch," the guard replied, "sleep in peace! You're out of your mind because you didn't eat well today." But when, toward midday, the saint of God still ordered him to get up, he saw the chains on his feet break and fall suddenly to the ground. Looking about the cell, he saw the timbers opened with their nails sprung outward: there was a clear path for his escape.

Once free, he was so astounded that he did not know enough to flee. Instead, he let out a cry and frightened all the guards. When the bishop was told that the man had been freed from his chains, he

---

a. In the province of Caserta.
b. For examples of Francis and heretics, see 1C 62; 2C 78-79.

thought that he had fled. Since he had not yet heard of the miracle, he was struck with fear and, since he was ill, fell from where he had been sitting. But once he understood what had happened, he devoutly went to the prison, and openly *acknowledging the power of God,* he there *worshiped the Lord.*

Mk 5:30
Gn 24:26

Later the chains were sent to the Lord Pope and the cardinals: on *seeing what had happened,* with much wonder *they blessed God.*

Lk 23:47; Dn 13:60

[94]Guidalotto of San Gimignano was falsely accused of poisoning a man, and further that he had intended to kill the man's son and the whole family with the same poison. He was arrested by the local podestà, who had him heavily chained and thrown into a ruined tower. The podestà thought about what punishment he could inflict on him, to obtain a confession of the crime through torture. He finally ordered him suspended from a revolving rack. He weighed him down with weights of iron until he fainted. Several times he ordered him let down and raised up again with the hope that one torment after another would more quickly bring him to confess his crime. But the man's face seemed joyful in an innocent way, showing no sign of sorrow in his pain. Then a rather large fire was lit beneath the man, but not a hair of his head was harmed while his head hung toward the ground. Finally, burning oil was poured over him, but he laughed through it all, because he was innocent and from the beginning had entrusted himself to blessed Francis. The night before he was to be punished, he had been visited by Saint Francis. He was surrounded by an immense bright light, and he remained in its light until morning, *filled with joy* and great confidence. *Blessed be God,* who does not allow the *innocent to perish,* and even in a *flood of many waters* is present to those who hope in Him.

Ps 126:20; Ps 66:20
Jb 4:7; Ps 32:6

Chapter XII
THOSE FREED FROM THE DANGERS OF CHILDBIRTH
AND THOSE WHO FAIL TO KEEP HIS FEAST

[95]A certain countess of Slavonia,[a] illustrious in nobility and a friend of goodness, had an ardent devotion to Saint Francis and a sincere affection for the brothers. She suffered severe pains at the time of childbirth; she was so overcome with pain that it appeared that the expected birth of the child would mean the demise of the mother. She seemed incapable of bringing the child into life unless she departed from life; and, by this effort, not to give birth but to

---

a. Used for Dalmatia and, more generally, Croatia; cf. 1C 55, FA:ED I 229 b.

Rv 19:1   perish. But the fame of Francis, his *glory and might,* sustained her
heart. Her faith aroused, her devotion kindled, she turned to the ef-
fective helper, the trusted friend, the comforter of those devoted to
Phlm 12   him, the refuge of the afflicted. "Saint Francis," she said, *"all my heart*
cries out to your mercy, and I vow in spirit what I cannot say aloud."
O the speed of mercy! The end of her speaking was the end of her suffering, and the end of her labor was the beginning of giving birth.
Just as soon as the pains ceased, she safely gave birth to a child. Nor
did she forget her vow or run away from her promise. She had a
beautiful church built and, once it was built, donated it to the brothers in honor of the saint.

[96]A certain Beatrice from the region of Rome was close to giving
birth. For four days she had been carrying a dead fetus in her womb.
She was much distressed and beset by deadly pain. The dead fetus
was causing the mother's death, and still the obvious threat to the
mother did not bring forth the abortive offspring. The help of doctors
Ps 127:1   proved fruitless; every human remedy *labored in vain.* Thus did the
Jer 20:17 ancient curse fall heavily upon the unfortunate woman. Her *womb*
Jb 3:21, 22 *became a grave,* and she certainly *awaited the grave* soon. Finally, by
means of messengers, she entrusted herself with great devotion to
the Lesser Brothers. She humbly requested in great faith some relic
of Saint Francis. By divine consent a piece of a cord was found, one
that the saint had once worn. As soon as the cord was placed on the
suffering woman, all her pain was relieved with ease. The dead fetus,
cause of death, was released and the woman was restored to her former health.

[97]Giuliana, wife of a nobleman of Calvi, passed a number of years
in mourning over the death of her children: she constantly mourned
those unhappy events. All the children she had borne were consigned to the earth; the axe cut down each new shoot. So when she
Mt 1:23   was four months *with child,* she was moved more by sorrow than joy,
because she feared that deceptive joy over birth would be changed
later to mourning over death.

Mt 1:20   Then one night as she slept, a woman *appeared* to her *in a dream.*
The woman carried a beautiful infant in her hands and joyfully offered him to her saying, "Take this child, my lady; Saint Francis
sends him to you!" But she was reluctant to accept something that
would soon perish, so she refused. "Why should I want this child,"
she said, "when I know it will soon die like all the others?" "Take it,"
Ez 18:9, 19 was the reply, "because the one Saint Francis sends you *shall surely
live!*" They spoke this way three times before the lady took the child
in her hands. She immediately awoke from her sleep and told her
husband about the vision. Both of them were thrilled with joy and

increased their vows for having a child. The *time for delivery arrived* and the woman *gave birth* to a son. He thrived to a lively age and made up for the grieving over those who had died.

⁹⁸A woman was near to childbirth in Viterbo, but perhaps nearer to death. She had severe abdominal pains and suffered the misfortunes that befall women. Doctors were consulted and the midwives summoned. They had no success, and only despair remained. The afflicted woman called upon blessed Francis, and promised, among other things, that she would celebrate his feast as long as she lived. She was immediately healed and joyfully finished giving birth.

But when she got what she wanted, she forgot what she promised. In fact, she did not so much forget her vow as despise it, since she went out to wash clothes on the feast of Saint Francis. Instantly an extraordinary *pain fell upon her* and, warned by the pain, she returned home.

But the pain passed, and because she was one of those who changes her mind ten times an hour, when she saw her neighbors at work, she foolishly set to work more strenuously than before. Suddenly she was unable to draw back the right arm she had extended to work; it was rigid and withered. When she tried to raise it with her other arm, that too withered with a similar curse. The pitiful woman now had to be fed by her son, and was unable to do any other tasks by herself. Her husband was puzzled and searched for the cause of what had happened; he concluded that her false faith toward Saint Francis was the cause of her torment. Both the man and his wife were *struck with fear* and without delay reaffirmed the vow. So the saint *had mercy* because *he was* always *merciful;* he restored the limbs to the one who repented, just as he had disabled them when she despised her vow. The woman's punishment made her sin known; she became an example to all who fail to keep their vows, and put fear into those who would presume to violate the feasts of the saints.

⁹⁹The wife of a judge in the city of Tivoli burned *with great fury,* since she had borne six daughters. She decided to stay away from her husband. Why should she continue to plant when she was so thoroughly displeased with the fruit? The woman bristled at always producing females, was worn out by the desire of the male sex, and even questioned God's will. But one should not bear reluctantly the judgment that the laws of *almighty God* impose on humans. In any case, she angrily remained separated from her husband for a year. A little later, *led to repentance,* she was told to be *reconciled to her husband.* The confessor persuaded her to request a son from blessed Francis, and to name it Francis because she would have the child through his merits. Not long after, the woman conceived and the one she had implored

Lk 1:57
Jb 20:22
Acts 10:4; Bar 3:2
Est 1:12
Rv 16:14
Mt 27:3
Mt 27:3; 1Cor 7:11

allowed her to bear twin boys, even though he had been asked for only one. One was named Francesco and the other Biagio.

Lv 23:7
[100]A noble woman of the city of Le Mans[a] had a lowly servant girl whom she forced to do *servile work* on the feast of Saint Francis. But the girl was of nobler mind and refused, out of reverence for the feast. Human fear, however, prevailed over fear of God, and the girl
Prv 31:19
did as she was told, even if unwillingly. *She put her hand* to the distaff, *her fingers plied the spindle*. But immediately her hands stiffened with pain and her fingers burned unbearably. The punishment revealed the fault as the sharpness of the pain made silence impossible. The girl hurried to the sons of Saint Francis,[b] revealed her offense, showed her punishment, and asked forgiveness. So the brothers marched in procession to the church and begged Saint Francis's mercy for the girl's health. As the sons begged their father she was healed, though a trace of the burning remained on her hands.

[101]A similar thing happened in Campania.[c] A certain woman was frequently rebuked by her neighbors for not abstaining from work on the saint's feast. On the vigil of blessed Francis she obstinately continued to work into the evening without ceasing. But after her work she was suddenly struck with pain and shock; a weakness in her hands kept her from even ordinary tasks. She soon arose and declared that the feast she had despised should be revered. In the hands of a priest she solemnly vowed that she would forever observe the saint's feast with reverence. After her vow she was taken to a church built in honor of Saint Francis. There, after many tears, she recovered her health.

[102]In the village of Olite[d] a neighbor warned a certain woman to observe the feast of Saint Francis, and not to do any work. But the woman impudently replied, "If there were one saint for every trade, the number of saints would be more than the number of days." At her foolish words she immediately fell ill by divine vengeance. For many days she lost her mind and memory until, through the prayers of many to blessed Francis, her madness subsided.

[103]In the town of Piglio in the province of Campania[e] a woman busily went about her work on the feast of Saint Francis. A noble-woman sternly rebuked her for this, since everyone should observe

---

a. In France, north of Tours.

b. On the brothers' presence there see AF IV, 307, 543.

c. Either the Champagne region of France or the Campagna (Terra di Lavoro) in Italy. Cf. AF IV, 307, n. 3.

d. This site has not been identified with certainty: perhaps Olite in the custody of Navarre or Vallodolid in the province of Castille (AF IV, 536, 537).

e. Roman Campagna (AF IV, 249, 345, 517).

the feast out of divine reverence. She answered, "I only have a little of my work left to finish: *Let the Lord see* whether I'm doing wrong!" She soon saw the harsh judgment, in her daughter, who was sitting nearby. The girl's mouth twisted back to her ears and her eyes bulged, pitifully distorted. Women gathered quickly from all around and cursed the mother's ungodliness on account of the innocent daughter. The mother was overcome with sorrow and fell to the ground, promising to observe the feast annually, and further to feed the poor on that day out of reverence for the saint. Her daughter's troubles subsided without delay, once the mother had repented of her offense.

[104] Matteo of Tolentino had a daughter named Francesca. He was quite upset when the brothers moved to another place, and he took to calling his daughter Mattea, depriving her of Francis's name. Soon she lost her health as well as her name. Because his action involved contempt for the father and hatred for his sons, his daughter fell gravely ill to the point of being in danger of death. Thereupon the man suffered bitter sorrow over the passing of his daughter. When his wife rebuked him for his hatred of the servants of God and his contempt of the saint's name, he quickly returned devoutly to the first name and reinstated to the daughter the title of which she had been deprived. Then, with fatherly tears, he took his daughter to the place of the brothers where she recovered her health as well as her name.

[105] A woman of Pisa, unaware that she was pregnant, put in a hard day of work on a church of Saint Francis being built in that city. Saint Francis, led by two brothers carrying candles, *appeared* to her *in the night and said,* "Daughter, *behold: you have conceived and are bearing a son.* You will rejoice over him if you give him my name." When her *time for delivery arrived, she gave birth to a son.* "He will be named Enrico," said her mother-in-law, "after one of our relatives." "*No,*" said his mother, "*he is to be called* Francesco." The mother-in-law scoffed at this noble name as if it were for peasants. A few days later when the baby was to be baptized, he became weak almost to the point of death. The whole household was saddened, their *joy turned into sorrow.* The mother's distress kept her awake that night. Saint Francis came with the two brothers as before and, as if disturbed, said to her, "Did I not tell you that you would not rejoice over this son unless you gave him my name?" She began to shout and swear that she would give him no other name. In the end the boy, graced with the name Francesco, was both baptized and healed. The boy was given the grace of not crying; his infant years passed happily.

1 Chr 24:22

2 Chr 1:7
Lk 1:31
Lk 1:57

Lk 1:60

Jas 4:9

[106]A woman from the region of Arezzo in Tuscany bore the pains of labor through seven days, and was turning black. In her death throes, when everyone had despaired of her, she made a vow to Saint Francis and called on his aid. When she had made her vow, she quickly fell asleep, and Saint Francis appeared to her. He called her by her name, "Adelasia," and asked her whether she recognized his face. She replied, "Yes, father, I do recognize you." The saint went on, "Can you recite the *Salve Regina?*" "Yes, father," she answered. "Start," said the saint, "and before you finish you will safely give

Mt 27:46 birth." Then the saint *cried out in a loud voice* and disappeared. At that cry, the woman woke up and anxiously began *"Salve regina . . ."* When she reached the words *"illos misericordes oculos,"* before she had finished, she suddenly gave birth to a beautiful child in joy and good health.

[107]Although she knew that it was the solemn feast day of blessed

Lv 23:7 Francis, a woman in Sicily nevertheless failed to abstain from *servile work.* She took a baker's mixing bowl, put in some flour and, with bare arms, she began to knead it. Right away the dough appeared to be flecked with blood. When the stunned woman saw this, she began to call her neighbors. The more the spectators gathered, the more the trickles of blood increased in the dough. The woman repented of

Ps 132:2 what she had done, and *swore a vow* never again to do servile work on his feast. Once her promise was confirmed, the flow of blood left the dough.

[108]While the saint was still living in the flesh, a woman in the

1C 63

Arezzo area was pregnant and at the time of childbirth she was in labor for several days with extraordinary distress. Blessed Francis was on his way to a hermitage, and was on horseback because of

Acts 28:6 the weakness of his body. *They were* all *waiting* for him to pass by the place where the woman was suffering. But the saint was already staying in the hermitage, and a brother was returning through that village with the horse on which the saint had ridden. When the

Tb 10:3 inhabitants of the place realized that he was not Saint Francis, *they*

Lk 22:23 *were greatly saddened* and they began to inquire among themselves if they could find some item that the servant of God had touched with his own hand. Discovering the bridle reins, which he had held in his hands, they quickly pulled the bridle from the horse's mouth. And when the woman felt the reins placed upon her, she gave birth in great joy and good health.

Chapter XIII
Ruptures Repaired

[109]Brother Giacomo of Iseo, a man of considerable fame and re-
nown in our Order,[a] *testifies of himself* and gives thanks to God's saint   Jn 1:15
for the grace of his health to the glory of our father. When he was a
tender youth in his parental home his body suffered a serious rupture. With great suffering from the injury, the body's inner parts
poured out: things that nature had placed inside were now in a place
that was not theirs. His father and family, who were aware of the
cause, were concerned and repeatedly sought medical help, but to no
avail. Inspired by the divine Spirit the youth began to reflect *about his*   1 Pt 1:9
salvation and to seek with a sincere mind the God *who heals the broken-*   Ps 147:3
hearted and binds up their wounds. He thus devoutly entered the Order
of Saint Francis without revealing to anyone the infirmity that trou-
bled him. After *he stayed* in the Order a short time, the brothers be-   Mt 25:5
came aware of his infirmity; and they intended to make the painful
decision to send him back to his parents.[b] But the boy's determination was strong enough to overcome this unpleasant decision. The
brothers took the youth into their care until, *strengthened by grace,* his   Lk 2:40
sound way of life proved him a good man. He undertook the care of
souls among them and was praiseworthy for his religious discipline.

It happened that when the body of blessed Francis was transferred to its place,[c] this same brother was among the many who joyfully celebrated the translation. He approached the tomb in which
the body of the most holy father rested and prayed at length for his
long-standing infirmity. His inner parts suddenly and wonderfully
returned to their proper place and he felt himself healed. He laid
aside his truss and was from then on totally free of his pain.

[110]A man from Pisa suffered bitter pain and terrible shame be-
cause he eliminated all the *hidden things of his bowels* by way of his pri-   Prv 20:27
vate parts, and he contemplated diabolical action against himself: in
the depth of his despair he resolved to end his life by hanging himself. But before that, the sting of his not yet deadened conscience led
him to impress on his memory the name of Saint Francis and, however weakly, to invoke him with his mouth. He soon experienced a

a. He served as Minister of the Roman province of the Order: cf. Salimbene, *Chronicle,* 67-8.
b. This reflects the legislation concerning those entering the Order which became more refined as the
   fraternity grew. For information on these developments, see Saint Bonaventure, *Writings Concerning*
   The Franciscan Order, introduction and translation by Dominic Monti (St. Bonaventure, NY:
   Franciscan Institute Publications, 1994): 76-77.
c. That is, on May 25, 1230; see 3C 48, supra, 342 b.

speedy conversion from his damnable intention and a full cure of his great misfortune.

[111]The son of a man from the town of Cisterna in Marittima[a] was horribly burdened with a rupture of the genitals and no device could hold back his intestines. For the truss, which usually supports such ruptures, caused many new ones. His parents were tormented, and the horrible spectacle provided their friends and neighbors with ample grounds for tears. They tried every remedy and cure with no success whatever. Finally his father and mother vowed their son to Saint Francis.

On the feast day of Saint Francis they took him to the church at Velletri built in his honor. They laid him out before the saint's image and, making their vows along with a crowd of many others, offered many tears for him. When the gospel was being sung, at the words *"what you have hidden from the learned you have revealed to the merest children,* his truss suddenly broke, and the useless remedies fell away. A scar quickly formed and the full health desired was restored. A great cry went up from those *praising the Lord* and venerating his saint.

[112]A sacristan named Niccolò one morning was entering his church in Ceccano, a town in Campania, when he took *a sudden fall.* The sad result was that all his intestines poured out at his private parts. The clergy and other neighbors rushed to him, lifted him and carried him to his bed. He lay motionless for eight days, unable even to rise for his natural functions. Doctors were called and they applied their remedies, but his pain only increased: his illness was not healed, but heightened. His monstrous organs remained in their unnatural position with such pain that the poor fellow was unable to eat for eight days. The man was now desperate and destined for death. Then he turned to the help of blessed Francis.

He had a daughter who was *religious and God-fearing;* he asked her to beg the aid of Saint Francis for him. *The blessed daughter went out* a short distance and with many tears gave herself to prayer. She prayed to the father for her own father. O the power of prayer! Her father suddenly called out to her while she was still praying and joyfully informed her of his *unexpected healing.* Everything returned to its proper place, and the man felt in better condition now than before his fall. He vowed then that blessed Francis would always be his patron, and that he would annually observe his feast day.

[113]A man from the village of Spello **suffered for two years from such a severe rupture that** it seemed that all his bowels **protruded through the side of his body. He could not keep them in place for**

Mt 11:25

Lk 2:13

Ez 26:16

Acts 10:1

Jn 18:29; Ru 3:10

Wis 5:2

1C 144

---

a. Today, Cisterna di Latina, in Lazio.

any length of time, nor was the attention of doctors able to put them back into their proper place. When he gave up hope in the help of doctors, he turned to divine help. When he devoutly called upon the merits of blessed Francis, he experienced with wondrous speed that what was broken was made whole, what was deformed was restored.

[114]A young man named Giovanni from the diocese of Sora was afflicted by a severe intestinal hernia and could not be helped by any doctor's medicine. One day his wife happened to go to a church of blessed Francis. While she was praying, one of the brothers, a simple soul, said to her, "Go tell your husband to vow himself to blessed Francis, and to make the sign of the cross on his rupture!" She went home and told her husband. The man vowed himself to blessed Francis, signed the place of his injury, and his intestines immediately returned to their proper place. The man was amazed at the *suddenness of his unexpected healing,* and to test whether the healing he so suddenly enjoyed was real, he tried a number of exercises.

Once when this same man had a high fever, blessed Francis *appeared in a dream, called* him *by name and said, "Do not fear,* Giovanni, for you will be *healed of your sickness."* The trustworthiness of this miracle was confirmed when blessed Francis appeared to a certain religious man named Roberto. When the man asked who he was, he replied, "I am Francis who came to heal a friend of mine."

[115]In Sicily he wondrously freed a man named Pietro, who was suffering from a rupture of the genitals, after the man had promised to visit the saint's tomb.

Wis 5:2

Mt 1:20

Is 40:26;
Lk 5:10; 13:12

Chapter XIV
THE BLIND, THE DEAF AND THE MUTE

[116]A brother named Roberto of the residence[a] of the brothers in Naples had been blind for many years. Excess flesh grew in his eyes and impeded the movement and use of his eyelids. Many brothers from other places had gathered there on their way to different parts of the world. The blessed father Francis, that mirror and exemplar of holy obedience, in order to encourage them on their journey with a

---

a. This first appearance of the Latin word *conventus* [convent] indicates a change in vocabulary. Previously the words *locus* [place] and *eremitorum* [hermitage] were used to refer to the places where brothers stayed. While Thomas uses *conventus* elsewhere (1C 123, 124), he does so in his reference to the sacred gathering of the pope and cardinals. Niermeyer indicates that in the twelfth and thirteenth centuries *conventus* referred to a general assembly, synod, or church council. Its interpretation as a gathering place—*con-venire*—appears only sporadically to an assembly of monks. Cf. Jan Frederik Niermeyer, *Mediae Latinitatis Lexicon Minus* (Leiden, New York, Köln, E.J. Brill, 1976), 270. This the only instance of the word's use in these hagiographical documents.

new miracle, healed the aforesaid brother in their presence in this way.

One night Brother Roberto lay deathly ill and his soul had already been commended, when suddenly the blessed father appeared to him along with three brothers, perfect in holiness, Saint Anthony,[a] Brother Agostino,[b] and Brother Giacomo of Assisi.[c] Just as these three had followed him perfectly in their lives, so they readily accompanied him after death. Saint Francis took a knife and cut away the excess flesh, restored his sight and snatched him from the jaws of death, saying, "Roberto, my son, the favor I have done for you is a sign to the brothers on their way to distant countries that I go before

Ps 40:3 them and *guide their steps*. May they go forth joyfully and fulfill the charge of obedience with enthusiasm! Let the sons of obedience rejoice, who have left their own land, forgetting their earthly homeland: they have an active leader and caring forerunner!"

[117]In Zancato, a village near Anagni,[d] a knight named Gerardo had entirely lost his sight. It happened that two Lesser Brothers arriving from abroad sought out his home for hospitality. The whole household received them with honor and treated them with every kindness. The brothers gave no notice to the blindness of their host. After their stay, the two brothers journeyed to the brothers' place six miles away and stayed there eight days. One night blessed Francis

Mt 2:13 *appeared* to one of the brothers *in a dream* with the command: " *Get up*, hurry with your companion to the home of your host. He honored me through you and on account of me was so graciously kind! Show your thanks for your delightful reception and repay honor to the honorable! For the man is sightless and blind, and that is what he de-

Jb 3:5 serves for the sins he has not yet confessed. The *shadows of* eternal *death* await him, and unending torture is his lot. He is bound to this by the misdeeds he has not let go."

When the father had gone, the son got up stunned and hurried with his companion to carry out the command. Both of the brothers returned to their host together, and the one related what he had seen

Est 15:9 *all in order*. The man was quite astonished as he confirmed the truth of all he heard. He broke out in tears, freely made his confession and promised amendment. As soon as the inner man was thus renewed, he recovered the outer light of his eyesight. The greatness of this

---

a. Anthony of Padua; cf. 3C 1, supra 318 b; 3C 3.

b. See 2C 218.

c. According to *The Book of Praises* by Bernard of Besse 1 (hereafter BPr), he is the brother mentioned in 1C 110 and 2C 217a.

d. On the presence of the brothers in Anagni, see AF IV, 517.

miracle spread everywhere and encouraged all who heard of it to extend the gift of hospitality.

[118]A blind woman of Thebes in Romania,[a] spent the vigil of Saint Francis fasting on bread and water, and was led by her husband at early dawn of the feast to the church of the brothers.[b] During the celebration of the Mass, at the elevation of the Body of Christ, she opened her eyes, saw clearly, and devoutly adored. In the very act of adoration she broke into a loud cry, "Thanks be to God and to his saint," she cried, "I see the Body of Christ!" All those present broke *into cries of gladness*. After the Mass the woman *returned to her home* using her own sight.

Ps 47:2; Lk 1:56

> Christ was a light to Francis while he lived,
> and just as then he attributed all of his wonders to Christ,
> so now he wishes that all glory be given to His Body.

[119]A fourteen-year-old boy from the village of Pofi in Campania[c] suffered a sudden attack and completely lost use of his left eye. The acuteness of the blow thrust the eye out of its socket so that it hung by a weak, inch-long strip of flesh; after eight days it had nearly dried up. Cutting it off seemed the only choice when medical remedies proved hopeless. Then the boy's father turned his *whole mind* to the help of blessed Francis, and the tireless helper of the afflicted did not fail the prayers of his petitioner. He marvelously returned the dried eye to its socket and restored its former vigor with the rays of light so longed for.

Mk 12:30

[120]In the same province, at Castro dei Volsci, an immense beam fell from a high place and crushed the skull of a priest, blinding his left eye. Flat on the ground, he began to cry out mournfully to Saint Francis, "Help me, holy father, so that I can go to your feast as I promised your brothers!" It was the vigil of the saint's feast. He quickly got up fully recovered and broke into shouts of praise and joy. And all the bystanders who were lamenting his accident were amazed and jubilant. He went to the feast and there told everyone how he had experienced the power and mercy of the saint. This was a lesson to all that they should devoutly venerate the saint whom they know will so readily assist them.

---

a. See 3C 88, supra, 354 a.

b. Concerning the church, see AF IV, 533.

c. The same village appears in 50, above. This incident is briefly mentioned in *The Legend for Use in the Choir* 15 (hereafter LCh).

1C 67

[121]While blessed Francis was still alive, a woman of Narni, afflicted with blindness, miraculously received the sight she had lost when the man of God made the sign of the cross over her eyes.

[122]A man named Pietro Romano from Monte Gargano[a] was working in his vineyard and while he was cutting wood with a blade struck his own eye and sliced it in half, so that part of the pupil was hanging out. Since the danger was desperate and he despaired that human help could save him, he promised that he would eat nothing on the feast of Saint Francis if the saint would help him. Right then the saint of God replaced the man's eye to its proper place, closed the wound and restored his earlier sight.

Jn 9:1

[123]The son of a nobleman *was born blind* and obtained the sight he longed for through the merits of blessed Francis. He was called Illuminato,[b] named for the event. When he was old enough he joined the Order of Saint Francis and finally fulfilled a holy beginning with an even holier ending.

2C 114

[124]Bevagna is a noble town in the valley of Spoleto. In it there lived a holy woman with an even holier daughter, a virgin, and a niece very devoted to Christ. Saint Francis several times enjoyed their hospitality, for the woman had a son in the Order, a man of outstanding virtue. One of them, however, the niece, was deprived of bodily sight, though her inner sight, which sees God, was sharp and clear. Saint Francis was once asked to take pity on the girl's infirmity

Jn 9:1

and to consider all their hard work. He *smeared the eyes* of the blind girl *with* his *saliva* three times in the name of the Trinity, and thus restored to her the sight she desired.

1C 147-8

[125]In Città della Pieve there was a young man, a beggar who was

Jn 9:1

deaf and mute *from birth*. His tongue was so short and stubby that, to those who many times examined it, it seemed to be completely cut out. A man named Marco received him as a guest for God's sake. When the youth saw the good will shown him, he stayed on with him.

One evening that man was dining with his wife, while the boy stood by. He said to his wife, "I would consider it the greatest miracle if blessed Francis were to give back to this boy his hearing and

Ps 132:2

speech. I vow to God," he added, "that if Saint Francis in his goodness will do this, for the love of him I will support this boy as long as he lives." A marvelous promise indeed! Suddenly the boy's

Gn 8:15

tongue grew, and he spoke, saying, "Long live Saint Francis! I see him standing above me, and he has granted me speech and

---

a. Site of the important pilgrimage sanctuary of Saint Michael, in Apulia.
b. That is, "enlightened."

hearing! **What will I tell the people?"** His foster father replied, **"You**   Ps 69:31; 36:70
shall praise God, and you shall save many people." The people of
that region, who had known the youth previously, were filled with
the greatest wonder.

[126]A woman in the region of Apulia had long ago lost the ability to
speak and to breathe freely. One night while she slept the Virgin
Mary appeared to her and said, "If you want to be cured, go to the
church of Saint Francis in Venosa; there you will receive the cure you
desire." The woman got up, and since she could neither breathe nor
speak, she indicated by signs to her relatives that she wanted to
travel to Venosa. Her relatives agreed and accompanied her to the
place. When the woman entered the church of Saint Francis, she
poured out her heartfelt request, and immediately she vomited a
mass of flesh and was marvelously healed in the sight of all.

[127]A woman in the diocese of Arezzo had been mute for seven
years. She continually sent her wish to the ears of God, that He
would see fit to loose her tongue. Amazing! While she slept two
brothers dressed in red appeared and gently instructed her to vow
herself to Saint Francis. She willingly took their advice and vowed in
her heart, since she could not speak. She was soon roused, and on
waking her speech returned.

[128]People were amazed when a judge named Alessandro, who had
belittled the miracles of blessed Francis, was deprived of speech for
more than six years. Great repentance overcame him, when he rec-
ognized that a man *is tormented by the very things through which he sins,*   Wis 11:16
and he was sorry that he had ridiculed the saint's miracles. So the
saint's anger did not last, and he restored his favor by repairing the
man's speech, since he was repentant and humbly invoked him.
From then on the judge dedicated his blasphemous tongue to praise
of the blessed father. His suffering greatly increased his devotion.

[129]Since we have mentioned blasphemy, another event deserves
mention. A knight named Gineldo from Borgo in the province of
Massa shamelessly dismissed the works and miraculous signs of
blessed Francis. He taunted the pilgrims on their way to observe the
saint's feast, and he publicly babbled foolishness against the brothers.

One day while he was playing dice, in his madness and disbelief
he said to the bystanders, "If Francis is a saint, let's see the dice roll
eighteen!" On the next roll the dice showed three 6's, and for the
next nine rolls, three 6's appeared each time. But the madman persisted; he added sin upon sin and piled blasphemy upon blasphemy.
"If it's true that this Francis is a saint," he cried, "let my body fall by
the sword today, and if he's not a saint, I'll be unharmed!" Scarcely

Ps 78:21, 31; Ps 109:7
had the *anger of God risen* than by divine judgment *his prayer was turned to sin*! As the game ended, he insulted his nephew, and the latter drew his sword and bloodied it with his uncle's bowels. The accursed

1 Thes 5:5
man died the same day and became a slave of hell and a *son of darkness*.

Let blasphemers beware! Words do not fly off with the wind, and there is One who avenges insults to the saints.

[130]A woman named Sibilla suffered from blindness in her eyes for many years. She was led to the tomb of the man of God, blind and dejected. She recovered her sight and, rejoicing and exulting, returned home. 1C 136

[131]In the village of Vico Albo in the diocese of Sora, a girl who had been born blind was taken by her mother to an oratory of blessed Francis. Invoking the name of Christ, and through the merits of blessed Francis, she deserved to receive the sight that she never had.

[132]In the city of Arezzo, in the church of blessed Francis built near the city, a woman who had not been able to see for seven years recovered the sight she had lost.

[133]In the same city the son of a poor woman was granted sight by blessed Francis when she vowed him to the saint.

[134]At the tomb of the holy body, a blind man from Spello recovered his sight, which he had lost long before. 1C 136

[135]In Poggibonsi of the diocese of Florence there was a blind woman who, because of a revelation, began to visit an oratory dedicated to blessed Francis. When she was brought there and lay pitiably before the altar, she suddenly received her sight and found her way home without a guide.

[136]Another woman, from Camerino, was totally blind in her right eye. Her parents covered the damaged eye with a cloth that the blessed Francis had touched. After making a vow, they gave thanks to the Lord God and Saint Francis for restoring her sight. 1C 136

[137]A similar thing happened to a woman of Gubbio who, after making a vow, rejoiced on recovering her vision. 1C 136

[138]A citizen of Assisi was blind for five years. While the blessed Francis was still living, he was friendly to him, so whenever he prayed to the blessed man, he would recall their former friendship. He was cured as soon as he touched his tomb. 1C 136

[139]Albertino from Narni was totally blind for about a year, for his eyelids hung down over his eyes. Vowing himself to the blessed Francis, his sight was immediately restored; then he prepared himself and went to his glorious tomb. 1C 136

1C 149

¹⁴⁰A young man named Villa could neither walk nor speak. His mother made a wax image for him and carried it with great reverence to the resting place of the blessed father Francis. When she returned home, she found her son walking and talking.

1C 149

¹⁴¹There was a man in the diocese of Perugia who was unable to utter a word. His mouth was always open, and he gaped and gasped horribly, for his throat was swollen and inflamed. When he came to the place where the most holy body rested and started going down the steps to the tomb, he vomited much blood. And he was entirely cured and began to speak, opening and closing his mouth in a normal way.

1C 150

¹⁴²A woman had a stone in her throat. Due to a violently feverish condition, her tongue stuck to her palate. She could neither speak nor eat, nor drink. After many medicines were tried she felt no comfort or relief. She made a vow to Saint Francis in her heart, and suddenly the flesh opened and she spat the stone from her throat.

¹⁴³Bartholomew from the village of Arpino in the diocese of Sora had been deaf for seven years and recovered his hearing by invoking the name of blessed Francis.

¹⁴⁴A woman from the village of Piazza in Sicily was deprived of her speech. When she prayed to Saint Francis with the tongue of her heart she regained the desired gift of speech.

¹⁴⁵In the town of Nicosia, a priest arose as usual for matins and when asked by the lector for the usual blessing, he uttered some barbarous threat. He was then confined at home, out of his mind, and totally lost his speech for a month. At the suggestion of some man of God he vowed himself to Saint Francis, and was freed of his madness and regained his speech.

Chapter XV
LEPERS AND HEMORRHAGICS

1C 146

¹⁴⁶At San Severino there was a young man named Atto who was covered with leprosy. All his limbs were stretched and swollen; he looked at everything with an unpleasant expression. Spending all his time in misery on his sickbed, he brought great sorrow to his parents. One day his father came to him and suggested that he dedicate himself to blessed Francis. The youth happily agreed, so the father had the wick of a candle brought, and with it he measured his son's height. The youth then vowed each year to bring a candle of this length to blessed Francis. Having made his vow, he immediately rose from his bed, cleansed of his leprosy.

¹⁴⁷Another man, named Buonuomo, from the city of Fano was a   1C 146
leper and paralytic. His parents brought him to the church of blessed
Francis, and there he recovered his health completely of both illnesses.

Mt 9:20

Lk 11:38

¹⁴⁸A noblewoman named Rogata, from the diocese of Sora, had   LCh 16
suffered from hemorrhages for twenty-three years. One day she heard a
boy singing in Roman dialect a song about the miracles that God had
worked in those days through blessed Francis.^a Sadness overwhelmed her, and as she broke into tears her faith moved her *to say
within herself:* "O blessed father Francis, so many miracles radiate
from you: if only you would see fit to free me of my illness! You have
not yet done such a great miracle." For the flow of blood was so great
that it often appeared that the woman would soon breathe her last,
and whenever the flow of blood was stopped, her whole body swelled
up. What happened? A few days later she felt herself freed through
the merits of blessed Francis.

Her son Mario, who had a withered arm, after a single vow was
cured by the saint of God.

¹⁴⁹Blessed Francis, Christ's standard bearer, also healed a woman   LCh 16
from Sicily who was worn out by suffering a flow of blood for seven
years.

Chapter XVI
THE INSANE AND POSSESSED

¹⁵⁰There was a man from Foligno named Pietro, who went one   1C 137
time on a pilgrimage to the shrine of blessed Michael; he drank
from a fountain, when he saw himself drinking up demons. From
then he was possessed for three years, was physically run down,
vile in speech, and dreadful in expression. Finally, as soon as he
touched the tomb of the blessed father and humbly invoked his
power, he was marvelously delivered from the demons that so cruelly tormented him.

Mt 2:13

¹⁵¹Saint Francis appeared *in a dream* to a woman in the city of   1C 138
Narni who was possessed by a devil and commanded her to make the
sign of the cross. In her mental state the woman did not know how,
so the blessed father made the sign of the cross on her and released
her from the devil's control.

---

a. Such songs have not been preserved.

¹⁵²A woman in the Marittima[a] had lost her mind for five years and was unable to see or hear. She tore her clothes with her teeth and had no fear of the dangers of fire or water. And lately she suffered terribly from falling sickness she had contracted.

One night, as divine mercy prepared to show her mercy, she drifted into a healing sleep. She saw blessed Francis *seated on a* beautiful *throne,* and prostrate before him she humbly begged for her health. As he still had not granted her request, she made a vow, promising for love of him never to refuse alms, as long as she had them, to anyone who asked. The saint immediately recognized the same pact he had once made with God,[b] and signing her with the sign of the cross he restored her to full health.

¹⁵³A girl of Norcia appeared listless for some time and it was eventually clear she was troubled by a devil. For she would often gnash her teeth and tear at herself. She would not avoid dangerous heights, nor did she fear any hazard. Then she lost her speech and was deprived of the use of her limbs, and became totally irrational.

Her parents were tormented by the confusion of their offspring; they tied her on a stretcher mounted on a draft animal and took her to Assisi. During the celebration of Mass on the feast of the Lord's Circumcision, she lay prone before the altar of Saint Francis. Suddenly she vomited some damnable thing—I can't say what—and then got up on her feet. She kissed the altar of Saint Francis, and now fully free of her illness she shouted, *"Praise the Lord and His holy one!"*

¹⁵⁴The son of a nobleman was tormented by falling sickness, no less horrible than painful. He foamed at the mouth and he looked at everything with a wild expression, and from his abused limbs he would spit out—I can't say what—something diabolical. His parents cried out to the saint of God, begging a cure, and offering their pitiful son to his feelings of pity. So the friend of mercy appeared one night to the mother while she slept and said to her, "See, I have come now to save your son." The woman was awakened by his voice and got up trembling, and found her son fully cured.

¹⁵⁵What great power Francis demonstrated over demons in his lifetime, should not, in my judgment, be kept secret.

One time the man of God was proclaiming the good news of the kingdom of God in a village of San Gemini. He received hospitality from a God-fearing man whose wife was troubled by a demon, as all were aware. When blessed Francis was asked to help her, he refused, because he feared the peoples' applause. Since so many

Is 6:1

Ps 150:1

1C 69

Lk 8:1; Mt 5:20
Acts 10:1-2
Mt 15:22

a. See 3C 111, supra, 364 a.
b. Cf. 1C 17; 2C 5.

Jdt 6:16

people kept asking, he set the three brothers who were with him in three corners, and he went to the fourth to pray. When *the prayer was finished* Francis confidently approached the woman, who was twisting miserably, and ordered the demon to depart *in the name* of Jesus Christ. It left with such swiftness at his command that the man of God thought he was deceived, and for this reason he left that place, ashamed.

Acts 3:6

1 Kgs 4:9, 16

That is why when he passed through that same place on another occasion, that woman ran down the street and cried out after him. She kissed his footprints asking him to speak to her. Reassured by many of her deliverance, he finally acceded to the many who asked him to speak with her.

Mt 15:23

Est 13:13

1C 70

¹⁵⁶Another time, at Città di Castello, there was a woman who *had a demon.* She was led to the house where he was staying and stood outside, gnashing her teeth, disturbing everyone with her barking. Many people had in fact humbly asked the saint of God to free her, since they had for so long been disturbed by her madness. Blessed Francis sent out to her the brother who was with him, since he wished to check whether it was a demon or the woman's deception. But she knew that he was not the holy man, Francis, so she mocked and belittled him. The holy father was inside praying, and once his prayer was finished, he came outside to the woman. She could not bear his presence, and she shook and rolled on the ground. God's saint commanded the demon to leave her by virtue of obedience. It departed immediately and left the woman unharmed.

Lk 4:33

Jn 20:11

Chapter XVII
THE CRIPPLED AND LAME

¹⁵⁷In the county of Parma a man had a son born with a foot reversed, that is, with the heel forward and the toes at the back. The man was poor, but devoted to Saint Francis. He complained daily to Saint Francis about his son who was born to be ridiculed, constantly adding to his poverty. He had thought about forcibly returning the tender boy's foot to its proper place, and with the nurse's permission he prepared to do just that while the boy's limbs were softening in the bath. But before he could attempt anything so rash, as the boy was being unswaddled he was found, through the merits of Saint Francis, as sound as if he had never been deformed.

¹⁵⁸ At Scoppito in Amiternoᵃ a man and wife had but one son, but he was the cause of daily lament, a sort of disgrace to their family

---

a. The place is thought to have been near the ancient Amiterno, a town above Aquila.

line. For he appeared to be more monster than human, for, contrary
to the order of nature, his forward limbs were twisted to the back. His
forearms were joined to his neck, his knees to his chest, and his feet
joined to his buttocks, making him appear more like a ball than a
body. He was kept out of the sight of relatives and neighbors so they
could not see him: his parents certainly acted out of sadness, but
even more out of shame. In his sorrow the husband reproached his
wife for not producing children like other women, but monsters
worse than any dumb brutes. He perversely blamed his wife's sin for
this judgment of God. The wife was downcast and filled with shame.
She constantly poured out her sorrow to Christ, and invoked the help
of Saint Francis, to see fit to lift her from her unhappy and shameful
condition.

One night, while she was overcome with sad sleep because of her
sad state, Saint Francis appeared to her and kindly addressed these
soothing words to her: "Get up and take the boy to the place nearby
dedicated to my name.[a] There bathe the boy in the water of the well.
As soon as you pour that water over the boy, he will be restored to full
health." The woman failed to carry out the saint's command about
the boy, so Saint Francis appeared a second time with the same orders, but the woman still did not comply. The saint kindly took pity
on her simplicity and found a marvelous way to *increase his mercy*. He   Hos 1:6
appeared to her a third time, this time accompanied by the glorious
Virgin and the noble band of the holy Apostles. He took her, together
with her son, and in an instant transported them to the door of that
place.

Dawn was breaking and the bodily vision had completely disappeared. The woman was stunned and wondering beyond belief as
she knocked at the door. Her story aroused no little wonder among
the brothers, since she was totally confident of a cure for her son: it
was promised three times through an oracle. Then a group of noble
women from the area arrived there out of devotion, and when they
heard what had happened they too were in awe. They immediately
drew some water from the well, and the noblest among them bathed
the child with her own hands. The boy instantly appeared healthy,
with all his limbs in their proper place. The greatness of this miracle
aroused wonder in them all.

[159]In the village of Cori of the diocese of Ostia, a man had so totally
lost the use of a leg that he could not walk or move at all. He was thus
confined in bitter agony and had lost hope in any human assistance.

---

a. Probably the church at Aquila; cf. AF IV, 530.

One night he began to spell out his complaint to blessed Francis as if he saw him there present. "Help me, Saint Francis! Think of all my service and devotion to you. I carried you on my donkey; I kissed your holy hands and feet. I was always devoted to you, always gracious, and, as you see, I am dying of the torture of this harsh suffering." The saint was moved by his complaint and gratefully recalled his good deeds and devotion. Along with one brother he appeared to the man keeping vigil, saying that he had come to him because he had been called, and that he brought the means of healing with him. He touched the source of the pain with a small stick bearing the figure of the "Tau." The abscess healed quickly, his full health was restored, and to this day the sign of the "Tau" remains on the spot.[a]

Saint Francis signed his letters with this sign whenever charity or necessity led him to send something in writing.

[160]A young girl was brought to his tomb who, for over a year, had suffered a deformity in her neck so hideous that her head rested on her shoulder and she could only look sideways. She put her head for a little while beneath the coffin in which the precious body of the saint rested, and through the merits of that most holy man she was immediately able to straighten her neck, and her head was restored to its proper position. At this the girl was so overwhelmed at the sudden change in herself that she started to run away and to cry. There was a depression in her shoulder where her head had been when it was twisted out of position by her prolonged affliction.

1C 128

[161]In the district of Narni there was a boy whose leg was bent back so severely that he could not walk at all without the aid of two canes. He had been burdened with that affliction since his infancy; he had no idea who his father and mother were, and had become a beggar. This boy was completely freed from his affliction by the merits of our blessed father Francis so that he could freely go where he wished without a cane.

1C 129

[162]A certain Niccolò, a citizen of Foligno, was so crippled in his left leg that it caused him extreme pain; as a result he spent so much on doctors in his endeavor to restore his health that he went more deeply into debt than he could ever hope to pay. Finally, when the help of physicians had proven worthless, he was suffering such extreme pain that his neighbors could not sleep at night because of his moaning cries. Then dedicating himself to God and to Saint Francis, he had himself carried to the tomb of the saint.

1C 127

---

a. Cf. 2C 106, supra, 235 b; 3C 3.

After spending a night in prayer at the saint's tomb, his crippled leg was cured and, overflowing with joy, he returned home without a cane.

1C 130 [163]A boy had one leg so deformed that his knee was pressed against his chest and his heel against his buttocks. He was carried to the tomb of the blessed Francis, while his father was mortifying his own flesh with a hair shirt and his mother was performing severe penance for him. Suddenly the boy had his health fully restored.

1C 131 [164]In the city of Fano there was a man who was crippled with his legs doubled up under him. They were covered with sores that gave off such a foul odor that the hospice staff refused to take him in or keep him. But then he asked the blessed father Francis for mercy and, through his merits, in a short time he rejoiced in being cured.

1C 132 [165]There was also a little girl in Gubbio; her hands and all her limbs were so crippled that for over a year she was totally unable to use them. Carrying a wax image, her nurse brought her to the tomb of the blessed father Francis to seek the favor of a cure. After she had been there for eight days, on the last day all her limbs were restored to their proper functions so that she was considered well enough to return to her activities.

1C 133 [166]There was another boy from Montenero lying for several days in front of the doors of the church where the body of Saint Francis rested. He could not walk or sit up, since he was completely paralyzed from the waist down. One day he got into the church and touched the tomb of the blessed father Francis. When he came back outside, he was completely cured. Moreover, the young boy himself reported that while he was lying in front of the tomb of the glorious saint, a young man was there with him clothed in the habit of the brothers, on top of the tomb. The young man was carrying some pears in his hands, and he called the boy. Offering him a pear, he encouraged him to get up. The boy took the pear from the young man's hand, and answered: "See, I am crippled and cannot get up at all!" He ate the pear given to him, and then started to put out his hand for another pear that the young man offered him. The young man again encouraged him to stand up, but the boy, feeling weighed down with his illness, did not get up. But while the boy reached out his hand, the young man holding out the pear took hold of his hand and led him outside. Then he vanished from sight. When the boy saw that he was cured, he began to cry at the top of his voice, telling everyone what had happened to him.

1C 134

¹⁶⁷After another citizen from Gubbio brought his crippled son on a stretcher to the tomb of the glorious father, he received him back whole and sound, though before he had been so crippled and deformed that his legs were completely withered and drawn up under him.

¹⁶⁸In the diocese of Volterra a man named Riccomagno could scarcely drag himself along the ground with his hands. His own mother had abandoned him on account of his monstrous swelling. He humbly vowed himself to blessed Francis and was instantly healed.

¹⁶⁹Two women named Verde and Sanguigna, from the same diocese, were so crippled that they could not move about unless carried by others. They had stripped the skin from their hands attempting to move themselves. By their vow alone were they restored to health.

¹⁷⁰A certain Giacomo from Poggibonsi was so pitiably bent and crippled that his mouth touched his knees. His widowed mother took him to an oratory of blessed Francis and poured out her prayer to the Lord for his recovery; she brought him home healthy and whole.

¹⁷¹A woman from Vicalvi with a withered hand had it restored to match the other through the merits of the holy father.

¹⁷²In the city of Capua a woman vowed to visit in person the tomb of blessed Francis. Because of the press of household matters she forgot her vow, and suddenly lost the use of her right side. On account of pinched nerves she was unable to turn her head or arm in any direction. She had so much pain that she wore her neighbors out with her constant wailing. Two of the brothers happened to pass by her home, and at a priest's request they stopped to visit the pitiful woman. She confessed to them her unfulfilled vow, and when she received their blessing she at once arose healthy. And now that she was made wiser by punishment, she fulfilled her vow without delay.

1C 135

¹⁷³Bartolomeo, from Narni, was sleeping in the shade of a tree when a diabolical seizure left him without use of a leg and a foot. Since he was a very poor man, he did not know where to turn. But that lover of the poor, Francis, Christ's standard bearer, *appeared to him in a dream* and ordered him to go to a certain place. He set out to drag himself there, but had left the direct route when he heard a voice saying to him: *"Peace be with you! I am the one to whom you vowed yourself."* Then leading him to the spot, it seemed that he placed one hand upon his foot and the other upon his leg, and thus restored his crippled limbs. This man *was advanced in years* and had been crippled for six years.

Mt 2:13

Acts 9:4; Dn 10:

Jos 13:1

¹⁷⁴He also performed many such powerful signs while he was still living in the flesh.

Thus when he was once passing through the diocese of Rieti he came to a village where a tearful woman carried her eight-year-old son in her arms and laid him at his feet. The boy for four years had been so hugely swollen that he could not see his legs. The saint took him kindly and passed his truly holy hands over his abdomen. The swelling went down at his touch and the boy was soon healthy. He joined his joyous mother in giving boundless thanks to God and to his saint.

¹⁷⁵**A knight of the city of Tuscanella took in blessed Francis as his guest.** The man *had only one son, who was lame and had no bodily strength. Although the young boy was no longer being breast fed, he was still sleeping in a cradle. The knight humbly* fell down at his feet, begging him for his son's health. The saint considered himself unworthy of such grace, and said so, but at last was overcome by the persistence of the father's entreaties; he prayed, he signed the boy and blessed him. Immediately the boy stood up and, with the onlookers rejoicing, began to walk all around.

¹⁷⁶Another time when he came to Narni, a man of that city named Pietro was bedridden as a paralytic. Hearing that God's saint had come to Narni, he sent a message to the bishop of the city requesting him to send the servant of the most high God to heal him. This man had been so deprived of the use of all his members, that he could only move his tongue and blink his eyes. The blessed Francis came to him, made the sign of the cross over him from head to toe, and, as the affliction vanished, immediately restored him to his earlier health.

¹⁷⁷At Gubbio, there was a woman with both hands so crippled that she was unable to handle anything with them. When she knew that the man of God had entered the city, she immediately ran to him. With a sad and mournful face, she showed him her crippled hands and begged him to touch them. He was moved by great pity. He touched her hands and healed them. The woman immediately returned home full of joy, made a cheesecake with her own hands, and offered it to the holy man. He kindly took a little of that cake because of the woman's friendly devotion and told her to eat the rest of it with her family.

¹⁷⁸One time Francis went to stay as a guest in the city of Orte. There a boy named Giacomo, who had lain curled up for a long time, came to him with his parents and begged a healing from the saint. After his long infirmity the boy's head was bent to his knees and

some of his bones were broken. As soon as Saint Francis made a sign of blessing over him, he began to uncoil. He straightened up fully and was completely cured.

[179]A neighbor from that same city had a tumor the size of a large loaf of bread between his shoulders. When he was blessed by Saint Francis he was instantly so fully cured that not a trace of his tumor remained.

[180]There was a young man whom everyone knew in the hospital at Città di Castello. He had been crippled for seven years and dragged himself along the ground like an animal. His mother implored Saint Francis for him many times, asking him to restore her snake-like son to a normal walk. When the saint heard the mother's mournful plea and accepted her vow, he immediately loosed the horrible bonds and restored her son to his natural freedom.

[181]Prassede was among the best known religious women in the City and in Roman circles. From her tender infancy she had, for love of her eternal Spouse, withdrawn for nearly forty years to a narrow cell. She earned the favor of a special friendship with Saint Francis. He did for her what he did for no other woman: he received her to obedience,[a] and with pious devotion gave her the habit of the Religion, that is, the tunic and cord.

One day in the course of her tasks, under some imaginary impulse, she went up to the attic of her cell, and by a cruel accident fell to the ground. Her foot and leg were both broken and her shoulder was totally separated from its joint. This virgin of Christ had for many years been withdrawn from the view of everyone, and she firmly intended to remain so. But she now lay on the ground like a tree trunk without anyone to help her, and she did not know where to turn. She had been advised by religious persons and ordered by a cardinal to break her confinement and to accept the assistance of some religious women, and thus to guard against the danger of death that could occur from negligence or neglect. She steadfastly refused to do this, and resisted every way she could to avoid breaking her vow even slightly. She thus cast herself with urgency at the feet

Mk 6:47 of divine mercy, and *as evening drew on* she poured out her pious complaints to the blessed father Francis. "My holy father, you so kindly respond anywhere to the needs of so many whom you did not know while you were in the flesh, why do you not help me in my misery since I merited your sweet favor while you were alive? As you can see, blessed father, I must either change my promised way of life or submit to a death sentence." While she repeated these expressions with

---

a. Cf. ER XII 4, where this is prohibited.

her heart and mouth, and expressed her miserable condition with
rising sobs, she was suddenly overcome by sleep and fell *into a trance.*   Acts 11:5

Behold, her kindly father, clothed in white, *in glorious garments,*   Is 52:1
came down into her dark cell and began to speak to her in sweet
words, "Get up, *beloved daughter, get up and do not fear!* Receive the sign   Ru 3:10; Lk 6:8. 1:30
of complete healing and keep your promise intact!" Then *he took her*   Mk 9:27
by the hand and lifted her up, and disappeared. She turned here and
there in the cell, not realizing what the servant of God had done for
her. She still thought she was *seeing a vision.*   Acts 12:9

Finally she went to the window and made the usual sign. A monk
came right away, and marveling beyond belief said to her, "What
happened, mother, to enable you to get up?" But she still thought she
was dreaming and that it was not really he, so she told him to light
the fire. When the lamp was brought, she *recovered her senses.* She felt   Acts 12:11
no pain and proceeded to recount *in order all* that had happened.   Est 15:9

Chapter XVIII
Various Miracles

[182]An eighty-year-old woman from the diocese of Sabino had two
daughters. When one of them died, her infant son was given to the
other to nurse. Then when this one conceived a child with her husband, the milk in her breasts stopped. No one could be found to help
the orphaned child, no one to provide a drop of milk for the thirsty
baby. The fretful old woman was distressed over her grandson, but
since she was extremely poor, she did not know where to turn. As the
boy grew weaker and faded, the compassionate grandmother was
dying with him. The old woman *went about through streets and houses*   Sg 3:2
and no one could escape her cries.

One night she put her withered breast in the boy's mouth to alleviate his squalling, and tearfully begged for the help and advice of
blessed Francis. The lover of the age of innocence was immediately
there, to show his usual mercy to the miserable. "Woman," he said,
"I am Francis whom you called with so many tears. Put your breasts
in the baby's mouth, for the Lord will give you milk in abundance."
The old woman did what she was told, and straightaway her
eighty-year-old breasts filled with milk.

This became known to all who saw with their own eyes, to their
amazement, that the bent old woman glowed with the warmth of
youth. Many came to see; among them was the count of that province, who had to admit from experience what he doubted about the
rumor. When the count arrived and was investigating everything

that happened, the wrinkled old woman squirted a stream of milk on him, and chased him away with this sprinkling.

Ps 103:20; 136:4
Therefore, let *everyone bless the Lord, who alone does great wonders*, and venerate with eager homage His servant Saint Francis. The boy grew quickly on this marvelous nourishment and soon outgrew his need for it.

[183]A man named Martino took his oxen far from home to find pasture. The leg of one ox was accidentally broken so badly that Martin could think of no remedy. He was concerned about getting the hide, but since he had no knife, he returned home and left the ox in the care of Saint Francis, lest wolves devour it before his return. Early next morning he returned to the ox with his skinning knife, but found the ox grazing peacefully; its broken leg could not be distin-
Jn 10:11; Lk 10:34
guished from the other. He thanked *the good shepherd* who *took* such loving *care* of him, and procured the remedy.

[184]Another man from Amiterno had three years earlier lost one of his draft animals by theft, and he took his complaint to Saint Francis and threw himself lamenting before him.

One night, when he had fallen asleep, he heard a voice saying to
Acts 11:7
him: "Get up, go to Spoleto[a] and bring back your animal from there." When he woke up, he wondered about the voice, and went back to sleep. When he was called again and had the same vision, he turned to ask who it was. "I am," he said, "that Francis whom you requested." He still feared that it was all an illusion, so he put off doing what he was told. But when he was called a third time he devoutly obeyed the reminder.

He went to Spoleto; he found the animal, which was generously returned to him in good health, and he led it home. He told everyone everywhere about the incident and became a lasting servant of Saint Francis.

[185]A man of Antrodoco bought a beautiful bowl and gave it to his wife to treasure. One day the wife's maid took the bowl and put clothes in it with lye for washing. But the heat of the sun and the caustic lye broke the bowl to pieces and made it useless. The trembling maid took the bowl to her lady and showed her what had happened, more with tears than with words. The wife too was shaken; she feared her husband's anger and expected a beating. For the time being she carefully hid the bowl and called on the merits of Saint Francis, asking his favor. At the saint's command the broken parts came together, the cracks were sealed and the bowl was intact. The

---

a. The town here and below should probably be "Scopleto," which is about five miles or nine kilometers from Amiterno, not "Spoleto," which is too far away to go looking for an ox.

neighbors who had first feared for the woman now rejoiced with her, and the wife was the first to tell the news of the amazing event to her husband.

[186]A man from Monte dell'Olmo[a] in the Marches one day was attaching the iron blade to his plow when the blade broke into several pieces. The man was saddened by the broken blade and even more by the loss of produce. So he cried, "O Blessed Francis, help me who trusts in your mercy! I will give your brothers an annual share of the grain, and I will do jobs for them, if I might now experience your favor that so many others have experienced." When he finished his prayer, the iron was rejoined and the blade was whole. Not a trace of the fracture remained.

LCh 16

[187]A cleric from Vicalvi named Matteo *drank* some *deadly poison.* He was obviously ill, and was so afflicted that he could not speak at all; he awaited only his end. Even a priest who encouraged him to confess could not pry a single word from him. But he humbly prayed to Christ *in his heart,* to save him through the merits of blessed Francis. Soon after, he tearfully pronounced the name of blessed Francis, and with witnesses present, he vomited up the poison.

Mk 16:18

Ps 14:1

[188]Lord Trasmondo Anibaldi was a consul of the Romans. When he exercised his office in Siena in Tuscany,[b] he had by his side an assistant named Niccolò who was dear to him and always ready for household tasks. When a sudden deadly disease invaded Niccolò's jaw, doctors predicted death was near. The Virgin Mother of Christ appeared while he slept and instructed him to vow himself to Saint Francis and to visit his tomb without delay. When *he got up in the morning,* he recounted the vision to his lord. That lord was amazed and hurried to put it into practice. So the lord accompanied him to Assisi, and before the tomb of Saint Francis he got his friend back quickly healed.

Gn 24:54

This recovery of health was wonderful;
even more wonderful the kindness of the Virgin
who both stooped so kindly to help a sick man
and also raised up the merits of our saint.

[189]This saint knew how to help *all who called upon* him, and he never considered anyone's needs beneath him.

Ps 145:18

---

a. Cf. AF IV, 514.

b. That is, in 1234; cf. *Annales Senenses,* in Muratori, *Rerum Italicarum Scriptores* XV (1729), 25; in *Monumenta Germaniae Historica Scriptum* XIX, 229.

In the Spanish town of San Facondo[a] a man had a cherry tree in his garden; it annually bore *abundant fruit* that *produced a profit* for the gardener. Then the tree dried up and withered from its roots. The master wanted to *cut it down,* so it would not *clutter the ground* any longer, but a neighbor suggested that he put it under blessed Francis's care, and the man agreed. In marvelous fashion, *against hope,* it revived, produced leaves, blossomed, and *produced fruit* in its time, just as before. In thanks for this miracle the owner annually gave its fruit to the brothers.

[190] Around Villesilos an infestation of worms was devastating the vineyards. The townspeople asked the advice of a member of the Order of Preachers about a remedy for the pestilence. He told them to choose any two saints, whomever they wished, and to select one of them by lot and make him their advocate to eradicate the pest. They chose Saint Francis and Saint Dominic. The *choice fell to* Saint Francis, and the people directed their prayers to him, and the pest suddenly and totally disappeared. The people consequently held him in special reverence, and have great affection for his Order. In thanksgiving for the miracle in the vineyards, they each year send a special alms of wine to the brothers.

[191] Near Palencia[b] a priest owned a barn for storing grain, but to the priest's loss it was annually full of weevils, the worms found in grain.[c] The priest was upset with his loss, and searching for a remedy, he assigned blessed Francis to guard the storehouse. Shortly thereafter he found all the weevils dead and heaped outside the barn, and he no longer had to put up with such a pest. The priest felt himself blessed for being heard, and was quite grateful for the favor: for love of Saint Francis he provided an annual ration of grain for the poor.

[192] Some time back, when a plague of locusts devastated the kingdom of Apulia, the lord of the castle of Pietramala humbly put his land under the care of blessed Francis. That land remained, through the merits of the saint, totally unharmed by the vile plague, while the same pestilence devoured *all its surroundings.*

[193] A noble lady of the castle of Galete[d] suffered from an ulcer between her breasts, and it afflicted her both with its pain and its stench. She could find nothing to restore her health. One day by

Lk 2:52;Wis 15:12

Lk 13:7

Rom 4:18

Lk 21:30

Acts 1:26

Jer 21:14

---

a. Today Sahagún.

b. In Old Castile, where there was a friary; cf. AF IV, 536.

c. Classical authors had already identified these *curculiones*; cf. Vergil, *Georgics* I, 186; Pliny, *Historia Naturalis* XVIII, 73, 2.

d. The site cannot be identified; many villages and places in central and southern Italy have similar names.

chance she stopped to pray in the church of the brothers. There she caught sight of a booklet containing the life and miracles of Saint Francis,[a] and she looked through it carefully. When she learned the truth of its contents, she tearfully took it and spread it over the diseased area. "As the things written about you on this page are true, Saint Francis," she said, "may I now be freed of my affliction through your holy merits!" She continued her weeping and praying for awhile, then removed her bandages. She was so completely healed that not even a trace of a scar could be detected.

[194]A similar thing happened in the area of Romania [b] where a father stormed Saint Francis with his humble prayers for his son, who was sick with a serious ulcer. "Saint of God," he prayed, "if all those marvelous things said of you around the world are true, let me experience to the praise of God the kindness of your mercy in my son." Suddenly the bandage was torn away from above, and in the sight of all, pus spurted from the wound, and the boy's flesh appeared intact, so that no sign of his former illness remained.

[195]While blessed Francis was still living in the flesh, a brother suffered from a terrible affliction, because of which he would often fall. He would often have an attack in which all of his limbs were bent into a circle. Sometimes he would be all stretched out and rigid, with his feet level with his head, and then would be lifted up as high as a man stands, then suddenly bounce back to the ground, where he would *roll around foaming* at the mouth. The holy father took pity on him, prayed, and with the sign of the cross healed him, and he was never again troubled by that illness.

[196]After the blessed father's death, another brother had a painful ulcer in his side, so serious that all hope of a cure had been given up. When the brother asked permission of his minister to visit the tomb of blessed Francis, the minister would not give permission, for fear he would incur greater danger from the hardships of the journey. The brother was saddened by this, but blessed Francis one night stood by him and said, "My son, do not be sad any more. Take off the fur you are wearing, and remove that dressing from your wound. Obey your *Rule,* and you will soon be healed." Early *the next morning he rose* and did as the saint commanded, and was immediately healed.

[197] A man was seriously wounded in the head by a metal arrow. He could get no relief from doctors, because the arrow had gone through his eye socket and was embedded in his head. He turned

1C 68

Mk 9:20

1C 145

Gn 19:27

1C 143

---

a. Likely Celano's own 1C, or at least his LCh.
b. See 3C 88, *supra,* 354 a.

Gn 31:24

Sir 13:17

humbly and devoutly to blessed Francis, and while he was resting a bit and sleeping, he heard blessed Francis say *to him in a dream,* that he should have the arrow pulled out through the back of his head. The next day he did what he had *heard* in the dream and without great difficulty he obtained relief.

Chapter XIV
CONCLUSION
OF
THE MIRACLES OF BLESSED FRANCIS

Lk 2:11; Acts 15:11

Jn 20:30

Mk 16:20

1 Cor 4:3

[198]The boundless piety of *Christ the Lord* has confirmed as true
what has been written and published about His saint and our father,
through the signs which accompanied them.
Thus it truly seems absurd to submit *to human judgment*
what has been approved by divine miracle.
I, a humble son of the same father,
humbly beg everyone to receive them kindly,
and to hear them reverently.
Though some may not be worded worthily,
still they are in themselves most worthy
of being treated with reverence.
Do not look down on the author's awkwardness,
but consider his faith, his dedication, and his labor.
We cannot forge something new every day,
nor square circles,
nor bring to agreement
the innumerable variety of times and wishes
that we received in a single block.
We did not set out to write these things to satisfy our vanity.
Nor have we plunged into this set of such differing reports
of our own will.
The insistence of our brothers' requests extorted it,
and the authority of our prelates ordered it.

Rom 1:7

We expect our reward from *Christ the Lord;*
from you, brothers and fathers, we ask grace and love.
So let it be!
Amen.

At the end of this book,
To Christ be praise and glory.

Abbreviations

Writings of Saint Francis

Adm	The Admonitions	LtMin	A Letter to a Minister
BlL	A Blessing for Brother Leo	LtOrd	A Letter to the Entire Order
CtC	The Canticle of the Creatures	LtR	A Letter to Rulers of the Peoples
CtExh	The Canticle of Exhortation	ExhP	Exhortation to the Praise of God
1Frg	Fragments of Worchester Manuscript	PrOF	A Prayer Inspired by the Our Father
2Frg	Fragments of Thomas of Celano	PrsG	The Praises of God
3Frg	Fragments from Hugh of Digne	OfP	The Office of the Passion
LtAnt	A Letter to Brother Anthony of Padua	PrCr	The Prayer before the Crucifix
1LtCl	First Letter to the Clergy	ER	The Earlier Rule (*Regula non bullata*)
	(Earlier Edition)	LR	The Later Rule (*Regula bullata*)
2LtCl	Second Letter to the Clergy	RH	A Rule for Hermitages
	(Later Edition)	SalBV	A Salutation of the Blessed Virgin Mary
1LtCus	The First Letter to the Custodians	SalV	A Salutation of Virtues
2LtCus	The Second Letter to the Custodians	Test	The Testament
1LtF	The First Letter to the Faithful	TPJ	True and Perfect Joy
2LtF	The Second Letter to the Faithful		
LtL	A Letter to Brother Leo		

Franciscan Sources

1C	The Life of Saint Francis by Thomas of Celano	ScEx	The Sacred Exchange between Saint Francis and Lady Poverty
2C	The Remembrance of the Desire of a Soul	AP	The Anonymous of Perugia
		L3C	The Legend of the Three Companions .
3C	The Treatise on the Miracles by Thomas of Celano	LP	The Legend of Perugia
		AC	The Assisi Compilation
LCh	The Legend for Use in the Choir	UChL	An Umbrian Choir Legend
Off	The Divine Office of Saint Francis by Julian of Speyer	1-4Srm	The Sermons of Bonaventure
		LMj	The Major Legend by Bonaventure
LJS	The Life of Saint Francis by Julian of Speyer	LMn	The Minor Legend by Bonaventure
		BPr	The Book of Praises by Bernard of Besse
VL	The Versified Life of Saint Francis by Henri d'Avranches	IntR	The Intention of the Rule
1-3JT	The Praises by Jacopone da Todi	OL	An Old Legend
DCom	The Divine Comedy by Dante Alighieri	WSF	The Words of Saint Francis
		WBC	The Words of Brother Conrad
TL	Tree of Life by Ubertino da Casale	DBF	The Deeds of Blessed Francis and His Companions
1MP	The Mirror of Perfection, Smaller Version	LFl	The Little Flowers of Saint Francis
2MP	The Mirror of Perfection, Larger Version	KnSF	The Kinship of Saint Francis
		ChrTE	The Chronicle of Thomas of Eccleston
HTrb	The Book of Chronicles or of the Tribulations of the Order of Lesser Ones by Angelo di Clareno	ChrJG	The Chronicle of Jordan of Giano

Other Sources

AF	Analecta Franciscana	DEC	Decrees of the Ecumenical Councils
AFH	Archivum Franciscanum Historicum	DMA	Dictionary of the Middle Ages
AM	Annales Minorum	GR	Greyfriars Review
BFr	Bullarium Franciscanum	PL	Patrologia Latina
CCSL	Corpus Christianorum, Series Latina	PG	Patrologia Graeca
CSEL	Corpus Scriptorum Eccles. Latinorum	TM	Testimonia Minora Saeculi

Scripture abbreviations are from *The New American Bible*; the Psalms follow the modern numbering sequence. Scripture references accompanying non-italicized text imply *confer*, or cf. References to the volumes in *Francis of Assisi: Early Documents* will be abbreviated FA:ED I, II.